CRAZY FOOD TRUCK

2

STORY AND ART BY ROKUROU OGAKI

#5 CURRY

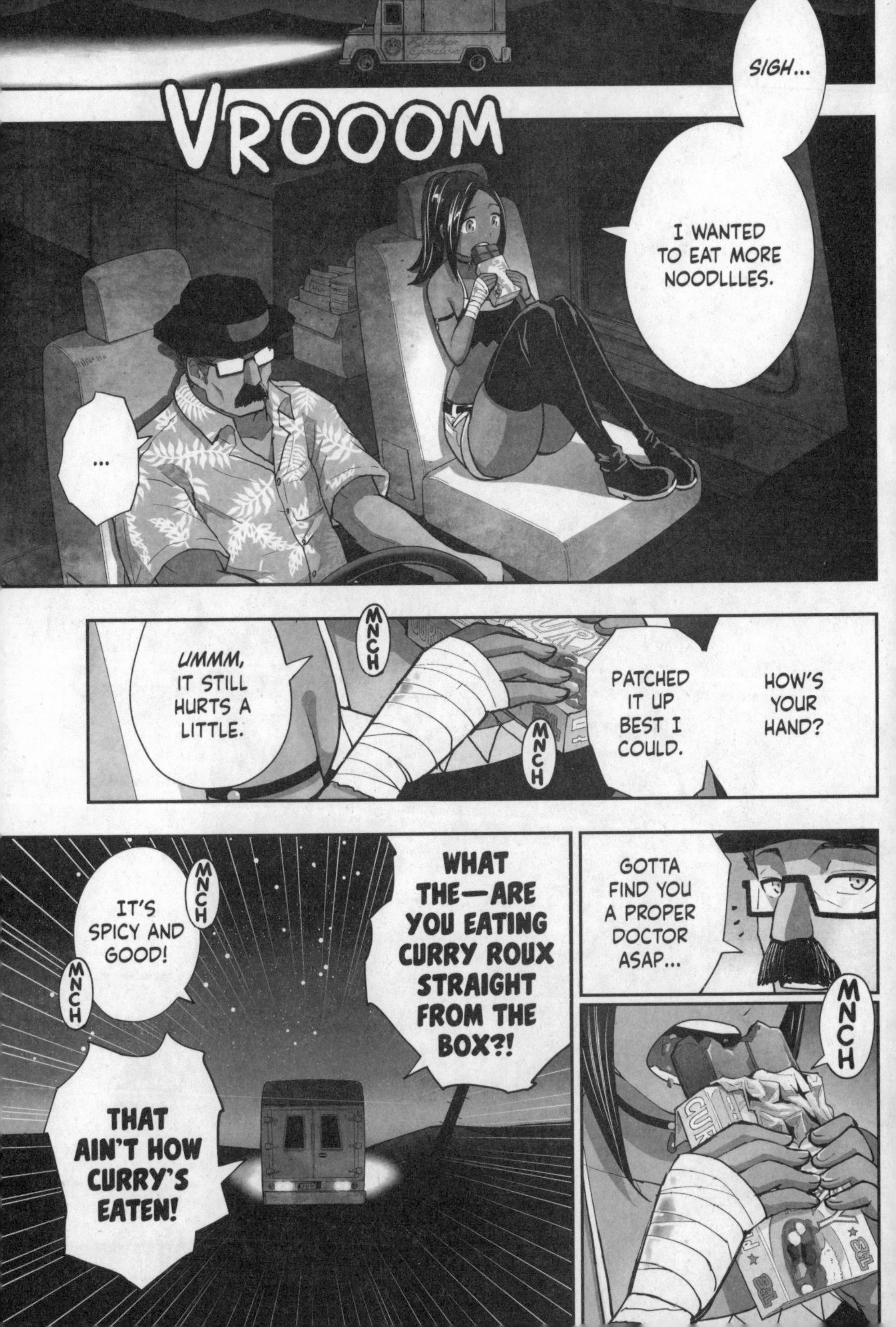
SIGH...
VROOOM
I WANTED TO EAT MORE NOODLLLES.
...
HOW'S YOUR HAND?
PATCHED IT UP BEST I COULD.
MNCH
MNCH
UMMM, IT STILL HURTS A LITTLE.
GOTTA FIND YOU A PROPER DOCTOR ASAP...
MNCH
WHAT THE—ARE YOU EATING CURRY ROUX STRAIGHT FROM THE BOX?!
MNCH
IT'S SPICY AND GOOD!
MNCH
THAT AIN'T HOW CURRY'S EATEN!

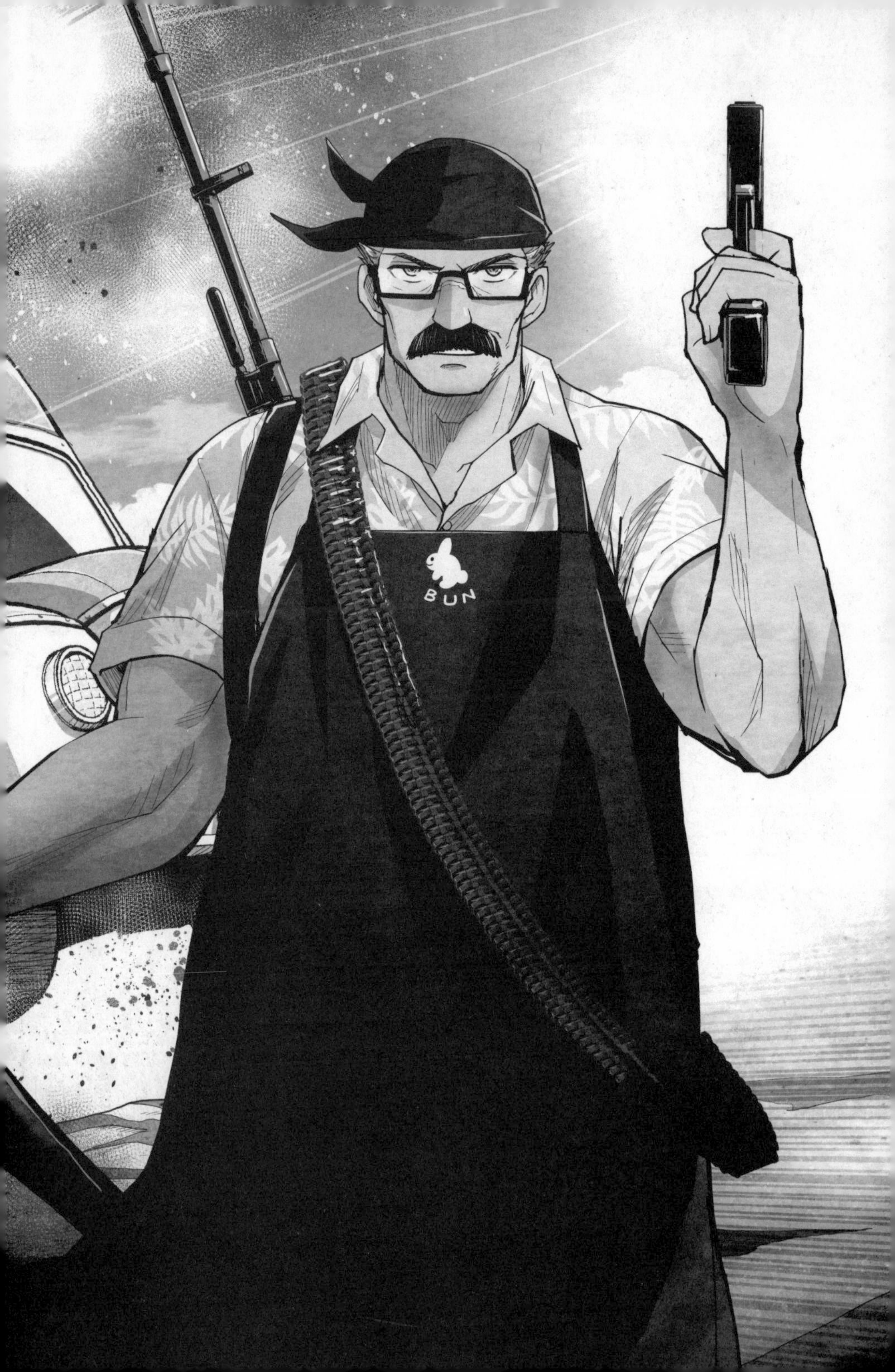
BUN

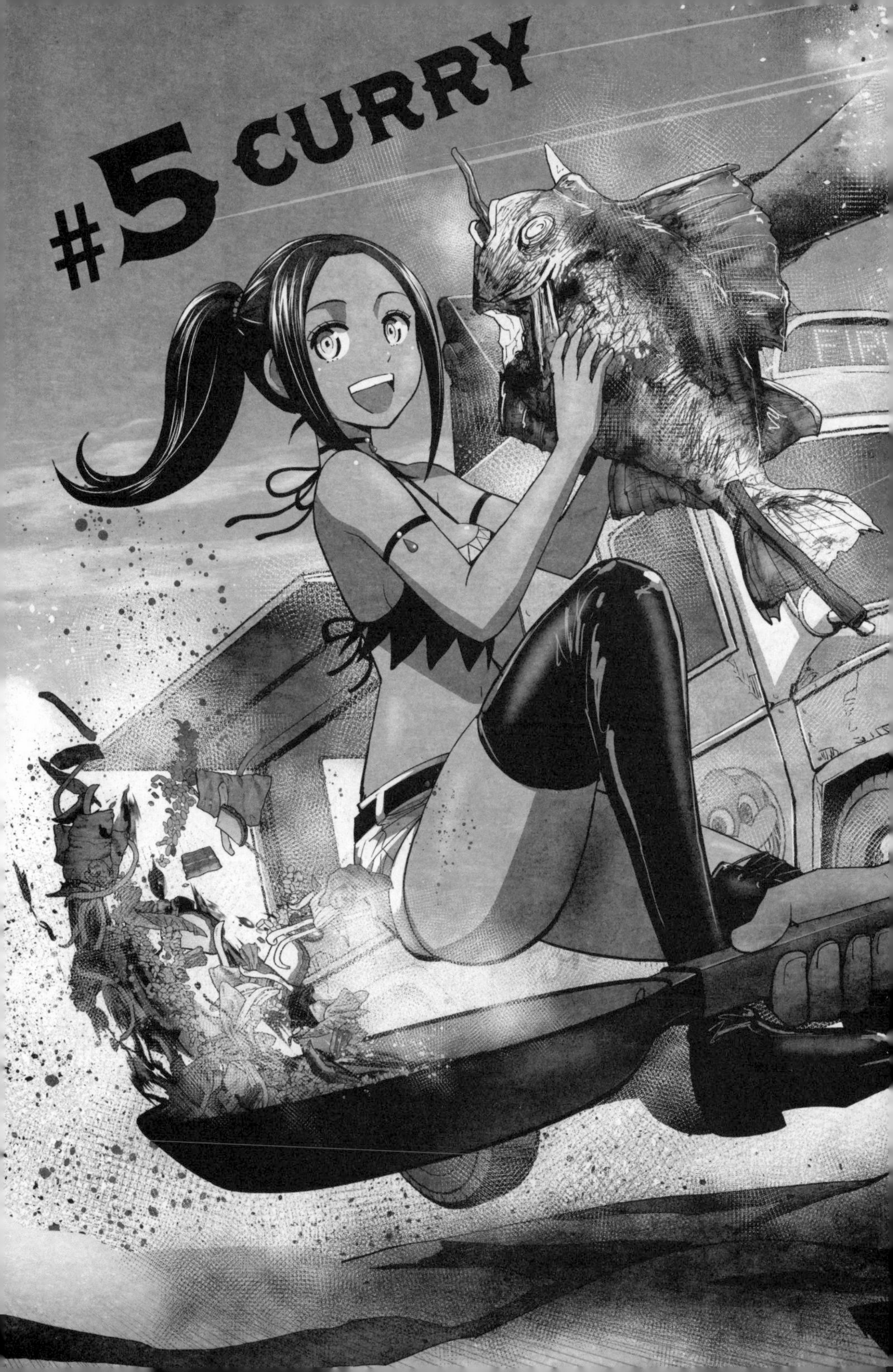
#5 CURRY

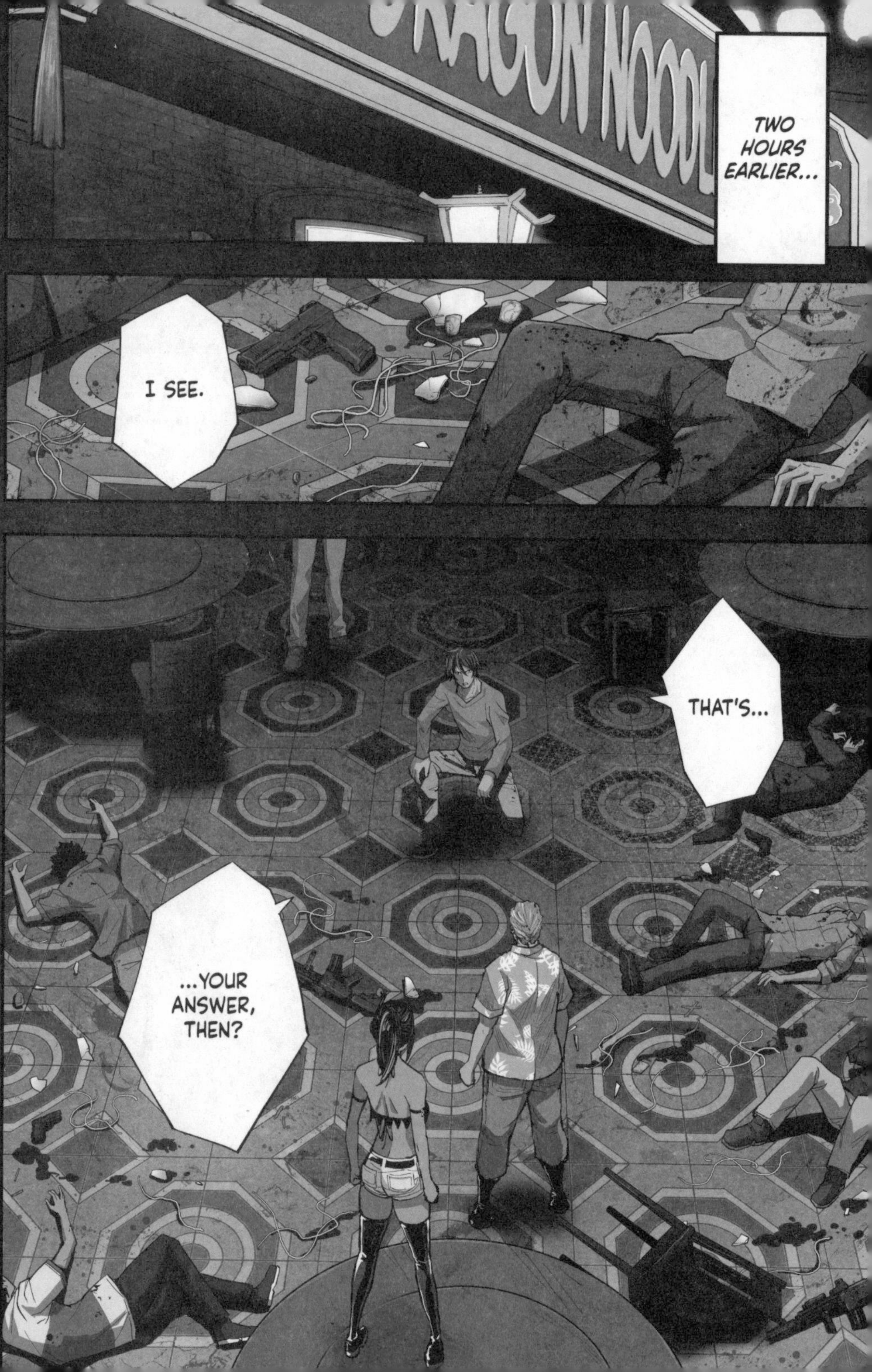
TWO HOURS EARLIER...
I SEE.
THAT'S...
...YOUR ANSWER, THEN?

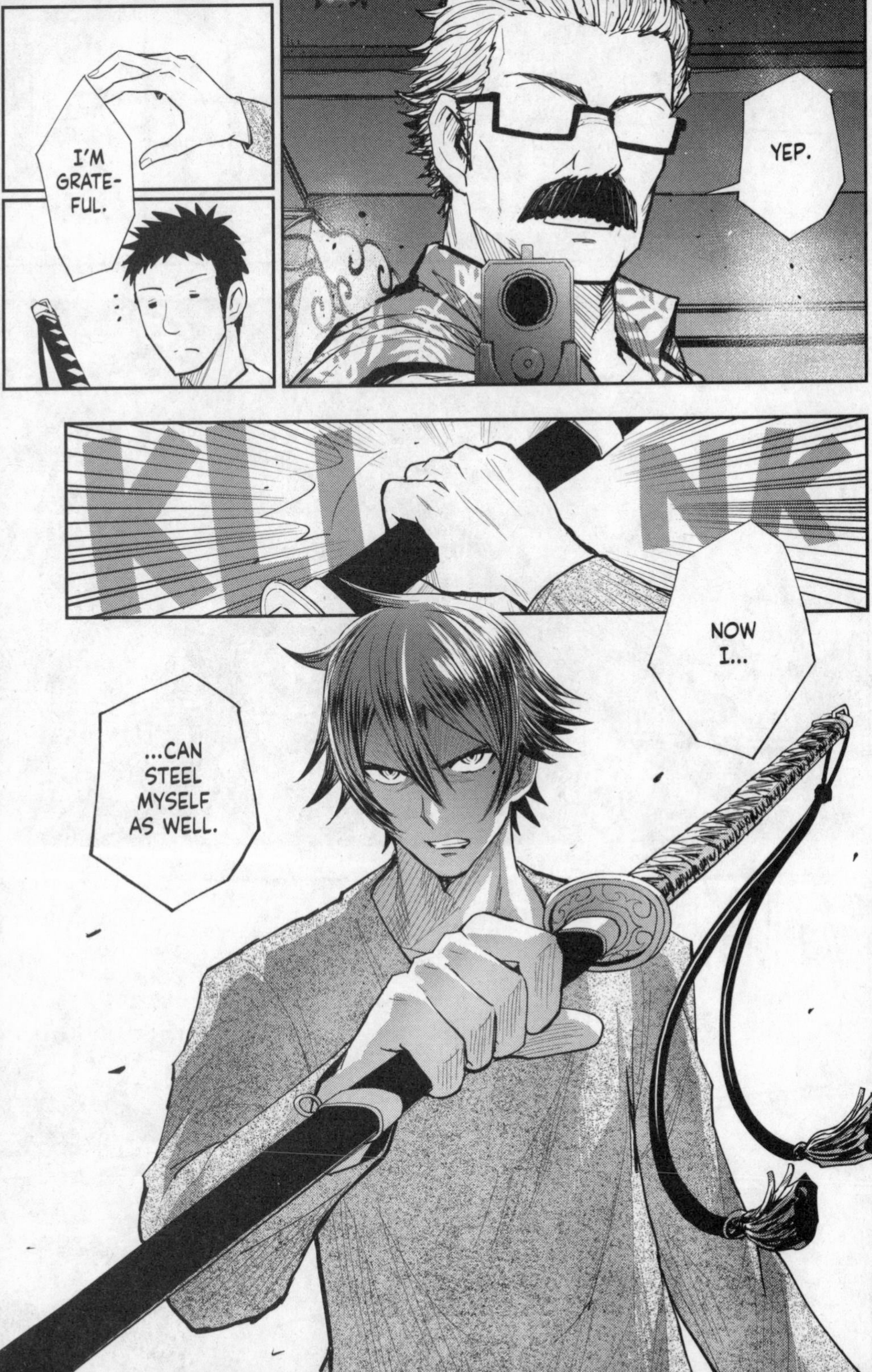
YEP.
I'M GRATE-FUL.
KLINK
NOW I...
...CAN STEEL MYSELF AS WELL.

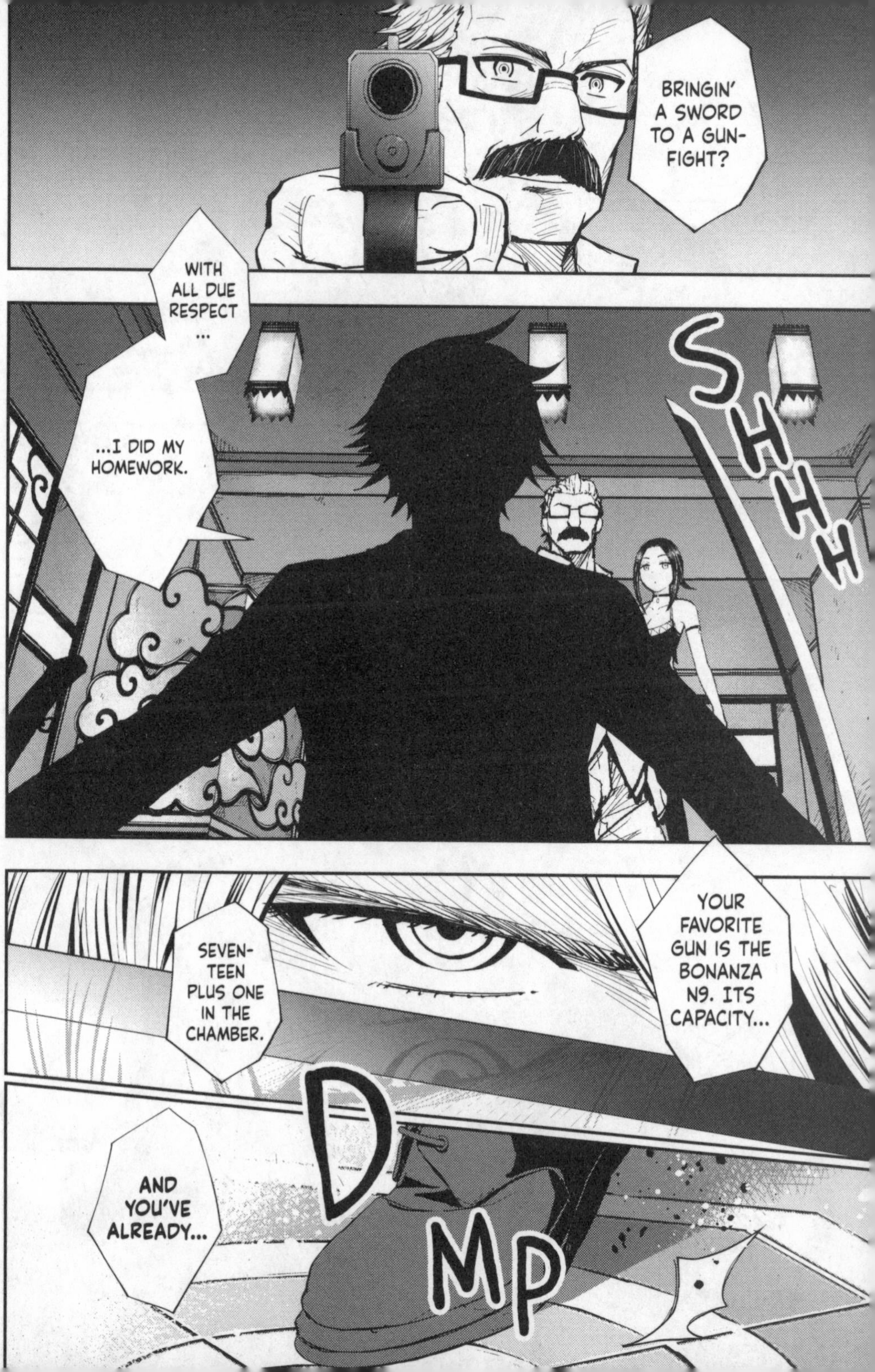
BRINGIN' A SWORD TO A GUN-FIGHT?
WITH ALL DUE RESPECT ...
SHHHH
...I DID MY HOMEWORK.
YOUR FAVORITE GUN IS THE BONANZA N9. ITS CAPACITY...
SEVEN-TEEN PLUS ONE IN THE CHAMBER.
DMP
AND YOU'VE ALREADY...

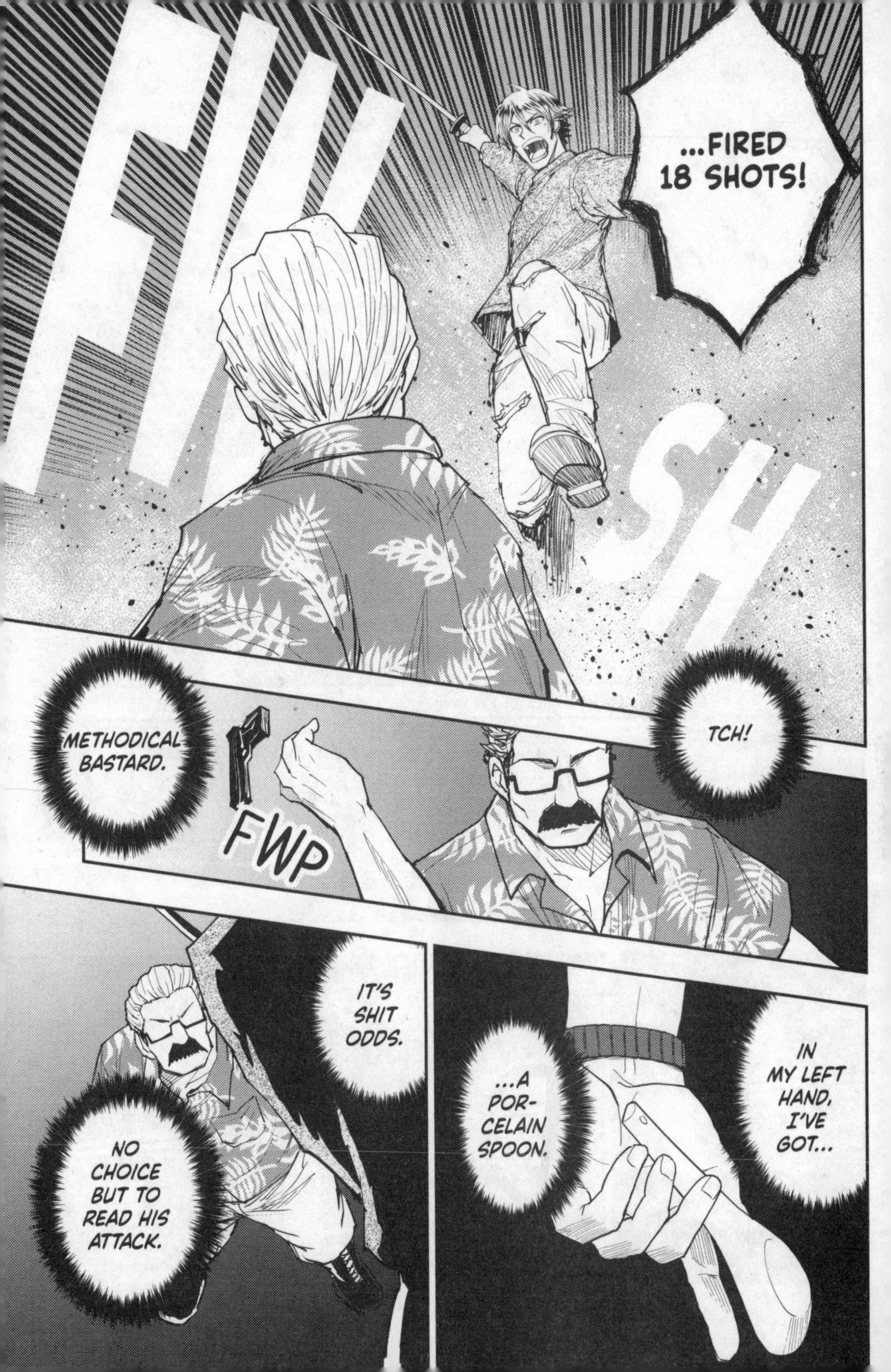
...FIRED 18 SHOTS!
SH
TCH!
METHODICAL BASTARD.
FWP
IN MY LEFT HAND, I'VE GOT...
...A POR-CELAIN SPOON.
IT'S SHIT ODDS.
NO CHOICE BUT TO READ HIS ATTACK.

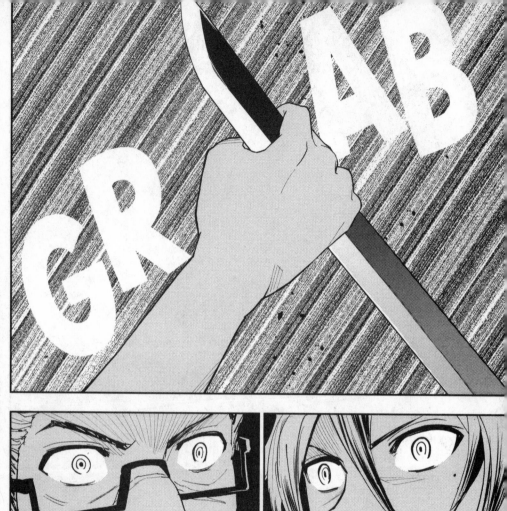

GRAB

MY SECONDS...

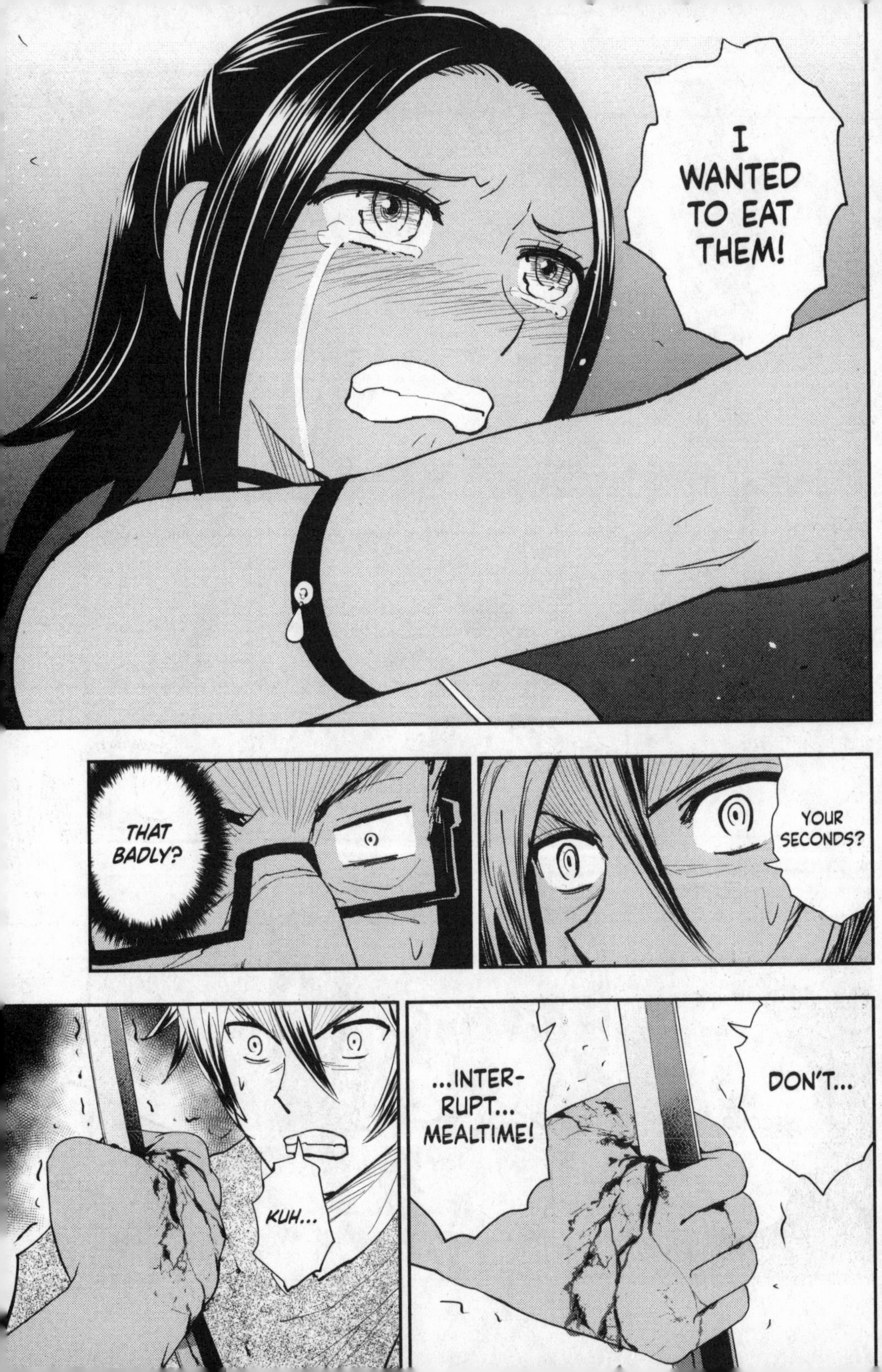
I WANTED TO EAT THEM!
YOUR SECONDS?
THAT BADLY?
DON'T...
...INTER-RUPT... MEALTIME!
KUH...

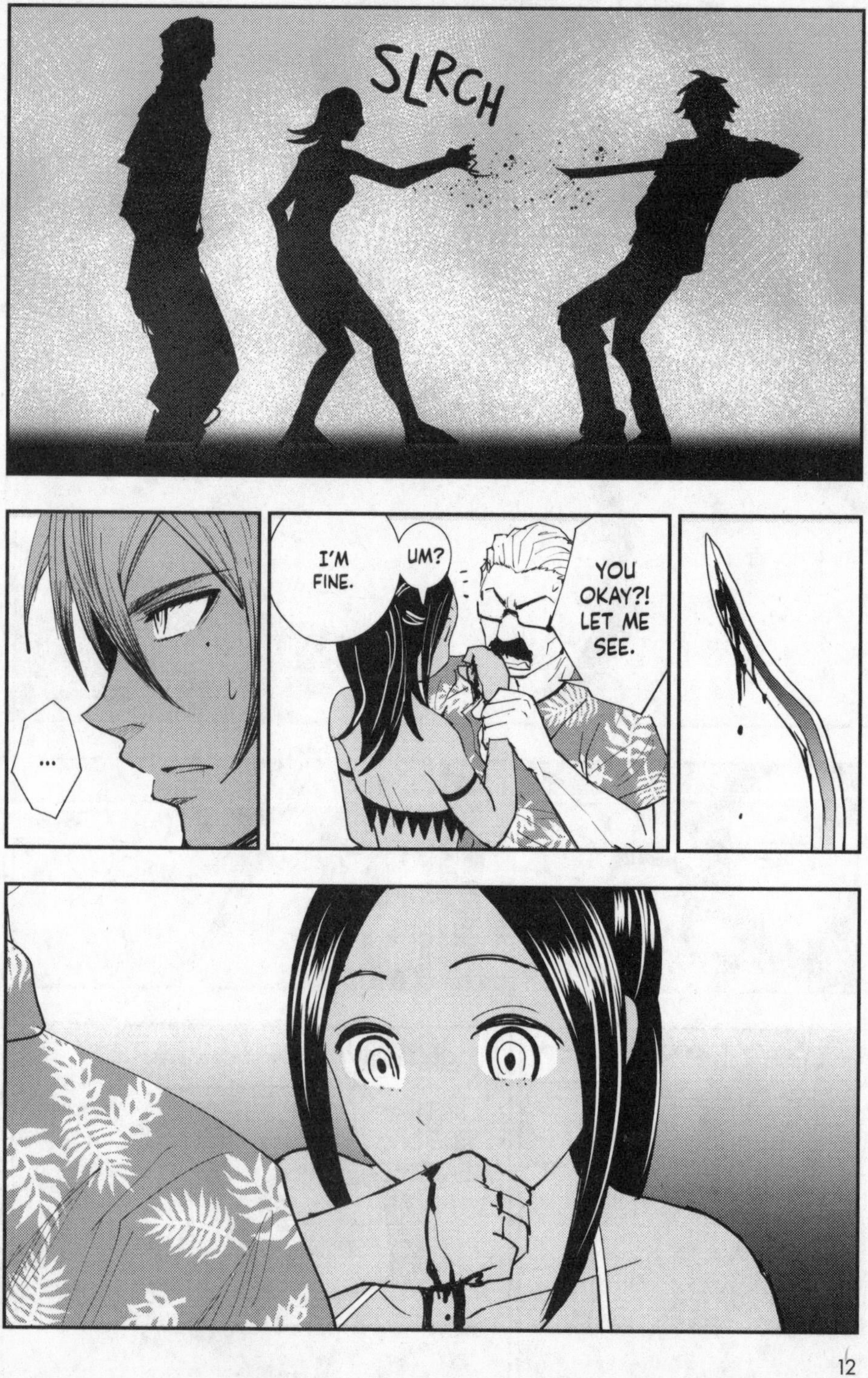
SLRCH
YOU OKAY?! LET ME SEE.
UM?
I'M FINE.
...

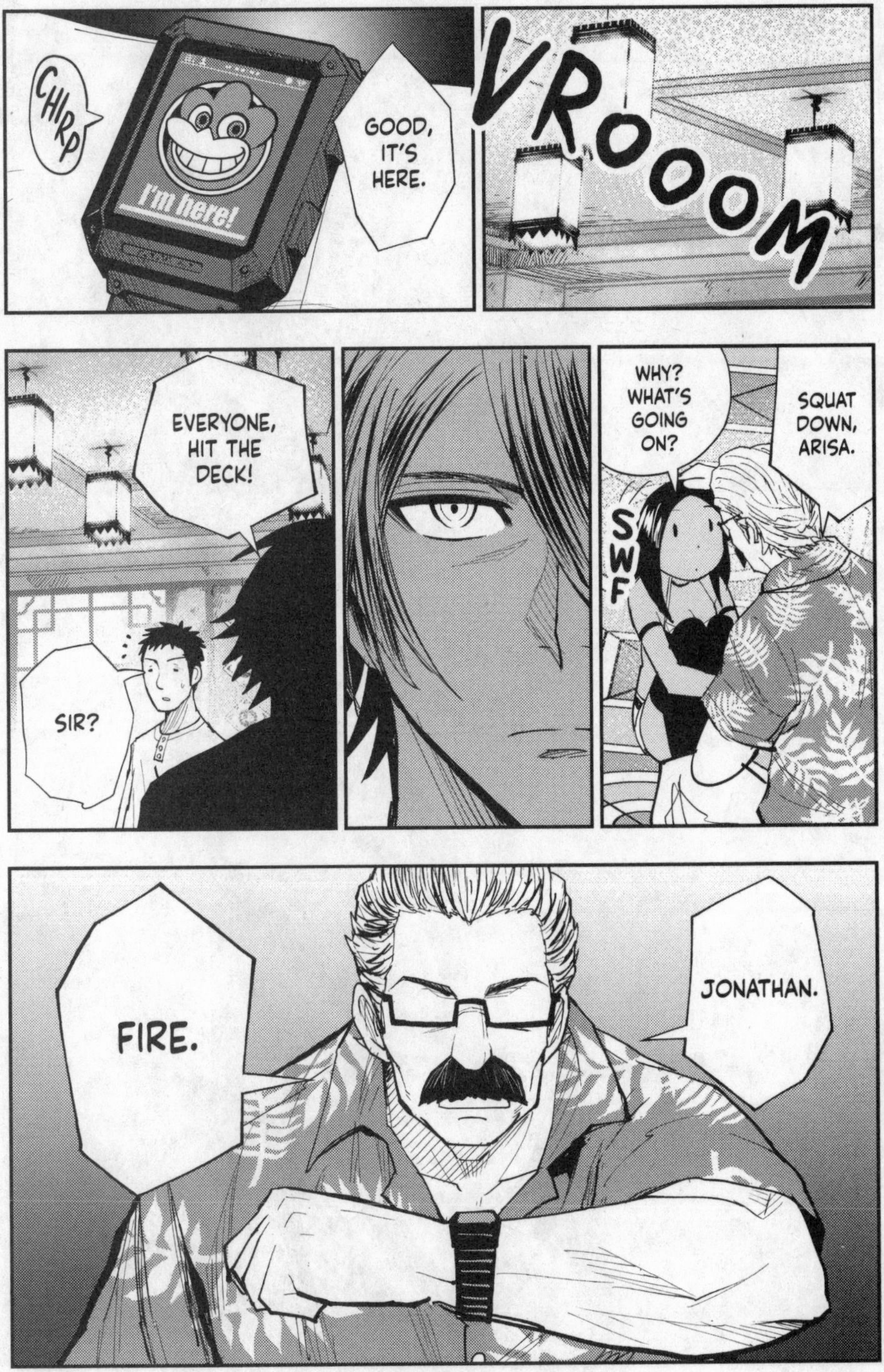
VROOOM
GOOD, IT'S HERE.
CHIRP
I'm here!
SQUAT DOWN, ARISA.
WHY? WHAT'S GOING ON?
SWF
EVERYONE, HIT THE DECK!
SIR?
JONATHAN.
FIRE.

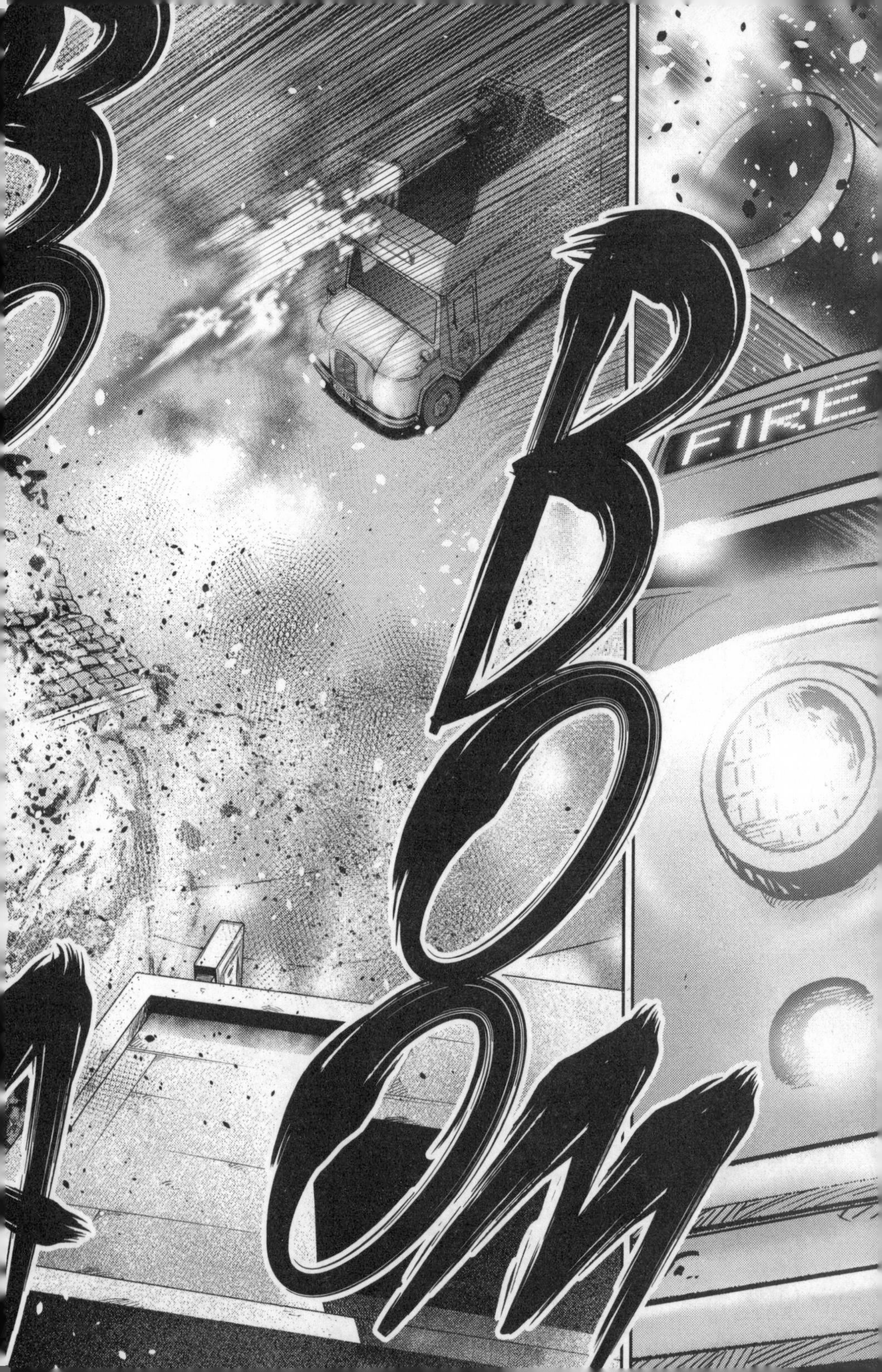
FIRE
BOOM

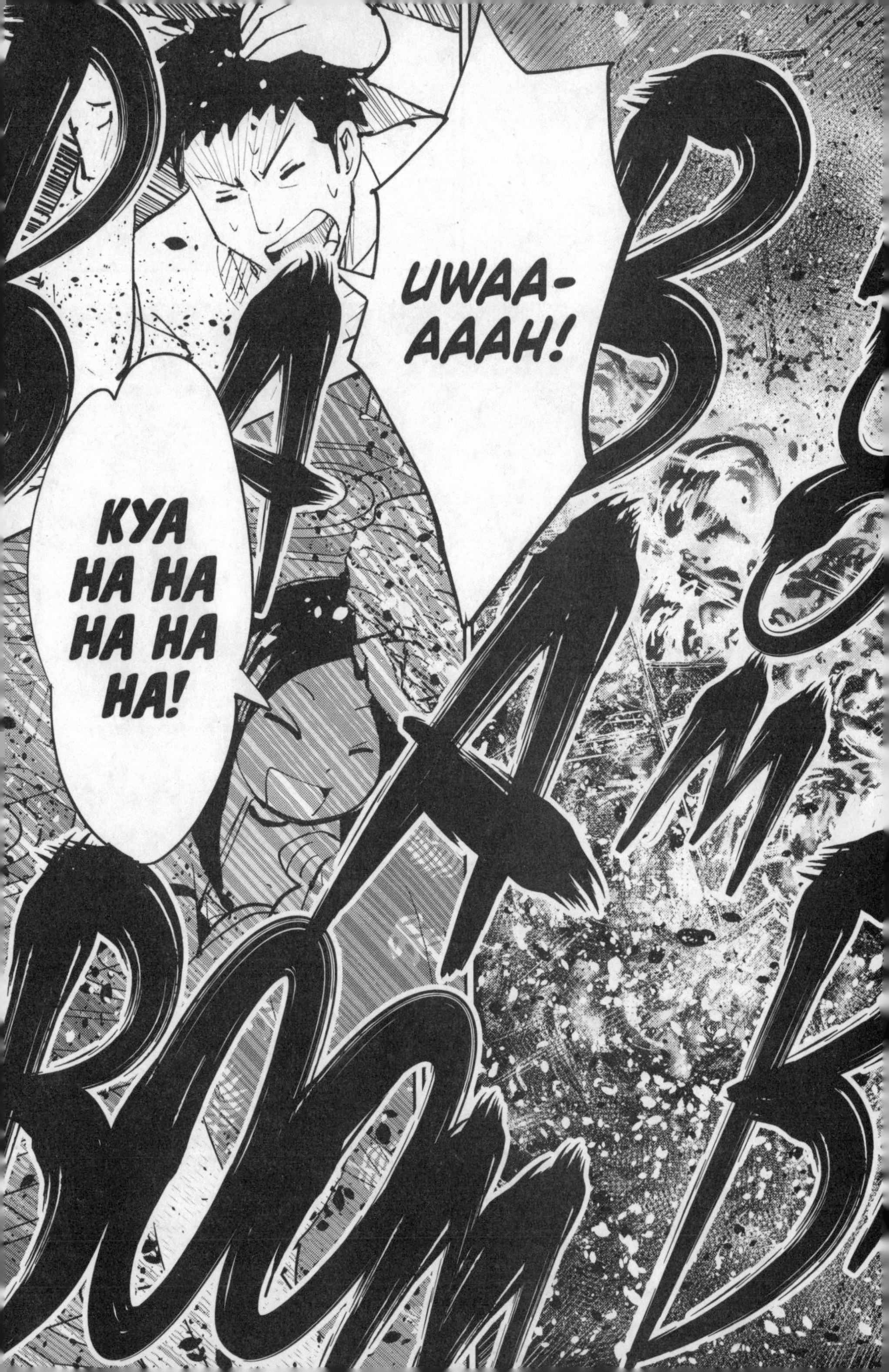
UWAA-AAAH!
KYA HA HA HA HA HA HA!

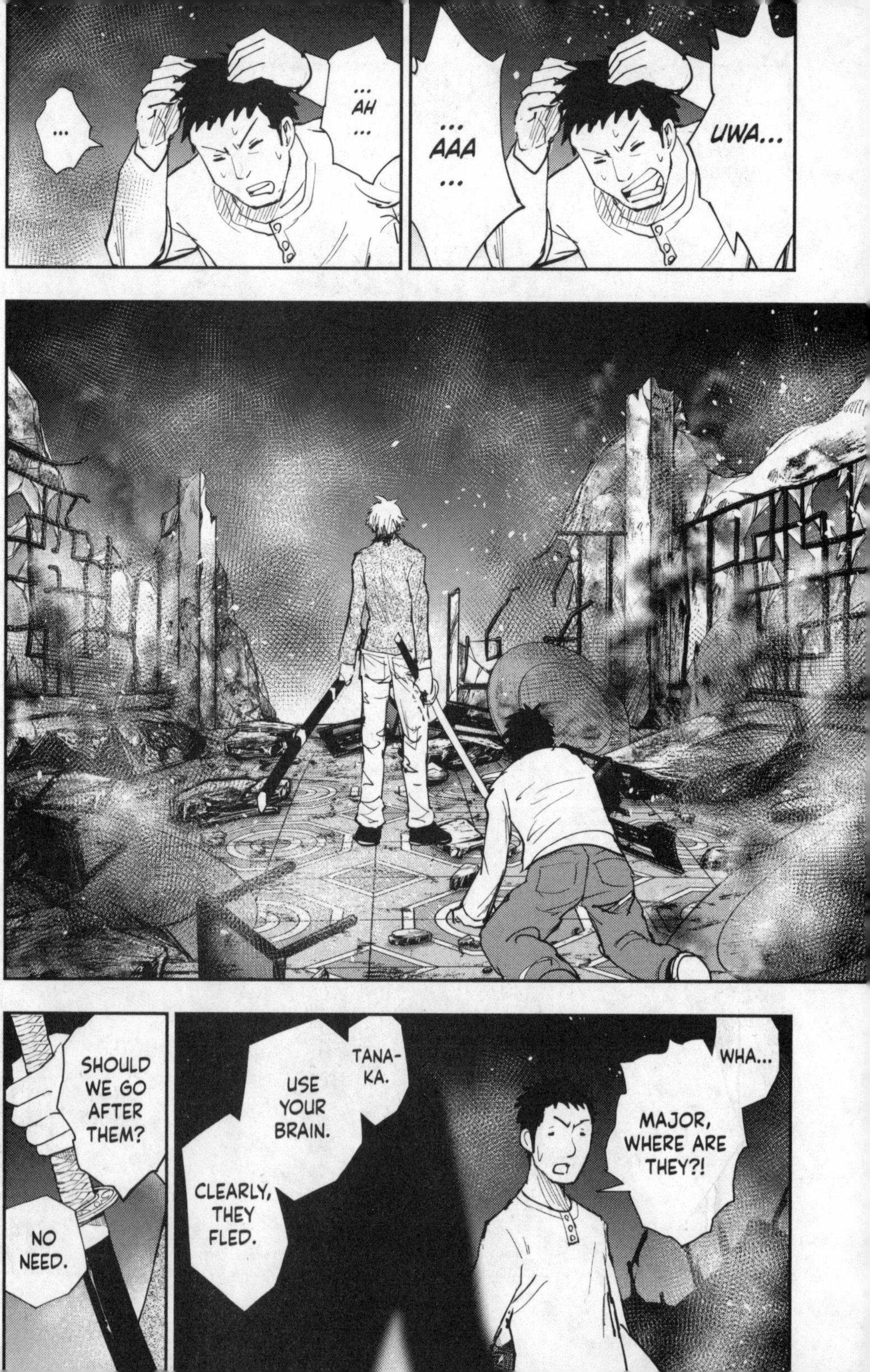
UWA...
...AAA...
...AH...
...
WHA...
MAJOR, WHERE ARE THEY?!
TANA-KA.
USE YOUR BRAIN.
CLEARLY, THEY FLED.
SHOULD WE GO AFTER THEM?
NO NEED.

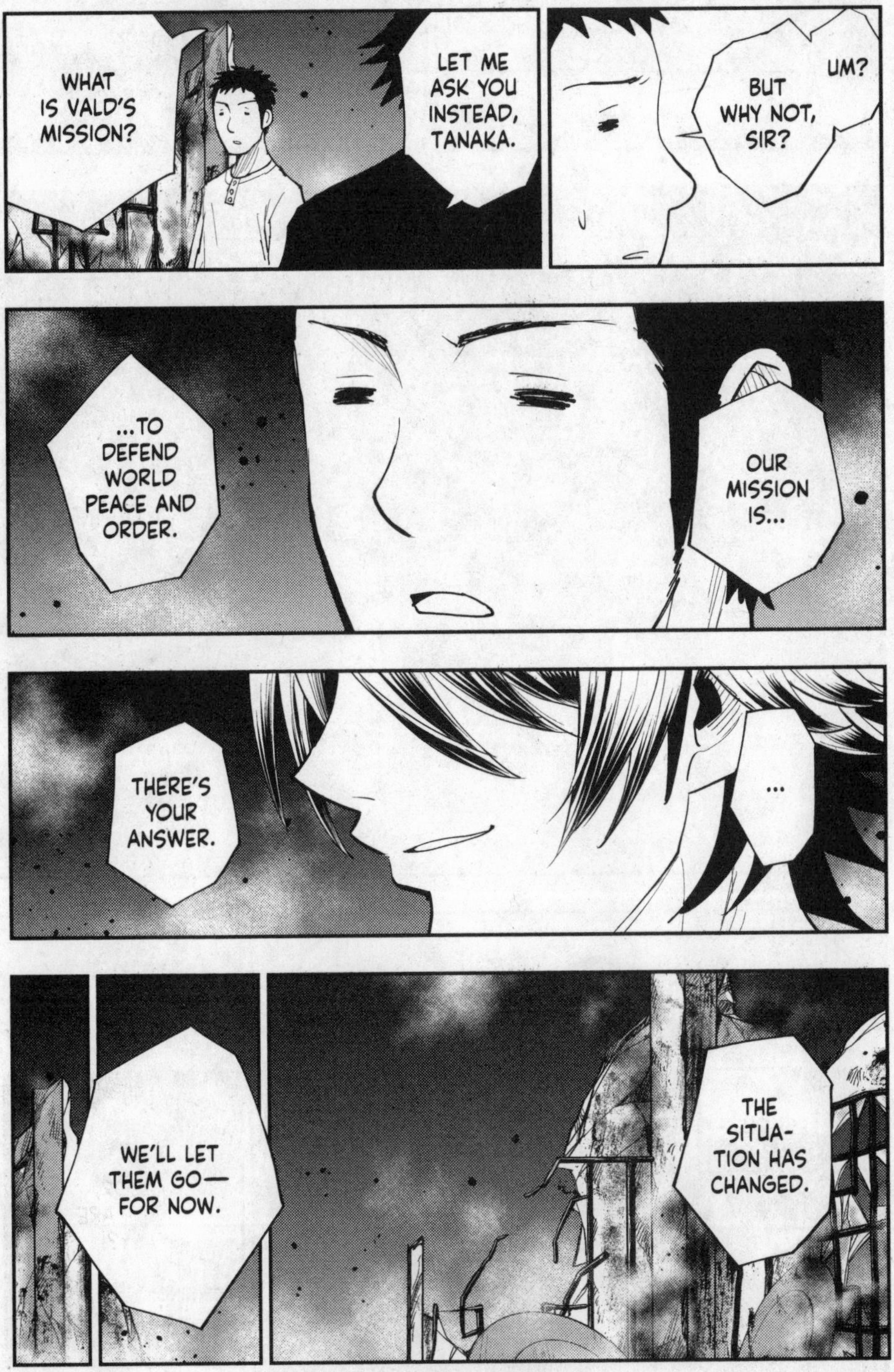
UM?
BUT WHY NOT, SIR?
LET ME ASK YOU INSTEAD, TANAKA.
WHAT IS VALD'S MISSION?
OUR MISSION IS...
...TO DEFEND WORLD PEACE AND ORDER.
...
THERE'S YOUR ANSWER.
THE SITUA-TION HAS CHANGED.
WE'LL LET THEM GO— FOR NOW.

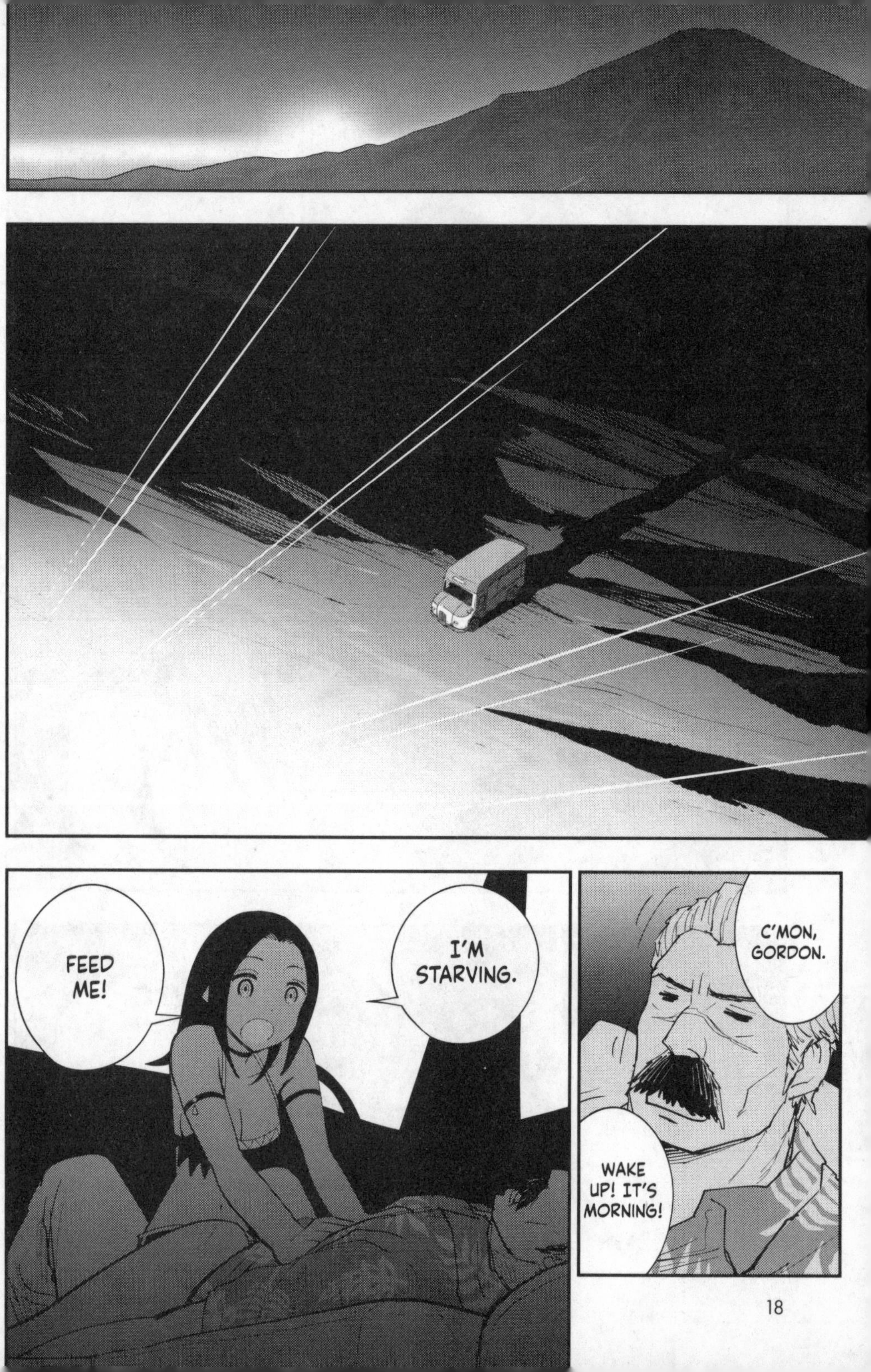
C'MON, GORDON.
WAKE UP! IT'S MORNING!
I'M STARVING.
FEED ME!

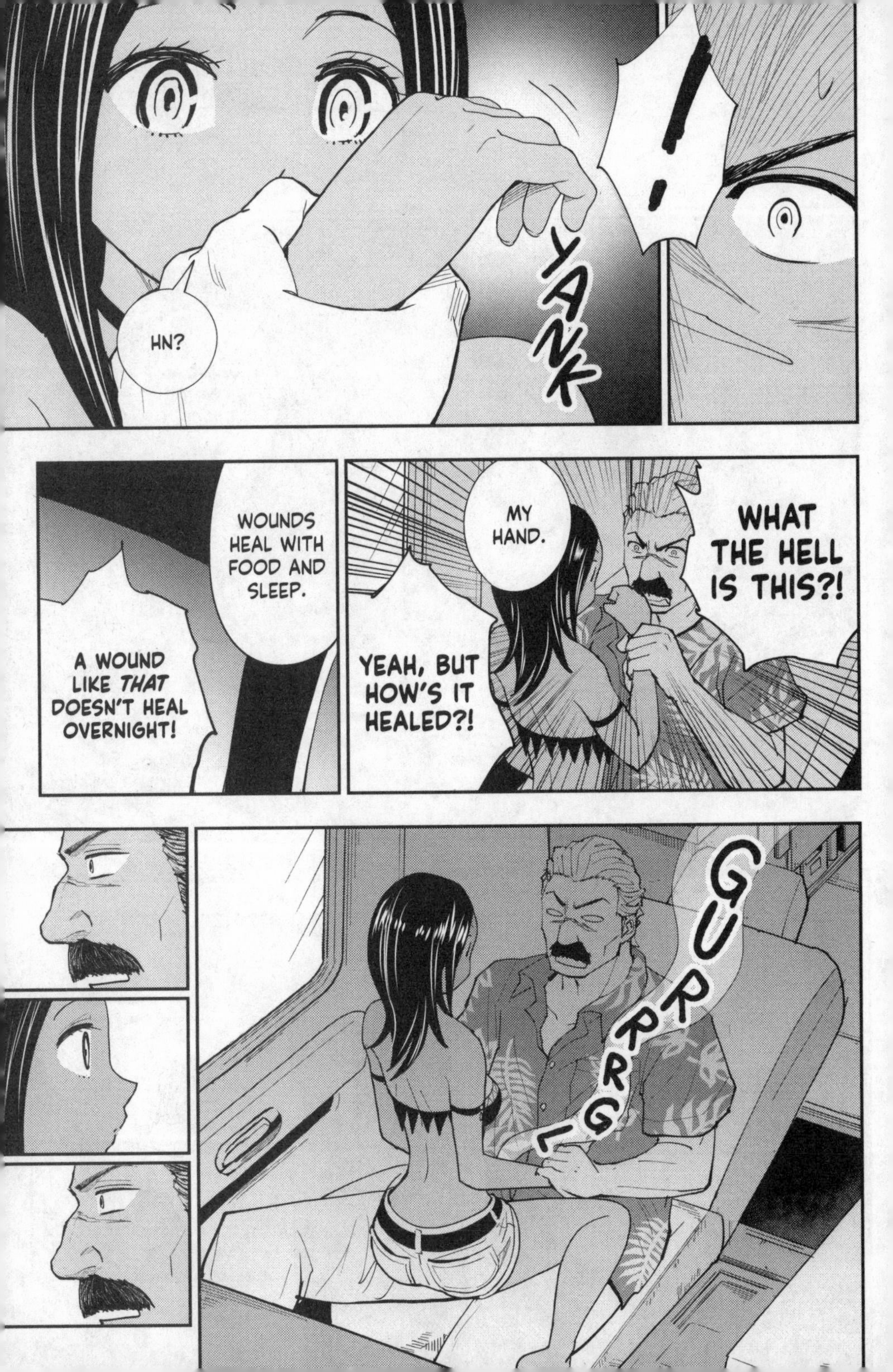
!
YANK
HN?
WHAT THE HELL IS THIS?!
MY HAND.
YEAH, BUT HOW'S IT HEALED?!
WOUNDS HEAL WITH FOOD AND SLEEP.
A WOUND LIKE *THAT* DOESN'T HEAL OVERNIGHT!
GURRRRGL

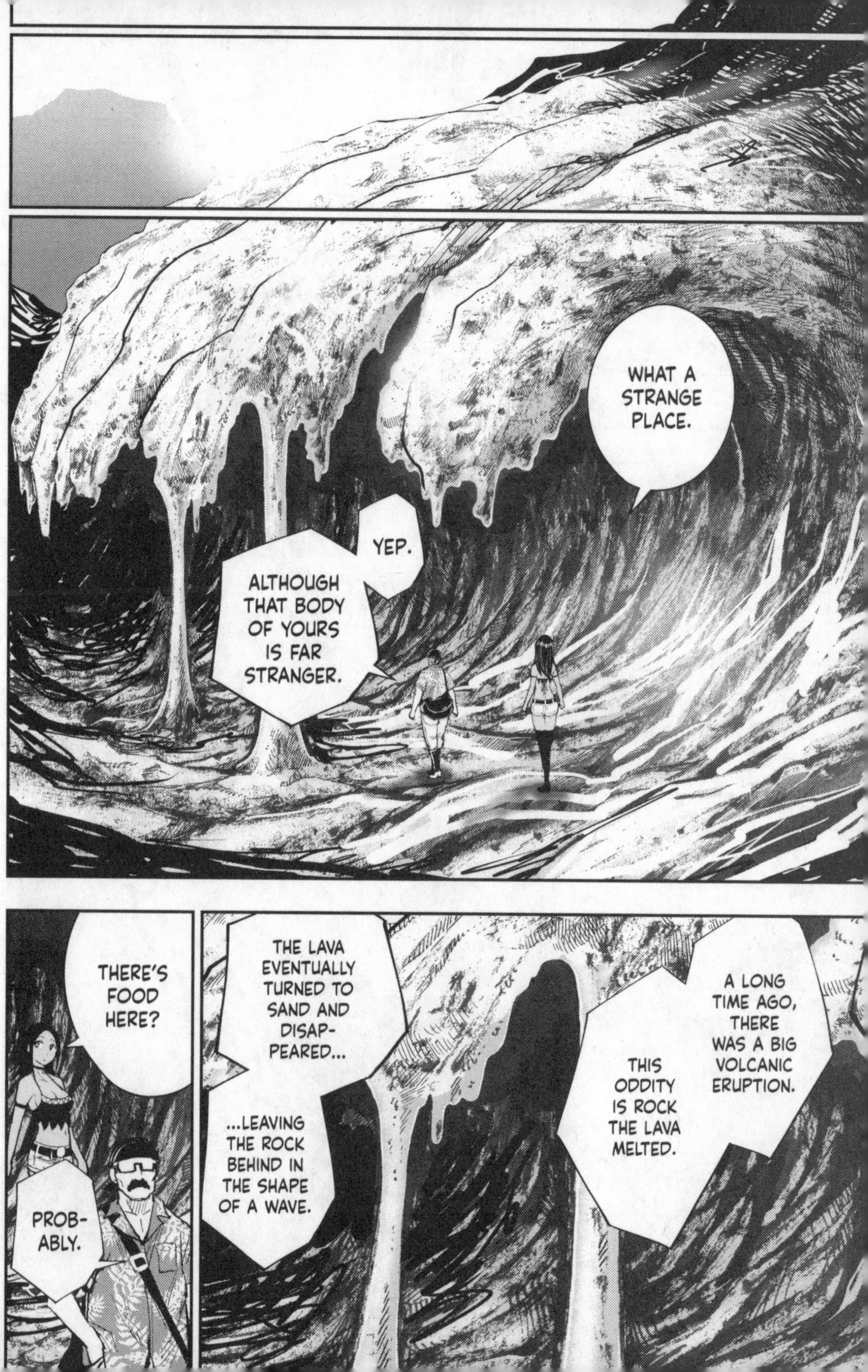
WHAT A STRANGE PLACE.
YEP.
ALTHOUGH THAT BODY OF YOURS IS FAR STRANGER.
A LONG TIME AGO, THERE WAS A BIG VOLCANIC ERUPTION.
THIS ODDITY IS ROCK THE LAVA MELTED.
THE LAVA EVENTUALLY TURNED TO SAND AND DISAP-PEARED...
...LEAVING THE ROCK BEHIND IN THE SHAPE OF A WAVE.
THERE'S FOOD HERE?
PROB-ABLY.

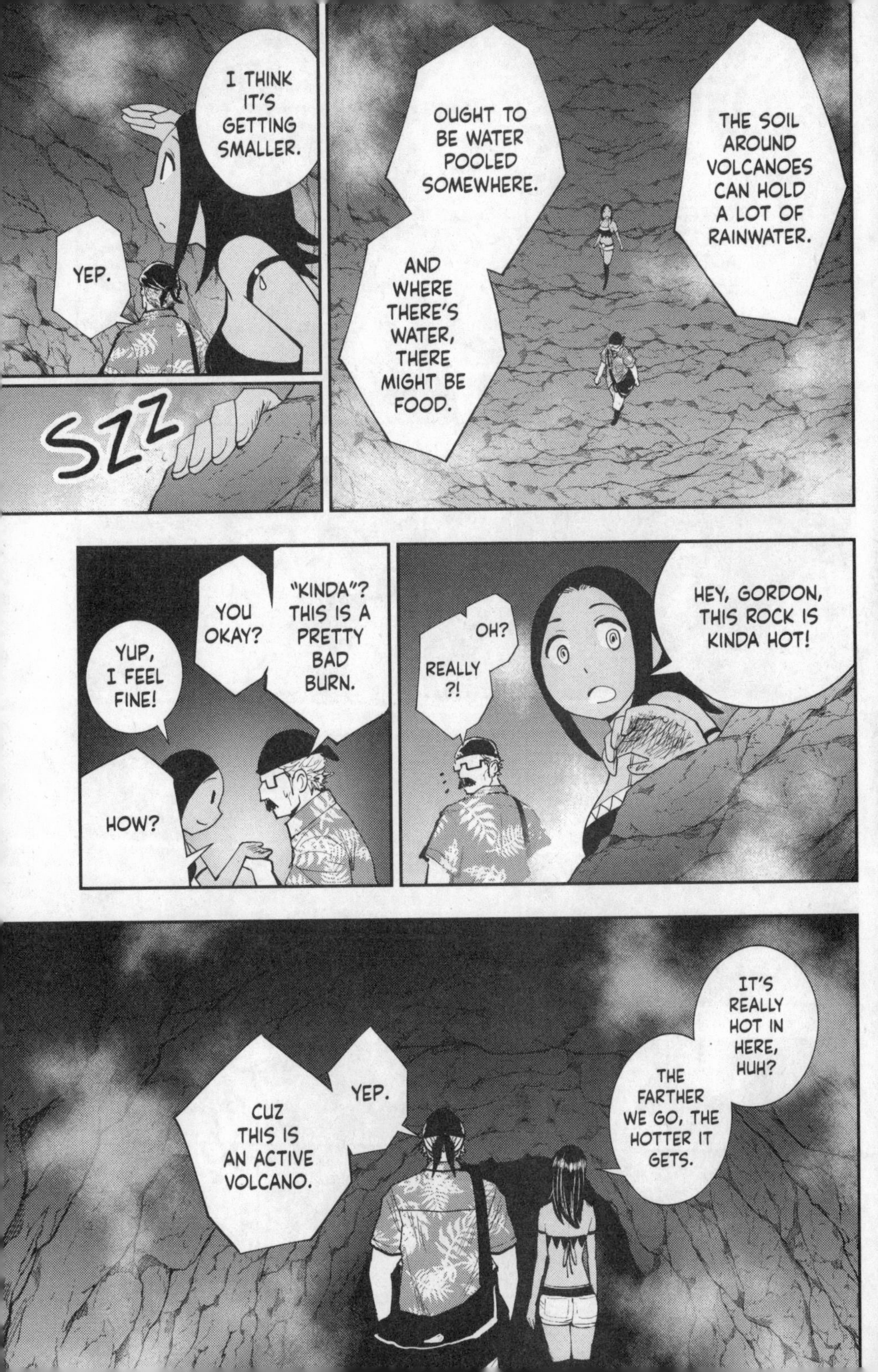
THE SOIL AROUND VOLCANOES CAN HOLD A LOT OF RAINWATER.
OUGHT TO BE WATER POOLED SOMEWHERE.
AND WHERE THERE'S WATER, THERE MIGHT BE FOOD.
I THINK IT'S GETTING SMALLER.
YEP.
SZZ
HEY, GORDON, THIS ROCK IS KINDA HOT!
OH?
REALLY?!
"KINDA"? THIS IS A PRETTY BAD BURN.
YOU OKAY?
YUP, I FEEL FINE!
HOW?
IT'S REALLY HOT IN HERE, HUH?
THE FARTHER WE GO, THE HOTTER IT GETS.
YEP.
CUZ THIS IS AN ACTIVE VOLCANO.

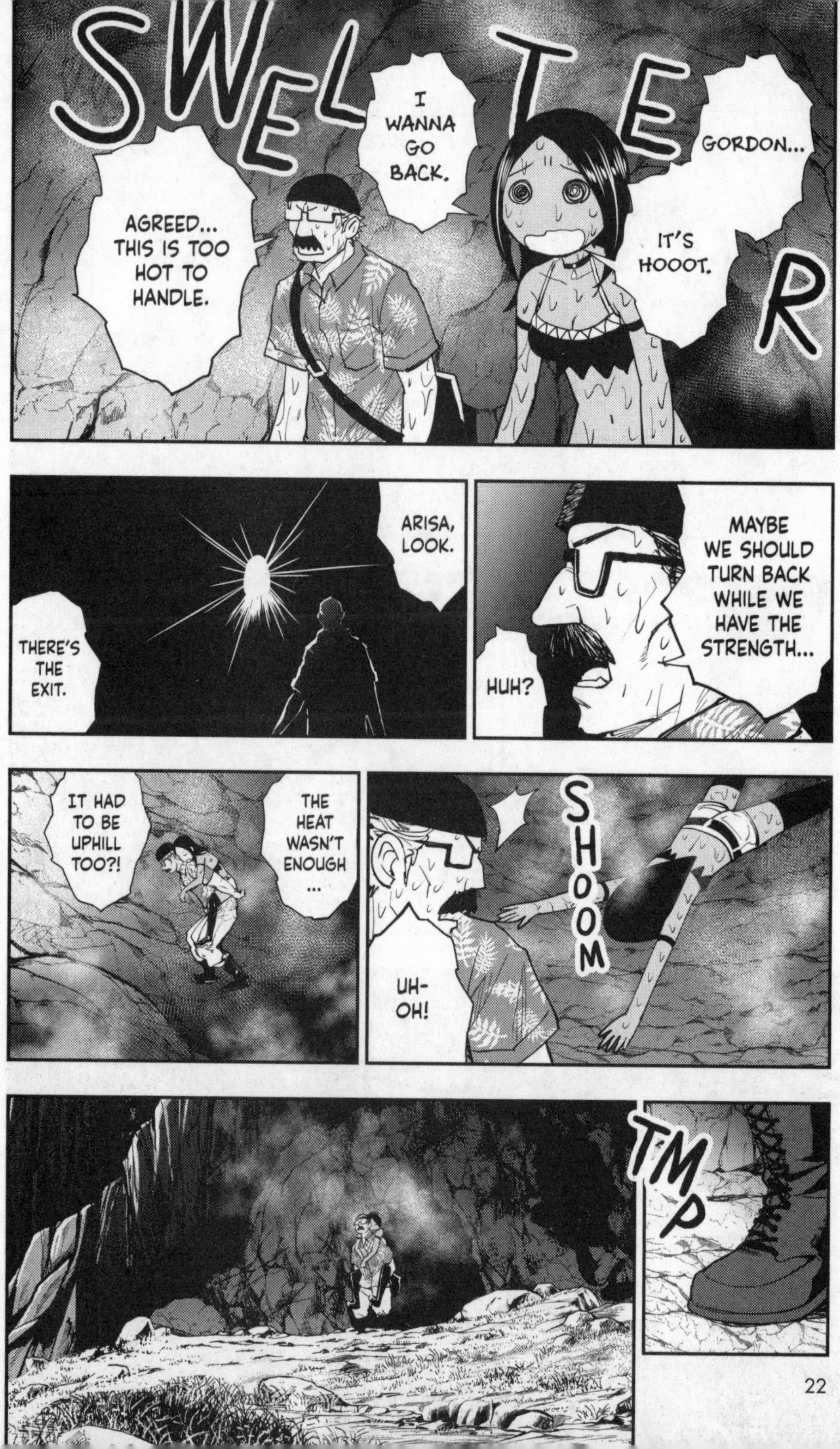
SWELTER
GORDON...
IT'S HOOOT.
I WANNA GO BACK.
AGREED... THIS IS TOO HOT TO HANDLE.
MAYBE WE SHOULD TURN BACK WHILE WE HAVE THE STRENGTH...
HUH?
ARISA, LOOK.
THERE'S THE EXIT.
SHOOM
UH-OH!
THE HEAT WASN'T ENOUGH...
IT HAD TO BE UPHILL TOO?!
TMP

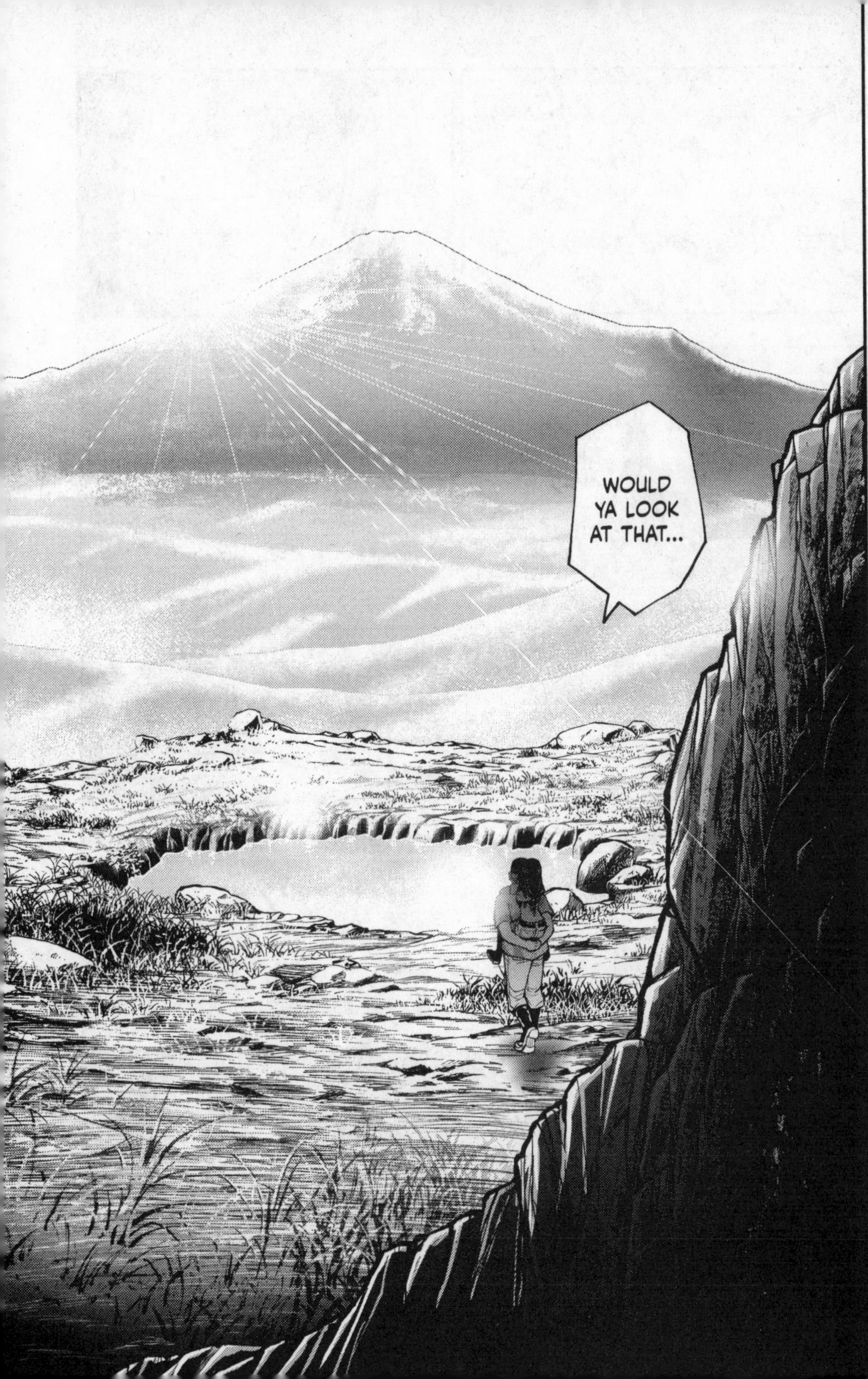
WOULD YA LOOK AT THAT...

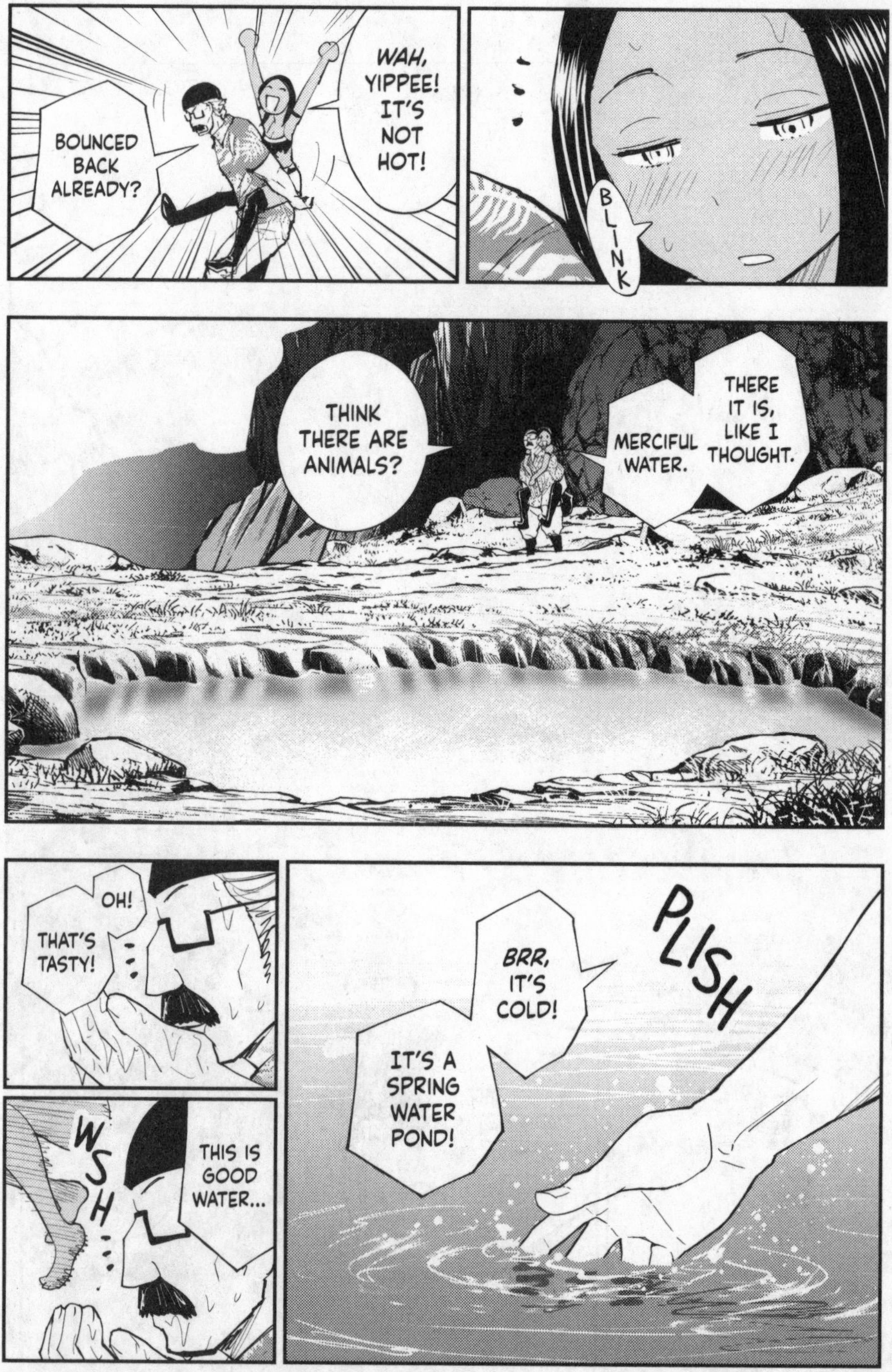
...
BLINK
WAH, YIPPEE! IT'S NOT HOT!
BOUNCED BACK ALREADY?
THERE IT IS, LIKE I THOUGHT.
MERCIFUL WATER.
THINK THERE ARE ANIMALS?
PLISH
BRR, IT'S COLD!
IT'S A SPRING WATER POND!
OH!
THAT'S TASTY!
...
WSH
THIS IS GOOD WATER...
...

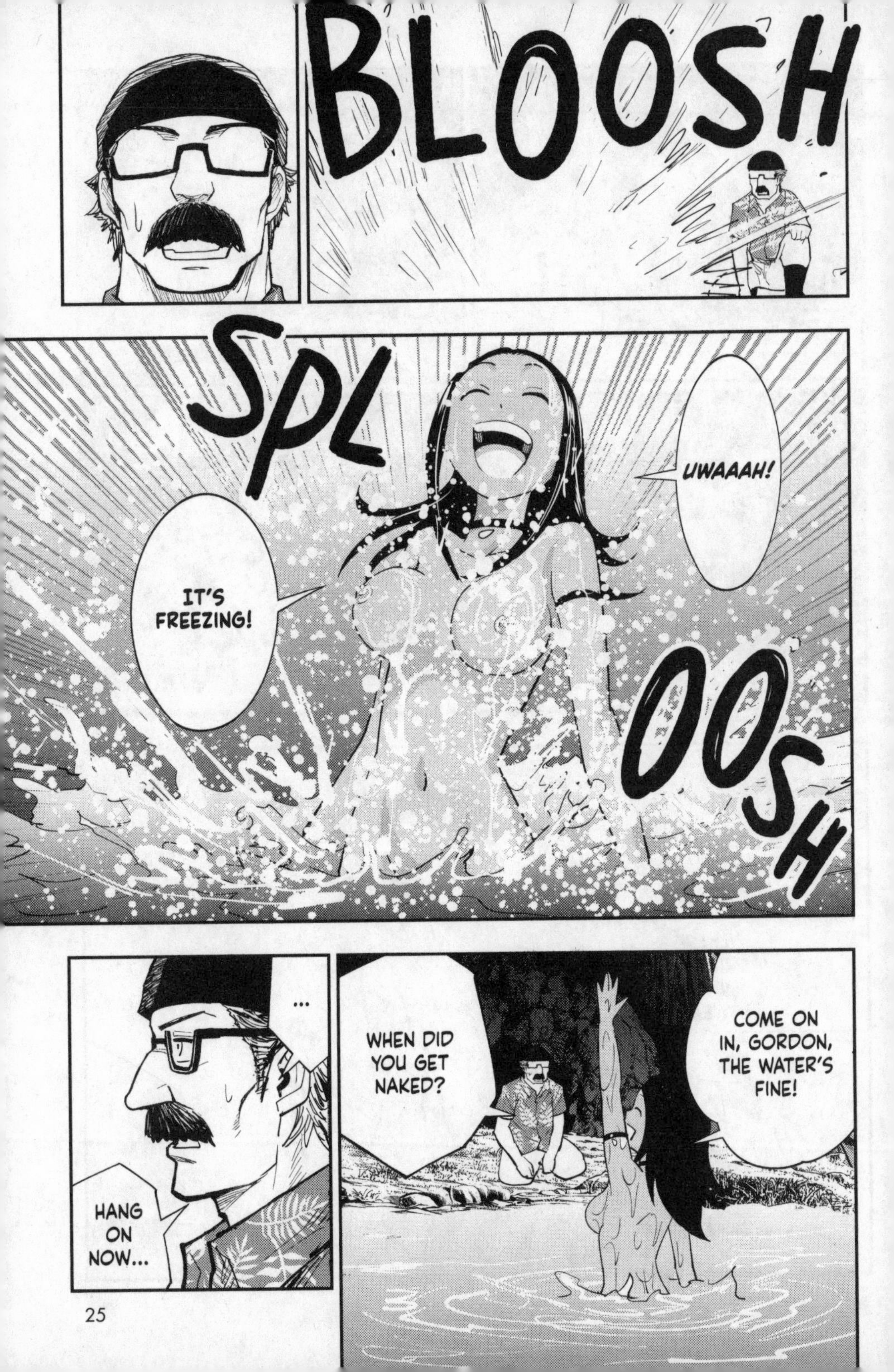
BLOOSH
UWAAAH!
SPL
IT'S FREEZING!
OOSH
COME ON IN, GORDON, THE WATER'S FINE!
WHEN DID YOU GET NAKED?
...
HANG ON NOW...

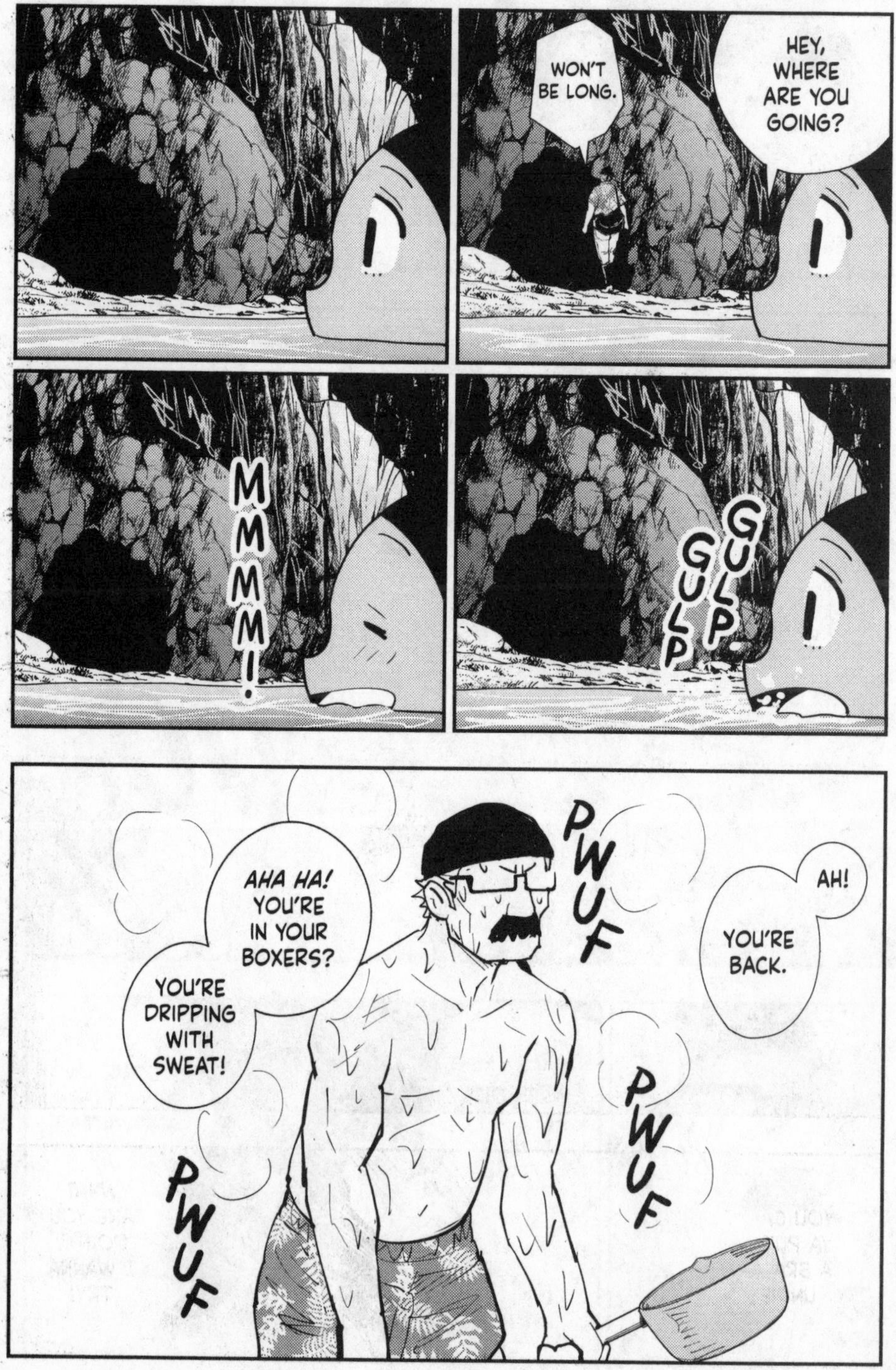
HEY, WHERE ARE YOU GOING?
WON'T BE LONG.
GULP GULP
MMMM!
AH!
YOU'RE BACK.
PWUF
AHA HA! YOU'RE IN YOUR BOXERS?
PWUF PWUF
YOU'RE DRIPPING WITH SWEAT!
PWUF

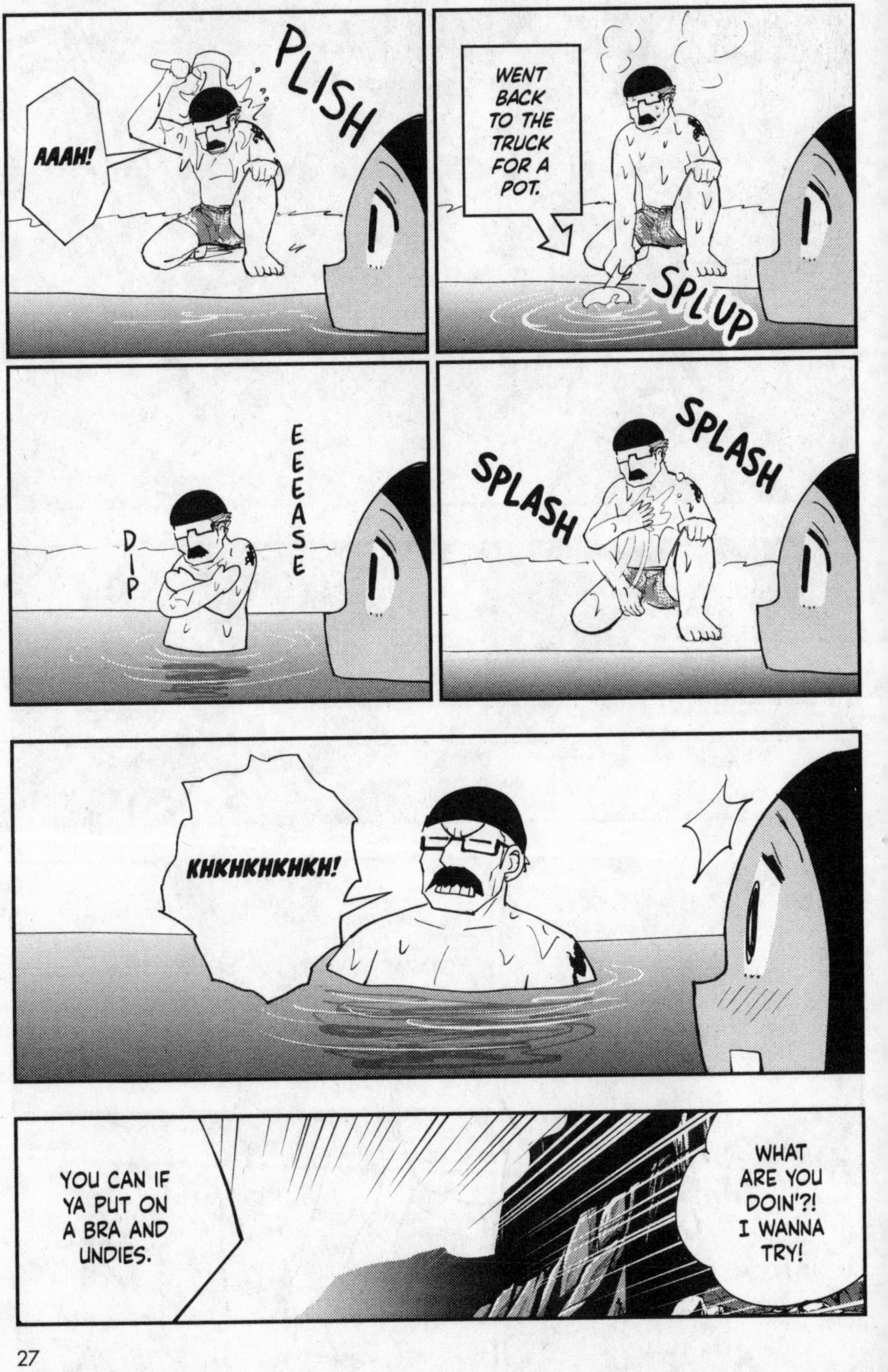
WENT BACK TO THE TRUCK FOR A POT.
SPLUP
PLISH
AAAH!
SPLASH
SPLASH
EEEASE
DIP
KHKHKHKHKH!
WHAT ARE YOU DOIN'?! I WANNA TRY!
YOU CAN IF YA PUT ON A BRA AND UNDIES.

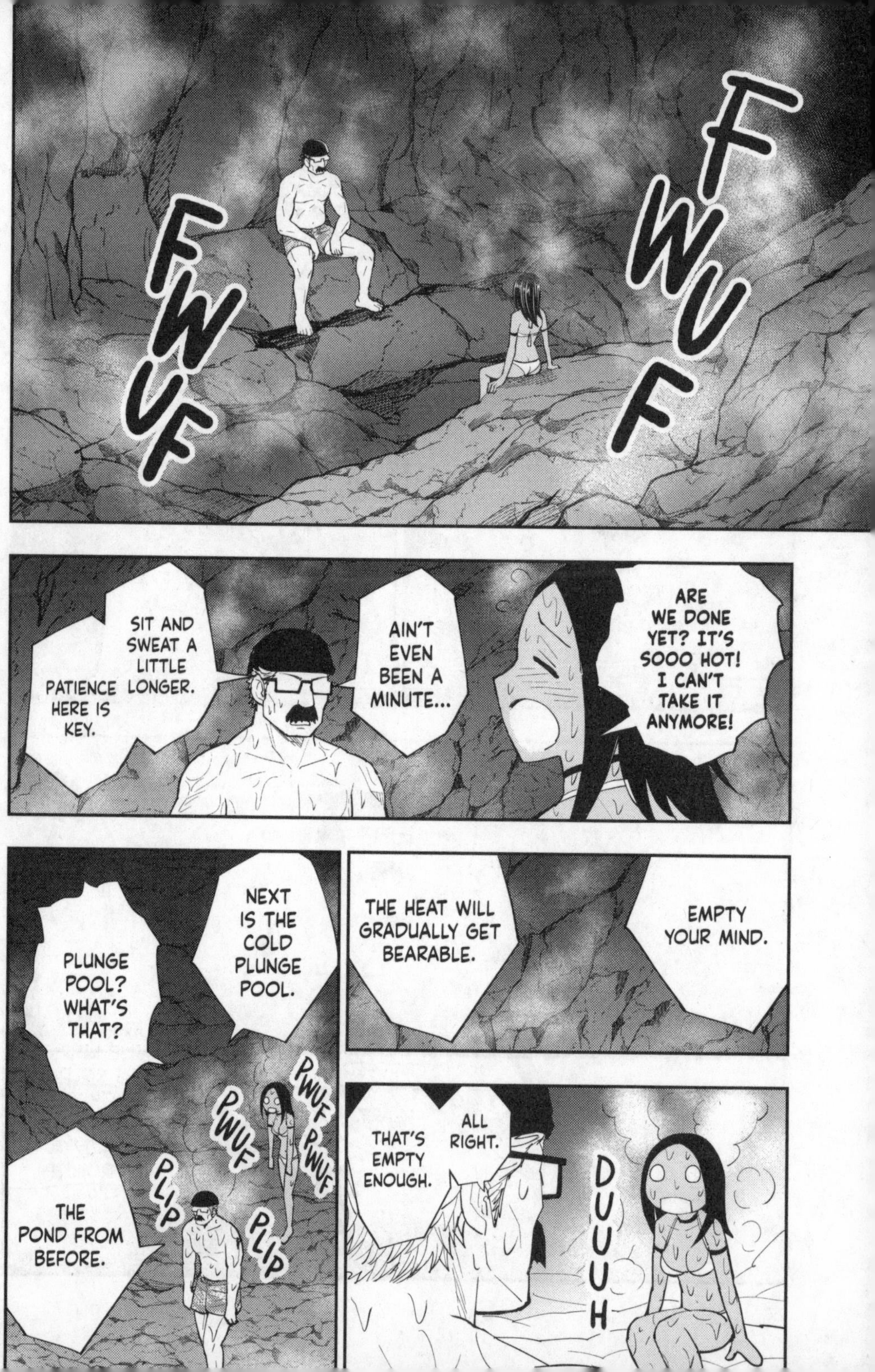
FWUF
FWUF
ARE WE DONE YET? IT'S SOOO HOT! I CAN'T TAKE IT ANYMORE!
AIN'T EVEN BEEN A MINUTE...
SIT AND SWEAT A LITTLE LONGER.
PATIENCE HERE IS KEY.
EMPTY YOUR MIND.
THE HEAT WILL GRADUALLY GET BEARABLE.
ALL RIGHT.
THAT'S EMPTY ENOUGH.
DUUUH
NEXT IS THE COLD PLUNGE POOL.
PLUNGE POOL? WHAT'S THAT?
PWUF PWUF
PWUF
PLIP
PLIP
THE POND FROM BEFORE.

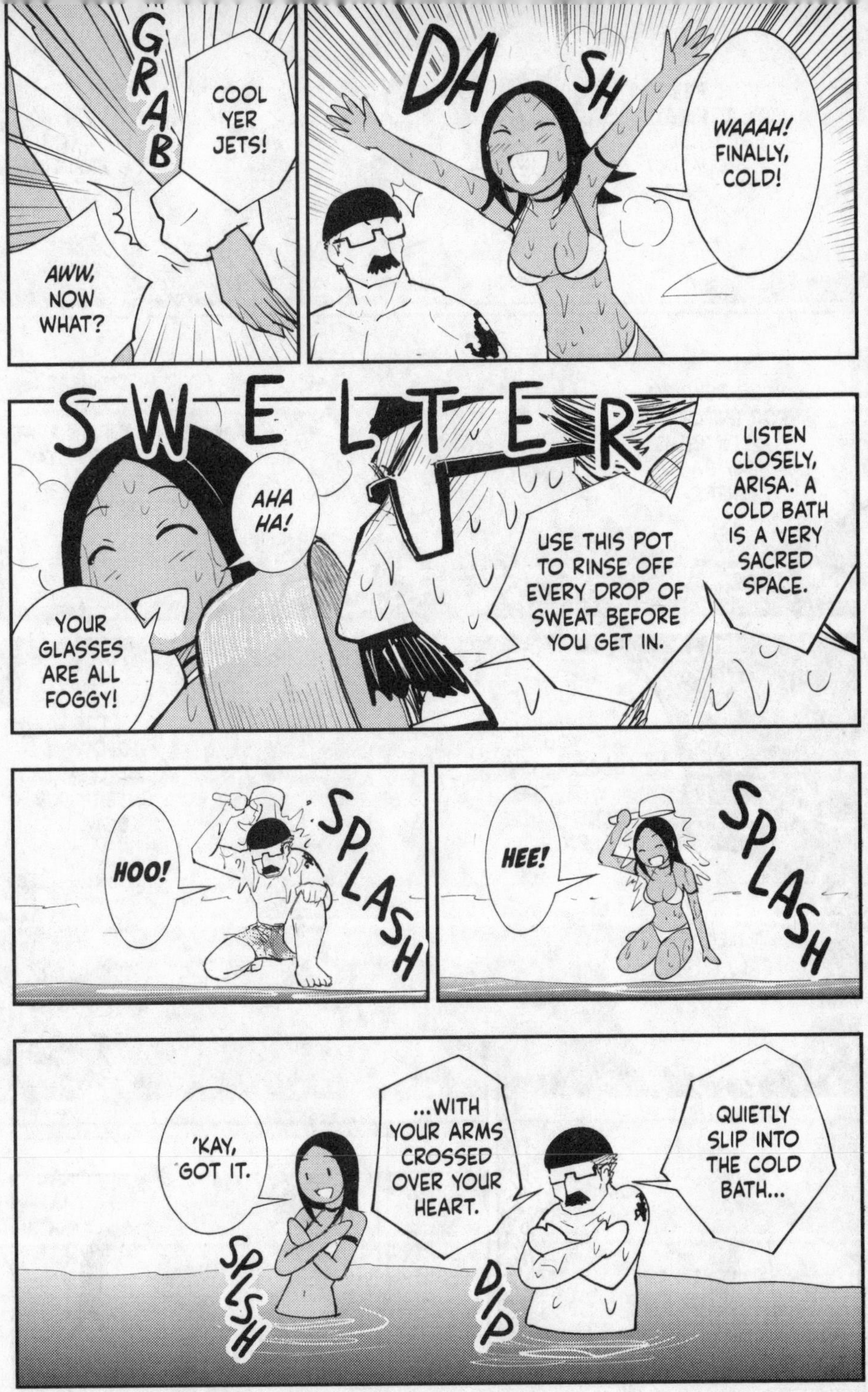
DASH
WAAAH! FINALLY, COLD!
COOL YER JETS!
GRAB
AWW, NOW WHAT?
SWELTER
LISTEN CLOSELY, ARISA. A COLD BATH IS A VERY SACRED SPACE.
USE THIS POT TO RINSE OFF EVERY DROP OF SWEAT BEFORE YOU GET IN.
AHA HA!
YOUR GLASSES ARE ALL FOGGY!
SPLASH
HEE!
SPLASH
HOO!
QUIETLY SLIP INTO THE COLD BATH...
...WITH YOUR ARMS CROSSED OVER YOUR HEART.
DIP
'KAY, GOT IT.
SPLSH

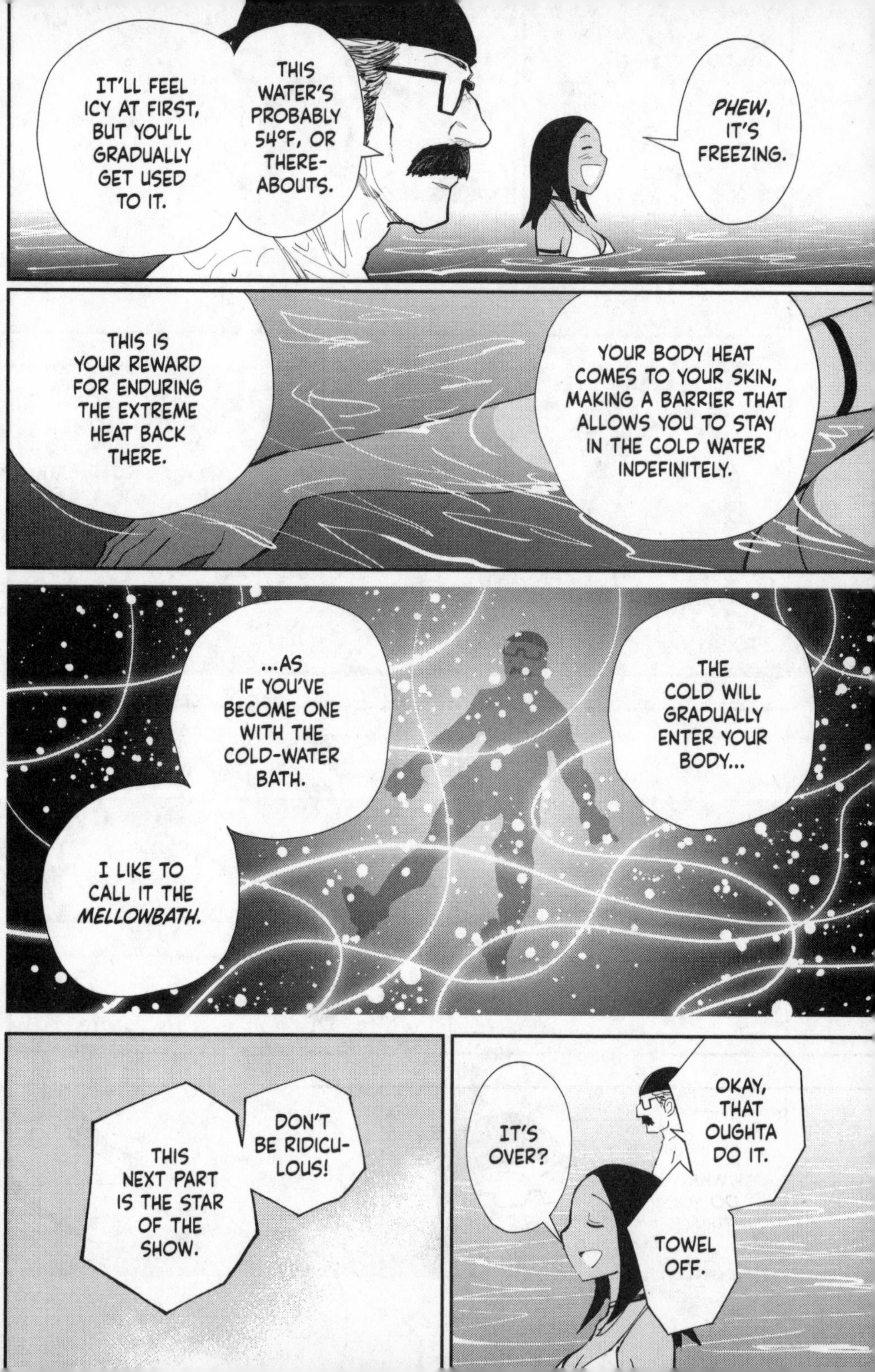
PHEW, IT'S FREEZING.
THIS WATER'S PROBABLY 54°F, OR THERE-ABOUTS.
IT'LL FEEL ICY AT FIRST, BUT YOU'LL GRADUALLY GET USED TO IT.
YOUR BODY HEAT COMES TO YOUR SKIN, MAKING A BARRIER THAT ALLOWS YOU TO STAY IN THE COLD WATER INDEFINITELY.
THIS IS YOUR REWARD FOR ENDURING THE EXTREME HEAT BACK THERE.
THE COLD WILL GRADUALLY ENTER YOUR BODY...
...AS IF YOU'VE BECOME ONE WITH THE COLD-WATER BATH.
I LIKE TO CALL IT THE *MELLOWBATH.*
OKAY, THAT OUGHTA DO IT.
IT'S OVER?
TOWEL OFF.
DON'T BE RIDICU-LOUS!
THIS NEXT PART IS THE STAR OF THE SHOW.

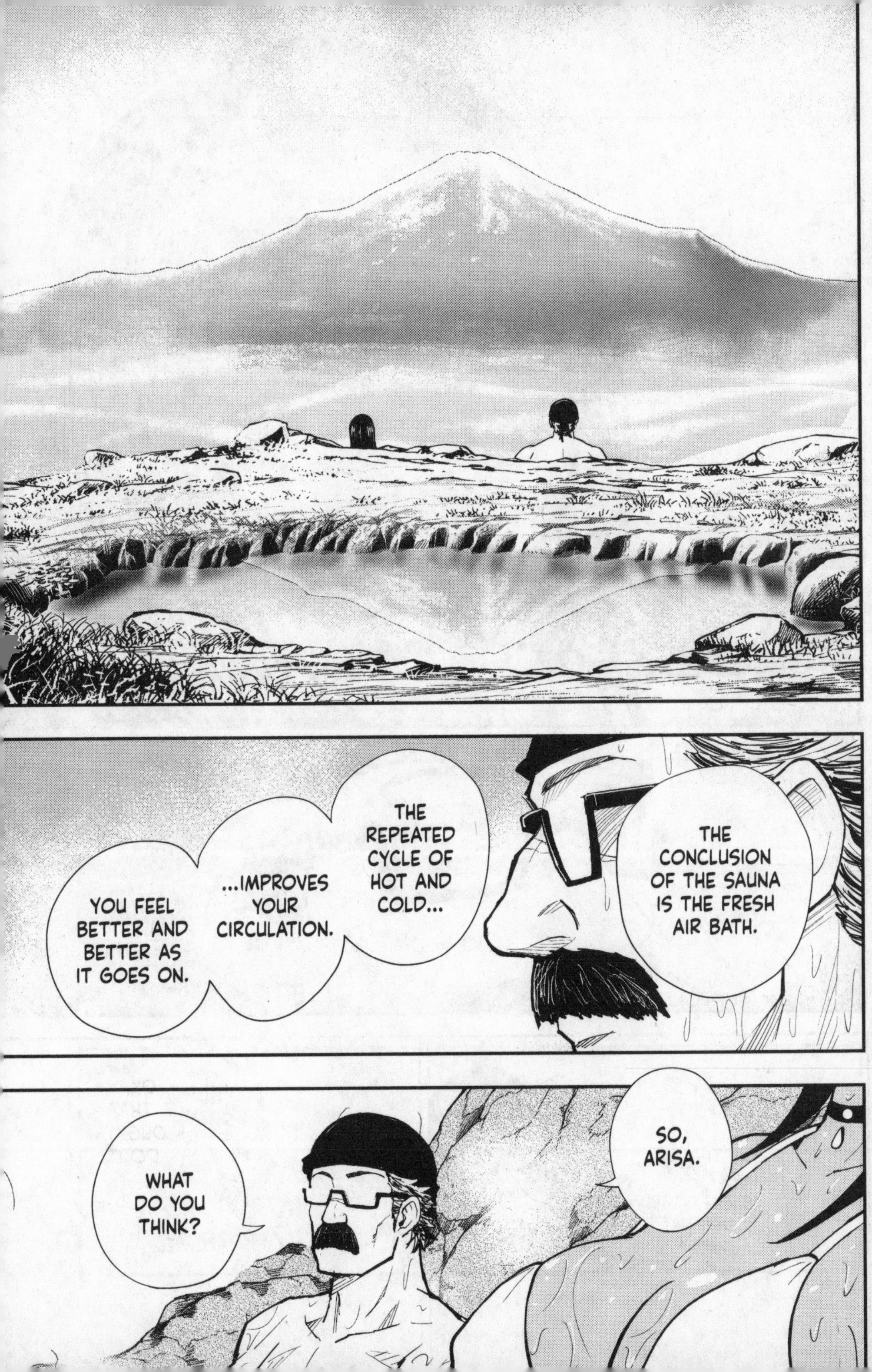
THE CONCLUSION OF THE SAUNA IS THE FRESH AIR BATH.
THE REPEATED CYCLE OF HOT AND COLD...
...IMPROVES YOUR CIRCULATION.
YOU FEEL BETTER AND BETTER AS IT GOES ON.
SO, ARISA.
WHAT DO YOU THINK?

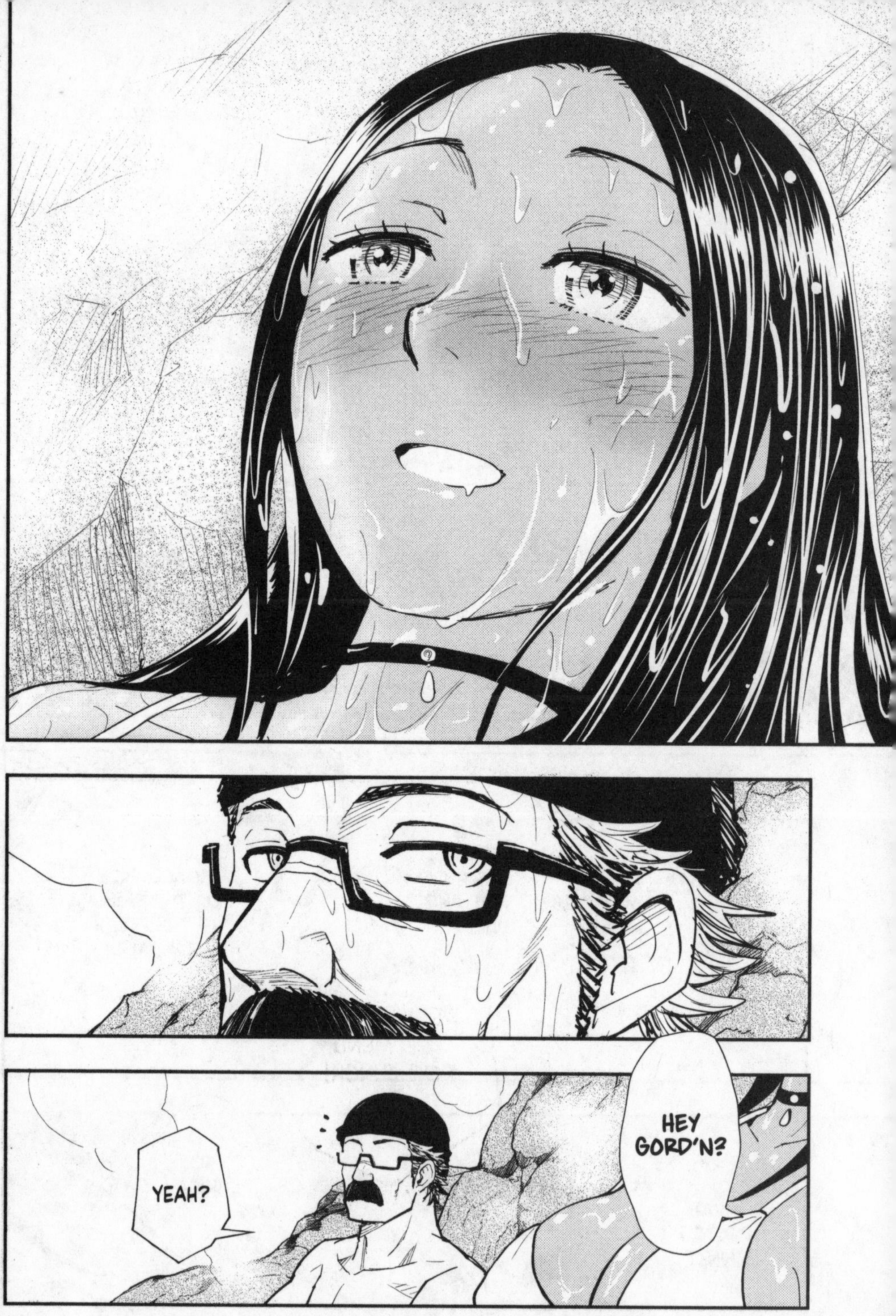
HEY GORD'N?
YEAH?

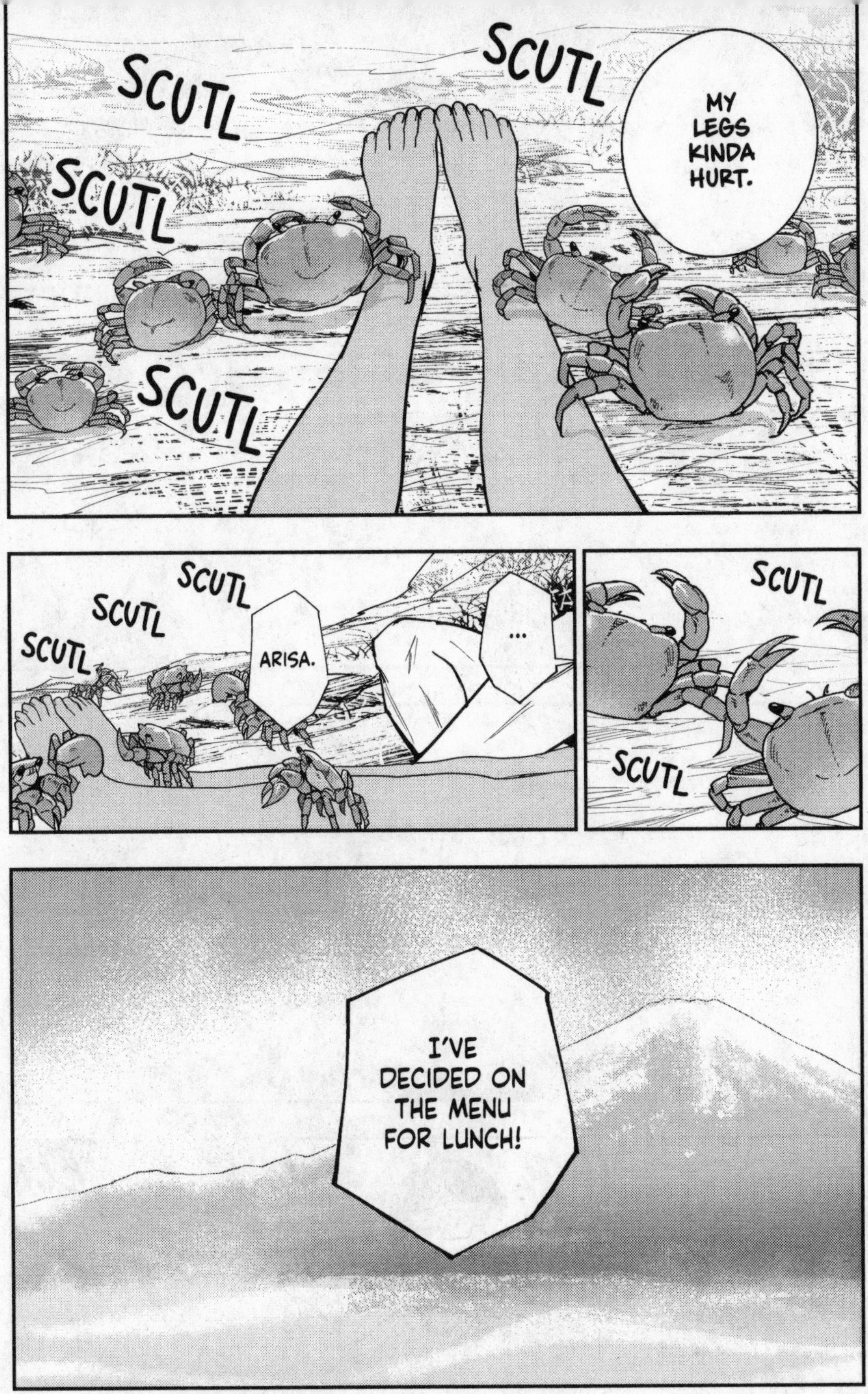
MY LEGS KINDA HURT.
SCUTL
SCUTL
SCUTL
SCUTL
SCUTL
SCUTL
...
ARISA.
SCUTL
SCUTL
SCUTL
I'VE DECIDED ON THE MENU FOR LUNCH!

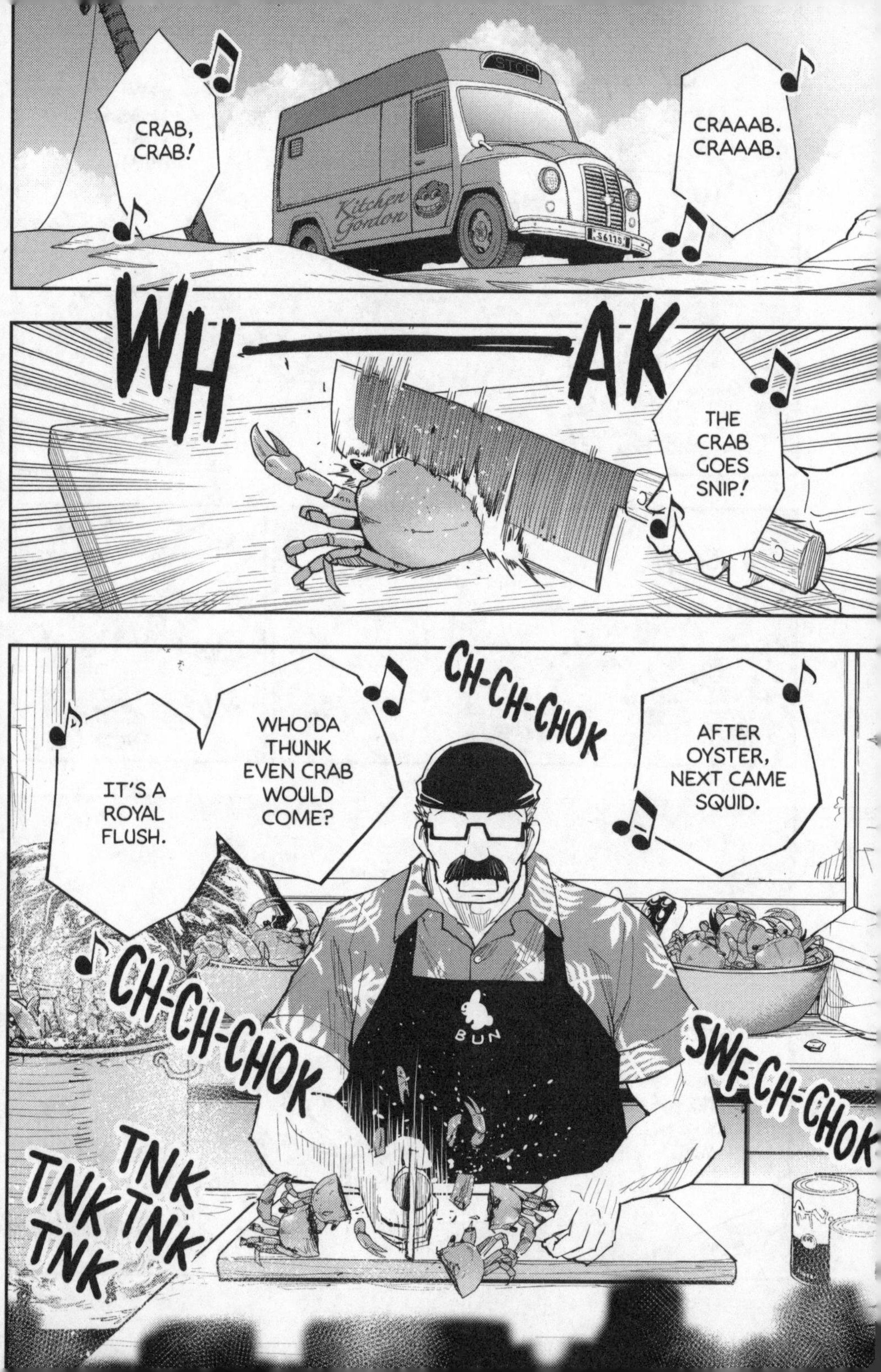
STOP
Kitchen Gordon
S6115
CRAAAB. CRAAAB.
CRAB, CRAB!
WH—AK
THE CRAB GOES SNIP!
CH-CH-CHOK
AFTER OYSTER, NEXT CAME SQUID.
WHO'DA THUNK EVEN CRAB WOULD COME?
IT'S A ROYAL FLUSH.
BUN
SWFCH-CH-CHOK
CH-CH-CHOK
TNK TNK TNK
TNK TNK

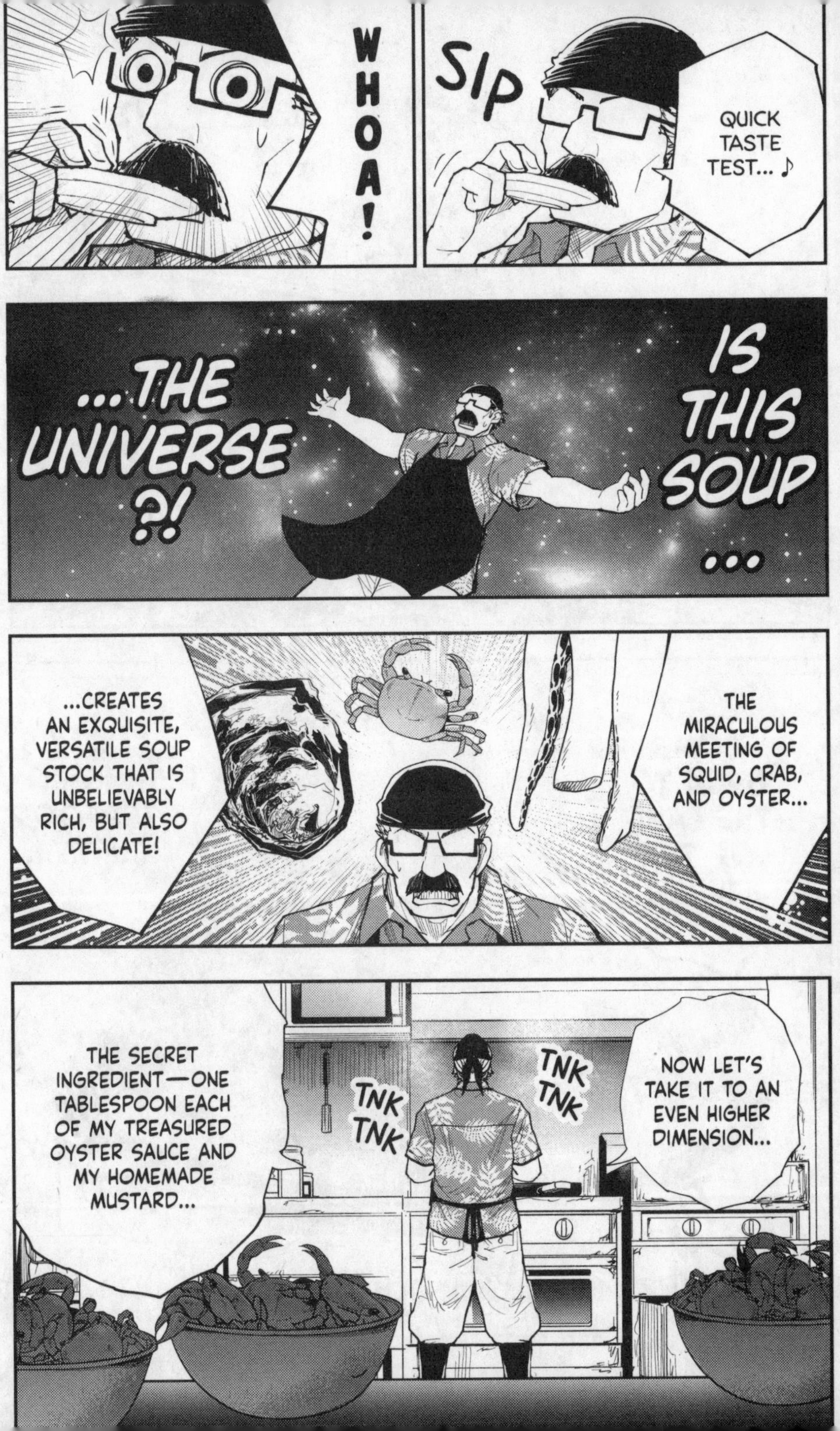
SIP
QUICK TASTE TEST... ♪
WHOA!
IS THIS SOUP...
...THE UNIVERSE?!
THE MIRACULOUS MEETING OF SQUID, CRAB, AND OYSTER...
...CREATES AN EXQUISITE, VERSATILE SOUP STOCK THAT IS UNBELIEVABLY RICH, BUT ALSO DELICATE!
NOW LET'S TAKE IT TO AN EVEN HIGHER DIMENSION...
TNK TNK
TNK TNK
THE SECRET INGREDIENT—ONE TABLESPOON EACH OF MY TREASURED OYSTER SAUCE AND MY HOMEMADE MUSTARD...

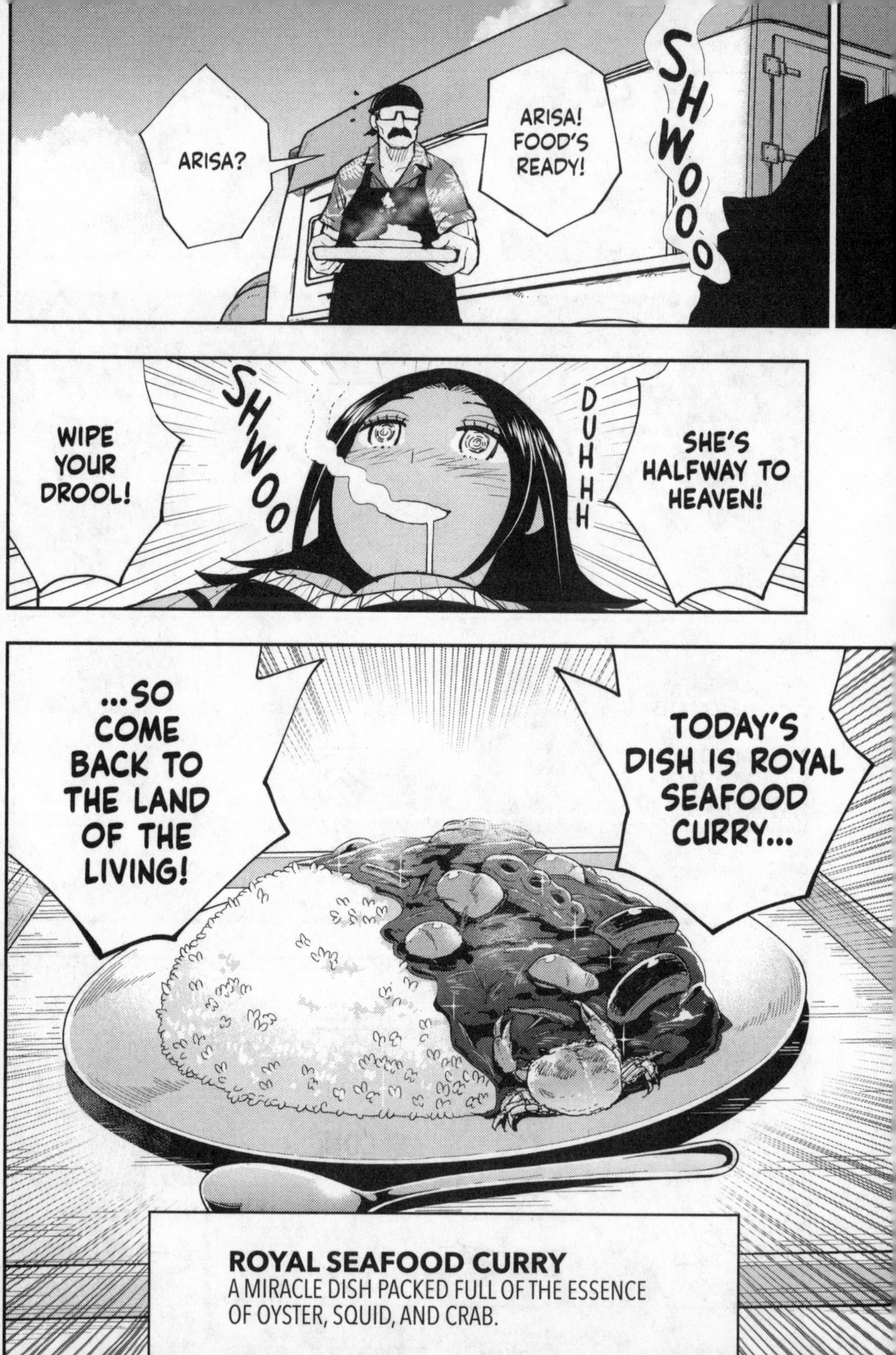
SHWOOO
ARISA! FOOD'S READY!
ARISA?
SHE'S HALFWAY TO HEAVEN!
DUHHH
SHWOO
WIPE YOUR DROOL!
TODAY'S DISH IS ROYAL SEAFOOD CURRY...
...SO COME BACK TO THE LAND OF THE LIVING!
ROYAL SEAFOOD CURRY
A MIRACLE DISH PACKED FULL OF THE ESSENCE OF OYSTER, SQUID, AND CRAB.

AAAH
NOM
!
SO, HOW DO YA LIKE CURRY THAT AIN'T A SOLID BLOCK?
GLUG
GLUG
GULP
NOW YOU'RE *DRINKIN'* IT?
SECONDS!
VWP
WELCOME BACK.

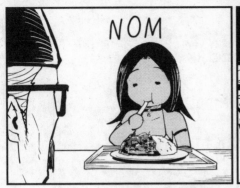

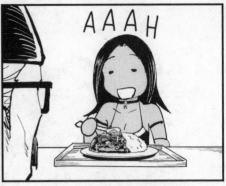

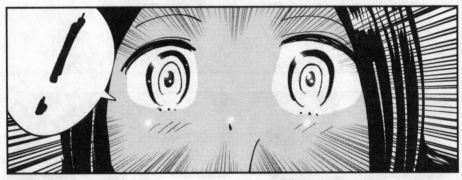

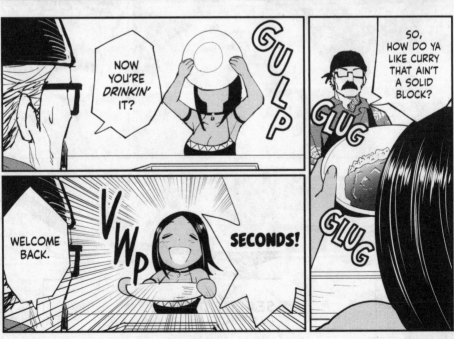

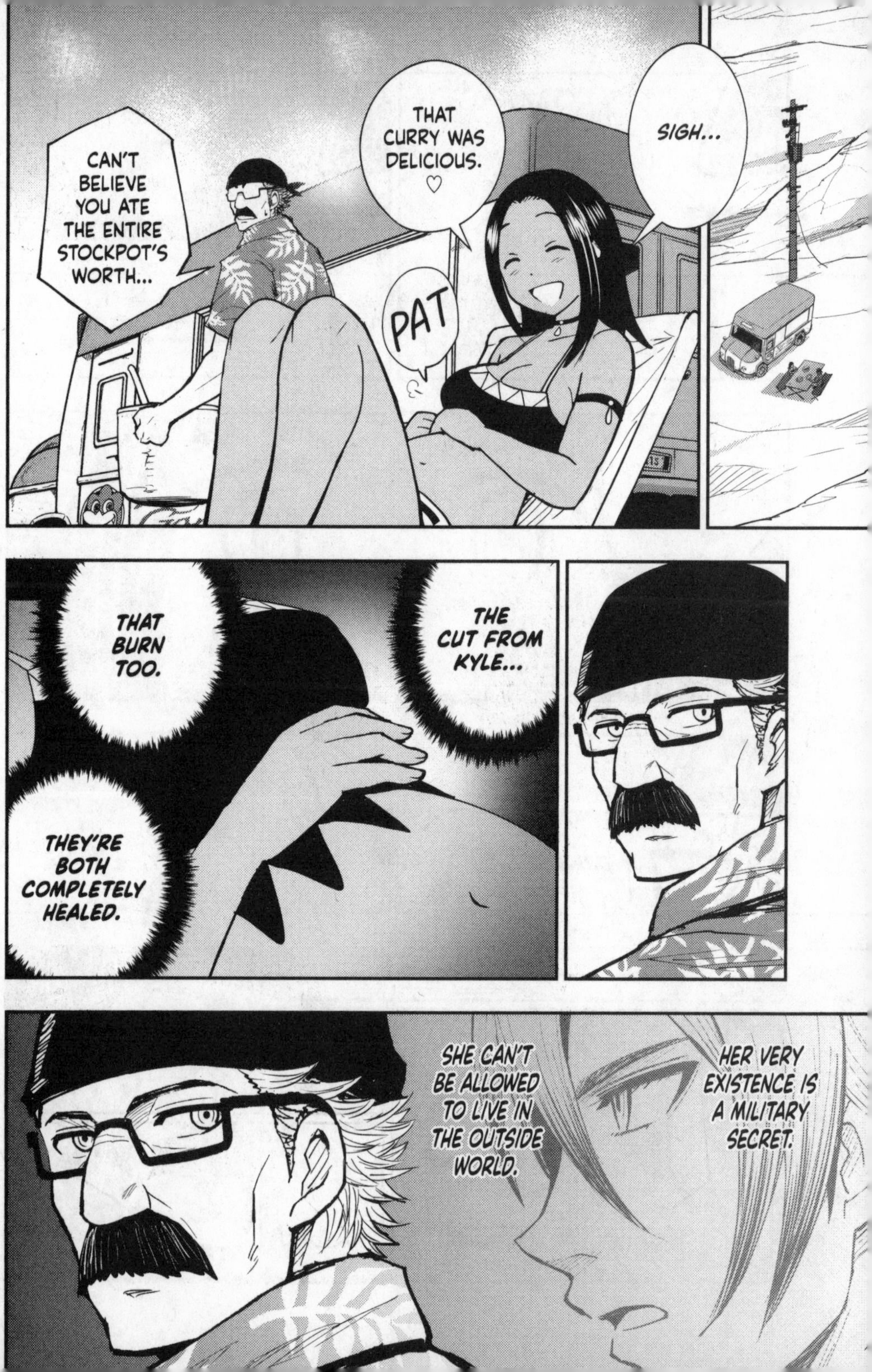
SIGH...
THAT CURRY WAS DELICIOUS. ♡
PAT
CAN'T BELIEVE YOU ATE THE ENTIRE STOCKPOT'S WORTH...
THE CUT FROM KYLE...
THAT BURN TOO.
THEY'RE BOTH COMPLETELY HEALED.
HER VERY EXISTENCE IS A MILITARY SECRET.
SHE CAN'T BE ALLOWED TO LIVE IN THE OUTSIDE WORLD.

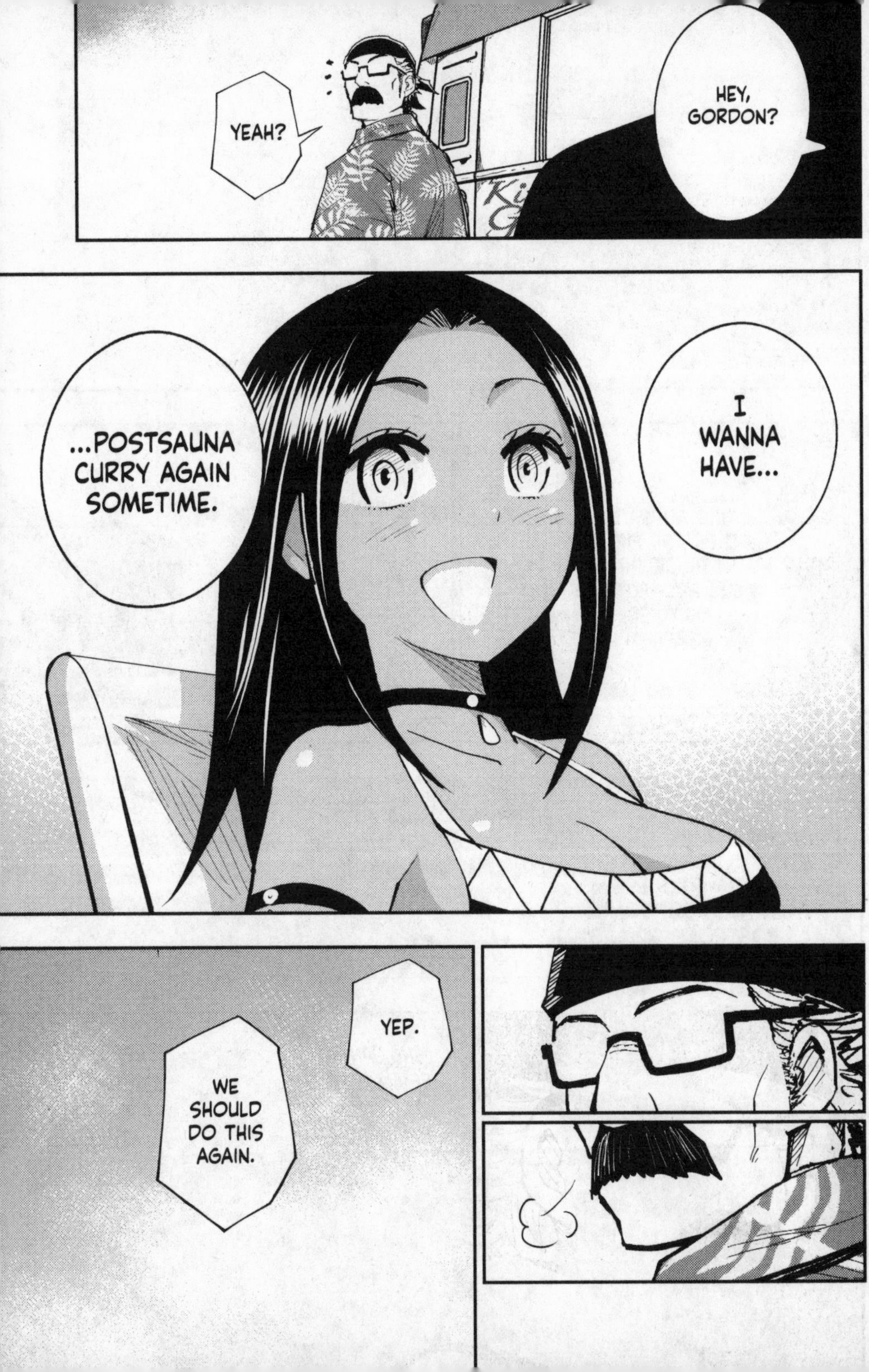
HEY, GORDON?
YEAH?
I WANNA HAVE...
...POSTSAUNA CURRY AGAIN SOMETIME.
YEP.
WE SHOULD DO THIS AGAIN.

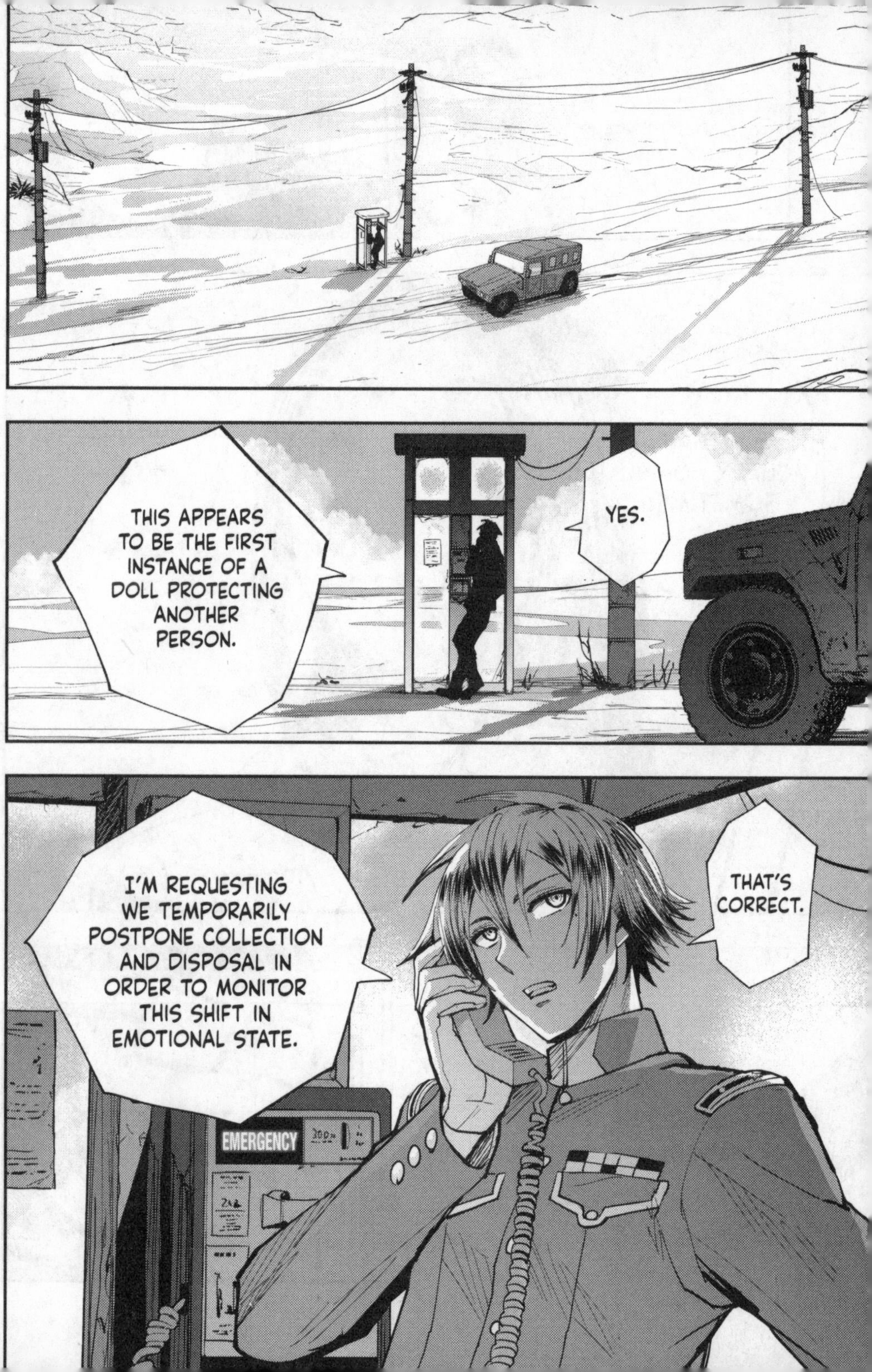
YES.
THIS APPEARS TO BE THE FIRST INSTANCE OF A DOLL PROTECTING ANOTHER PERSON.
THAT'S CORRECT.
I'M REQUESTING WE TEMPORARILY POSTPONE COLLECTION AND DISPOSAL IN ORDER TO MONITOR THIS SHIFT IN EMOTIONAL STATE.
EMERGENCY

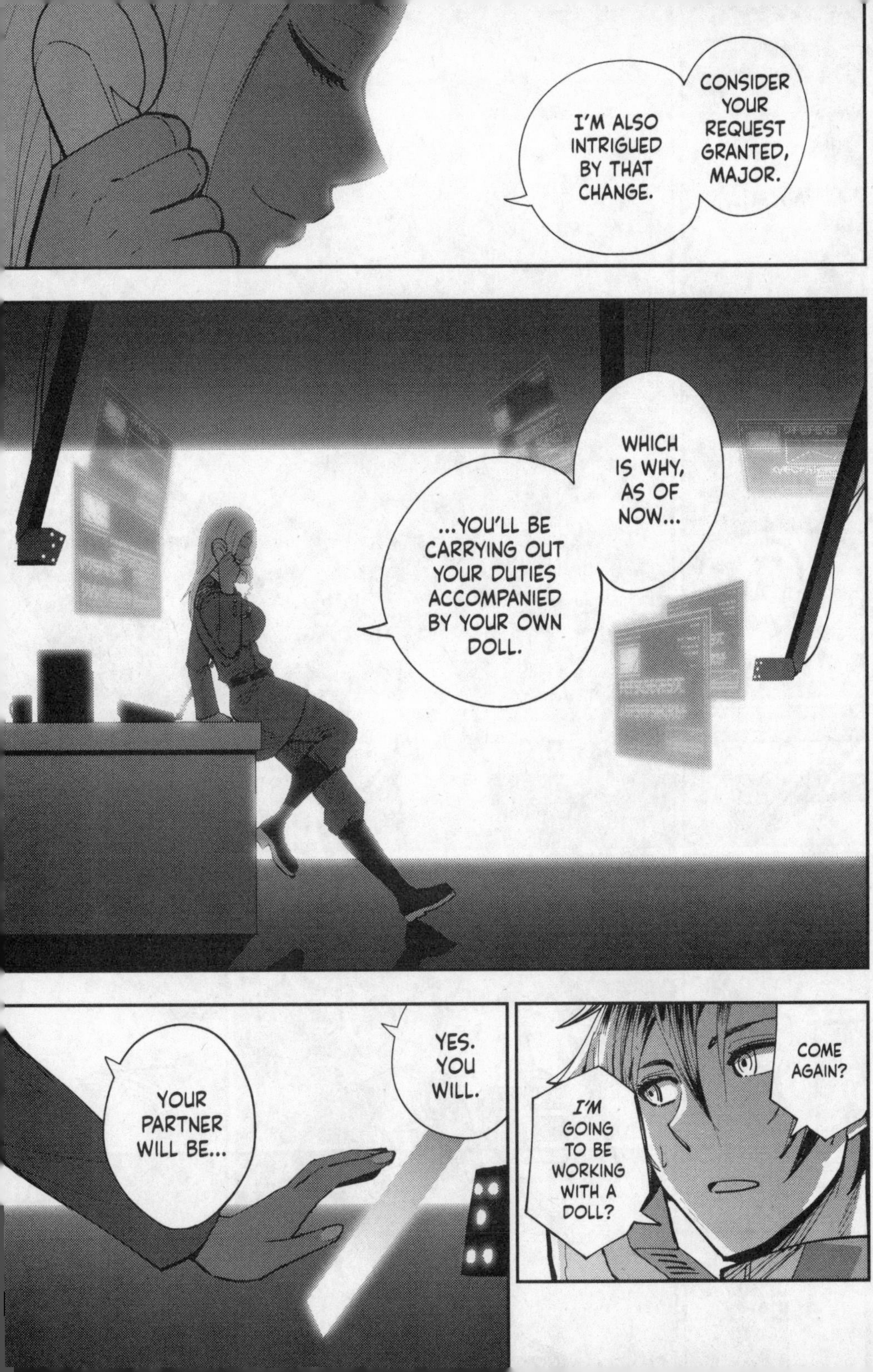
CONSIDER YOUR REQUEST GRANTED, MAJOR.
I'M ALSO INTRIGUED BY THAT CHANGE.
WHICH IS WHY, AS OF NOW...
...YOU'LL BE CARRYING OUT YOUR DUTIES ACCOMPANIED BY YOUR OWN DOLL.
COME AGAIN?
I'M GOING TO BE WORKING WITH A DOLL?
YES. YOU WILL.
YOUR PARTNER WILL BE...

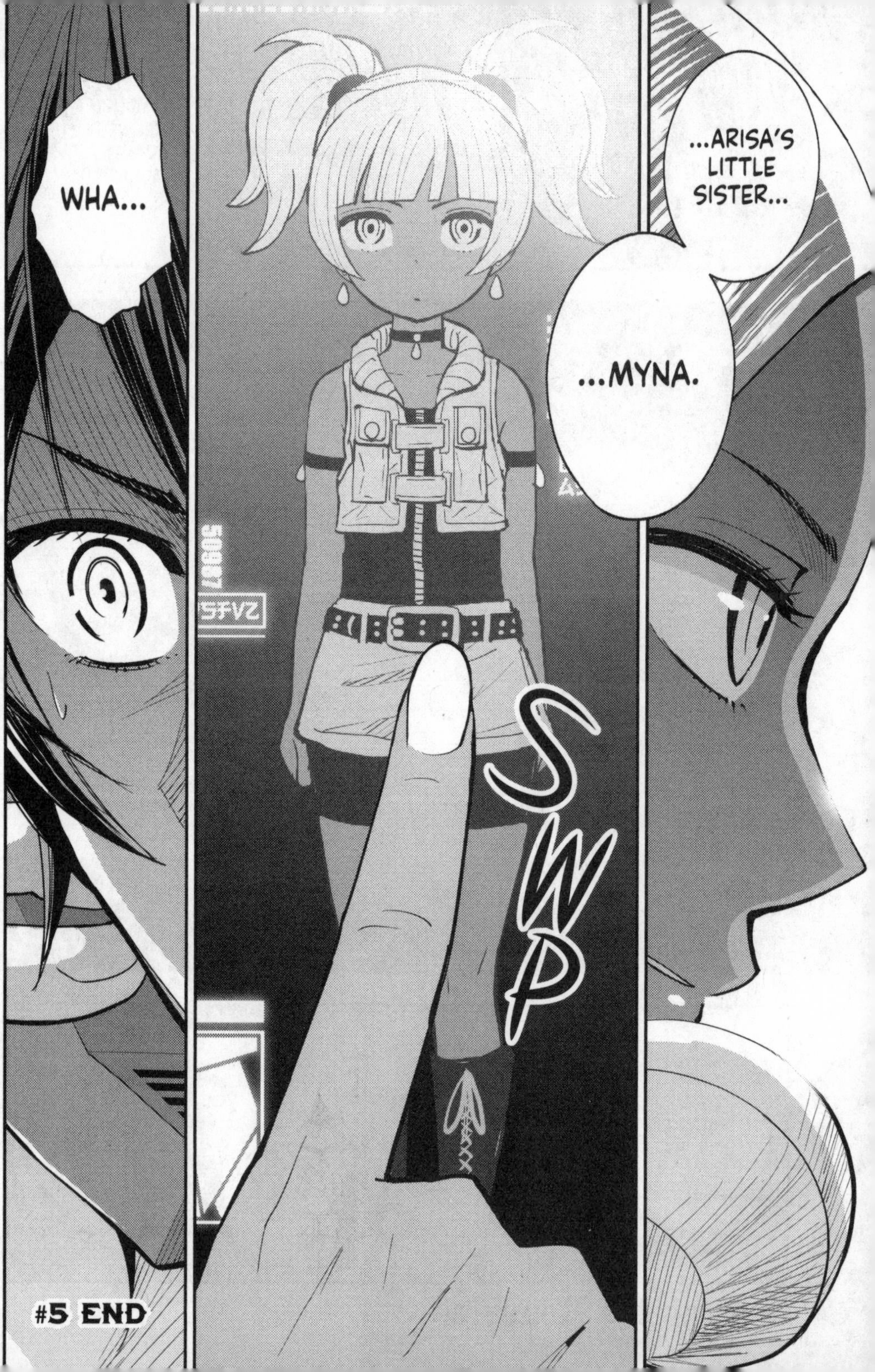
...ARISA'S LITTLE SISTER...
...MYNA.
SWP
WHA...
#5 END

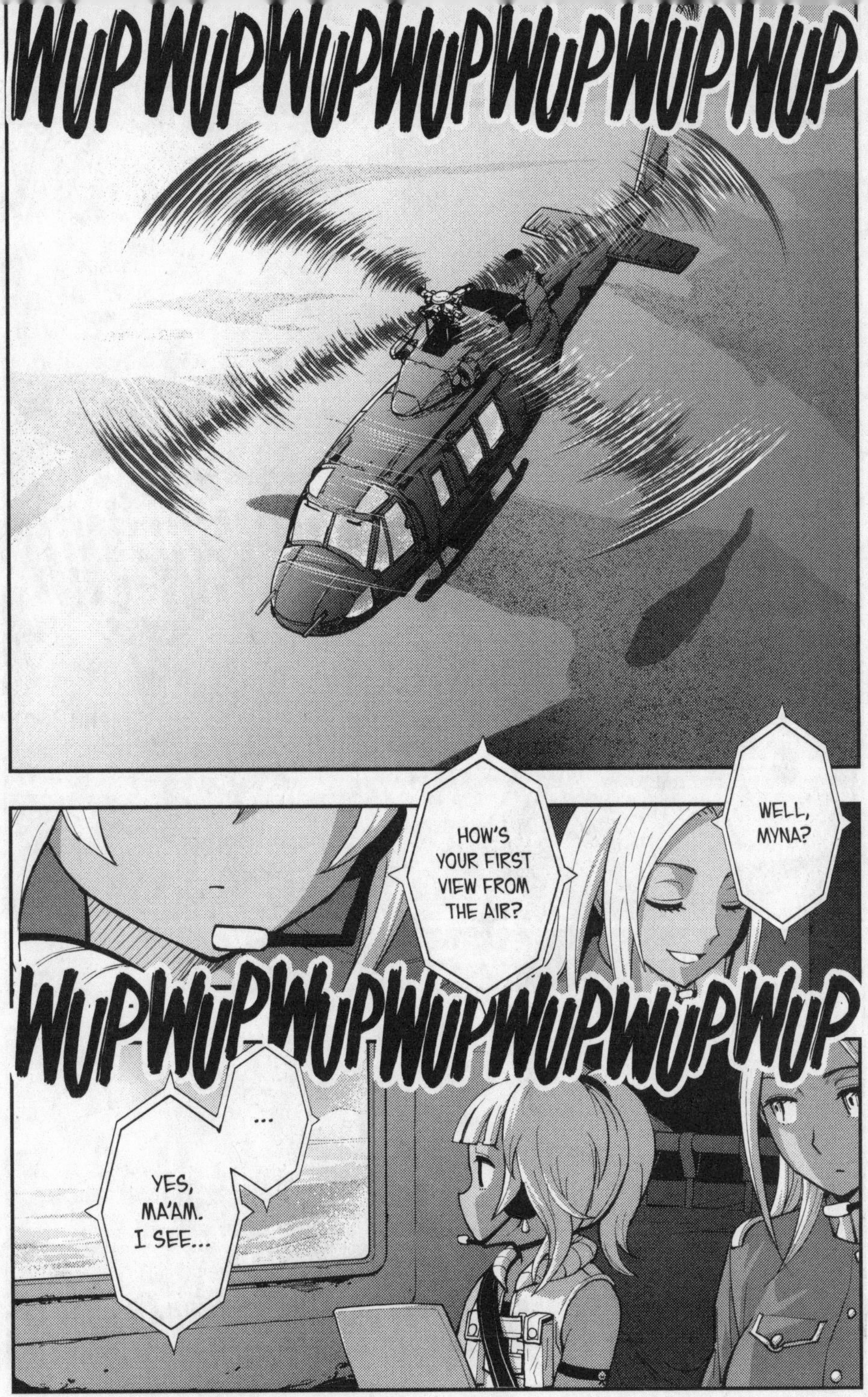
WUP WUP WUP WUP WUP WUP WUP
WELL, MYNA?
HOW'S YOUR FIRST VIEW FROM THE AIR?
WUP WUP WUP WUP WUP WUP WUP
...
YES, MA'AM. I SEE...

#6 B (NO LT) SANDWICH

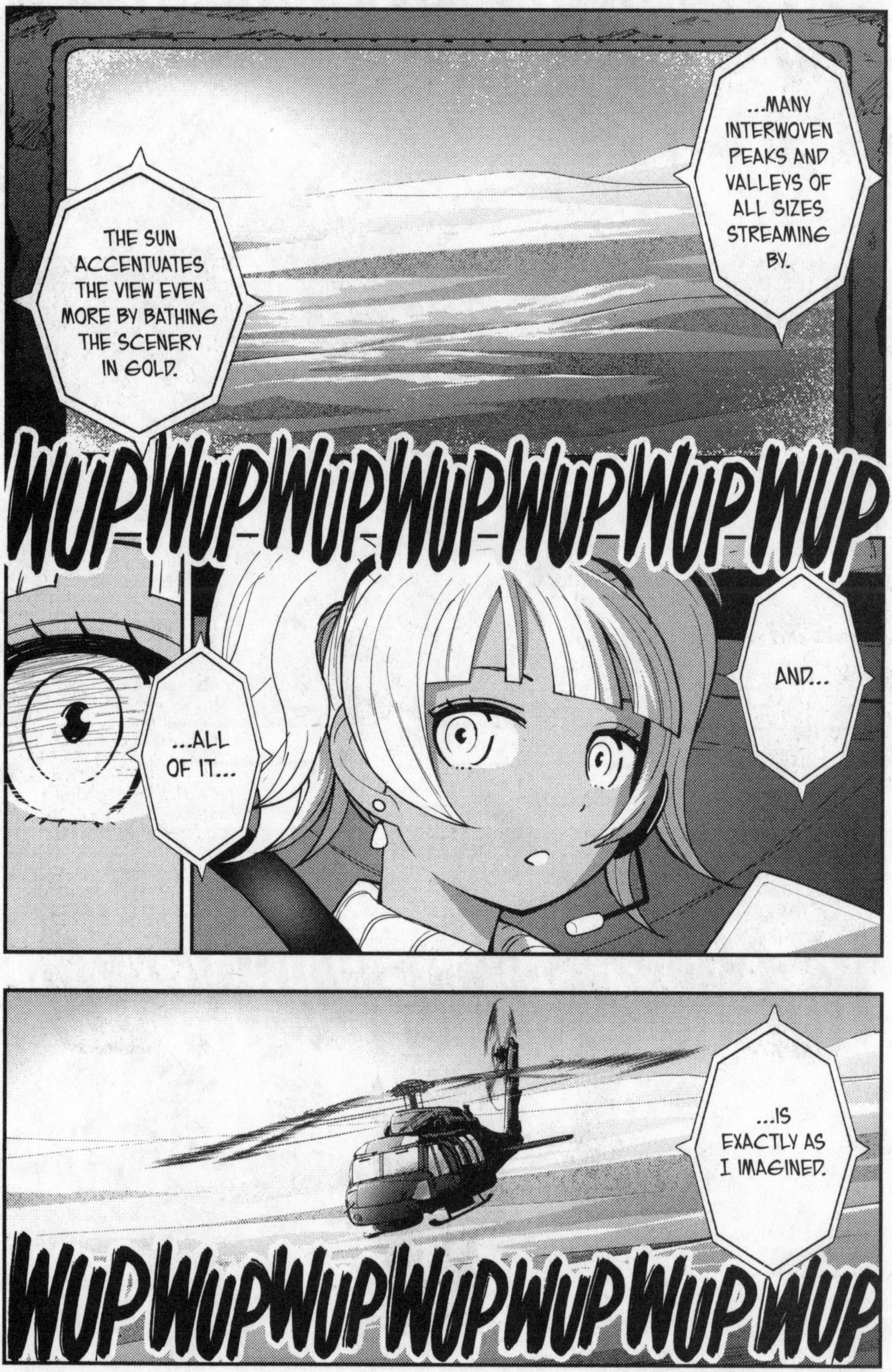
...MANY INTERWOVEN PEAKS AND VALLEYS OF ALL SIZES STREAMING BY.
THE SUN ACCENTUATES THE VIEW EVEN MORE BY BATHING THE SCENERY IN GOLD.
WUP WUP WUP WUP WUP WUP WUP
AND...
...ALL OF IT...
...IS EXACTLY AS I IMAGINED.
WUP WUP WUP WUP WUP WUP WUP

#6 B (NO LT) SANDWICH

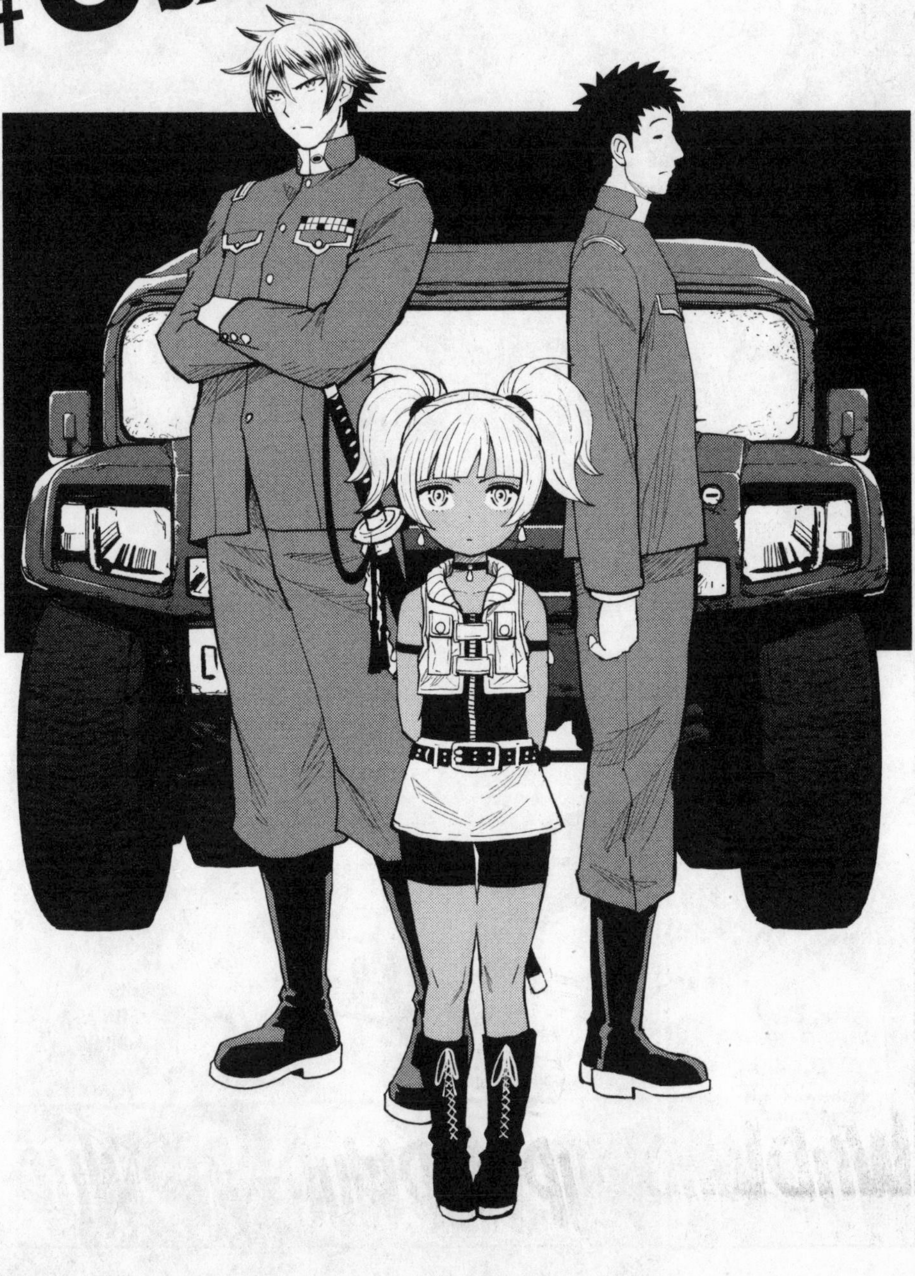

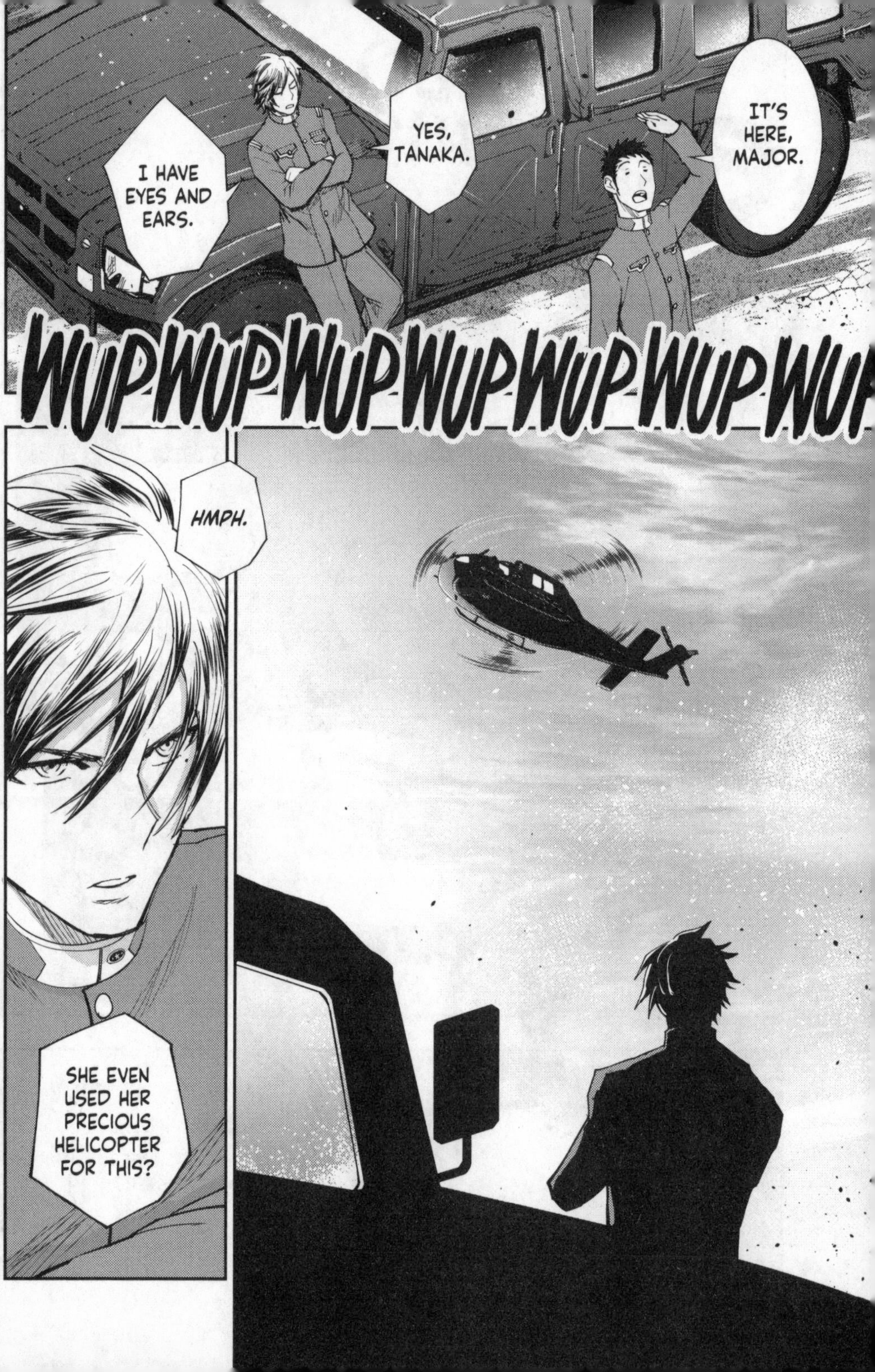
IT'S HERE, MAJOR.
YES, TANAKA.
I HAVE EYES AND EARS.
WUP WUP WUP WUP WUP WUP WUP
HMPH.
SHE EVEN USED HER PRECIOUS HELICOPTER FOR THIS?

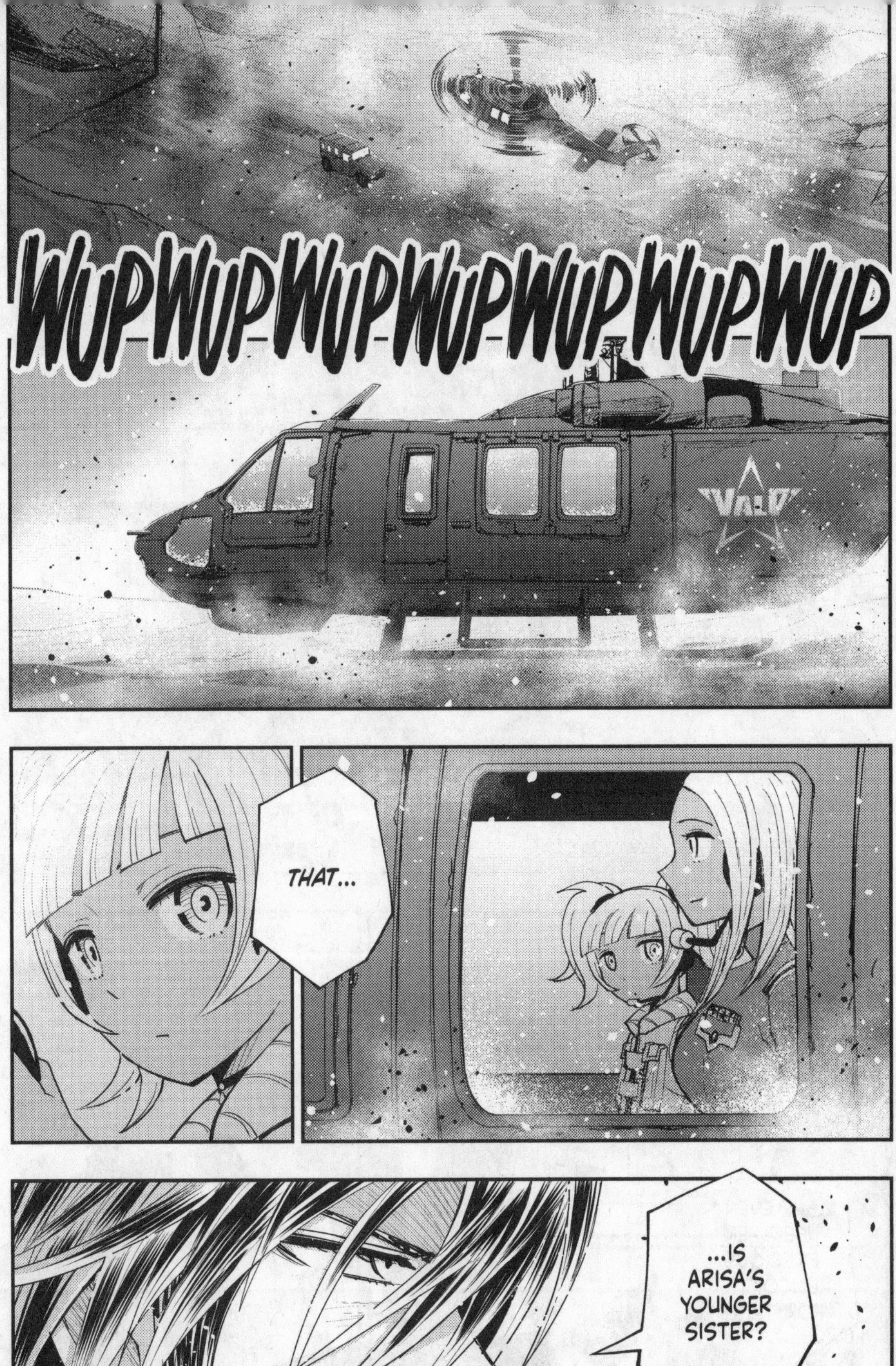
WUP WUP WUP WUP WUP WUP WUP
THAT...
...IS ARISA'S YOUNGER SISTER?

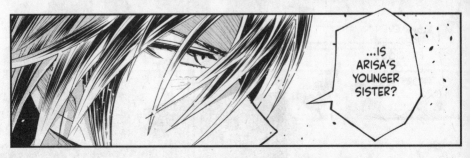

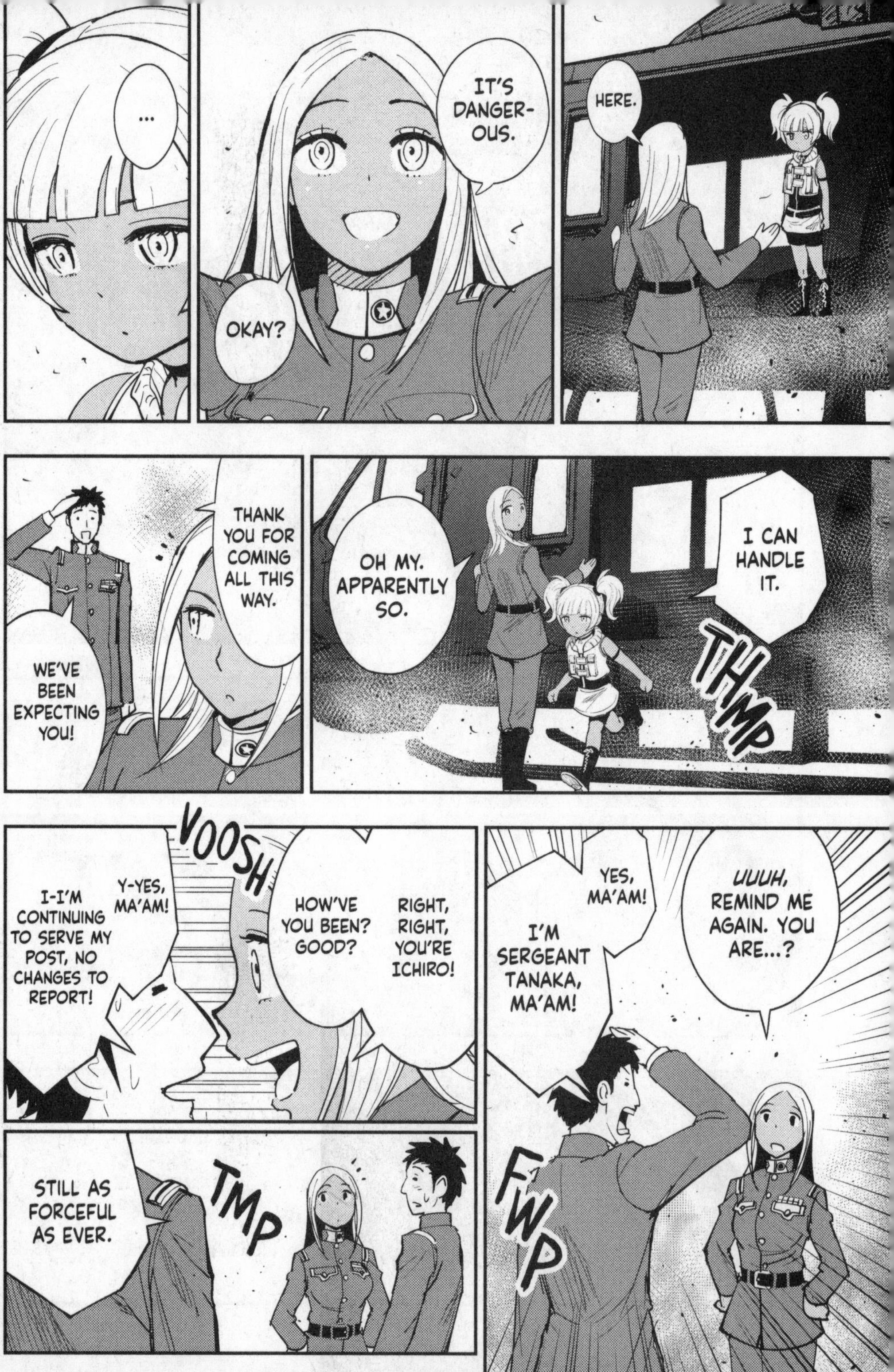
HERE.
IT'S DANGER-OUS.
OKAY?
...
I CAN HANDLE IT.
THMP
OH MY. APPARENTLY SO.
THANK YOU FOR COMING ALL THIS WAY.
WE'VE BEEN EXPECTING YOU!
UUUH, REMIND ME AGAIN. YOU ARE...?
YES, MA'AM!
I'M SERGEANT TANAKA, MA'AM!
FWP
RIGHT, RIGHT, YOU'RE ICHIRO!
HOW'VE YOU BEEN? GOOD?
VOOSH
Y-YES, MA'AM!
I-I'M CONTINUING TO SERVE MY POST, NO CHANGES TO REPORT!
TMP
STILL AS FORCEFUL AS EVER.

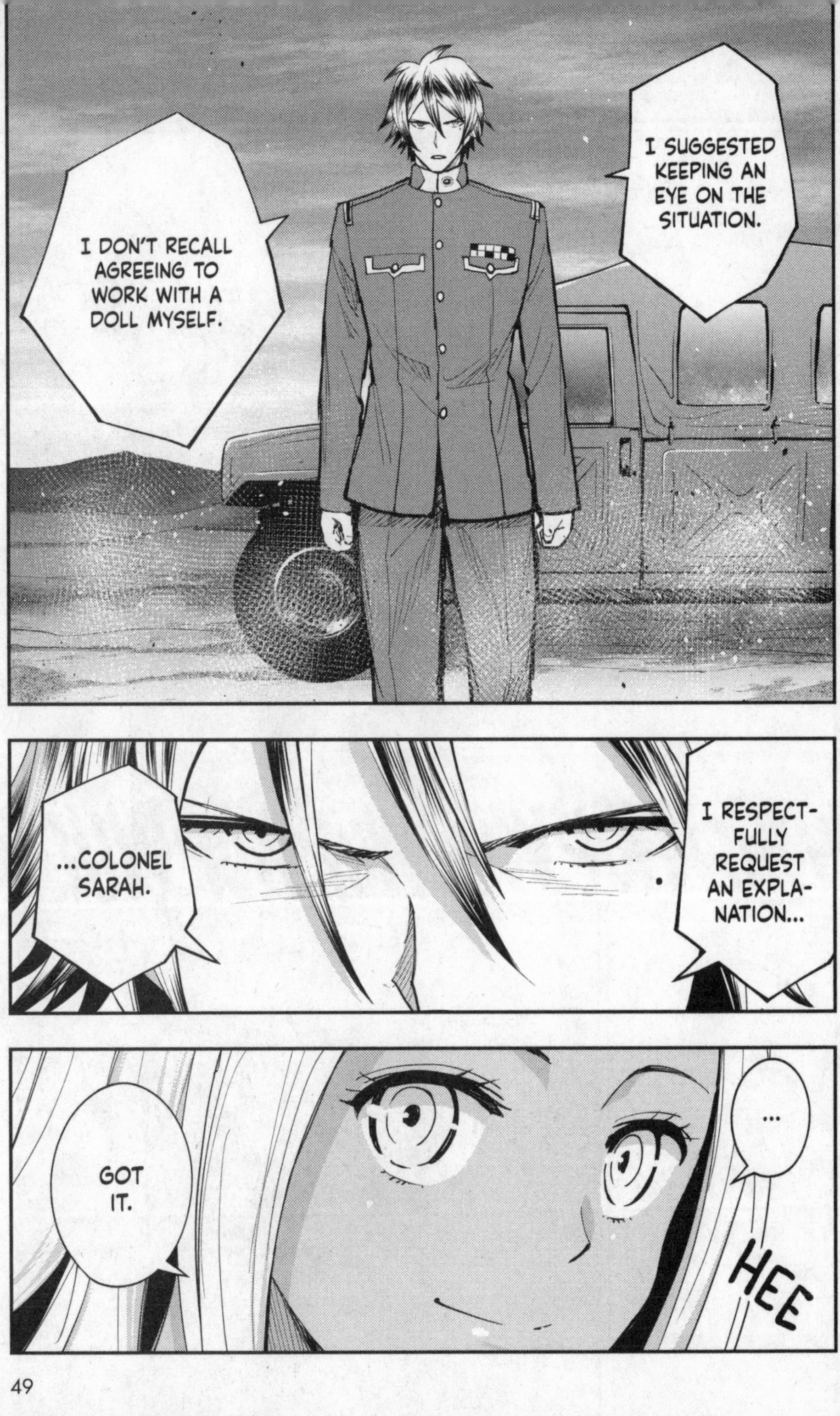
I SUGGESTED KEEPING AN EYE ON THE SITUATION.
I DON'T RECALL AGREEING TO WORK WITH A DOLL MYSELF.
I RESPECT-FULLY REQUEST AN EXPLA-NATION...
...COLONEL SARAH.
...
HEE
GOT IT.

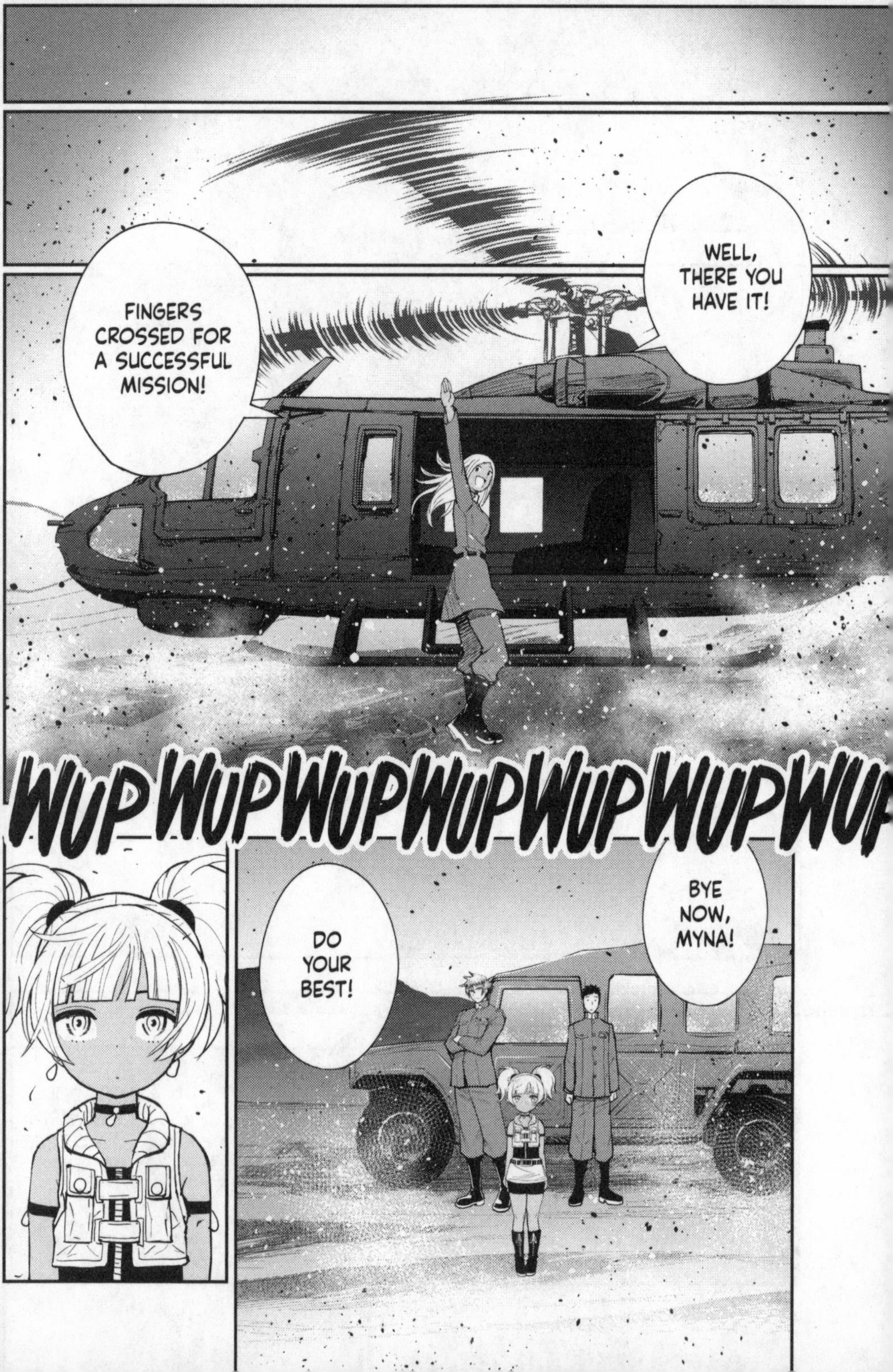
WELL, THERE YOU HAVE IT!
FINGERS CROSSED FOR A SUCCESSFUL MISSION!
WUP WUP WUP WUP WUP WUP WUP
BYE NOW, MYNA!
DO YOUR BEST!

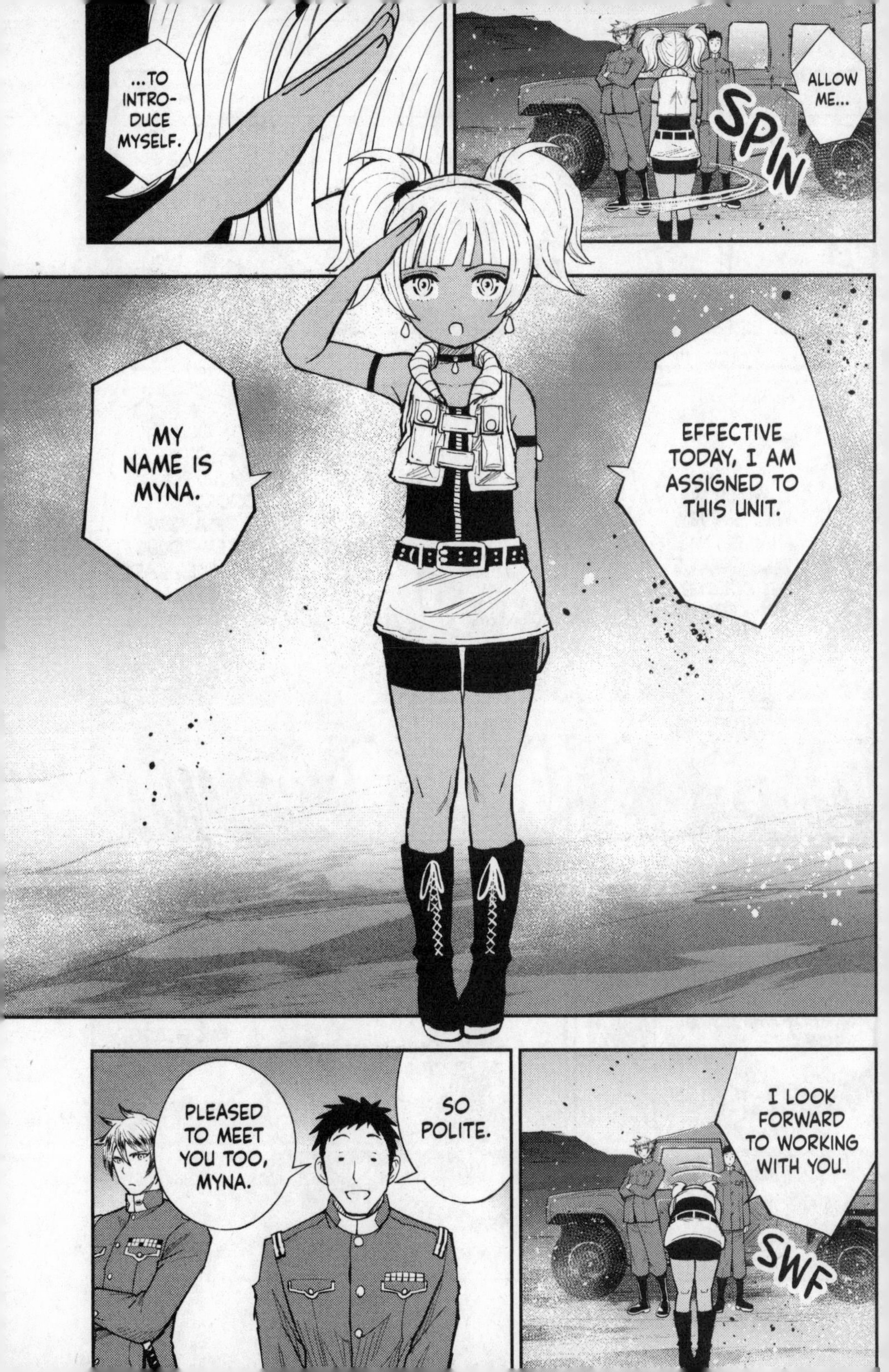
ALLOW ME...
SPIN
...TO INTRO-DUCE MYSELF.
EFFECTIVE TODAY, I AM ASSIGNED TO THIS UNIT.
MY NAME IS MYNA.
I LOOK FORWARD TO WORKING WITH YOU.
SWF
SO POLITE.
PLEASED TO MEET YOU TOO, MYNA.

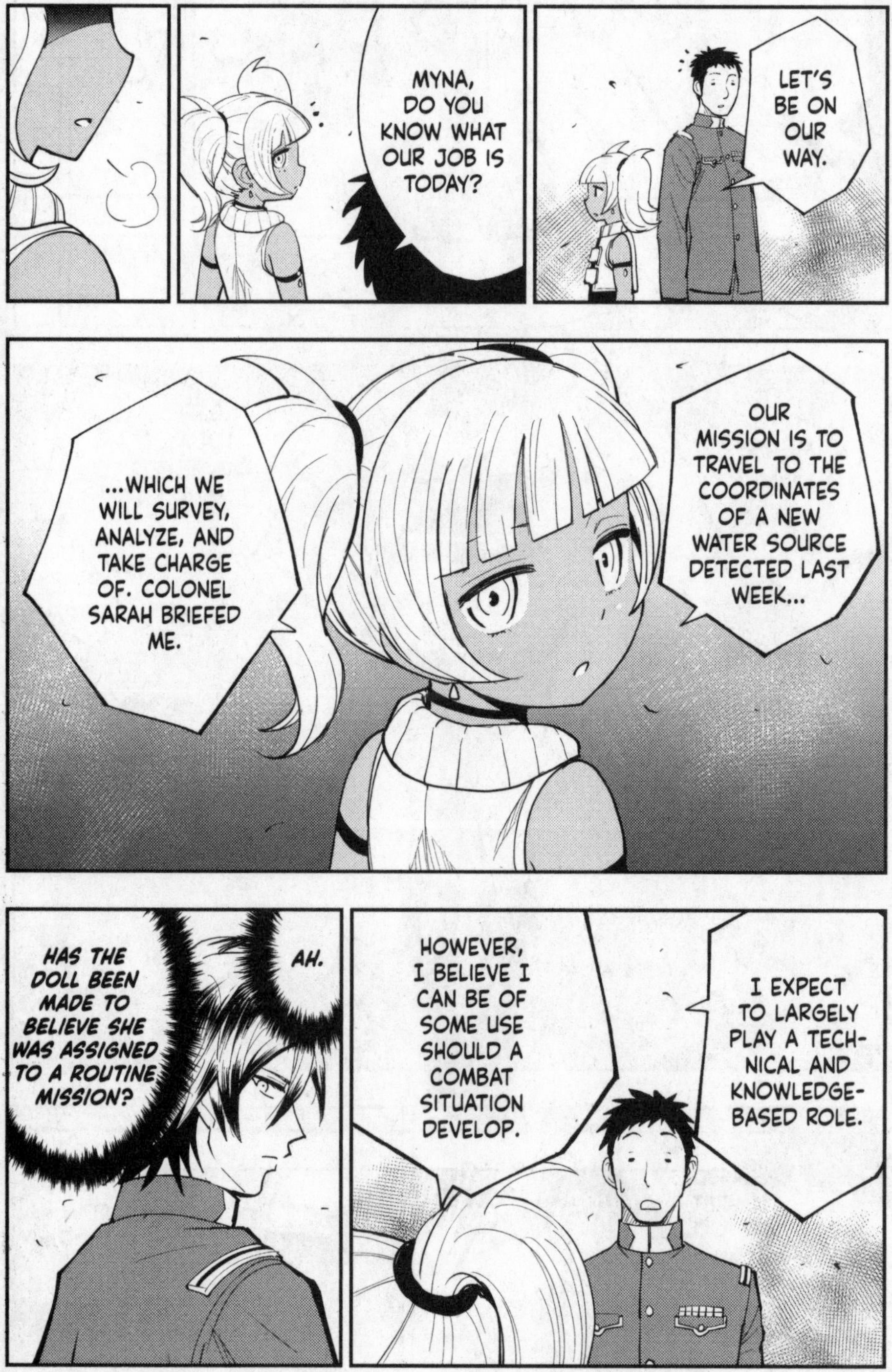
LET'S BE ON OUR WAY.
MYNA, DO YOU KNOW WHAT OUR JOB IS TODAY?
OUR MISSION IS TO TRAVEL TO THE COORDINATES OF A NEW WATER SOURCE DETECTED LAST WEEK...
...WHICH WE WILL SURVEY, ANALYZE, AND TAKE CHARGE OF. COLONEL SARAH BRIEFED ME.
I EXPECT TO LARGELY PLAY A TECH-NICAL AND KNOWLEDGE-BASED ROLE.
HOWEVER, I BELIEVE I CAN BE OF SOME USE SHOULD A COMBAT SITUATION DEVELOP.
AH.
HAS THE DOLL BEEN MADE TO BELIEVE SHE WAS ASSIGNED TO A ROUTINE MISSION?

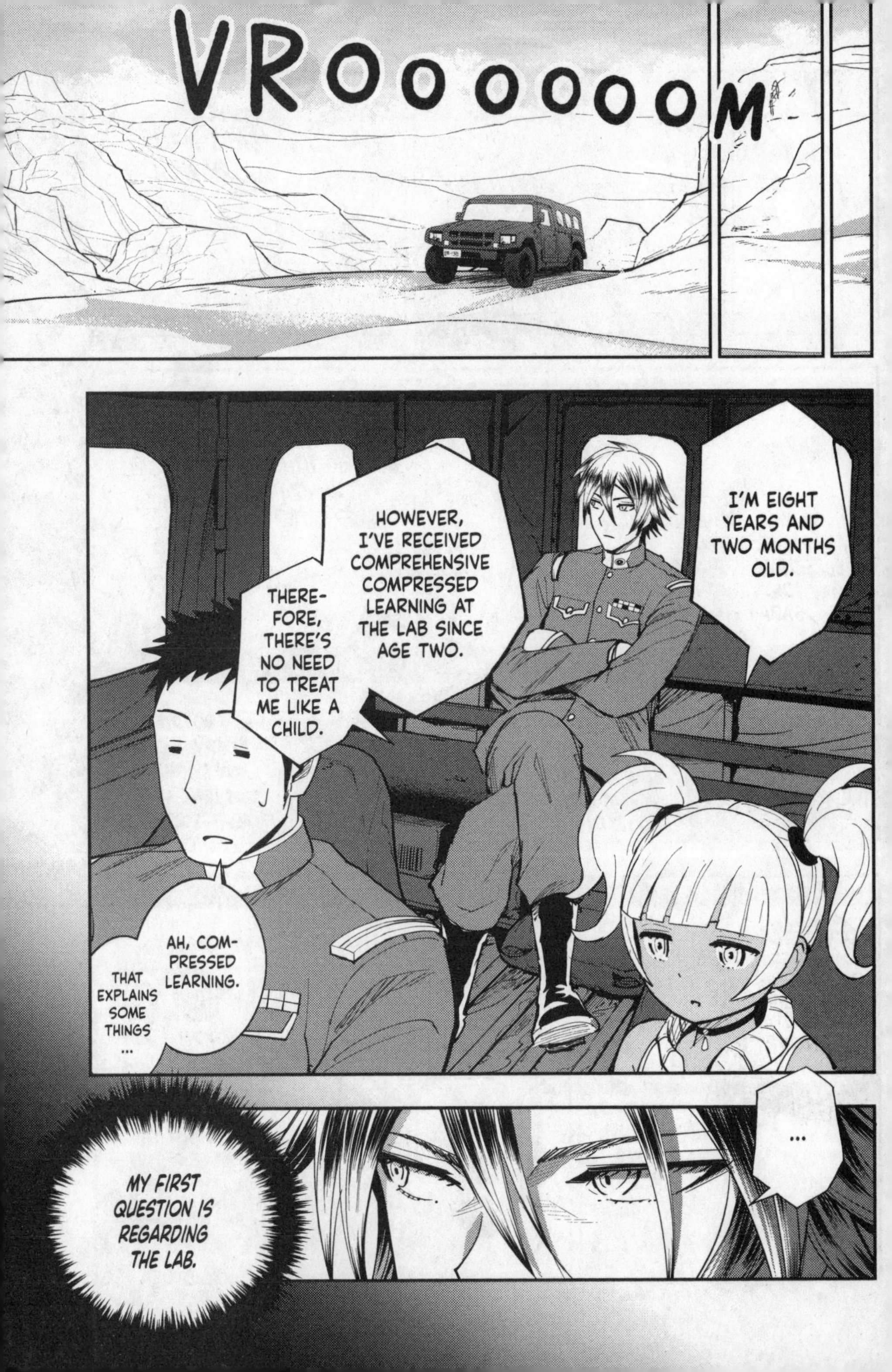
VROOOOOOM
I'M EIGHT YEARS AND TWO MONTHS OLD.
HOWEVER, I'VE RECEIVED COMPREHENSIVE COMPRESSED LEARNING AT THE LAB SINCE AGE TWO.
THERE-FORE, THERE'S NO NEED TO TREAT ME LIKE A CHILD.
AH, COM-PRESSED LEARNING.
THAT EXPLAINS SOME THINGS ...
...
MY FIRST QUESTION IS REGARDING THE LAB.

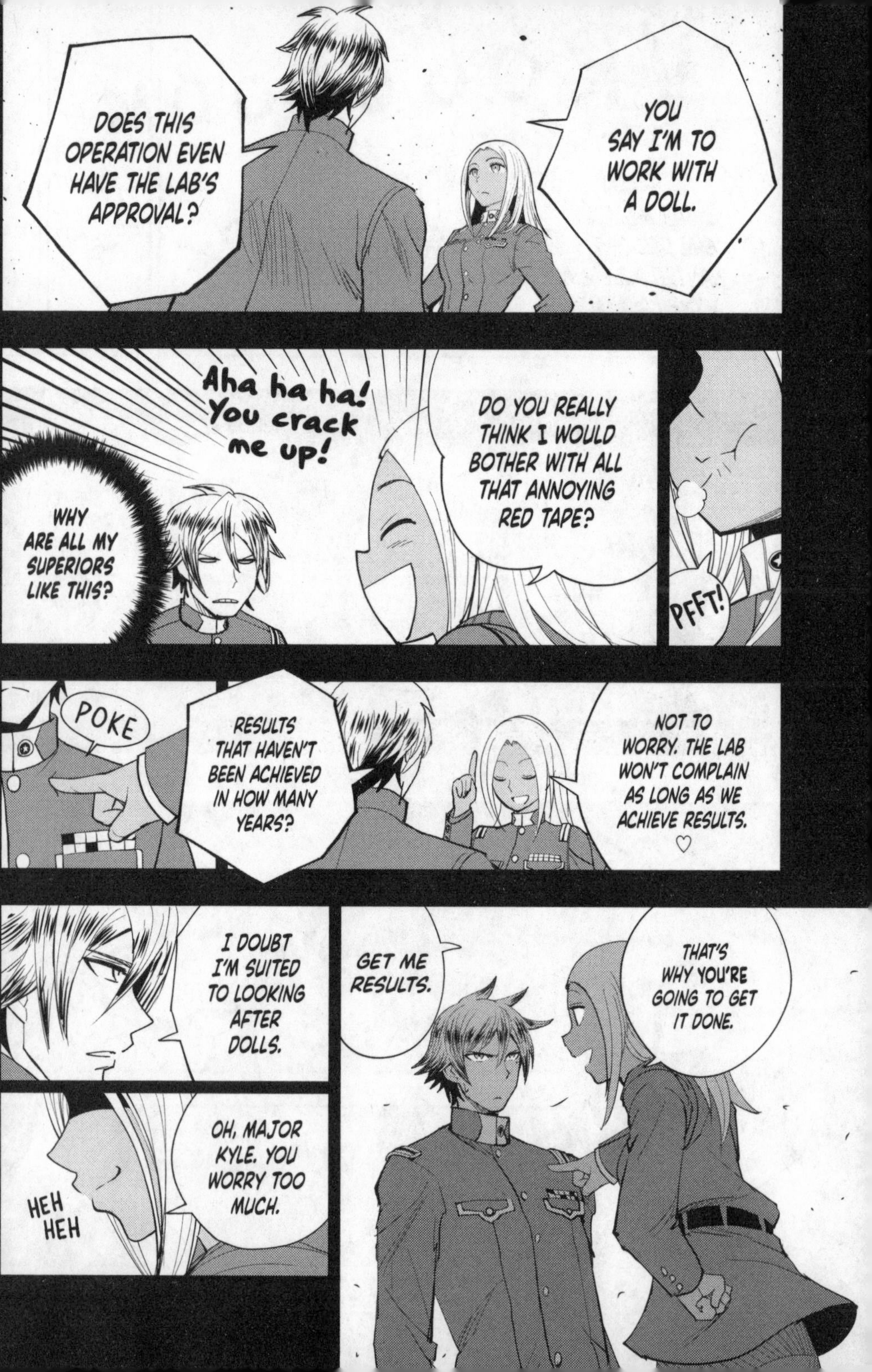
YOU SAY I'M TO WORK WITH A DOLL.
DOES THIS OPERATION EVEN HAVE THE LAB'S APPROVAL?
PFFT!
DO YOU REALLY THINK I WOULD BOTHER WITH ALL THAT ANNOYING RED TAPE?
Aha ha ha! You crack me up!
WHY ARE ALL MY SUPERIORS LIKE THIS?
NOT TO WORRY. THE LAB WON'T COMPLAIN AS LONG AS WE ACHIEVE RESULTS. ♡
RESULTS THAT HAVEN'T BEEN ACHIEVED IN HOW MANY YEARS?
POKE
THAT'S WHY YOU'RE GOING TO GET IT DONE.
GET ME RESULTS.
I DOUBT I'M SUITED TO LOOKING AFTER DOLLS.
OH, MAJOR KYLE. YOU WORRY TOO MUCH.
HEH HEH

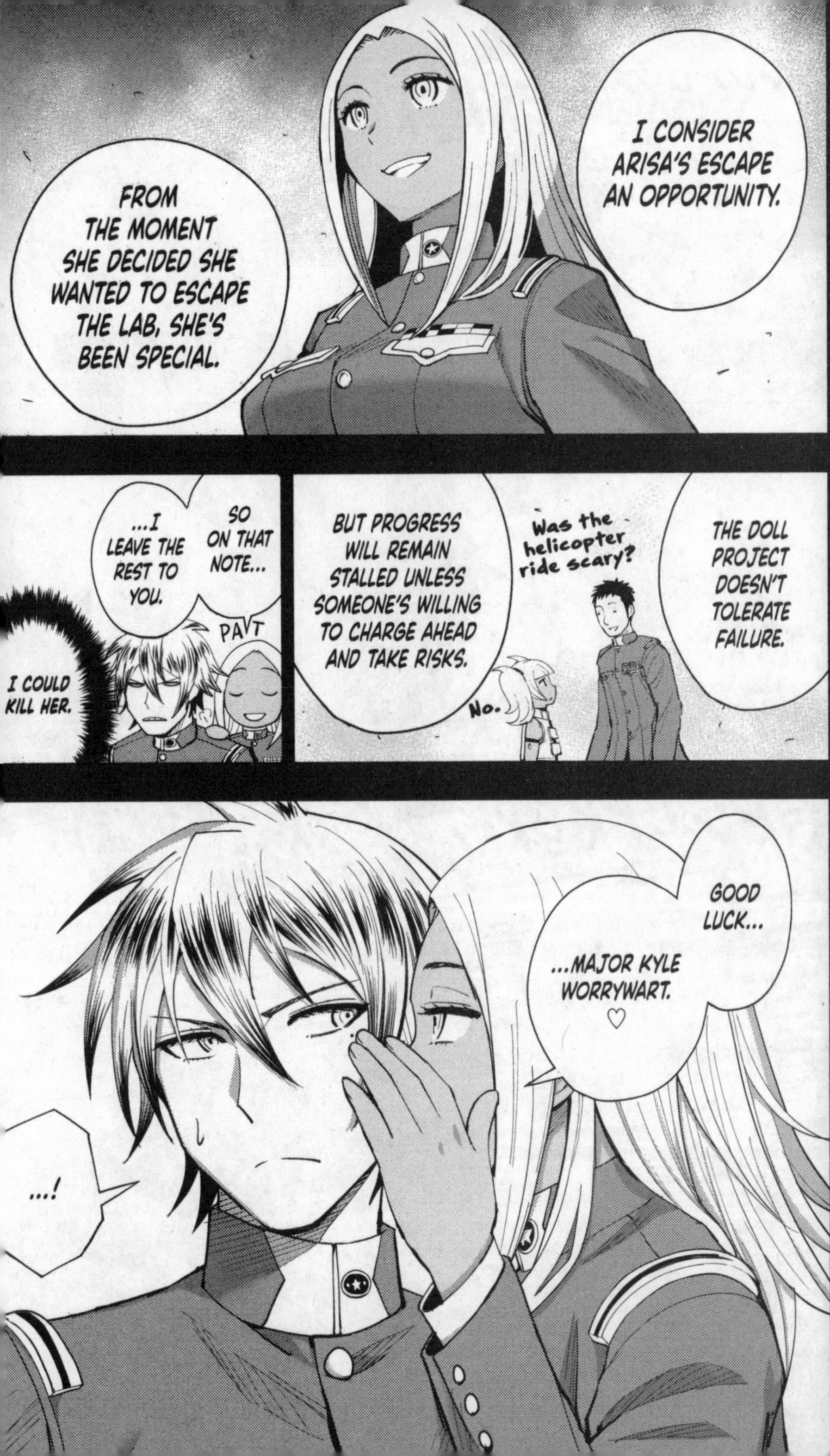
I CONSIDER ARISA'S ESCAPE AN OPPORTUNITY.
FROM THE MOMENT SHE DECIDED SHE WANTED TO ESCAPE THE LAB, SHE'S BEEN SPECIAL.
THE DOLL PROJECT DOESN'T TOLERATE FAILURE.
Was the helicopter ride scary?
No.
BUT PROGRESS WILL REMAIN STALLED UNLESS SOMEONE'S WILLING TO CHARGE AHEAD AND TAKE RISKS.
SO ON THAT NOTE...
...I LEAVE THE REST TO YOU.
PAT
I COULD KILL HER.
GOOD LUCK...
...MAJOR KYLE WORRYWART. ♡
...!

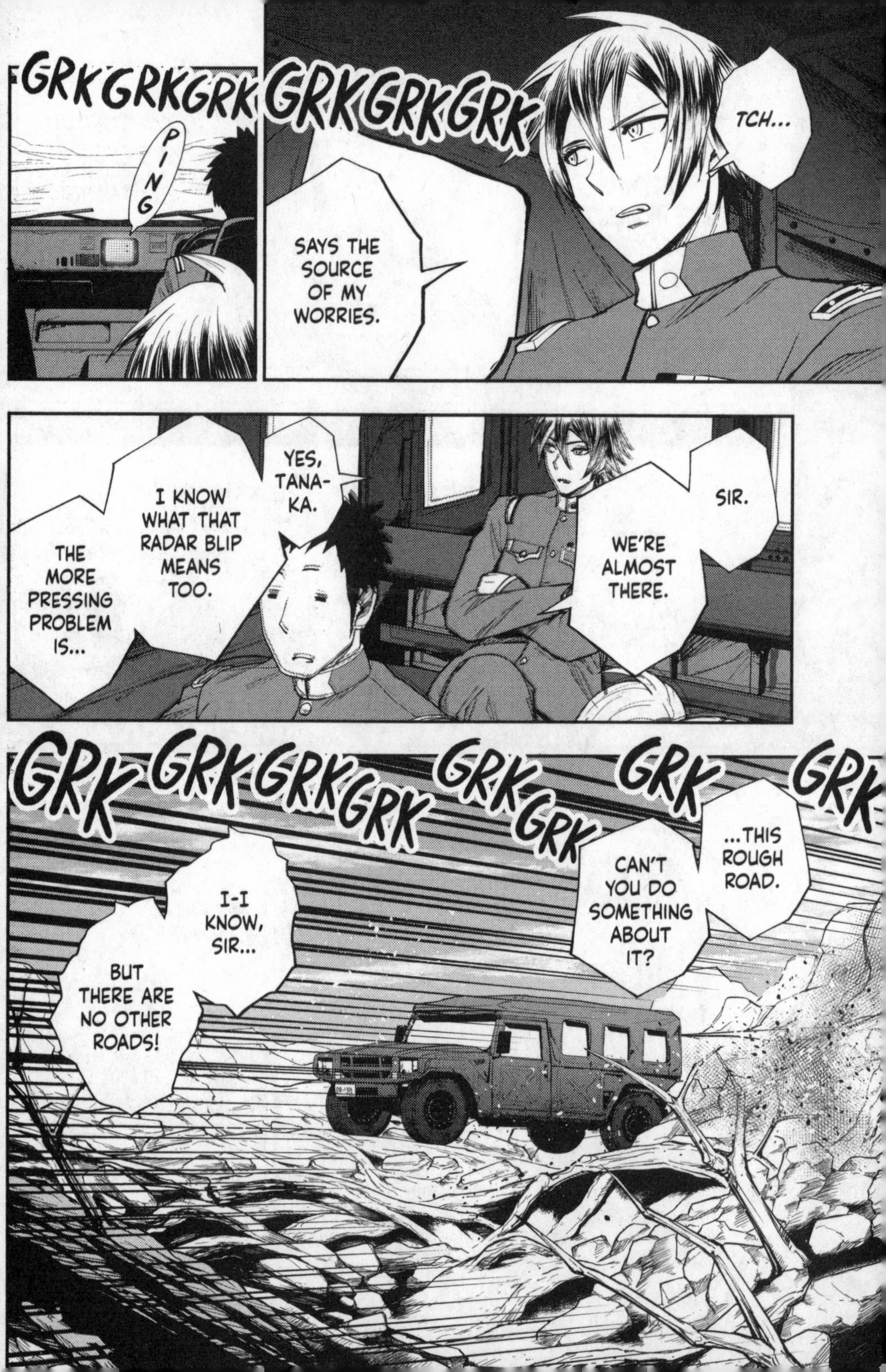
GRKGRKGRK
TCH...
SAYS THE SOURCE OF MY WORRIES.
GRKGRKGRK
PING
SIR.
WE'RE ALMOST THERE.
YES, TANAKA.
I KNOW WHAT THAT RADAR BLIP MEANS TOO.
THE MORE PRESSING PROBLEM IS...
GRK GRK GRK GRK GRK GRK GRK GRK
...THIS ROUGH ROAD.
CAN'T YOU DO SOMETHING ABOUT IT?
I-I KNOW, SIR...
BUT THERE ARE NO OTHER ROADS!

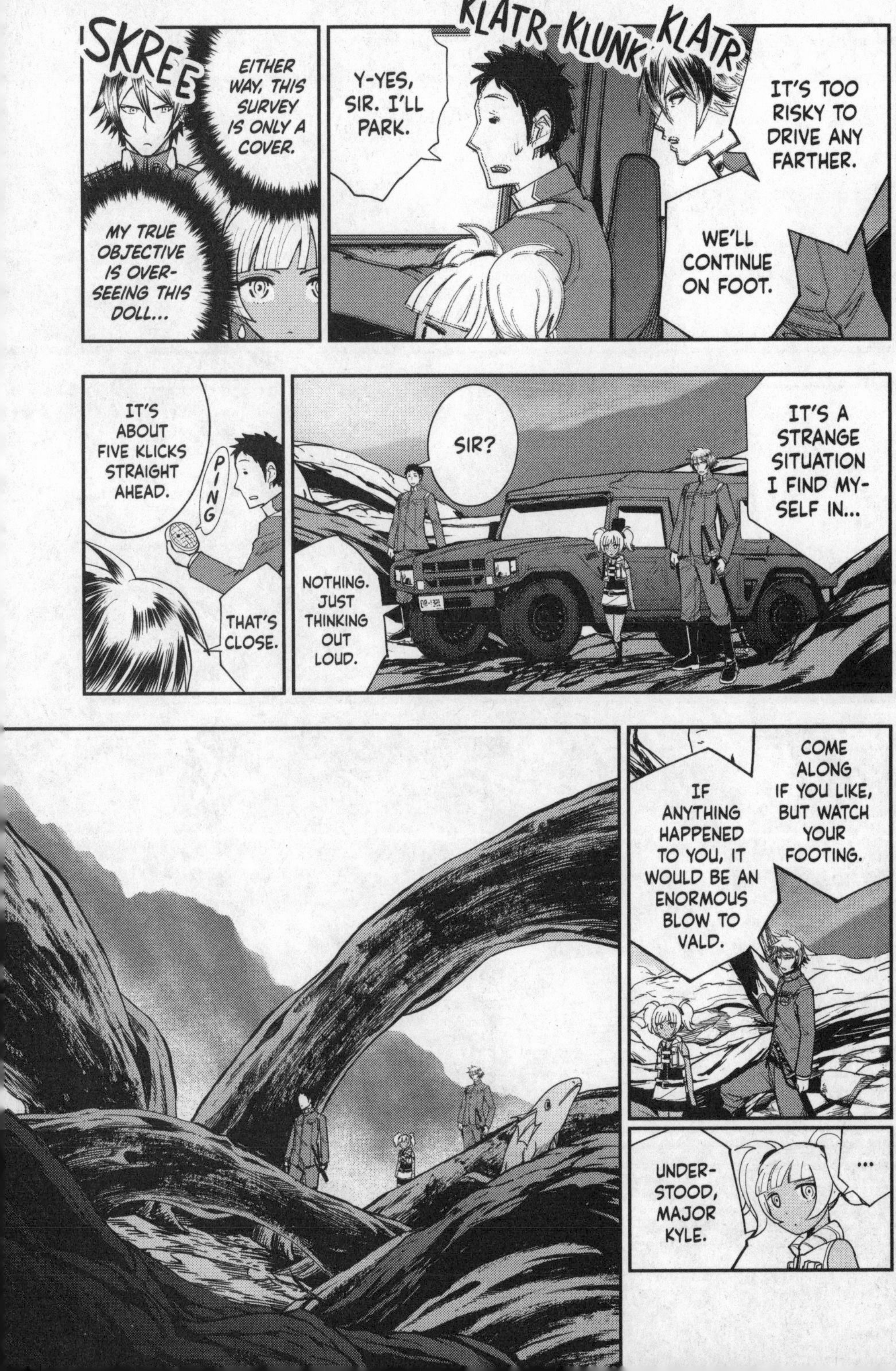
KLATR KLUNK KLATR
IT'S TOO RISKY TO DRIVE ANY FARTHER.
WE'LL CONTINUE ON FOOT.
Y-YES, SIR. I'LL PARK.
SKREE
EITHER WAY, THIS SURVEY IS ONLY A COVER.
MY TRUE OBJECTIVE IS OVER-SEEING THIS DOLL...
IT'S A STRANGE SITUATION I FIND MY-SELF IN...
SIR?
NOTHING. JUST THINKING OUT LOUD.
IT'S ABOUT FIVE KLICKS STRAIGHT AHEAD.
PING
THAT'S CLOSE.
COME ALONG IF YOU LIKE, BUT WATCH YOUR FOOTING.
IF ANYTHING HAPPENED TO YOU, IT WOULD BE AN ENORMOUS BLOW TO VALD.
...
UNDER-STOOD, MAJOR KYLE.

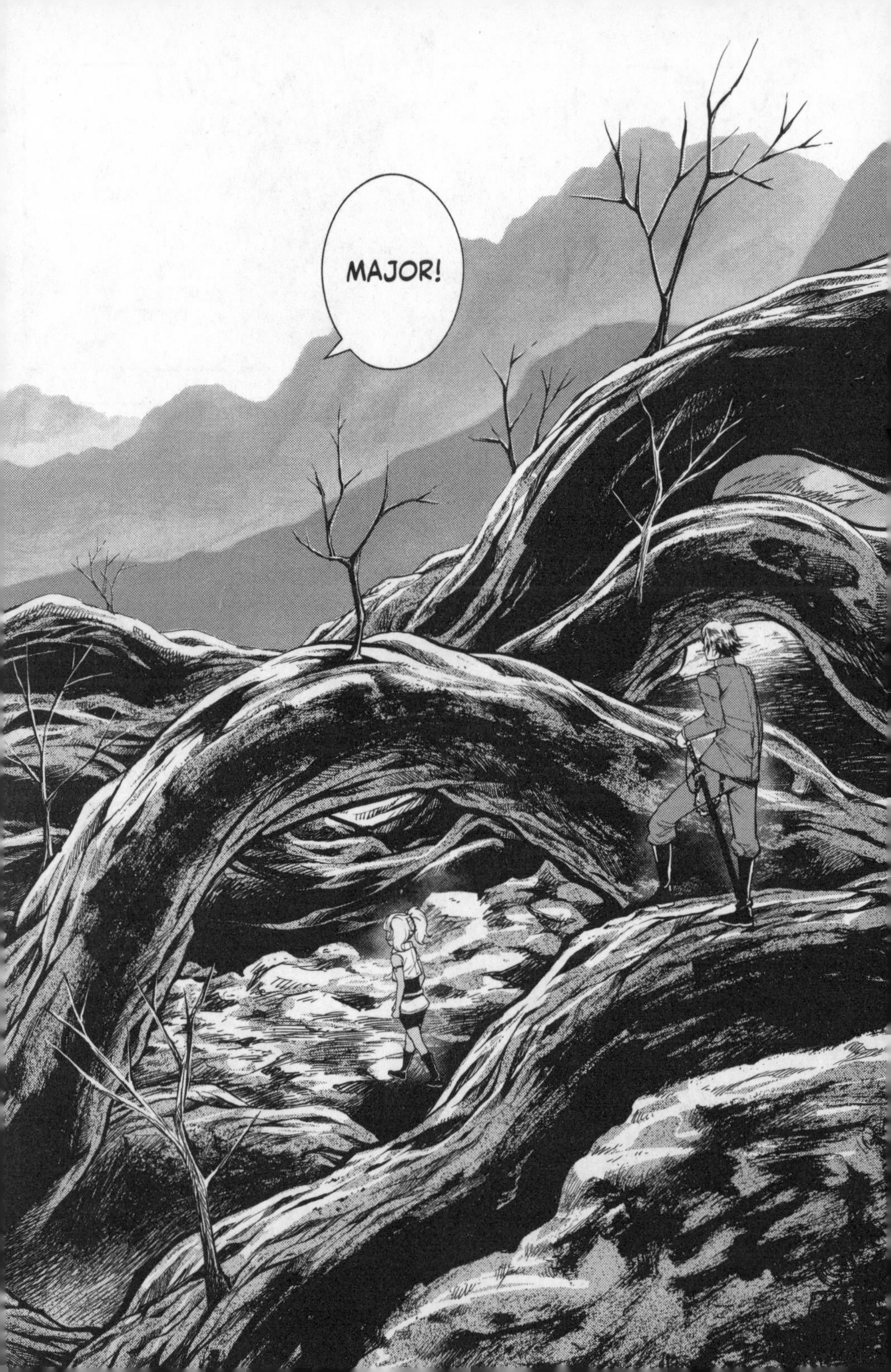
MAJOR!

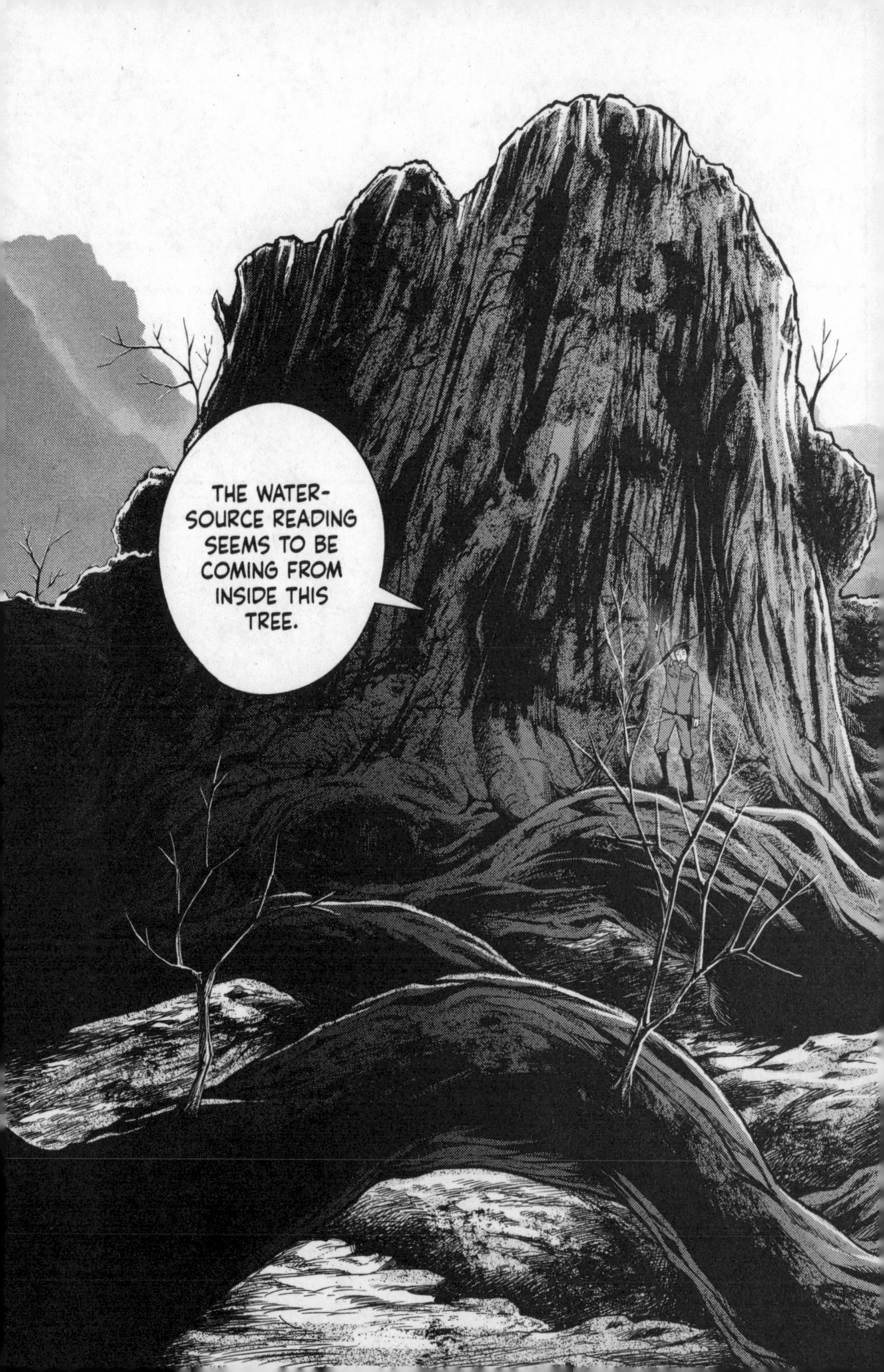
THE WATER-SOURCE READING SEEMS TO BE COMING FROM INSIDE THIS TREE.

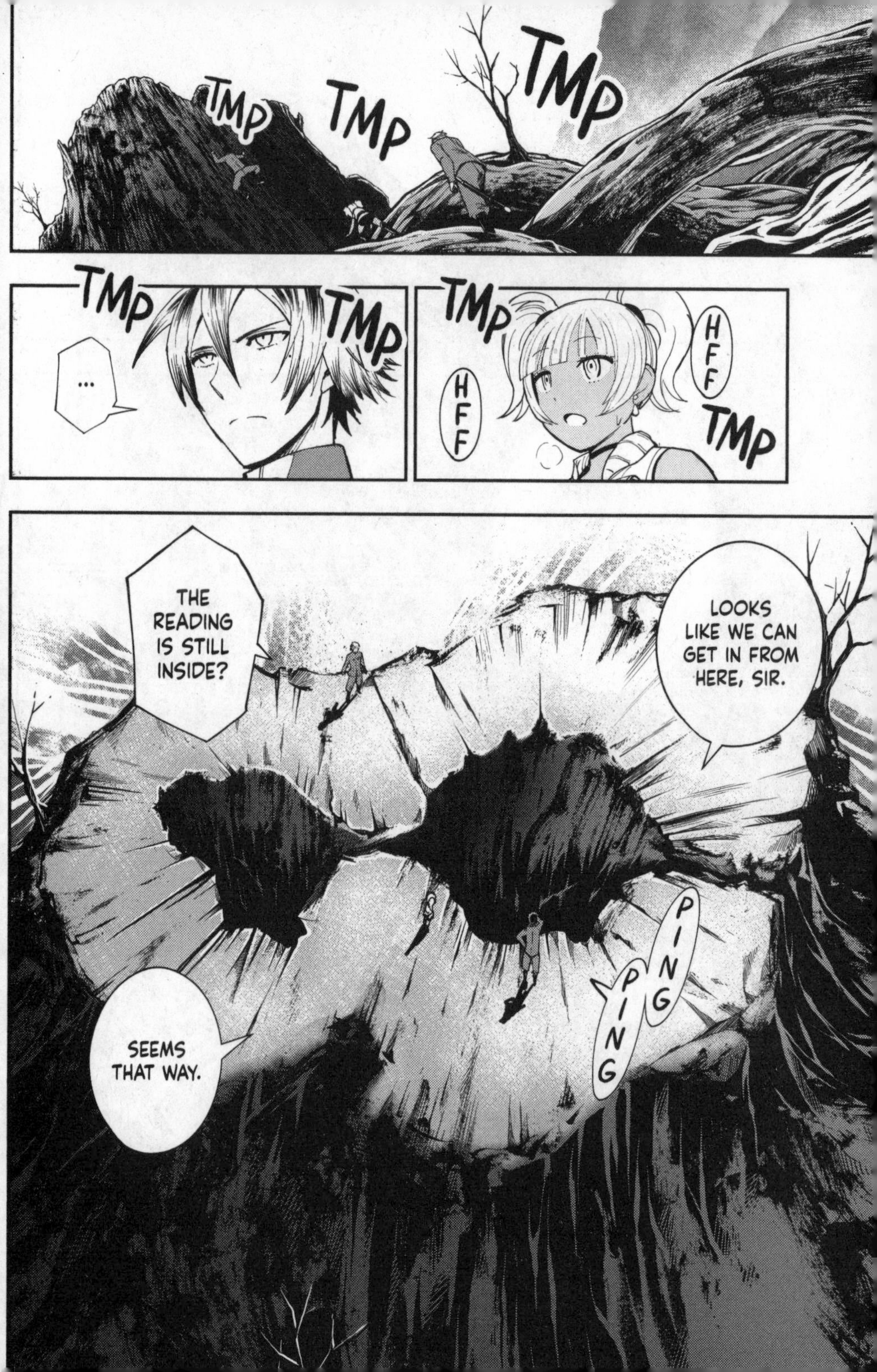
TMP
TMP
TMP
TMP
HFF
HFF
TMP
TMP
TMP
...
LOOKS LIKE WE CAN GET IN FROM HERE, SIR.
THE READING IS STILL INSIDE?
PING
PING
SEEMS THAT WAY.

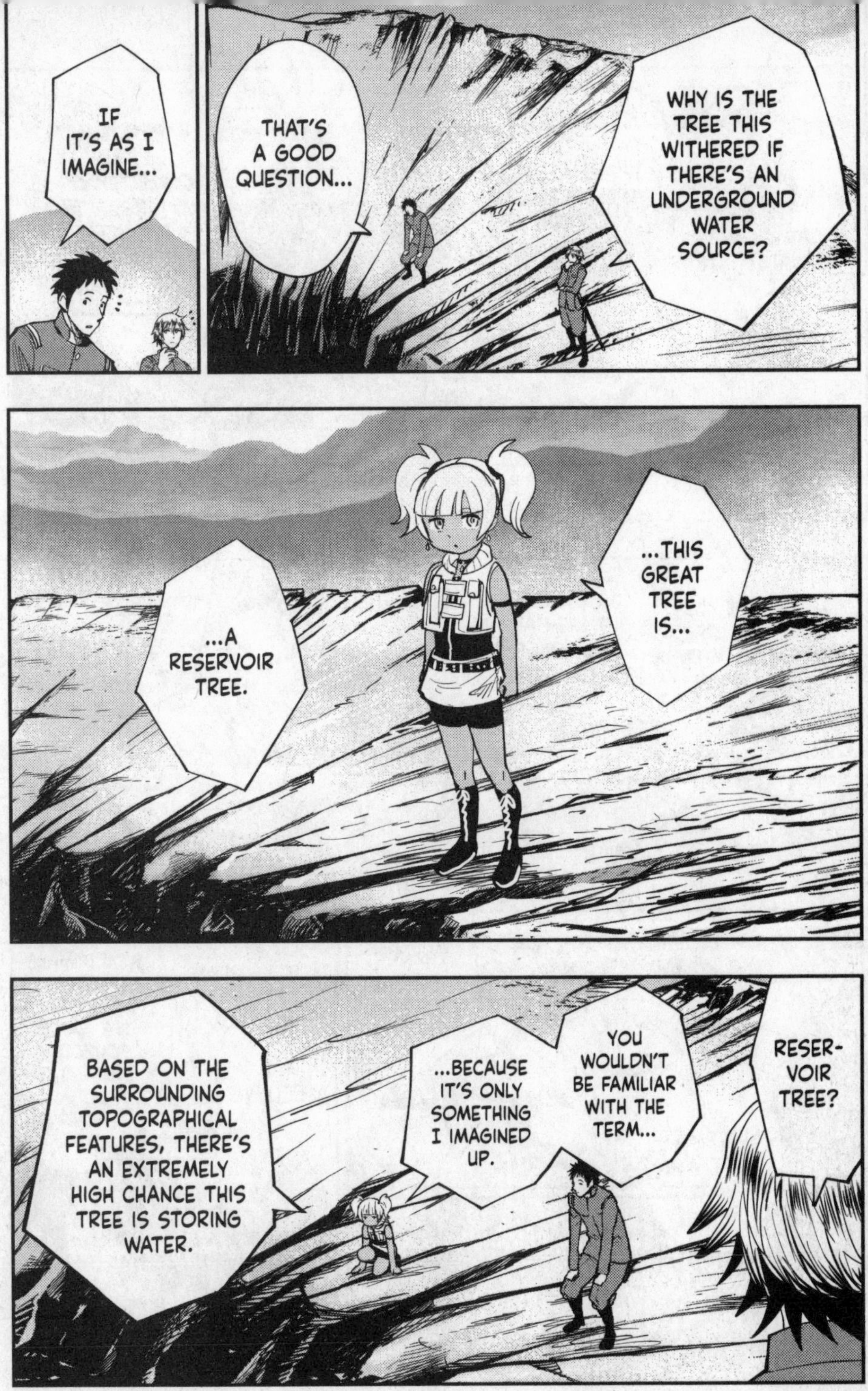
WHY IS THE TREE THIS WITHERED IF THERE'S AN UNDERGROUND WATER SOURCE?
THAT'S A GOOD QUESTION...
IF IT'S AS I IMAGINE...
...THIS GREAT TREE IS...
...A RESERVOIR TREE.
RESER-VOIR TREE?
YOU WOULDN'T BE FAMILIAR WITH THE TERM...
...BECAUSE IT'S ONLY SOMETHING I IMAGINED UP.
BASED ON THE SURROUNDING TOPOGRAPHICAL FEATURES, THERE'S AN EXTREMELY HIGH CHANCE THIS TREE IS STORING WATER.

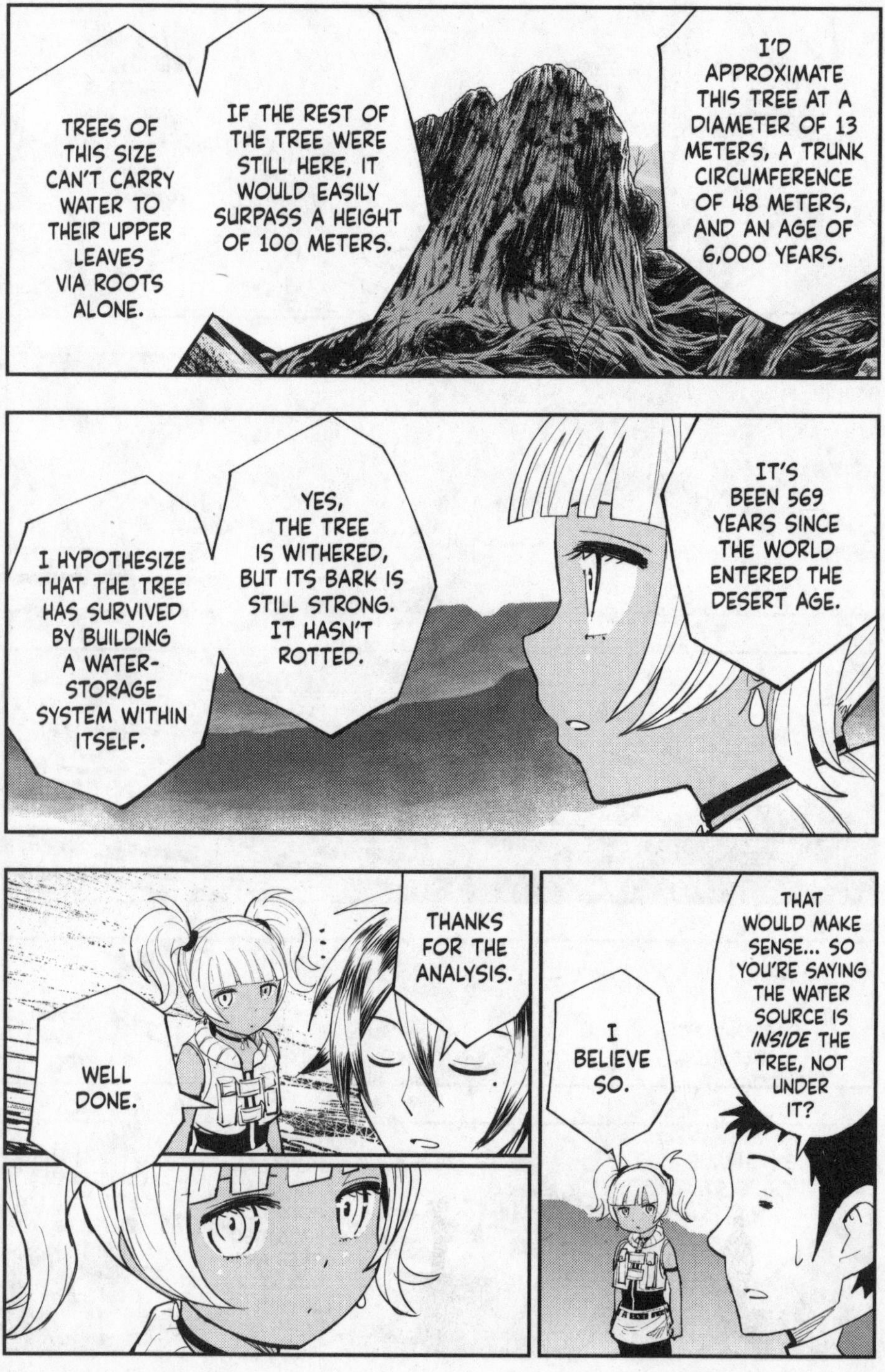
I'D APPROXIMATE THIS TREE AT A DIAMETER OF 13 METERS, A TRUNK CIRCUMFERENCE OF 48 METERS, AND AN AGE OF 6,000 YEARS.
IF THE REST OF THE TREE WERE STILL HERE, IT WOULD EASILY SURPASS A HEIGHT OF 100 METERS.
TREES OF THIS SIZE CAN'T CARRY WATER TO THEIR UPPER LEAVES VIA ROOTS ALONE.
IT'S BEEN 569 YEARS SINCE THE WORLD ENTERED THE DESERT AGE.
YES, THE TREE IS WITHERED, BUT ITS BARK IS STILL STRONG. IT HASN'T ROTTED.
I HYPOTHESIZE THAT THE TREE HAS SURVIVED BY BUILDING A WATER-STORAGE SYSTEM WITHIN ITSELF.
THAT WOULD MAKE SENSE... SO YOU'RE SAYING THE WATER SOURCE IS *INSIDE* THE TREE, NOT UNDER IT?
I BELIEVE SO.
THANKS FOR THE ANALYSIS.
WELL DONE.

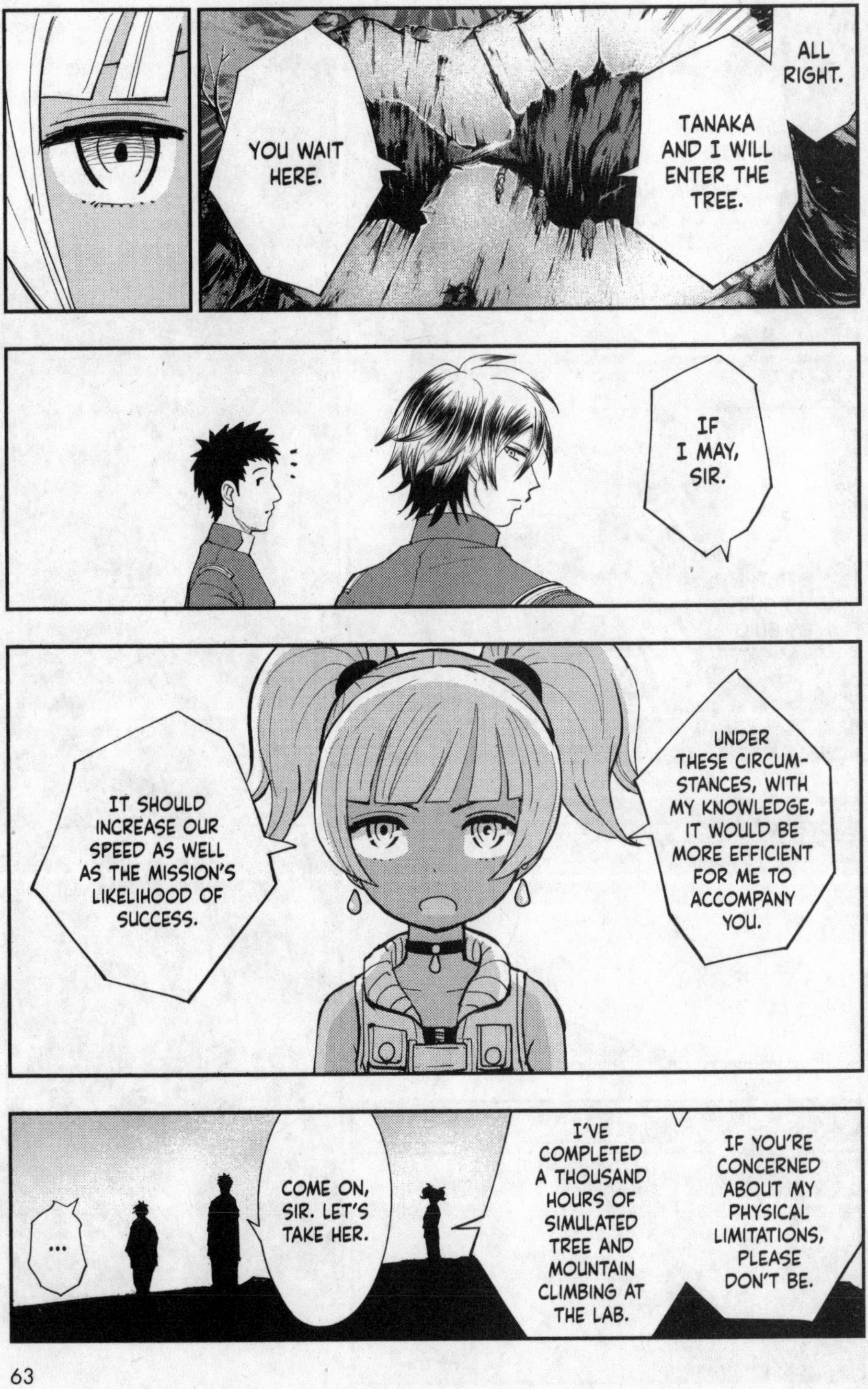
ALL RIGHT.
TANAKA AND I WILL ENTER THE TREE.
YOU WAIT HERE.
IF I MAY, SIR.
UNDER THESE CIRCUM- STANCES, WITH MY KNOWLEDGE, IT WOULD BE MORE EFFICIENT FOR ME TO ACCOMPANY YOU.
IT SHOULD INCREASE OUR SPEED AS WELL AS THE MISSION'S LIKELIHOOD OF SUCCESS.
IF YOU'RE CONCERNED ABOUT MY PHYSICAL LIMITATIONS, PLEASE DON'T BE.
I'VE COMPLETED A THOUSAND HOURS OF SIMULATED TREE AND MOUNTAIN CLIMBING AT THE LAB.
COME ON, SIR. LET'S TAKE HER.
...

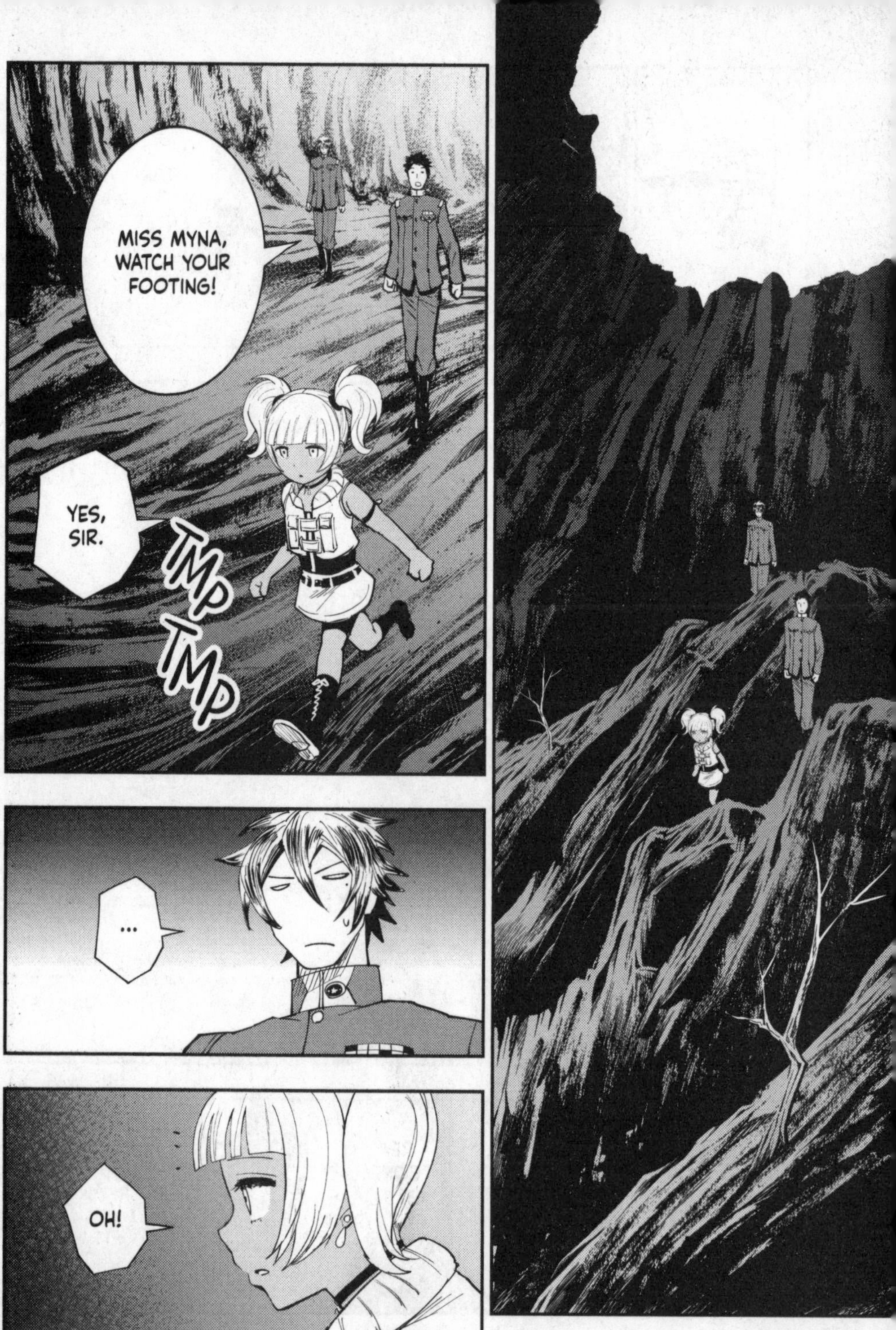
MISS MYNA, WATCH YOUR FOOTING!
YES, SIR.
TMP TMP
...
OH!

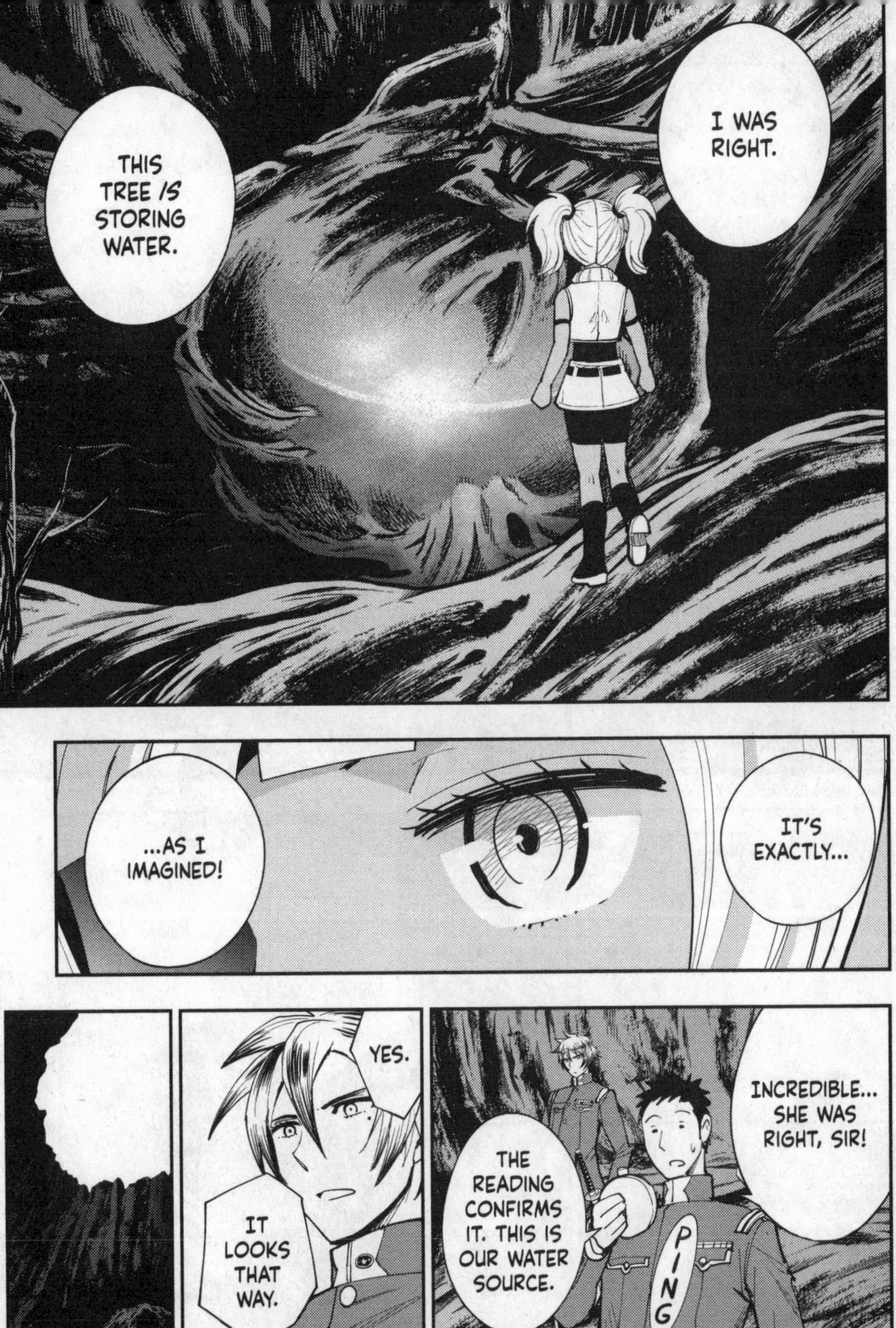
I WAS RIGHT.
THIS TREE IS STORING WATER.
IT'S EXACTLY...
...AS I IMAGINED!
INCREDIBLE... SHE WAS RIGHT, SIR!
PING
THE READING CONFIRMS IT. THIS IS OUR WATER SOURCE.
YES.
IT LOOKS THAT WAY.

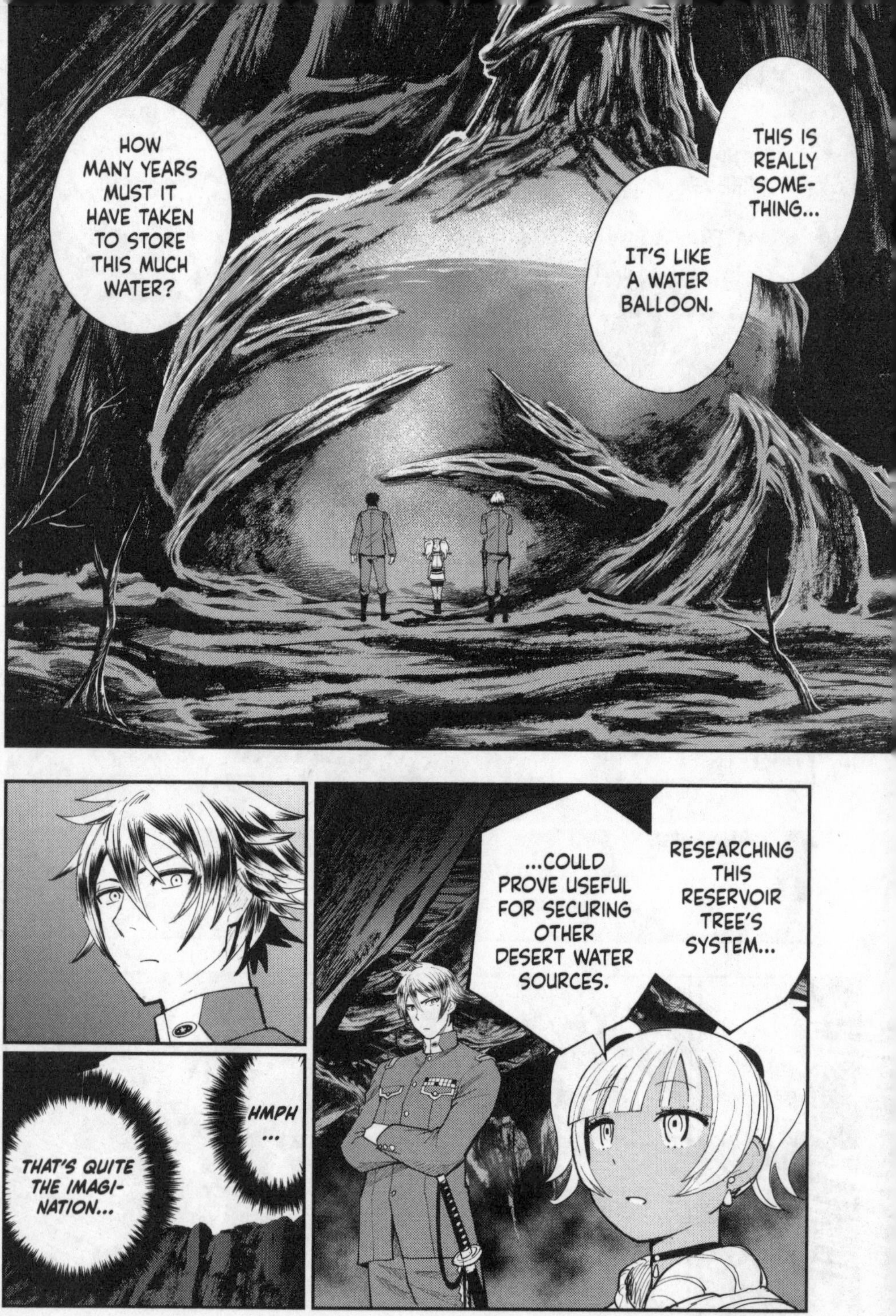
THIS IS REALLY SOME-THING...
IT'S LIKE A WATER BALLOON.
HOW MANY YEARS MUST IT HAVE TAKEN TO STORE THIS MUCH WATER?
RESEARCHING THIS RESERVOIR TREE'S SYSTEM...
...COULD PROVE USEFUL FOR SECURING OTHER DESERT WATER SOURCES.
HMPH...
THAT'S QUITE THE IMAGI-NATION...

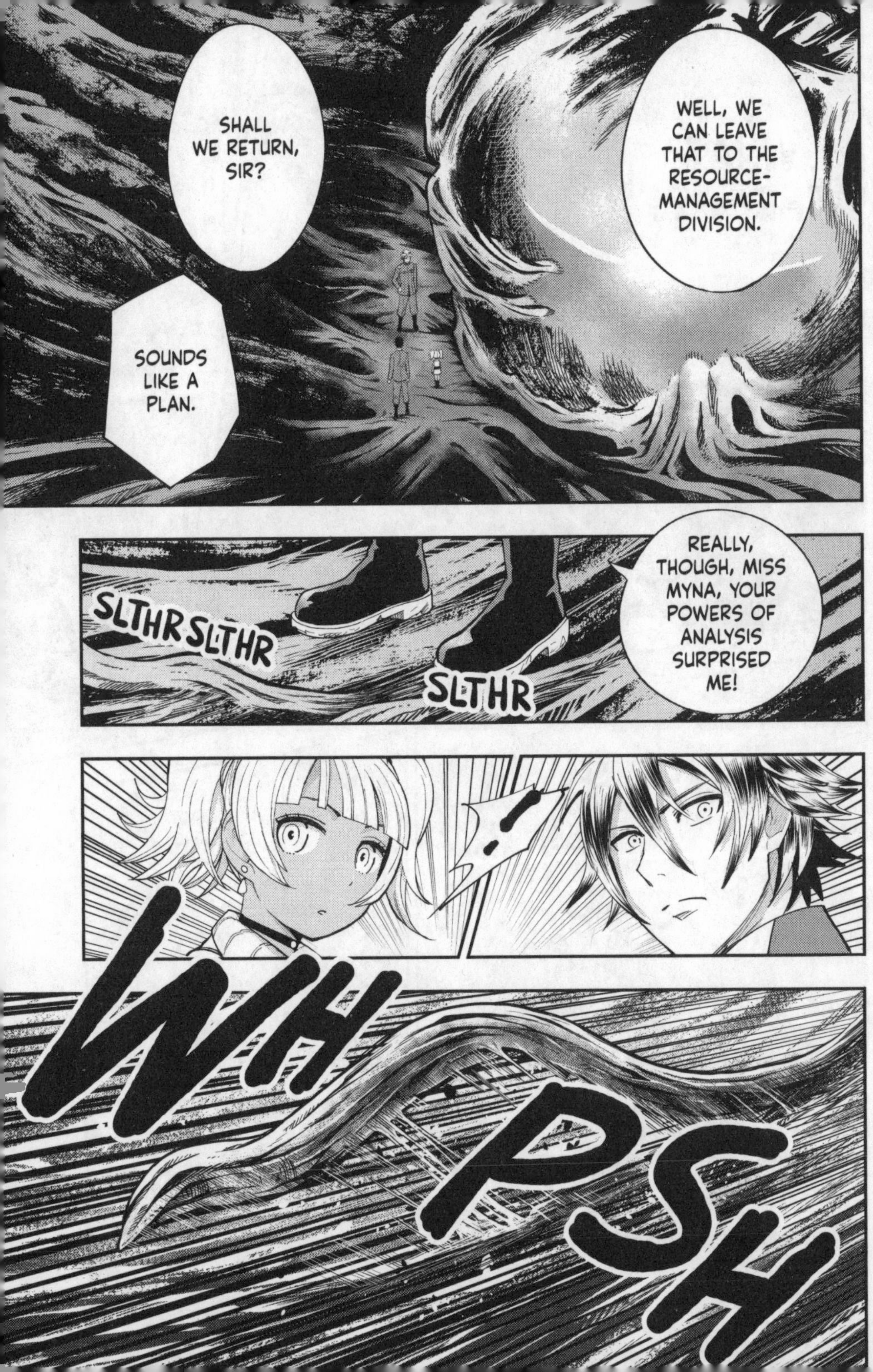
WELL, WE CAN LEAVE THAT TO THE RESOURCE-MANAGEMENT DIVISION.
SHALL WE RETURN, SIR?
SOUNDS LIKE A PLAN.
REALLY, THOUGH, MISS MYNA, YOUR POWERS OF ANALYSIS SURPRISED ME!
SLTHR
SLTHR SLTHR
!
WHPSH

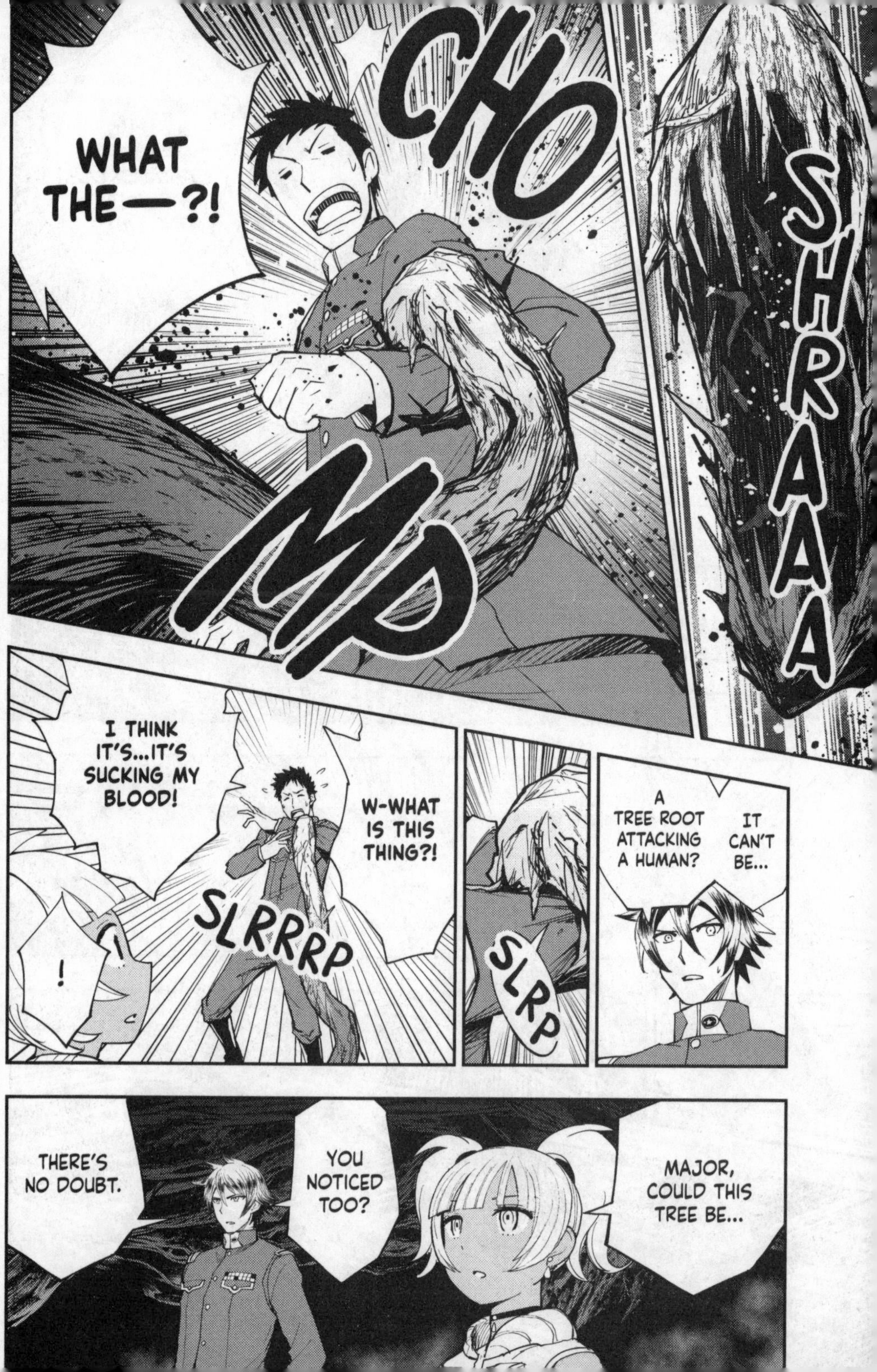
CHOMP
SHRAAA
WHAT THE—?!
IT CAN'T BE...
A TREE ROOT ATTACKING A HUMAN?
SLRP
W-WHAT IS THIS THING?!
I THINK IT'S...IT'S SUCKING MY BLOOD!
SLRRRP
!
MAJOR, COULD THIS TREE BE...
YOU NOTICED TOO?
THERE'S NO DOUBT.

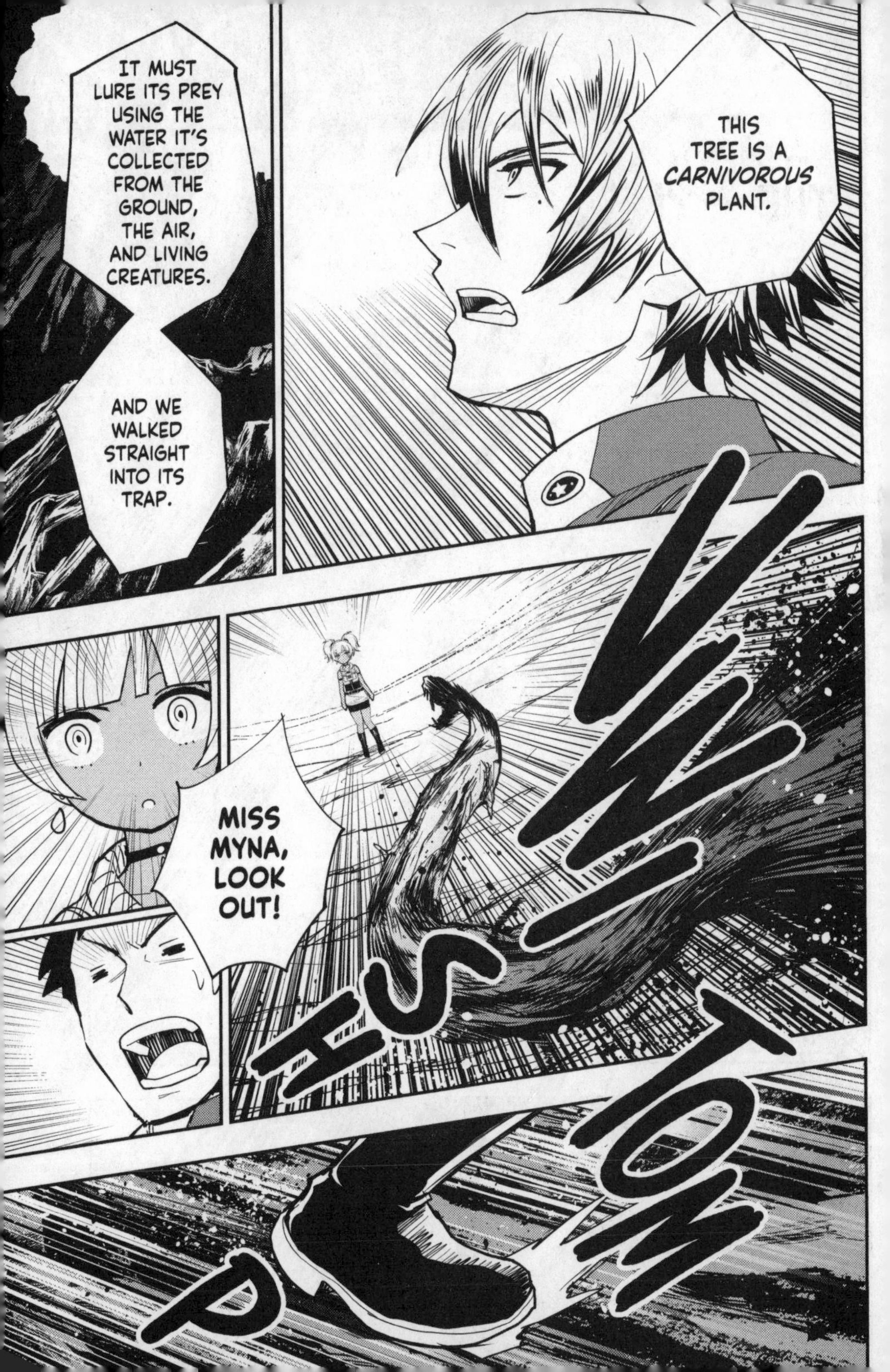
THIS TREE IS A *CARNIVOROUS* PLANT.
IT MUST LURE ITS PREY USING THE WATER IT'S COLLECTED FROM THE GROUND, THE AIR, AND LIVING CREATURES.
AND WE WALKED STRAIGHT INTO ITS TRAP.
MISS MYNA, LOOK OUT!

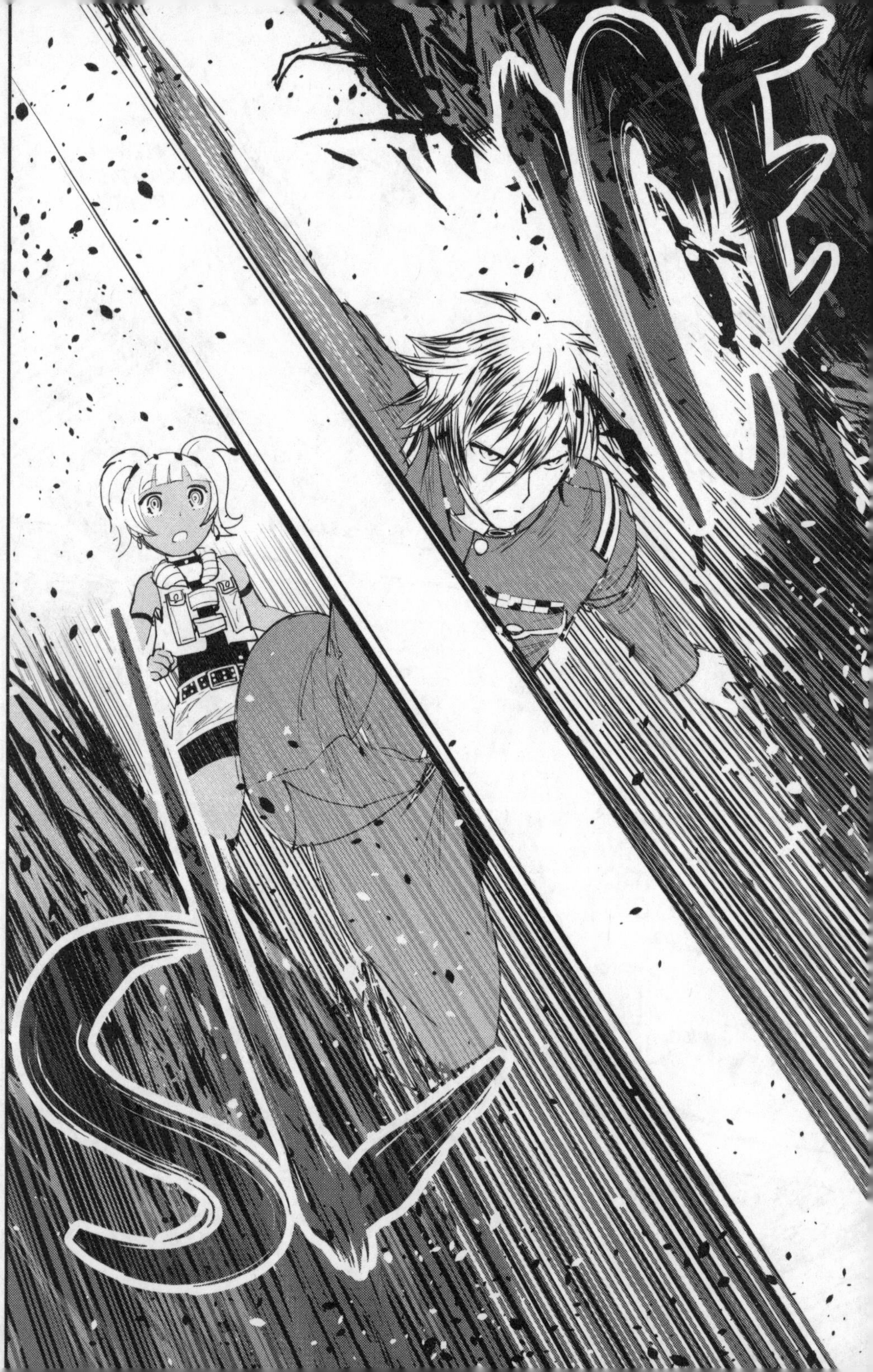
SLICE

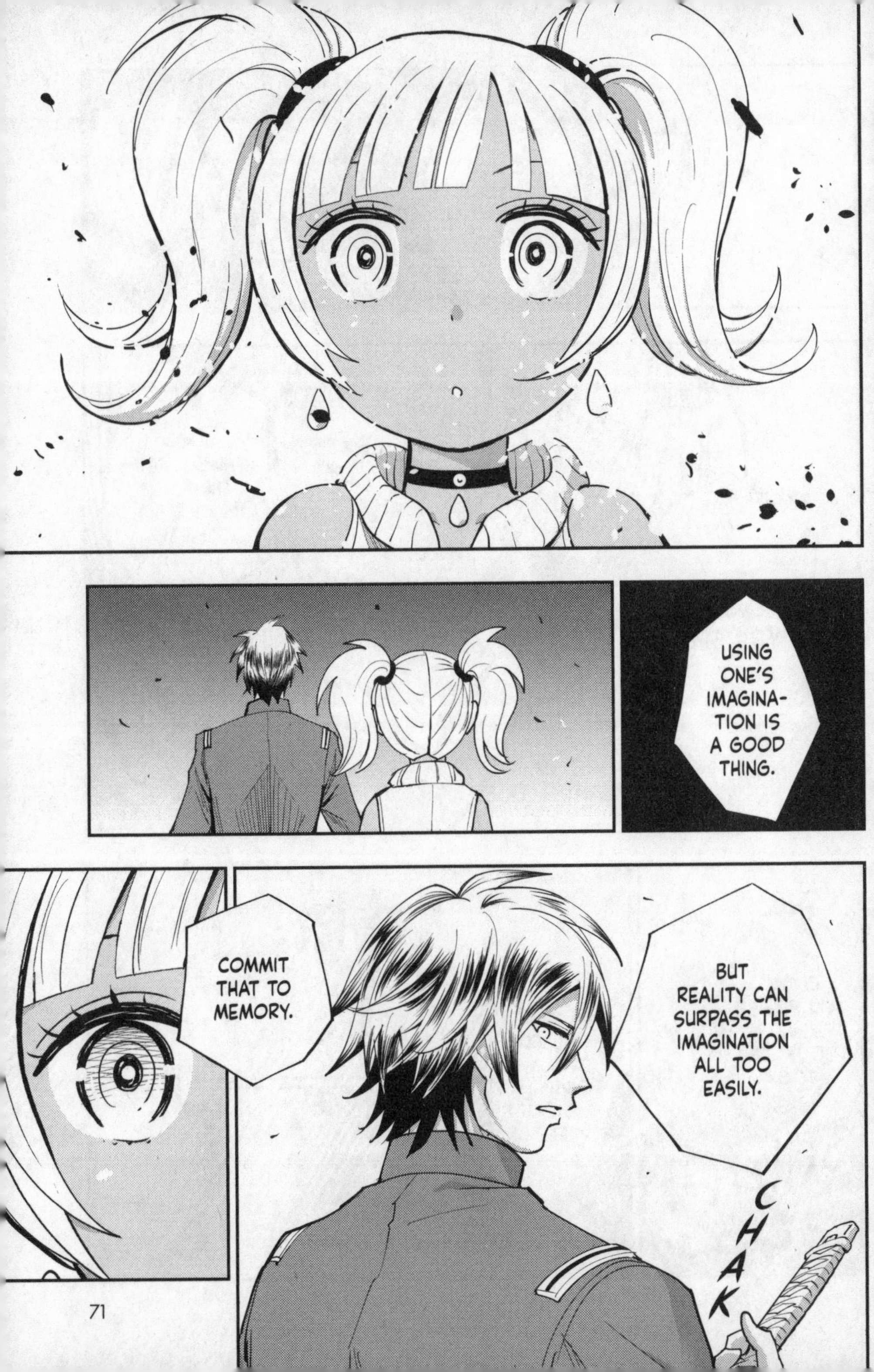
USING ONE'S IMAGINA-TION IS A GOOD THING.
BUT REALITY CAN SURPASS THE IMAGINATION ALL TOO EASILY.
COMMIT THAT TO MEMORY.
CHAK

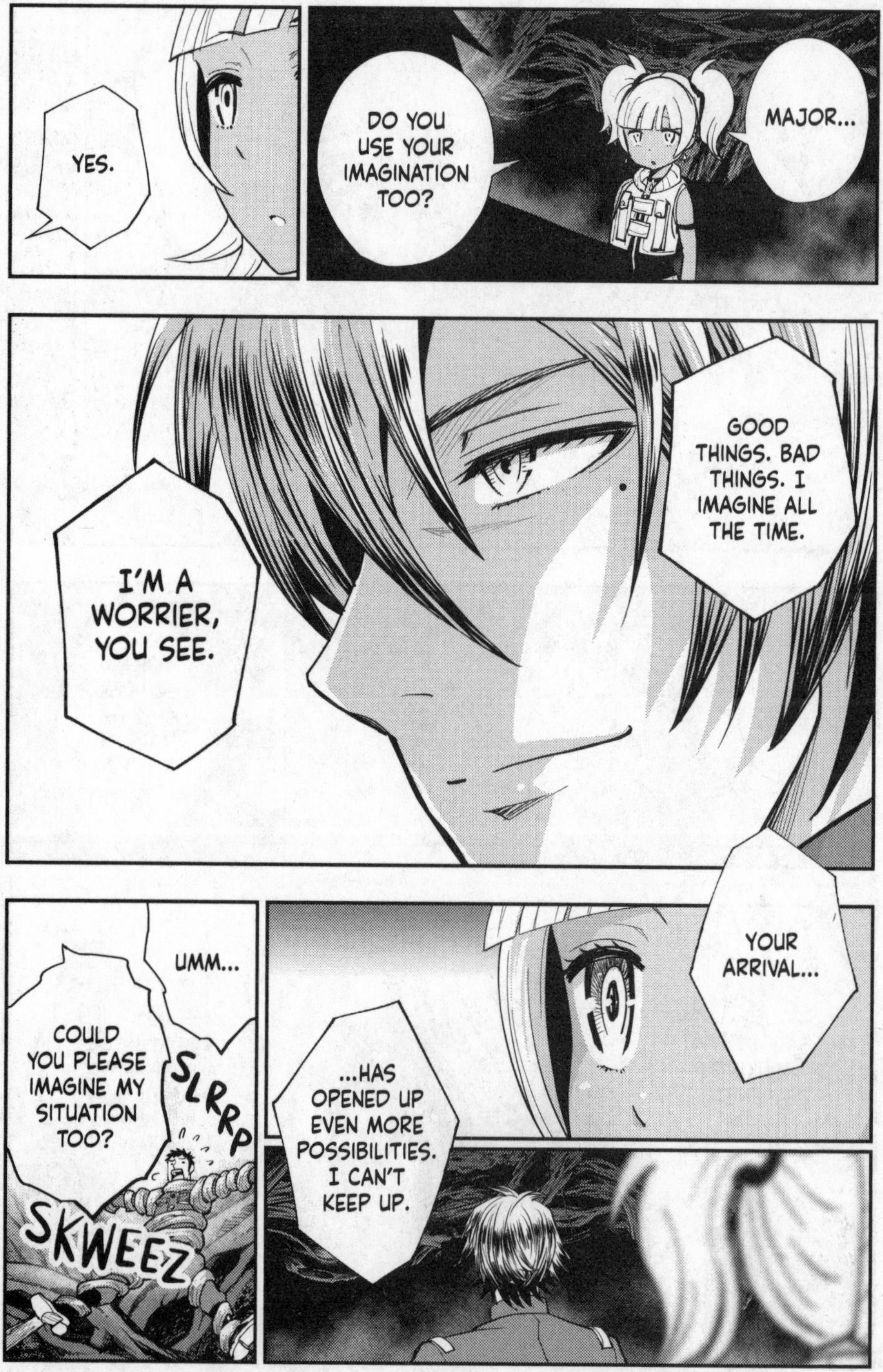
MAJOR...
DO YOU USE YOUR IMAGINATION TOO?
YES.
GOOD THINGS. BAD THINGS. I IMAGINE ALL THE TIME.
I'M A WORRIER, YOU SEE.
YOUR ARRIVAL...
...HAS OPENED UP EVEN MORE POSSIBILITIES. I CAN'T KEEP UP.
UMM...
COULD YOU PLEASE IMAGINE MY SITUATION TOO?
SLRRP
SKWEEZ

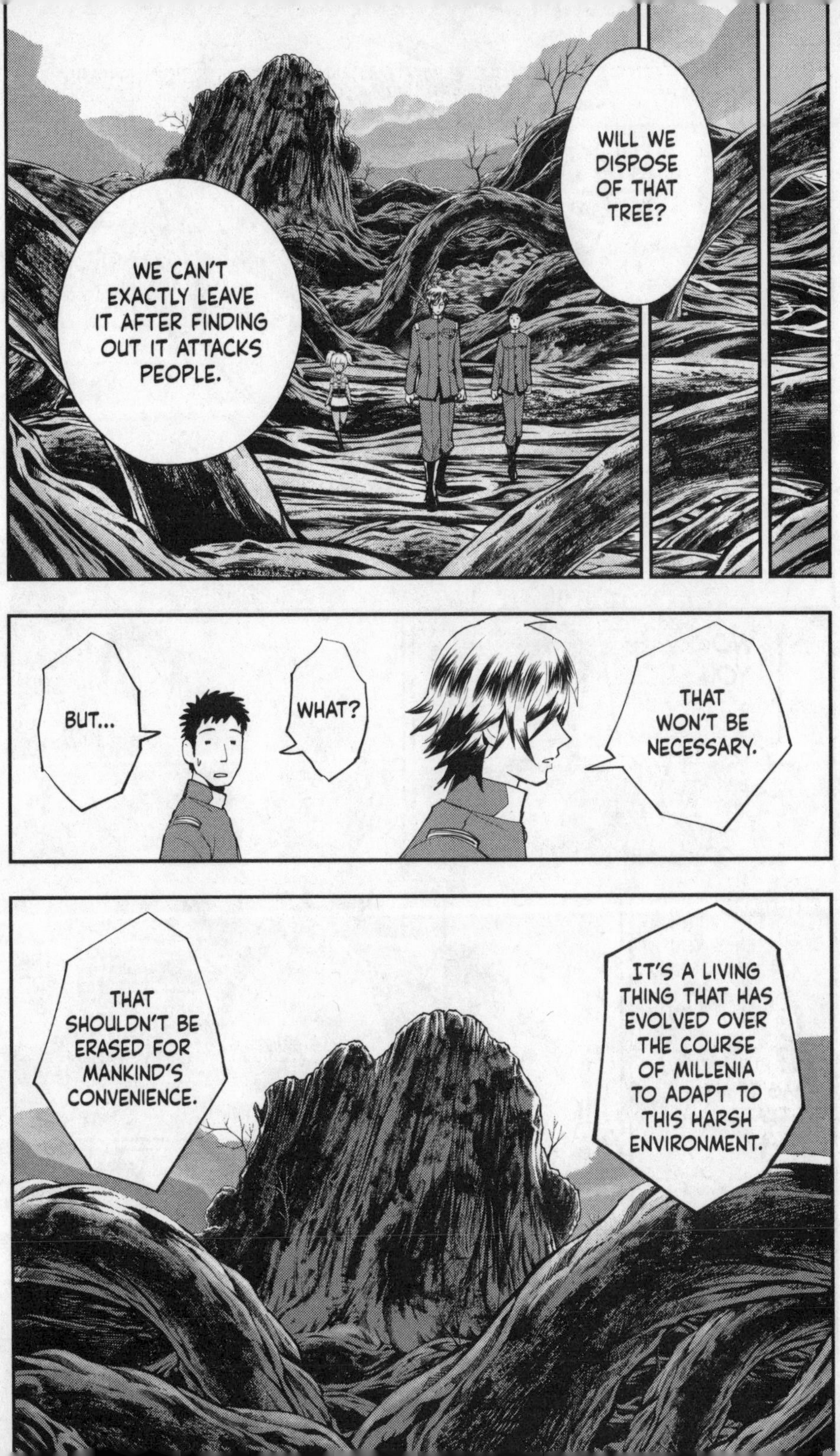
WILL WE DISPOSE OF THAT TREE?
WE CAN'T EXACTLY LEAVE IT AFTER FINDING OUT IT ATTACKS PEOPLE.
THAT WON'T BE NECESSARY.
WHAT?
BUT...
IT'S A LIVING THING THAT HAS EVOLVED OVER THE COURSE OF MILLENIA TO ADAPT TO THIS HARSH ENVIRONMENT.
THAT SHOULDN'T BE ERASED FOR MANKIND'S CONVENIENCE.

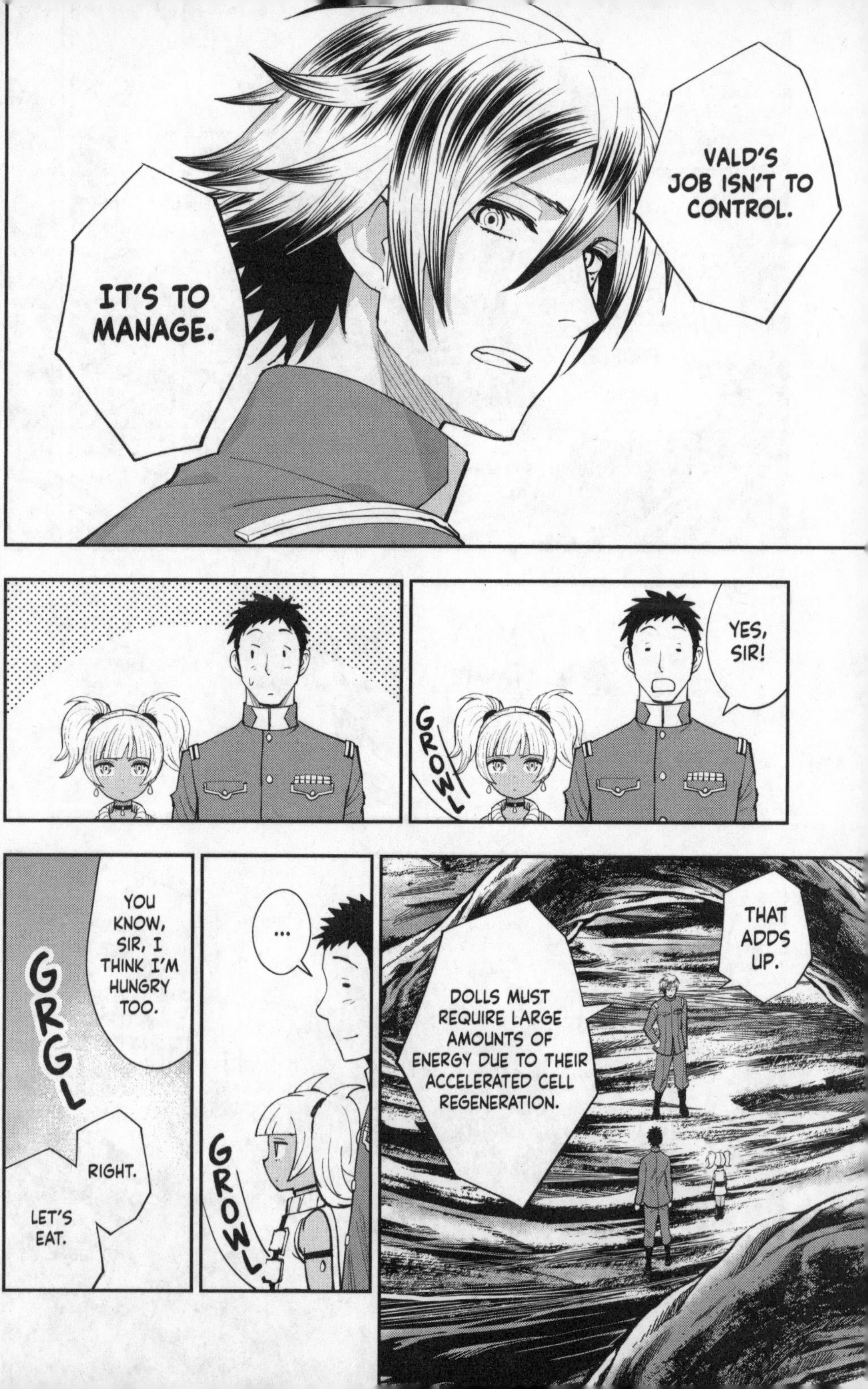
VALD'S JOB ISN'T TO CONTROL.
IT'S TO MANAGE.
YES, SIR!
GROWL
THAT ADDS UP.
DOLLS MUST REQUIRE LARGE AMOUNTS OF ENERGY DUE TO THEIR ACCELERATED CELL REGENERATION.
...
GROWL
YOU KNOW, SIR, I THINK I'M HUNGRY TOO.
GRGL
RIGHT.
LET'S EAT.

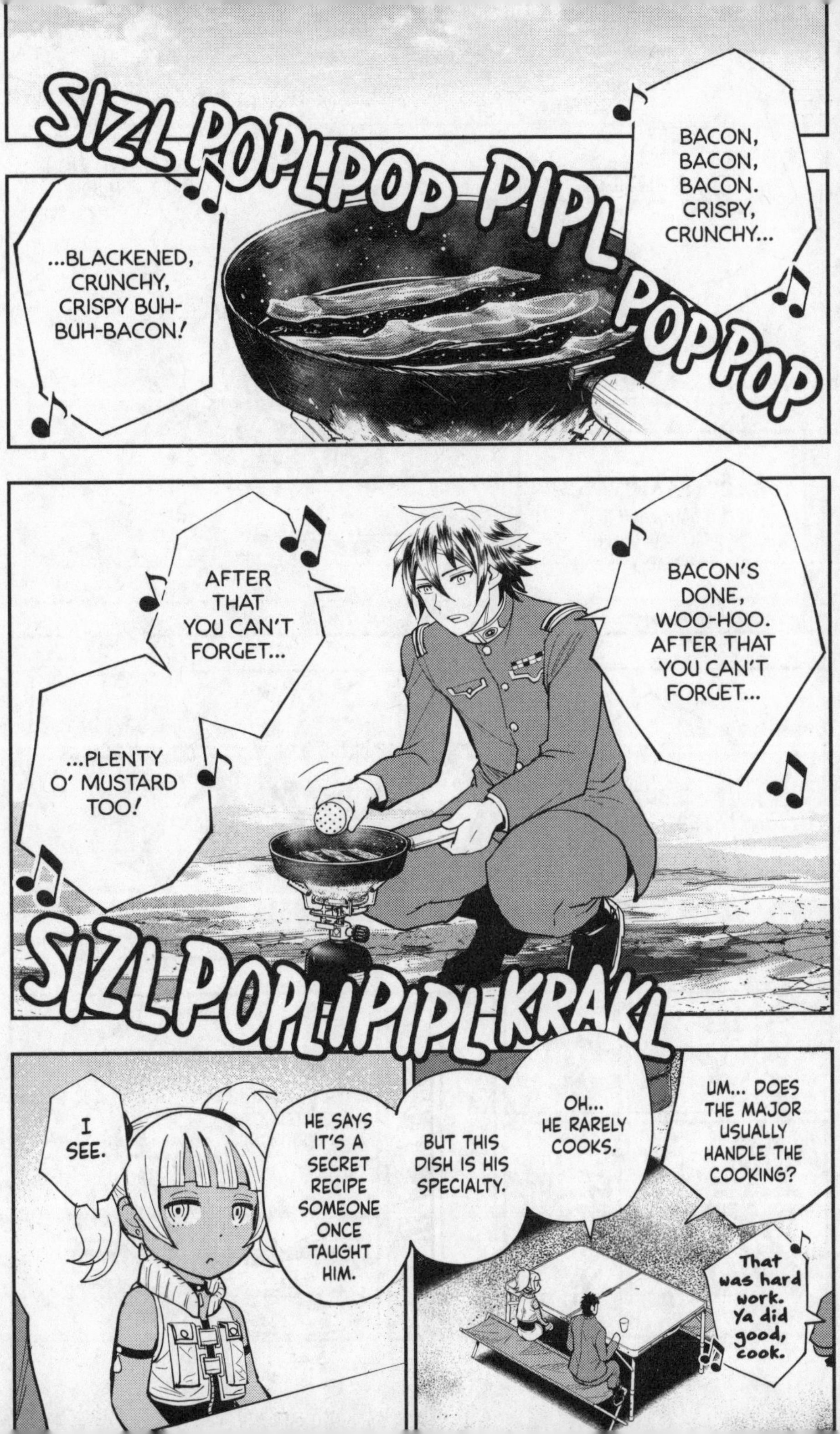
SIZL POPLPOP PIPL POPPOP
BACON, BACON, BACON. CRISPY, CRUNCHY...
...BLACKENED, CRUNCHY, CRISPY BUH-BUH-BACON!
BACON'S DONE, WOO-HOO. AFTER THAT YOU CAN'T FORGET...
AFTER THAT YOU CAN'T FORGET...
...PLENTY O' MUSTARD TOO!
SIZL POPLIPIPL KRAKL
UM... DOES THE MAJOR USUALLY HANDLE THE COOKING?
OH... HE RARELY COOKS.
BUT THIS DISH IS HIS SPECIALTY.
That was hard work. Ya did good, cook.
HE SAYS IT'S A SECRET RECIPE SOMEONE ONCE TAUGHT HIM.
I SEE.

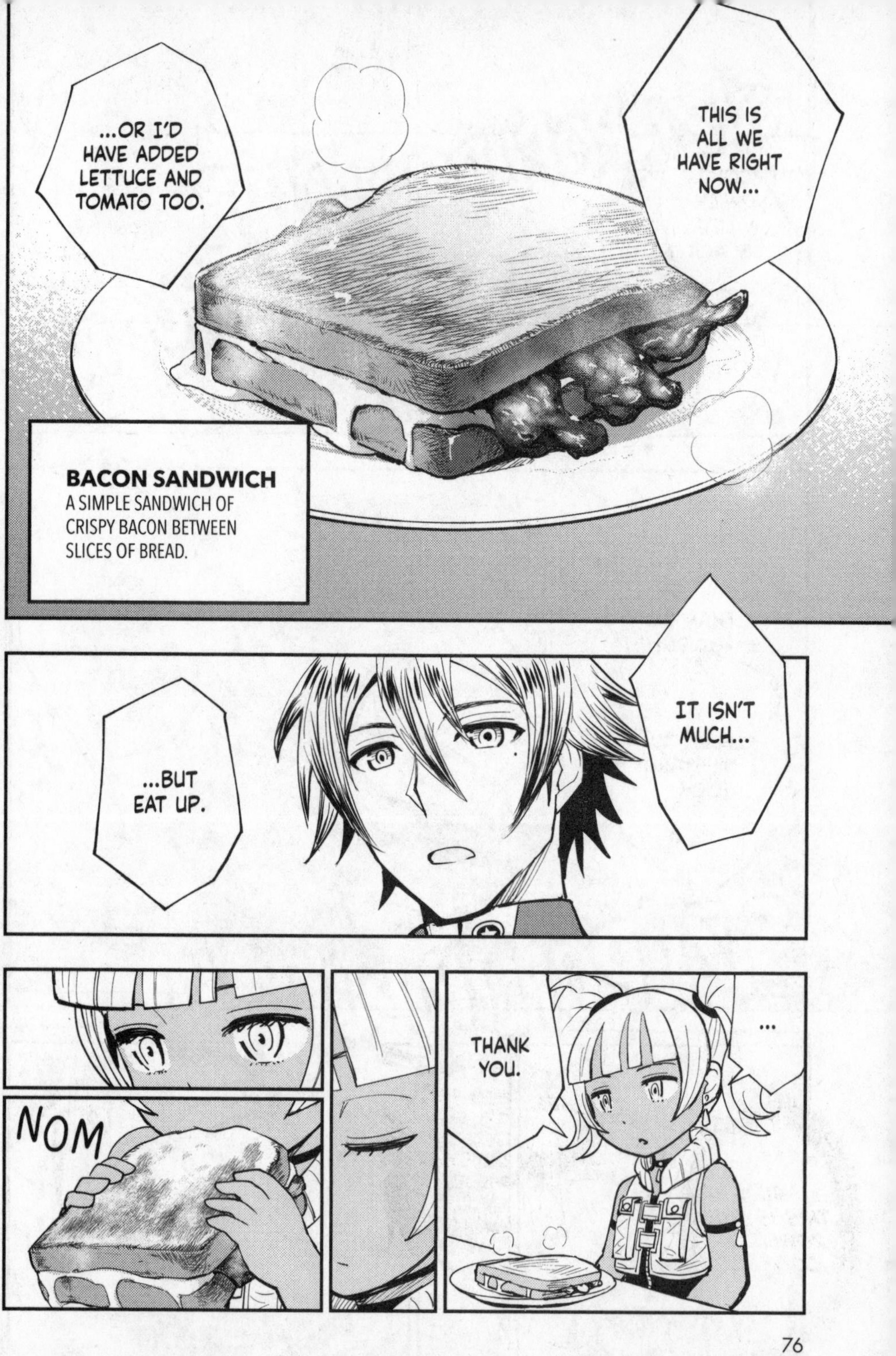
THIS IS ALL WE HAVE RIGHT NOW...
...OR I'D HAVE ADDED LETTUCE AND TOMATO TOO.
BACON SANDWICH
A SIMPLE SANDWICH OF CRISPY BACON BETWEEN SLICES OF BREAD.
IT ISN'T MUCH...
...BUT EAT UP.
...
THANK YOU.
NOM

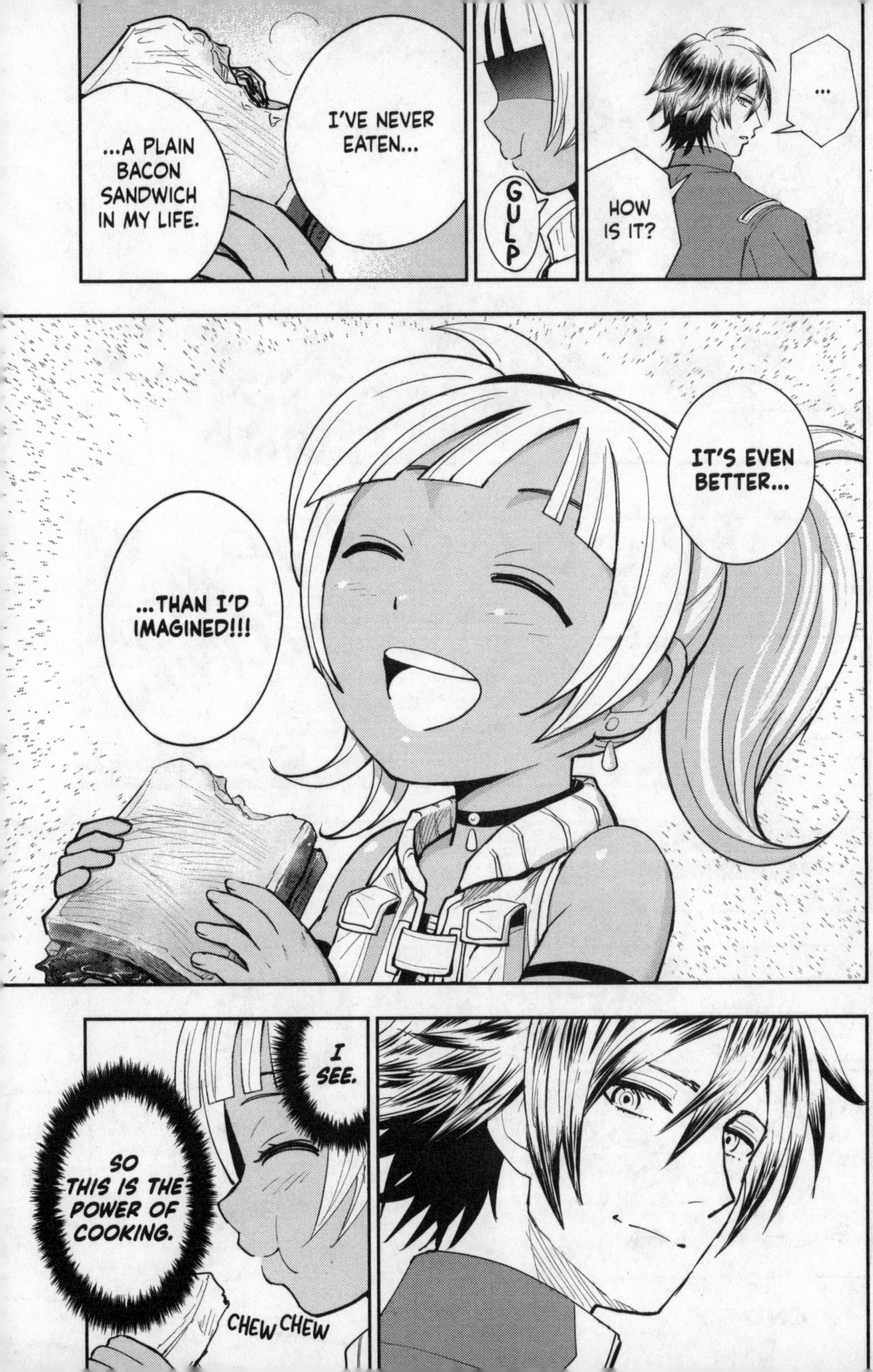
...
HOW IS IT?
GULP
I'VE NEVER EATEN...
...A PLAIN BACON SANDWICH IN MY LIFE.
IT'S EVEN BETTER...
...THAN I'D IMAGINED!!!
I SEE.
SO THIS IS THE POWER OF COOKING.
CHEW CHEW

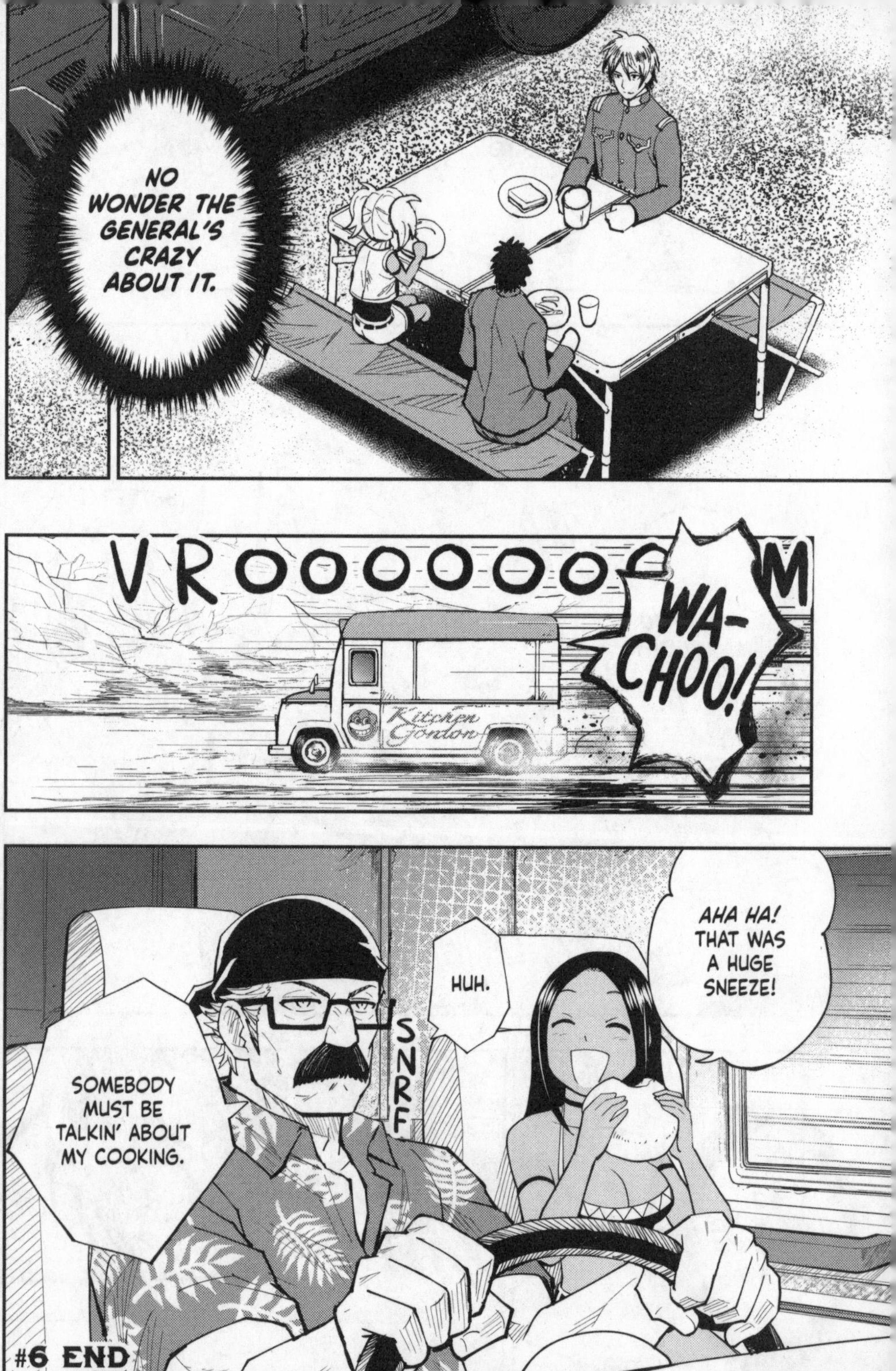
NO WONDER THE GENERAL'S CRAZY ABOUT IT.
VROOOOOOOOM
WA-CHOO!
Kitchen Gordon
AHA HA! THAT WAS A HUGE SNEEZE!
HUH.
SNRF
SOMEBODY MUST BE TALKIN' ABOUT MY COOKING.
#6 END

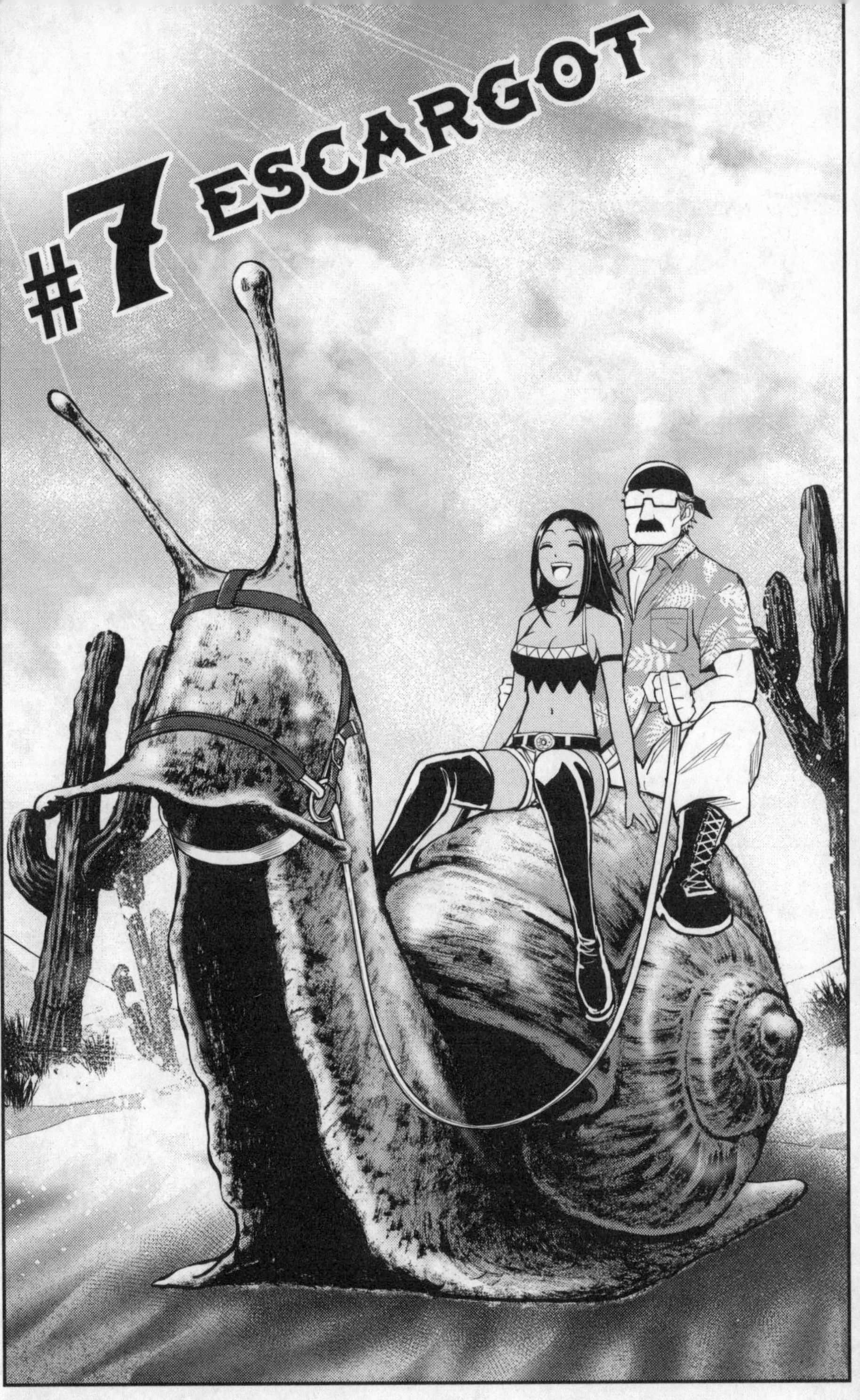
#7 ESCARGOT

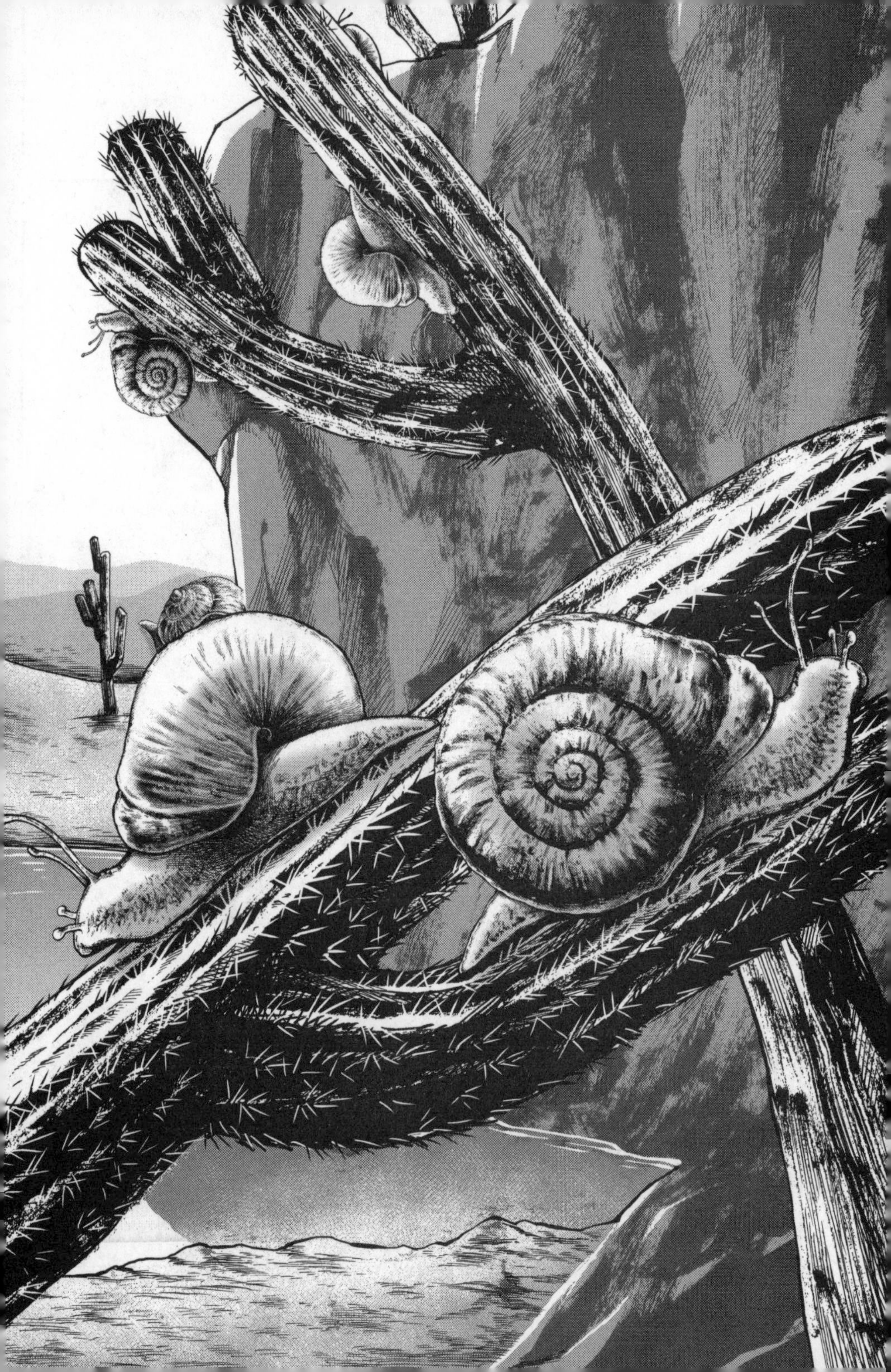

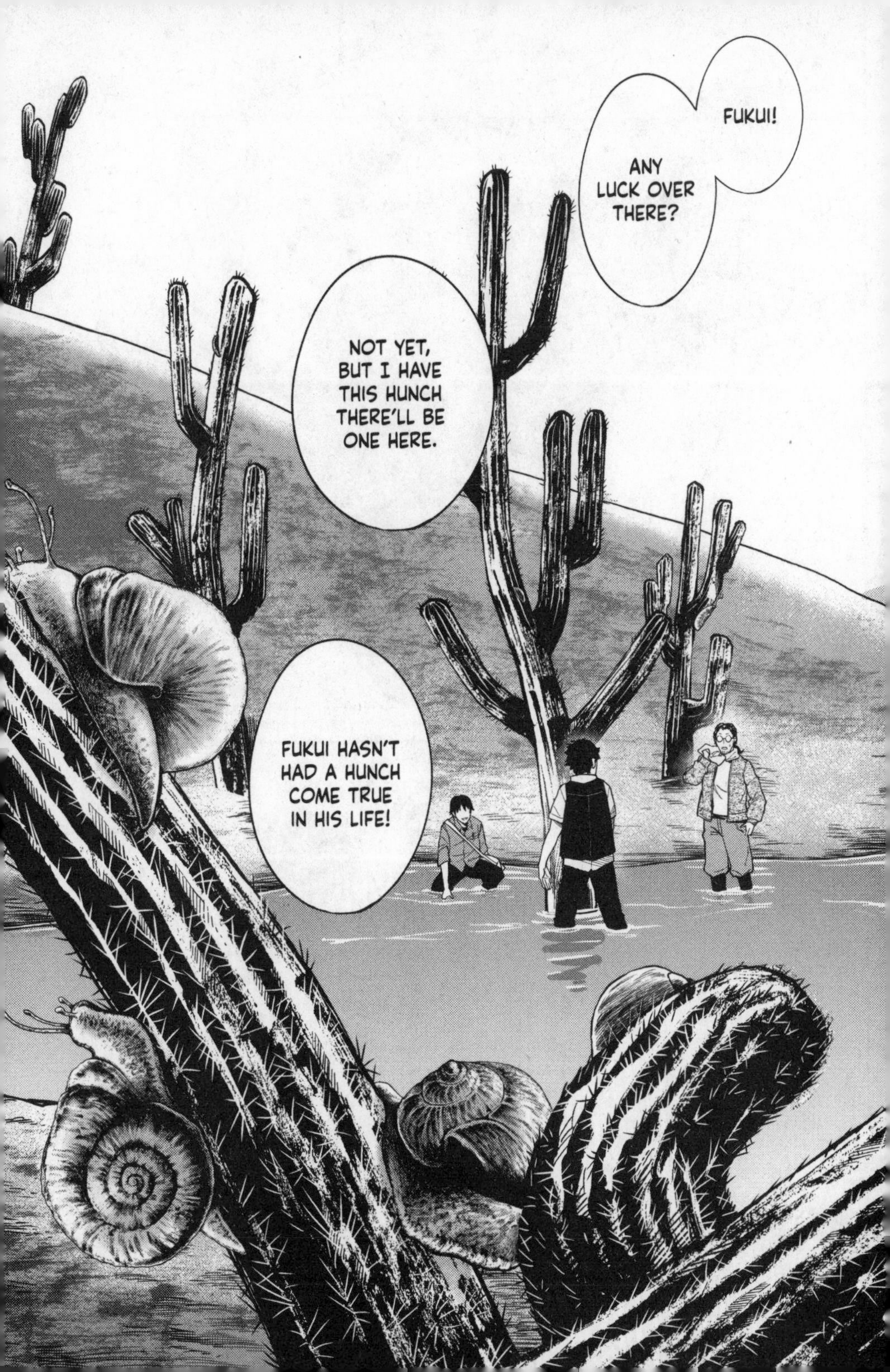
FUKUI! ANY LUCK OVER THERE?
NOT YET, BUT I HAVE THIS HUNCH THERE'LL BE ONE HERE.
FUKUI HASN'T HAD A HUNCH COME TRUE IN HIS LIFE!

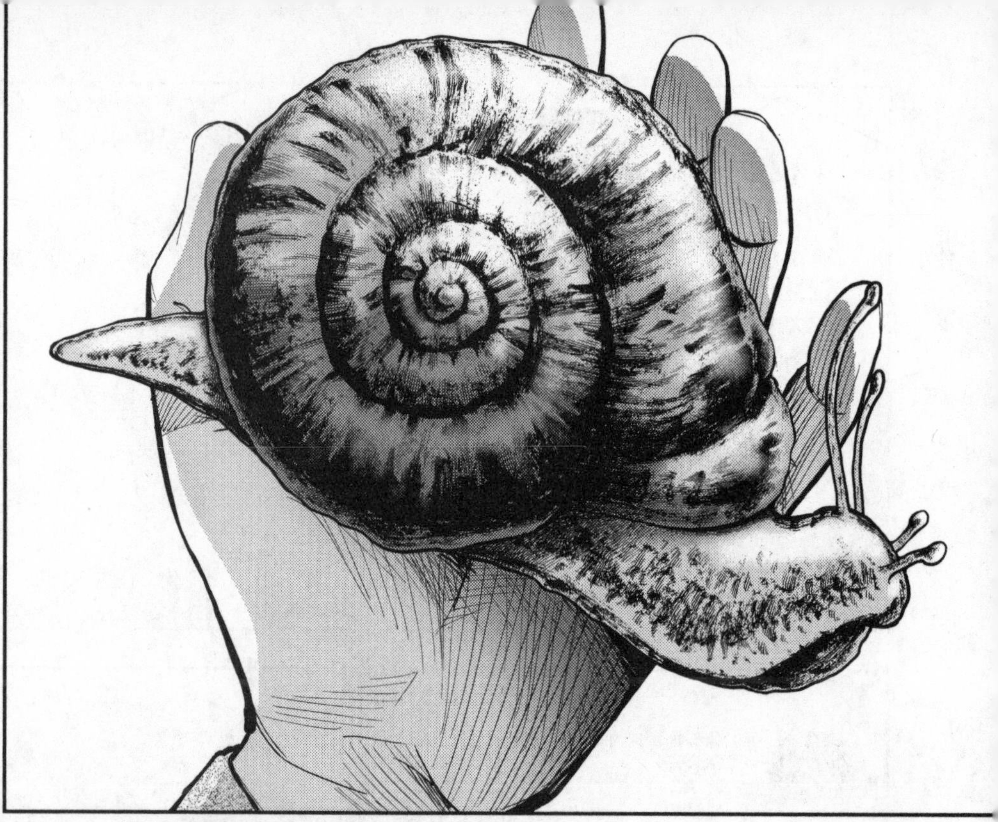

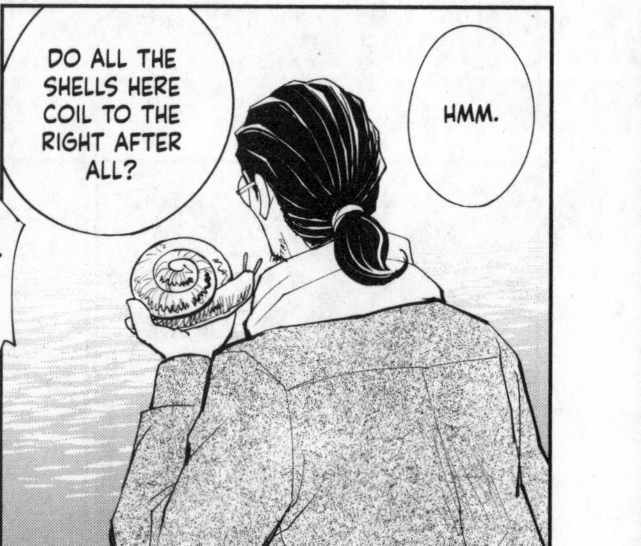
HMM.
DO ALL THE SHELLS HERE COIL TO THE RIGHT AFTER ALL?

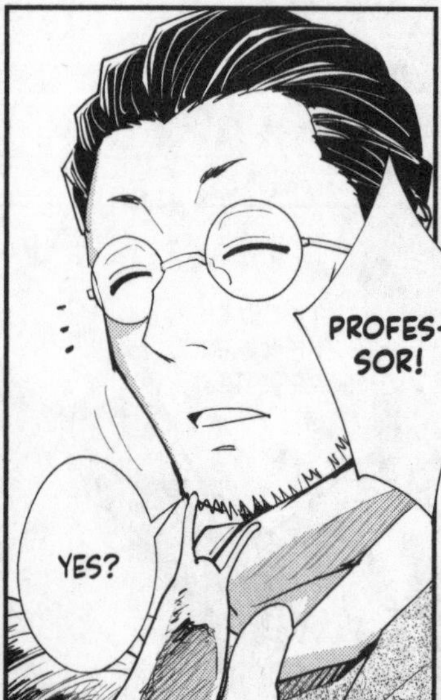
PROFES-SOR!
YES?

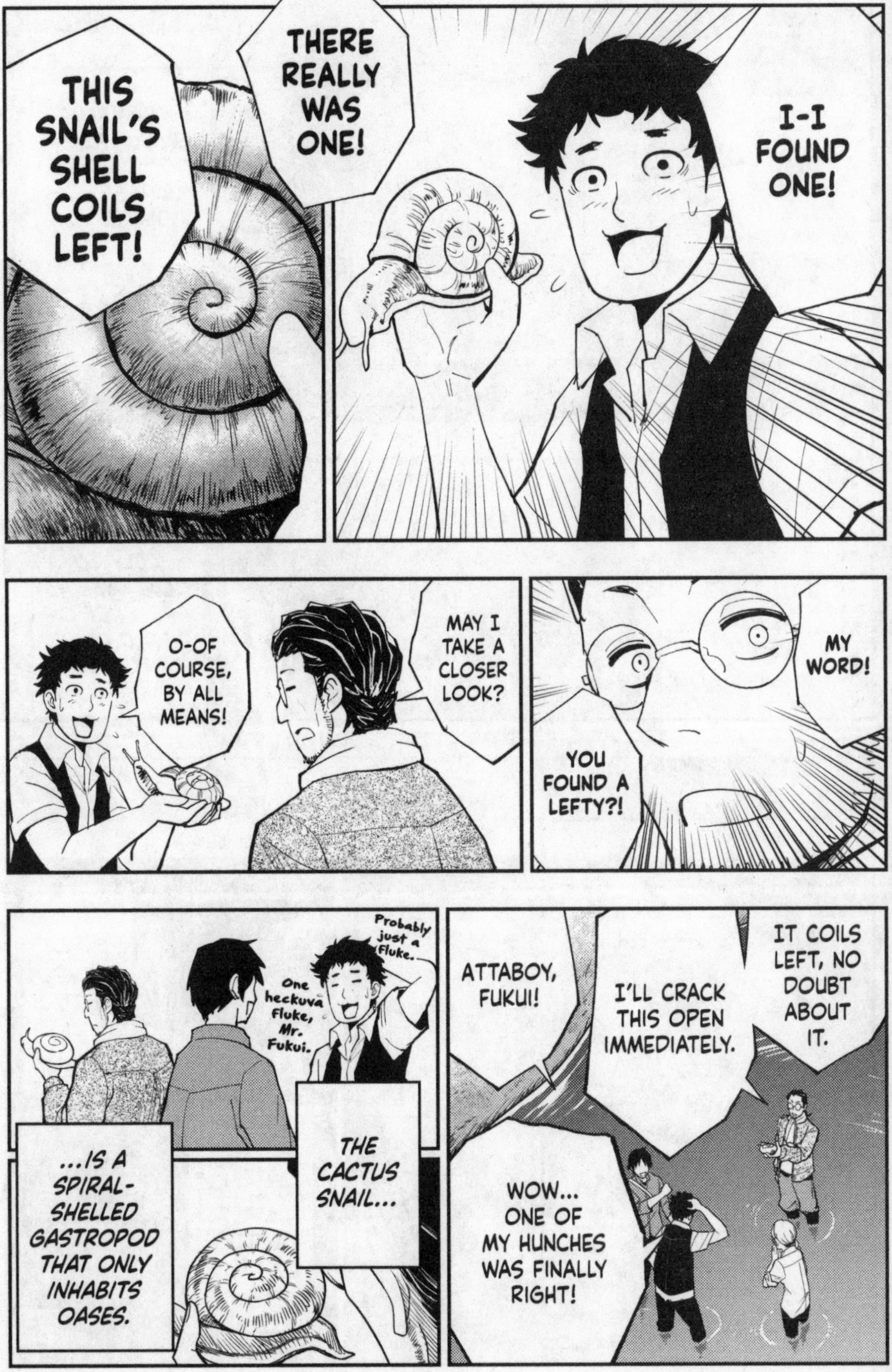
I-I FOUND ONE!
THERE REALLY WAS ONE!
THIS SNAIL'S SHELL COILS LEFT!
MY WORD!
YOU FOUND A LEFTY?!
MAY I TAKE A CLOSER LOOK?
O-OF COURSE, BY ALL MEANS!
IT COILS LEFT, NO DOUBT ABOUT IT.
I'LL CRACK THIS OPEN IMMEDIATELY.
ATTABOY, FUKUI!
WOW... ONE OF MY HUNCHES WAS FINALLY RIGHT!
Probably just a fluke.
One heckuva fluke, Mr. Fukui.
THE CACTUS SNAIL...
...IS A SPIRAL-SHELLED GASTROPOD THAT ONLY INHABITS OASES.

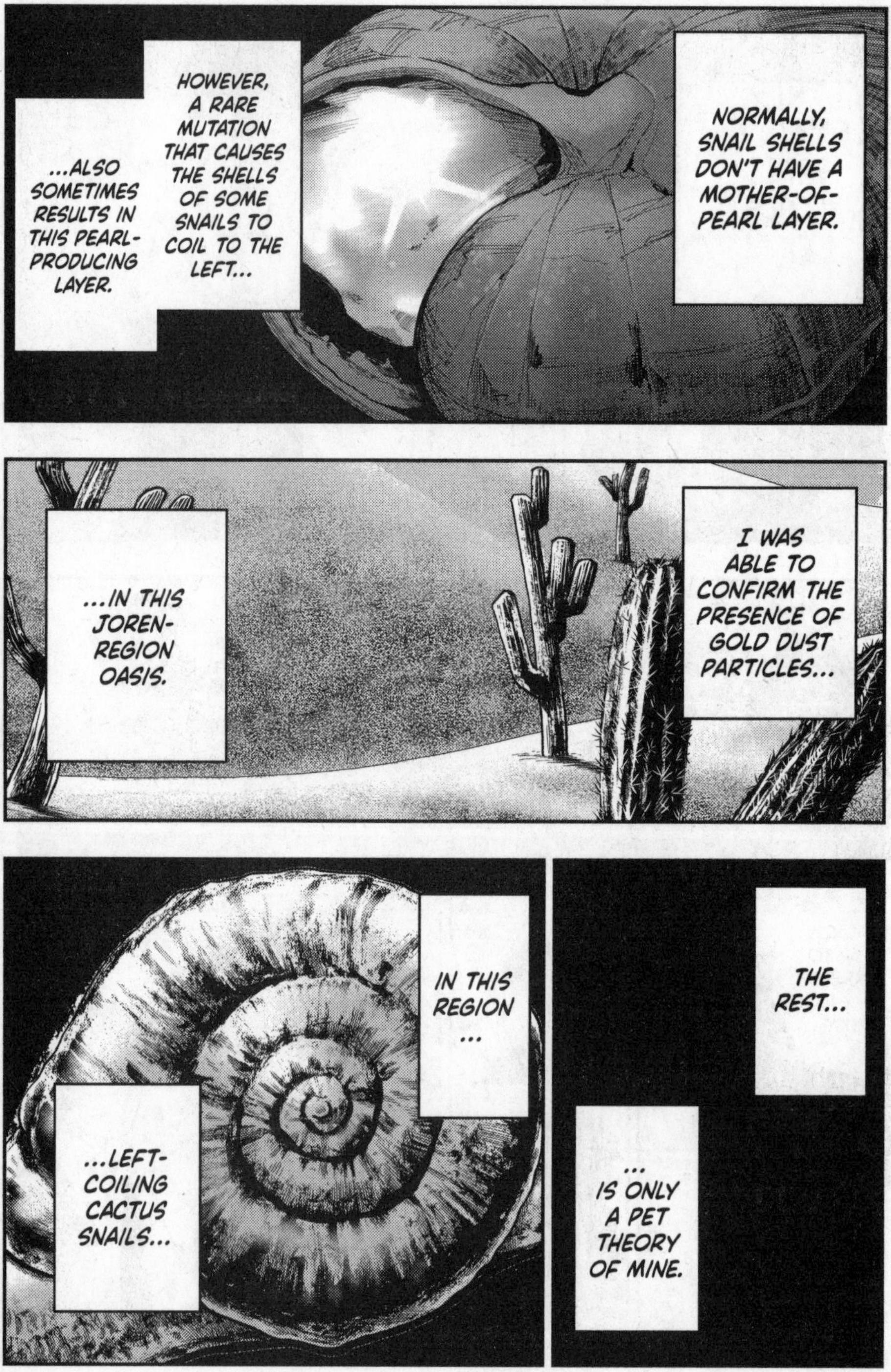
NORMALLY, SNAIL SHELLS DON'T HAVE A MOTHER-OF-PEARL LAYER.
HOWEVER, A RARE MUTATION THAT CAUSES THE SHELLS OF SOME SNAILS TO COIL TO THE LEFT...
...ALSO SOMETIMES RESULTS IN THIS PEARL-PRODUCING LAYER.
I WAS ABLE TO CONFIRM THE PRESENCE OF GOLD DUST PARTICLES...
...IN THIS JOREN-REGION OASIS.
THE REST...
...IS ONLY A PET THEORY OF MINE.
IN THIS REGION...
...LEFT-COILING CACTUS SNAILS...

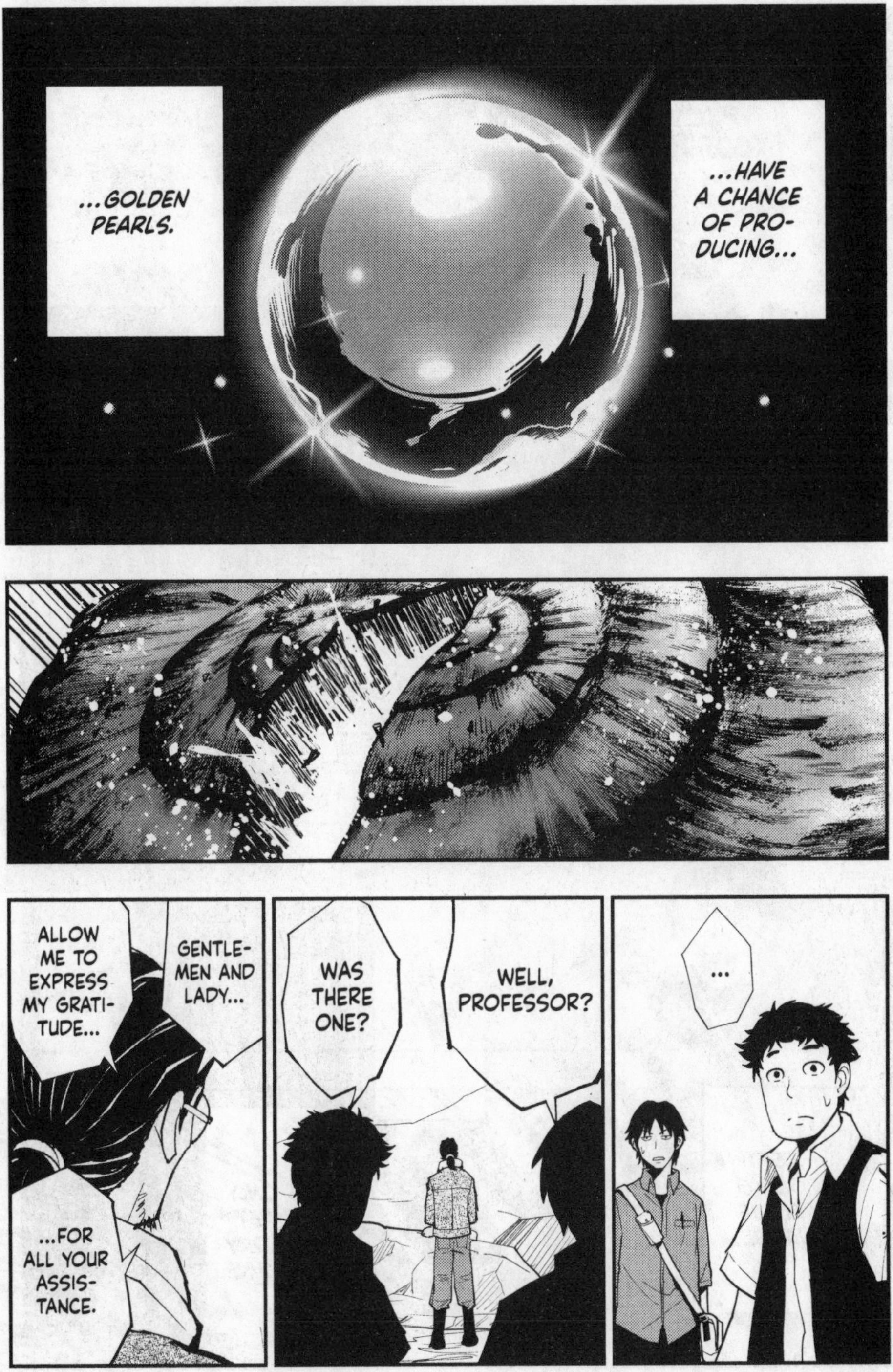
...HAVE A CHANCE OF PRO-DUCING...
...GOLDEN PEARLS.
...
WELL, PROFESSOR?
WAS THERE ONE?
GENTLE-MEN AND LADY...
ALLOW ME TO EXPRESS MY GRATI-TUDE...
...FOR ALL YOUR ASSIS-TANCE.

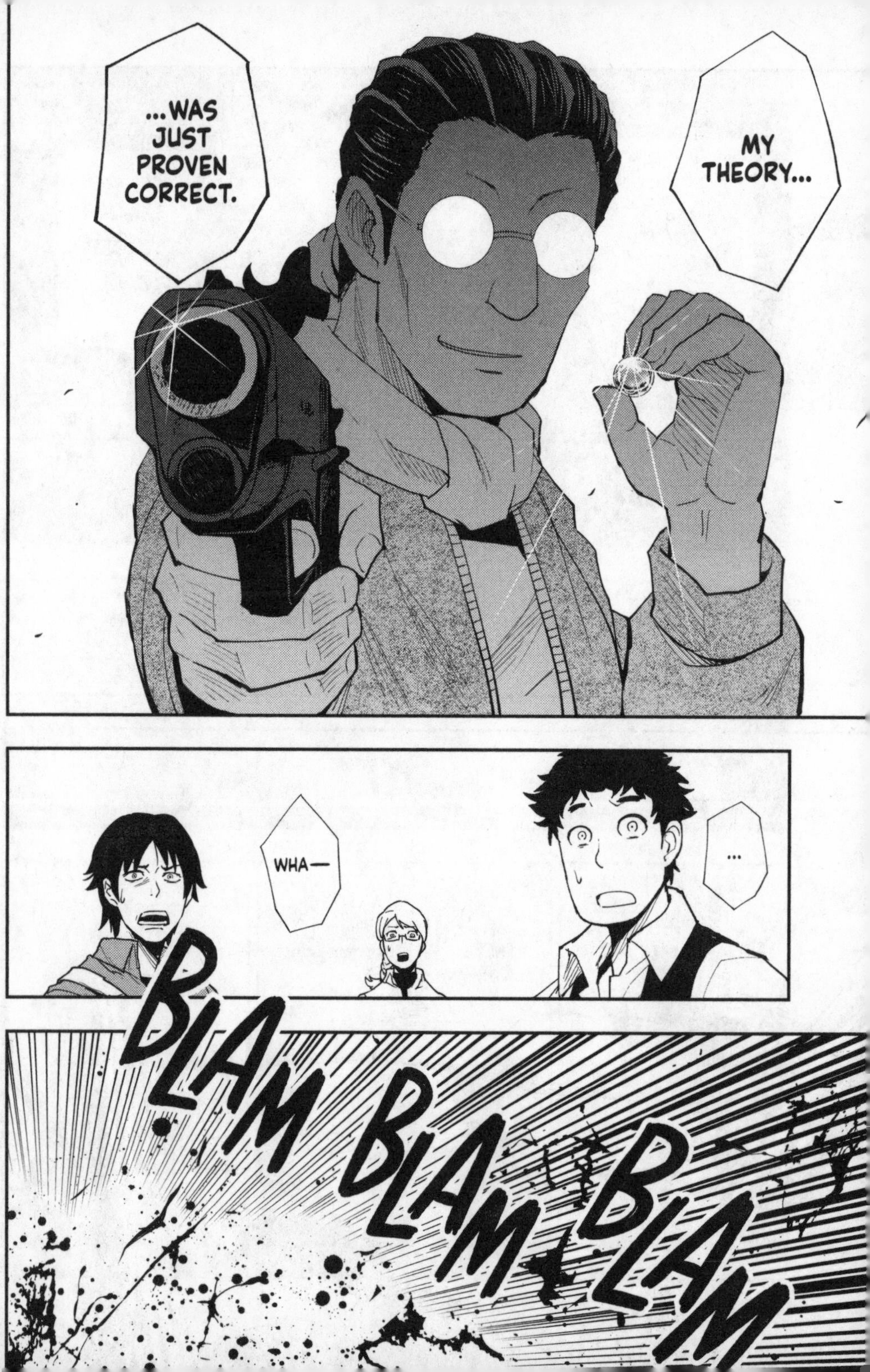
MY THEORY...
...WAS JUST PROVEN CORRECT.
...
WHA—
BLAM BLAM BLAM

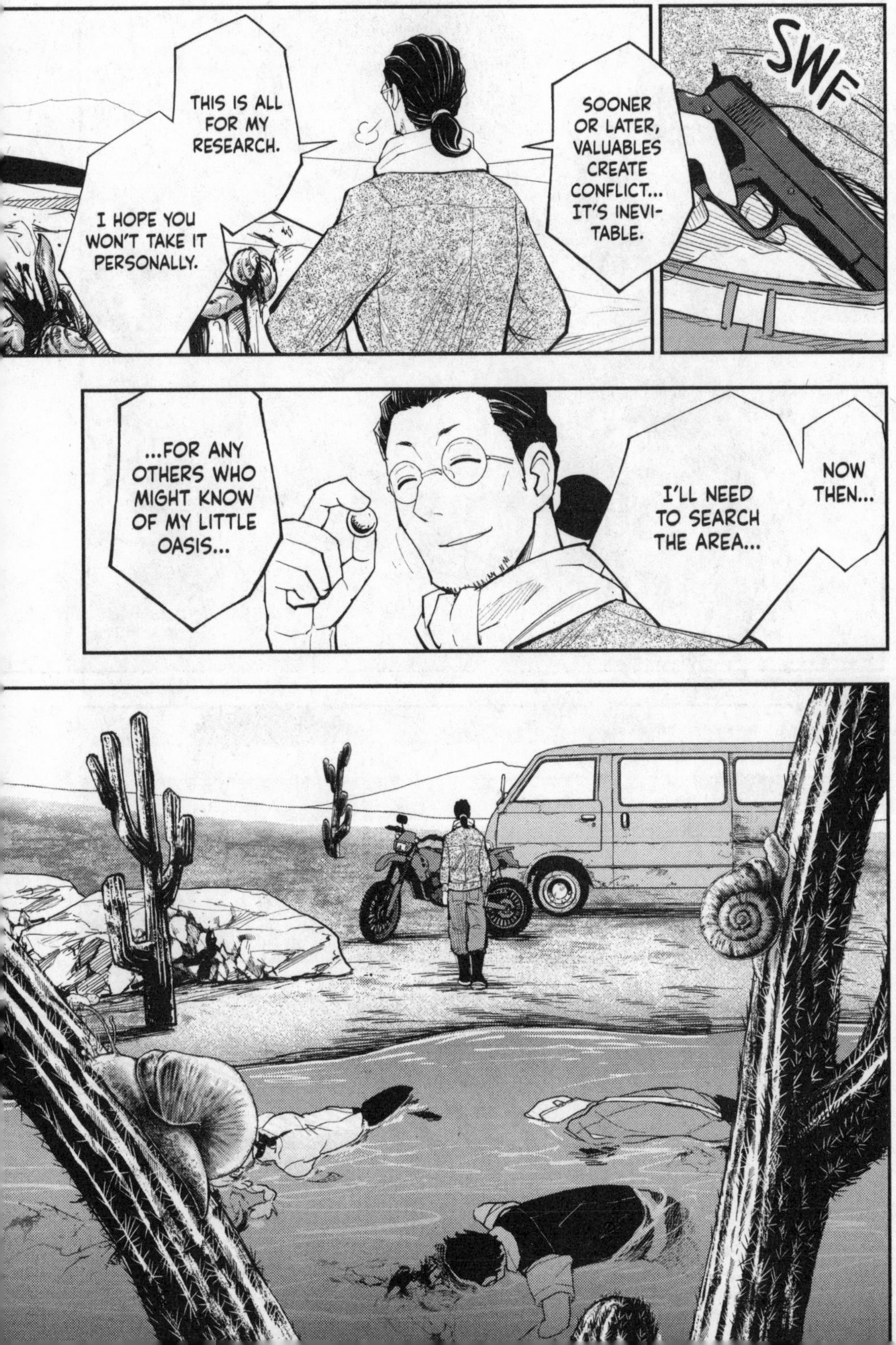
SWF
SOONER OR LATER, VALUABLES CREATE CONFLICT... IT'S INEVITABLE.
THIS IS ALL FOR MY RESEARCH.
I HOPE YOU WON'T TAKE IT PERSONALLY.
NOW THEN...
I'LL NEED TO SEARCH THE AREA...
...FOR ANY OTHERS WHO MIGHT KNOW OF MY LITTLE OASIS...

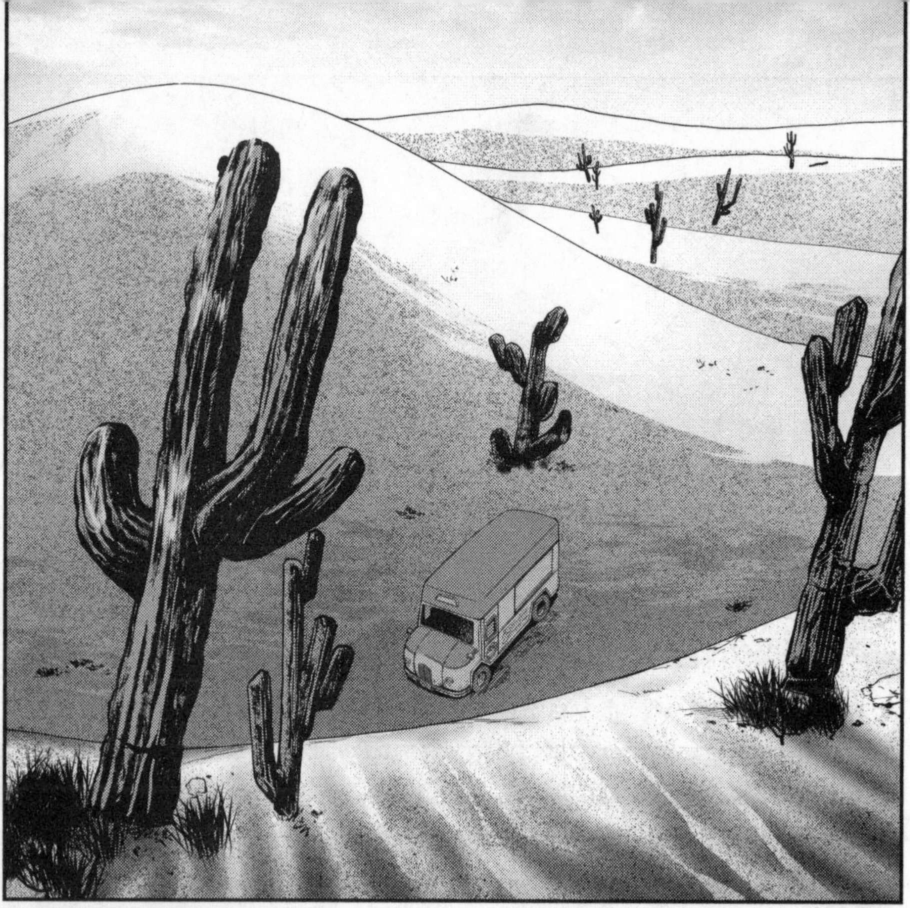

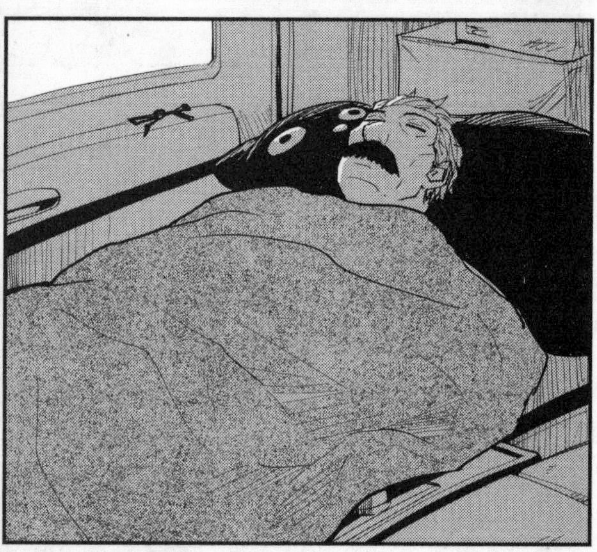

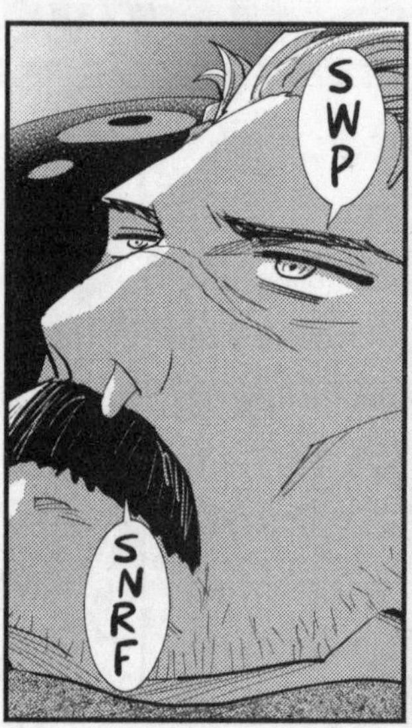
SWP
SNRF

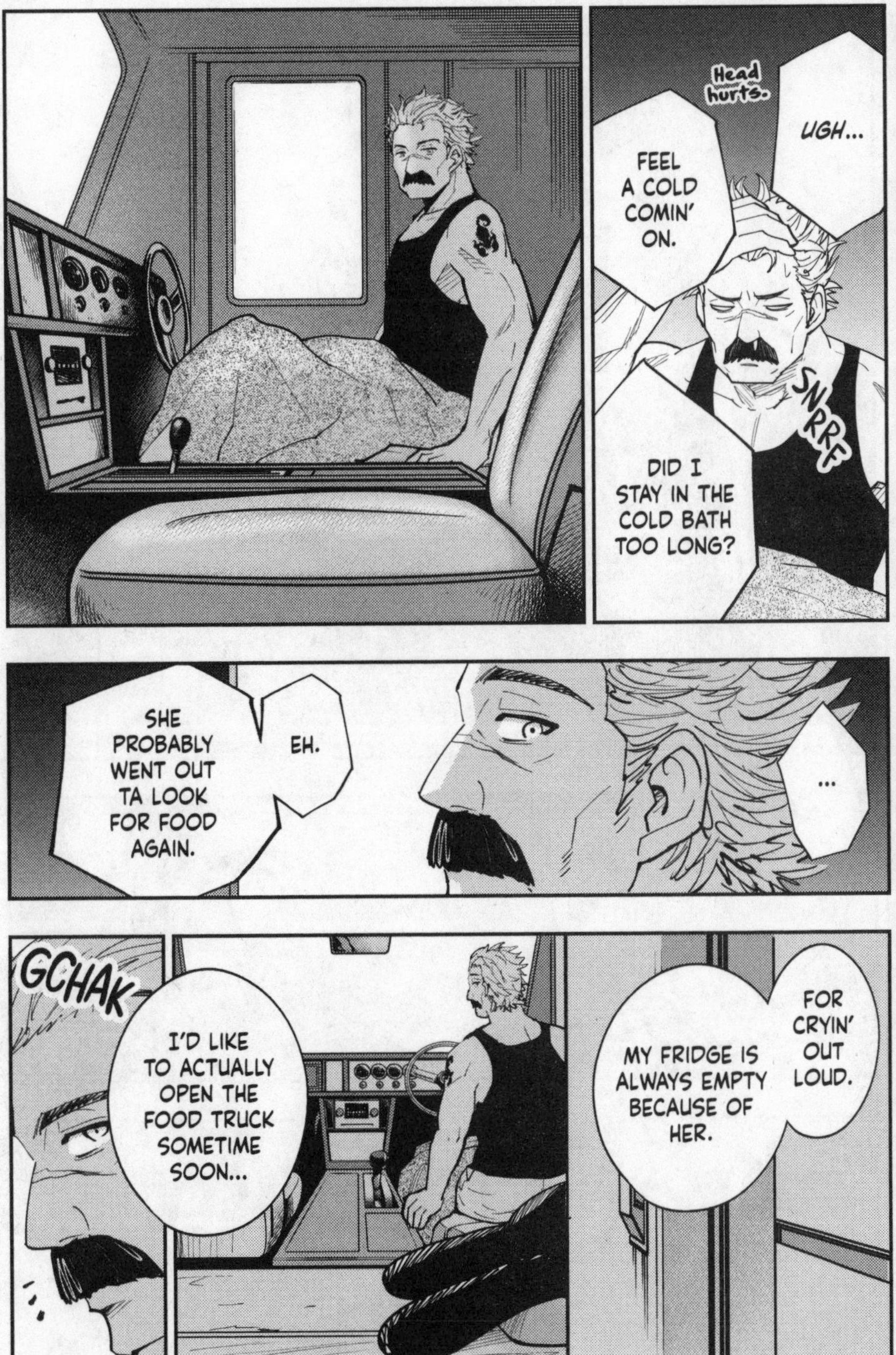
UGH...
Head hurts.
FEEL A COLD COMIN' ON.
SNRRF
DID I STAY IN THE COLD BATH TOO LONG?
...
EH.
SHE PROBABLY WENT OUT TA LOOK FOR FOOD AGAIN.
FOR CRYIN' OUT LOUD.
MY FRIDGE IS ALWAYS EMPTY BECAUSE OF HER.
GCHAK
I'D LIKE TO ACTUALLY OPEN THE FOOD TRUCK SOMETIME SOON...

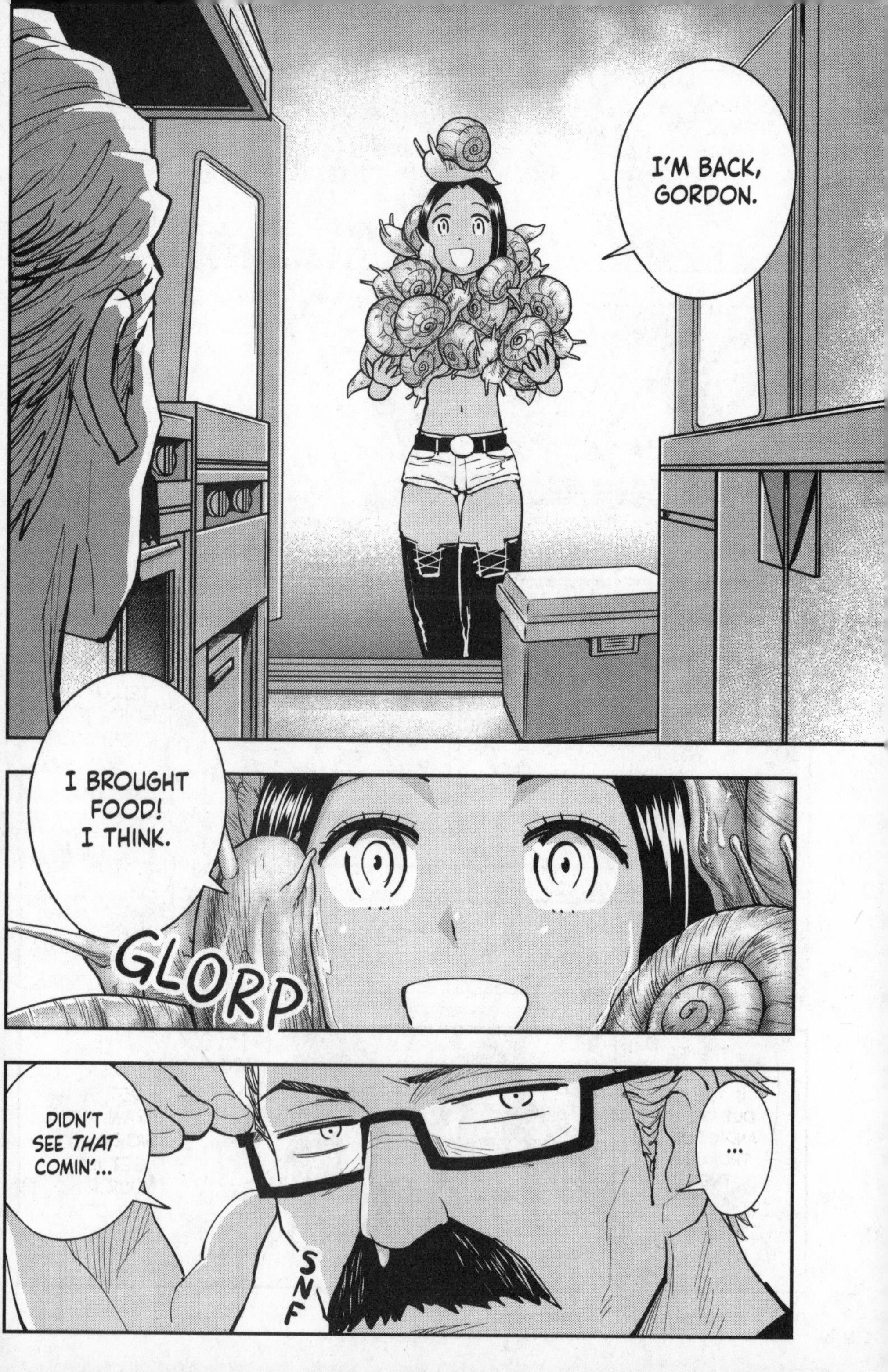
I'M BACK, GORDON.
I BROUGHT FOOD! I THINK.
GLORP
...
DIDN'T SEE *THAT* COMIN'...
SNF

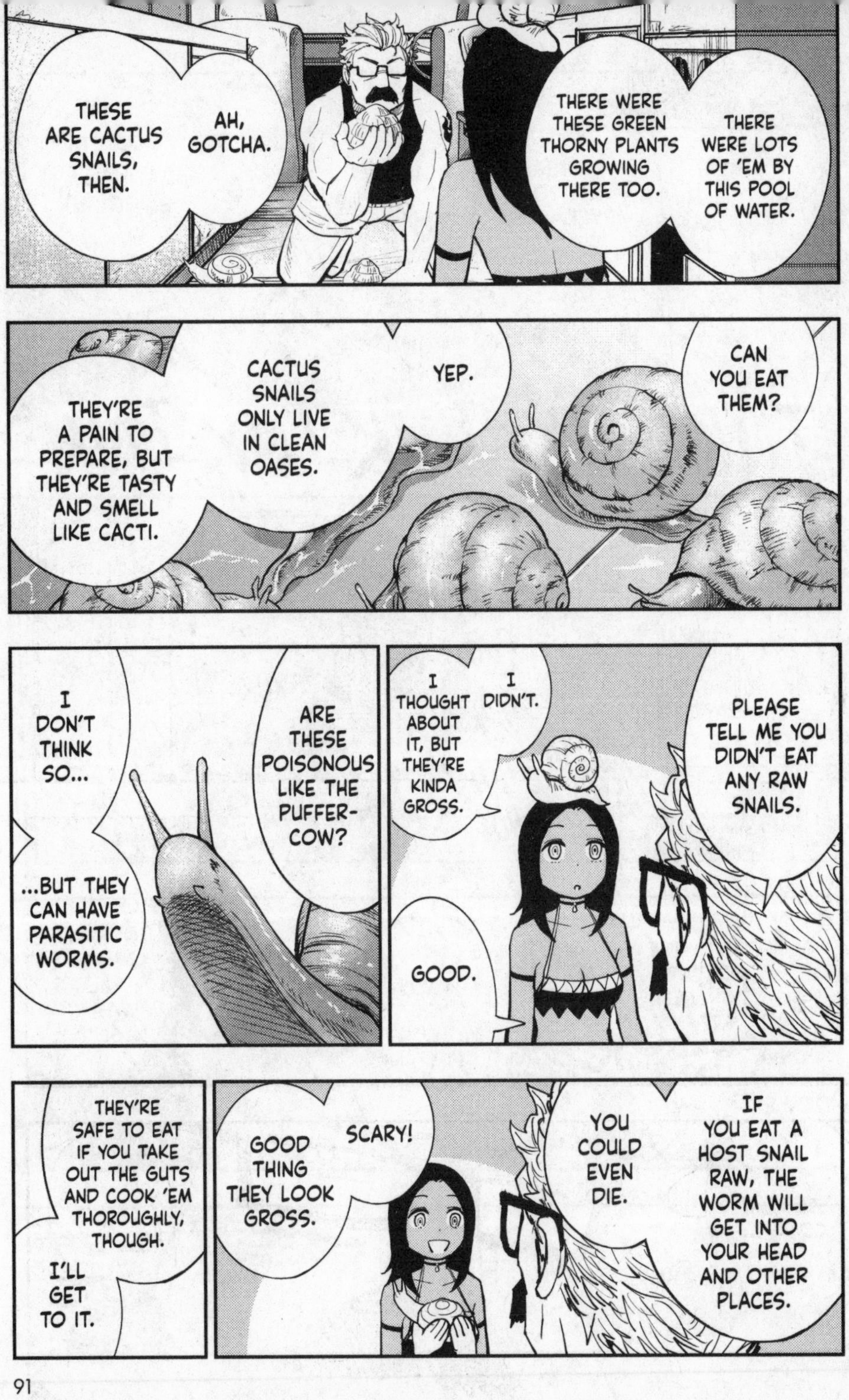
THERE WERE LOTS OF 'EM BY THIS POOL OF WATER.
THERE WERE THESE GREEN THORNY PLANTS GROWING THERE TOO.
AH, GOTCHA.
THESE ARE CACTUS SNAILS, THEN.
CAN YOU EAT THEM?
YEP.
CACTUS SNAILS ONLY LIVE IN CLEAN OASES.
THEY'RE A PAIN TO PREPARE, BUT THEY'RE TASTY AND SMELL LIKE CACTI.
PLEASE TELL ME YOU DIDN'T EAT ANY RAW SNAILS.
I DIDN'T.
I THOUGHT ABOUT IT, BUT THEY'RE KINDA GROSS.
GOOD.
ARE THESE POISONOUS LIKE THE PUFFER-COW?
I DON'T THINK SO...
...BUT THEY CAN HAVE PARASITIC WORMS.
IF YOU EAT A HOST SNAIL RAW, THE WORM WILL GET INTO YOUR HEAD AND OTHER PLACES.
YOU COULD EVEN DIE.
SCARY!
GOOD THING THEY LOOK GROSS.
THEY'RE SAFE TO EAT IF YOU TAKE OUT THE GUTS AND COOK 'EM THOROUGHLY, THOUGH.
I'LL GET TO IT.

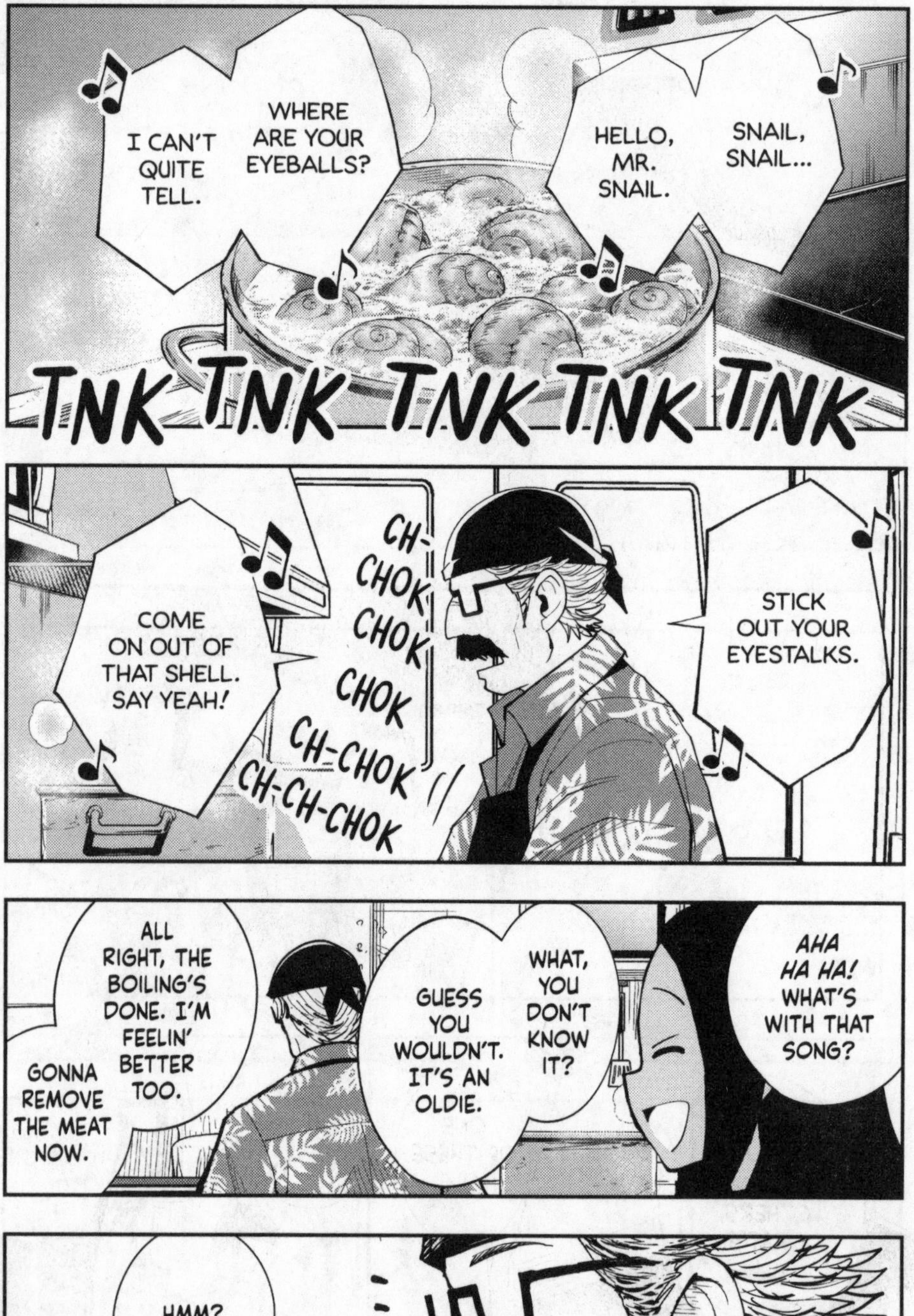
SNAIL, SNAIL...
HELLO, MR. SNAIL.
WHERE ARE YOUR EYEBALLS?
I CAN'T QUITE TELL.
TNK TNK TNK TNK TNK
STICK OUT YOUR EYESTALKS.
CH-CHOK CHOK CHOK CH-CHOK CH-CH-CHOK
COME ON OUT OF THAT SHELL. SAY YEAH!
AHA HA HA! WHAT'S WITH THAT SONG?
WHAT, YOU DON'T KNOW IT?
GUESS YOU WOULDN'T. IT'S AN OLDIE.
ALL RIGHT, THE BOILING'S DONE. I'M FEELIN' BETTER TOO.
GONNA REMOVE THE MEAT NOW.
HMM?

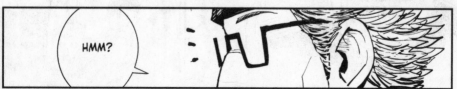

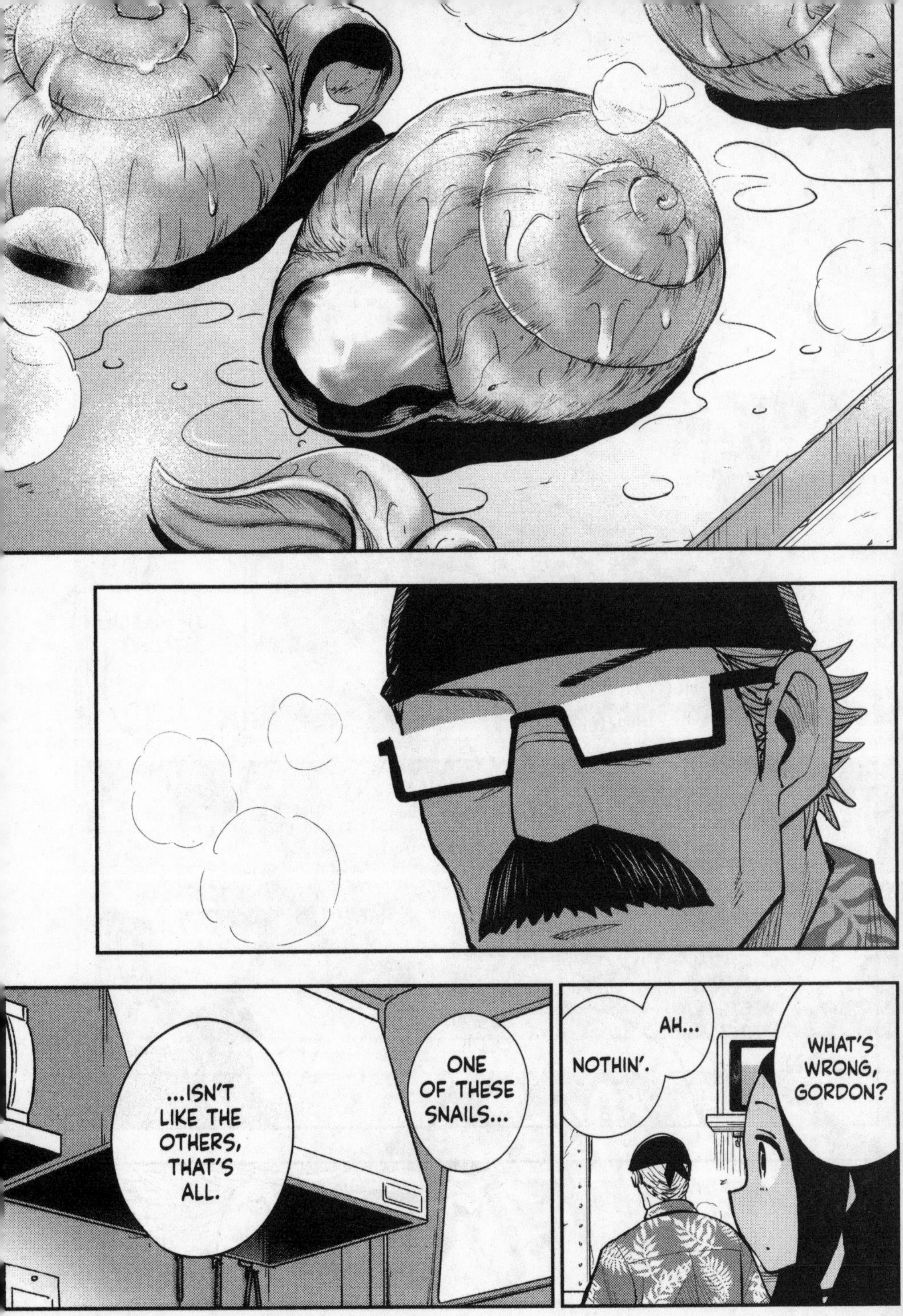
WHAT'S WRONG, GORDON?
AH...
NOTHIN'.
ONE OF THESE SNAILS...
...ISN'T LIKE THE OTHERS, THAT'S ALL.

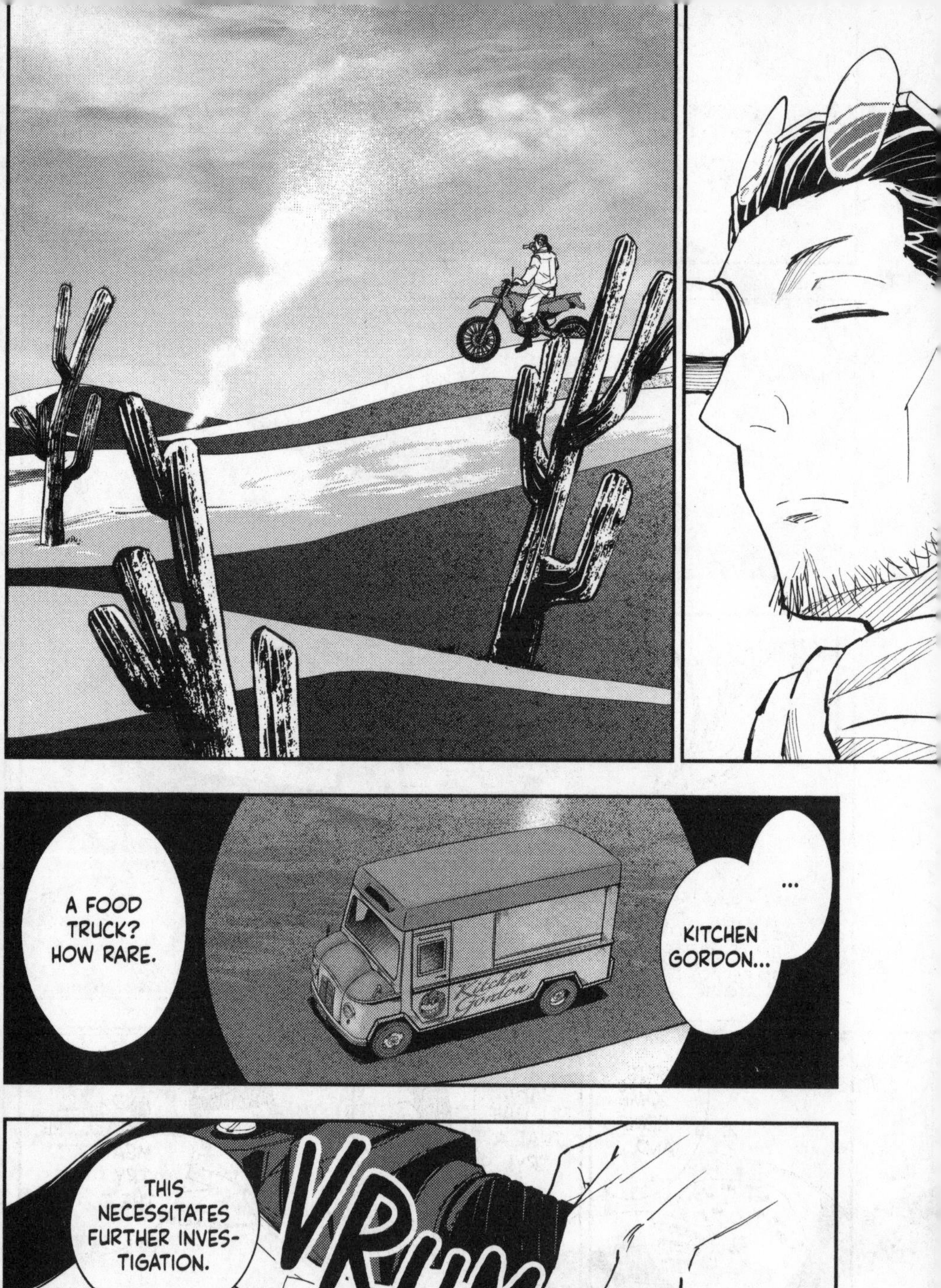
...
KITCHEN GORDON...
Kitchen Gordon
A FOOD TRUCK? HOW RARE.
VRUM
THIS NECESSITATES FURTHER INVES-TIGATION.

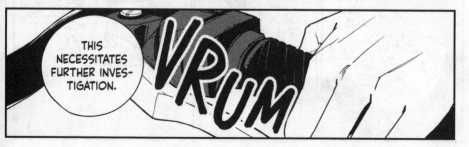

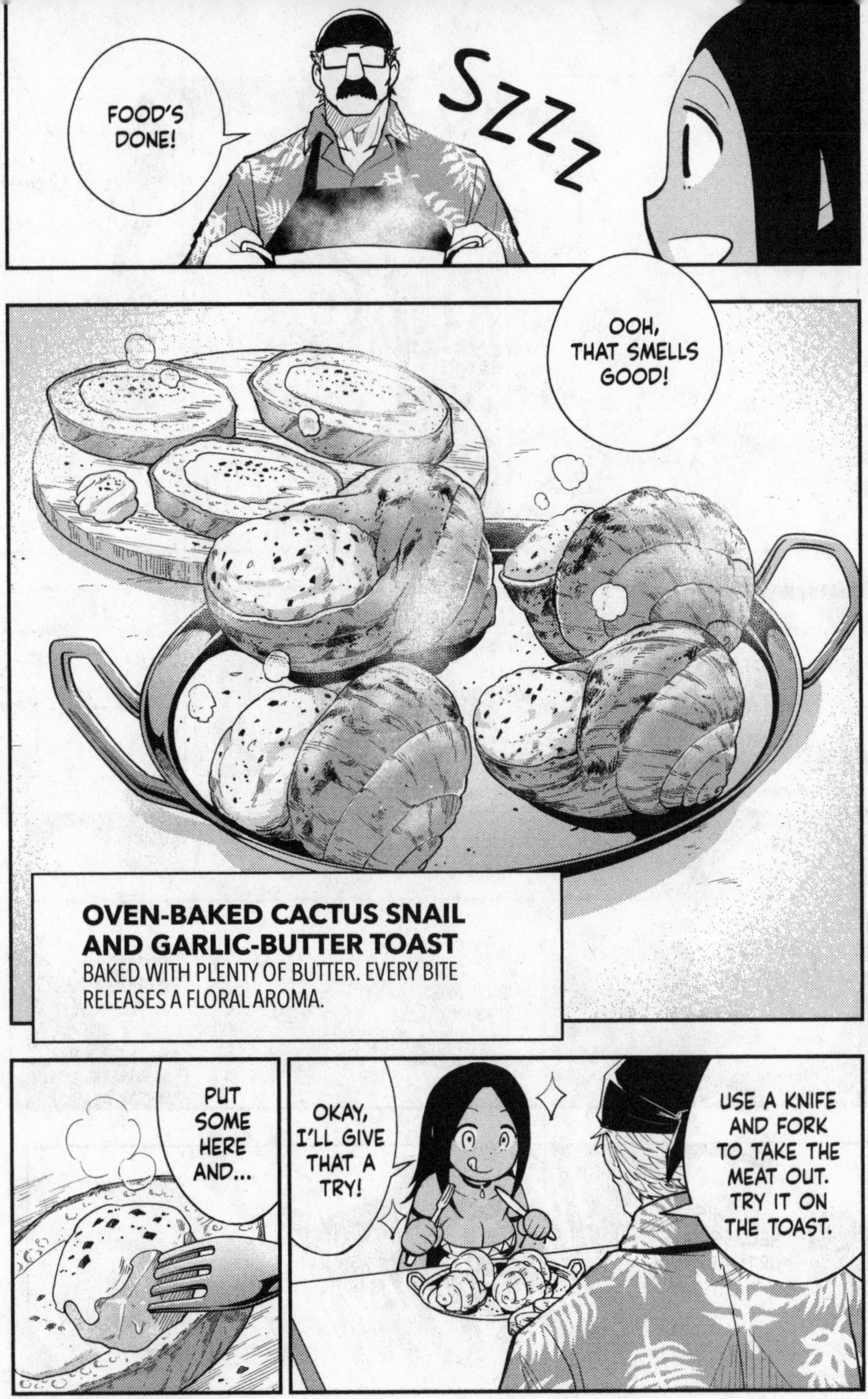
SZZZ
FOOD'S DONE!
OOH, THAT SMELLS GOOD!
OVEN-BAKED CACTUS SNAIL AND GARLIC-BUTTER TOAST
BAKED WITH PLENTY OF BUTTER. EVERY BITE RELEASES A FLORAL AROMA.
USE A KNIFE AND FORK TO TAKE THE MEAT OUT. TRY IT ON THE TOAST.
OKAY, I'LL GIVE THAT A TRY!
PUT SOME HERE AND...

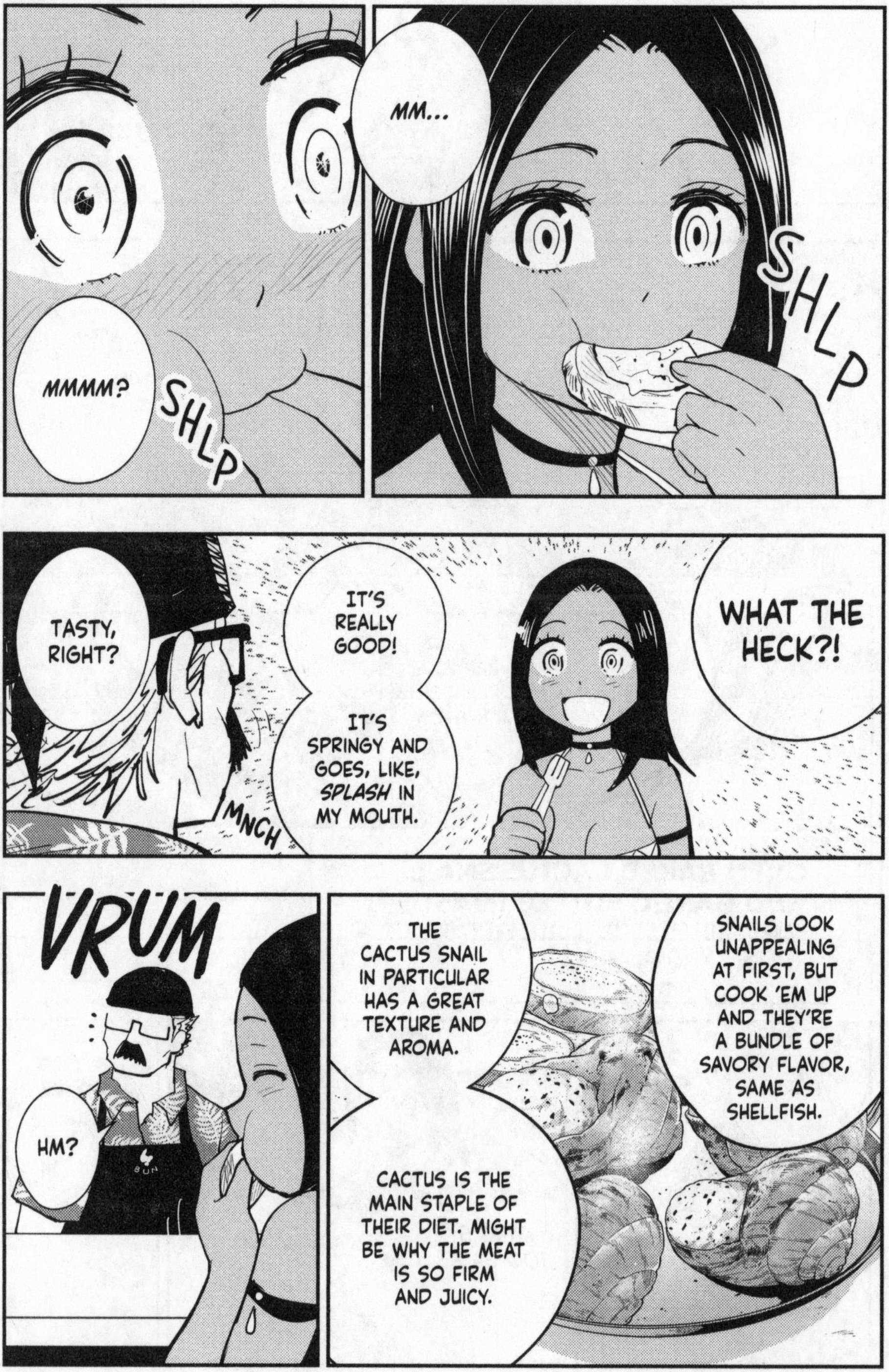
MM...
SHLP
MMMM?
SHLP
WHAT THE HECK?!
IT'S REALLY GOOD!
IT'S SPRINGY AND GOES, LIKE, *SPLASH* IN MY MOUTH.
MNCH
TASTY, RIGHT?
SNAILS LOOK UNAPPEALING AT FIRST, BUT COOK 'EM UP AND THEY'RE A BUNDLE OF SAVORY FLAVOR, SAME AS SHELLFISH.
THE CACTUS SNAIL IN PARTICULAR HAS A GREAT TEXTURE AND AROMA.
CACTUS IS THE MAIN STAPLE OF THEIR DIET. MIGHT BE WHY THE MEAT IS SO FIRM AND JUICY.
VRUM
HM?

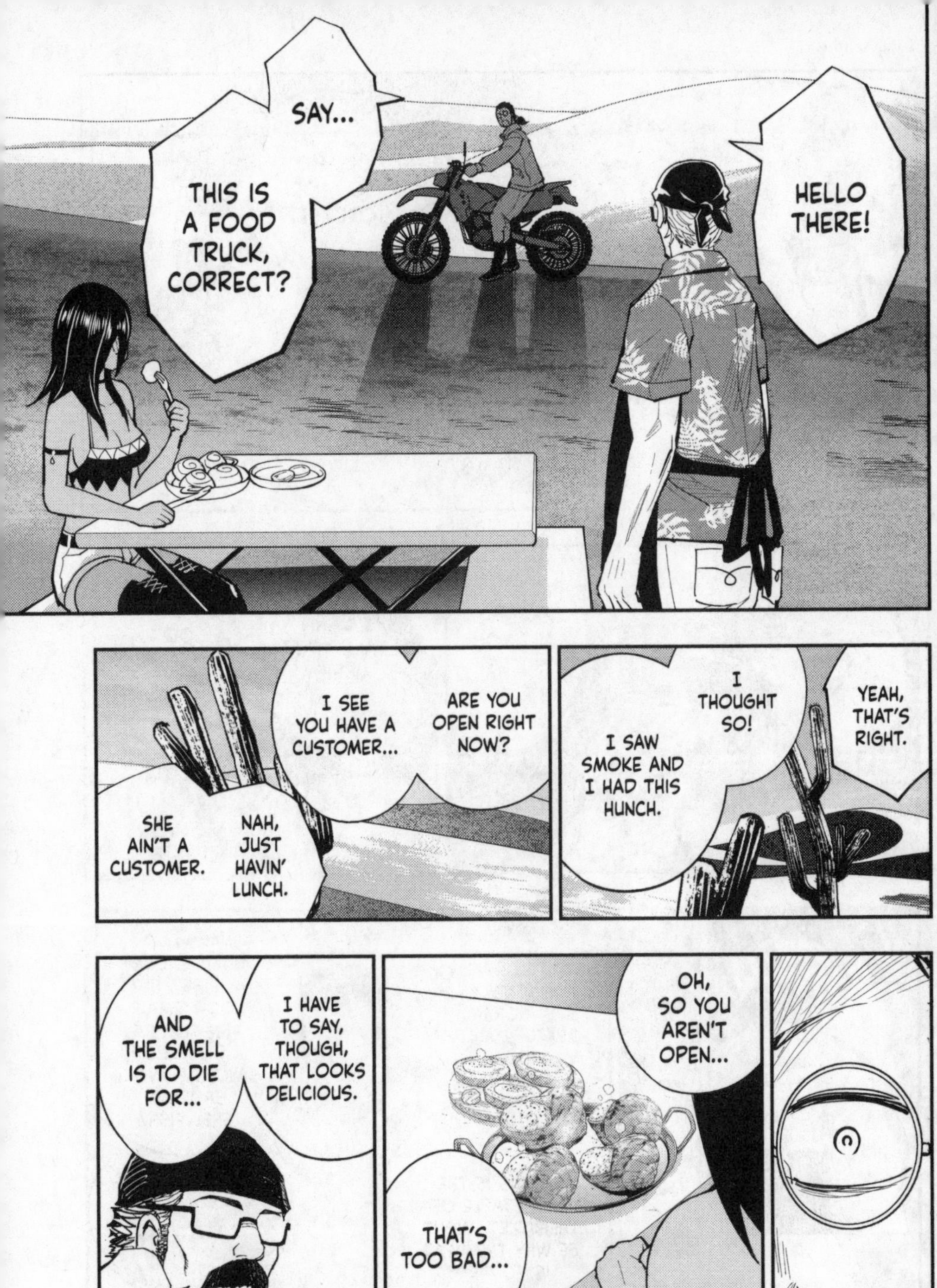
HELLO THERE!
SAY... THIS IS A FOOD TRUCK, CORRECT?
YEAH, THAT'S RIGHT.
I THOUGHT SO!
I SAW SMOKE AND I HAD THIS HUNCH.
ARE YOU OPEN RIGHT NOW?
I SEE YOU HAVE A CUSTOMER...
NAH, JUST HAVIN' LUNCH.
SHE AIN'T A CUSTOMER.
OH, SO YOU AREN'T OPEN...
THAT'S TOO BAD...
I HAVE TO SAY, THOUGH, THAT LOOKS DELICIOUS.
AND THE SMELL IS TO DIE FOR...
...

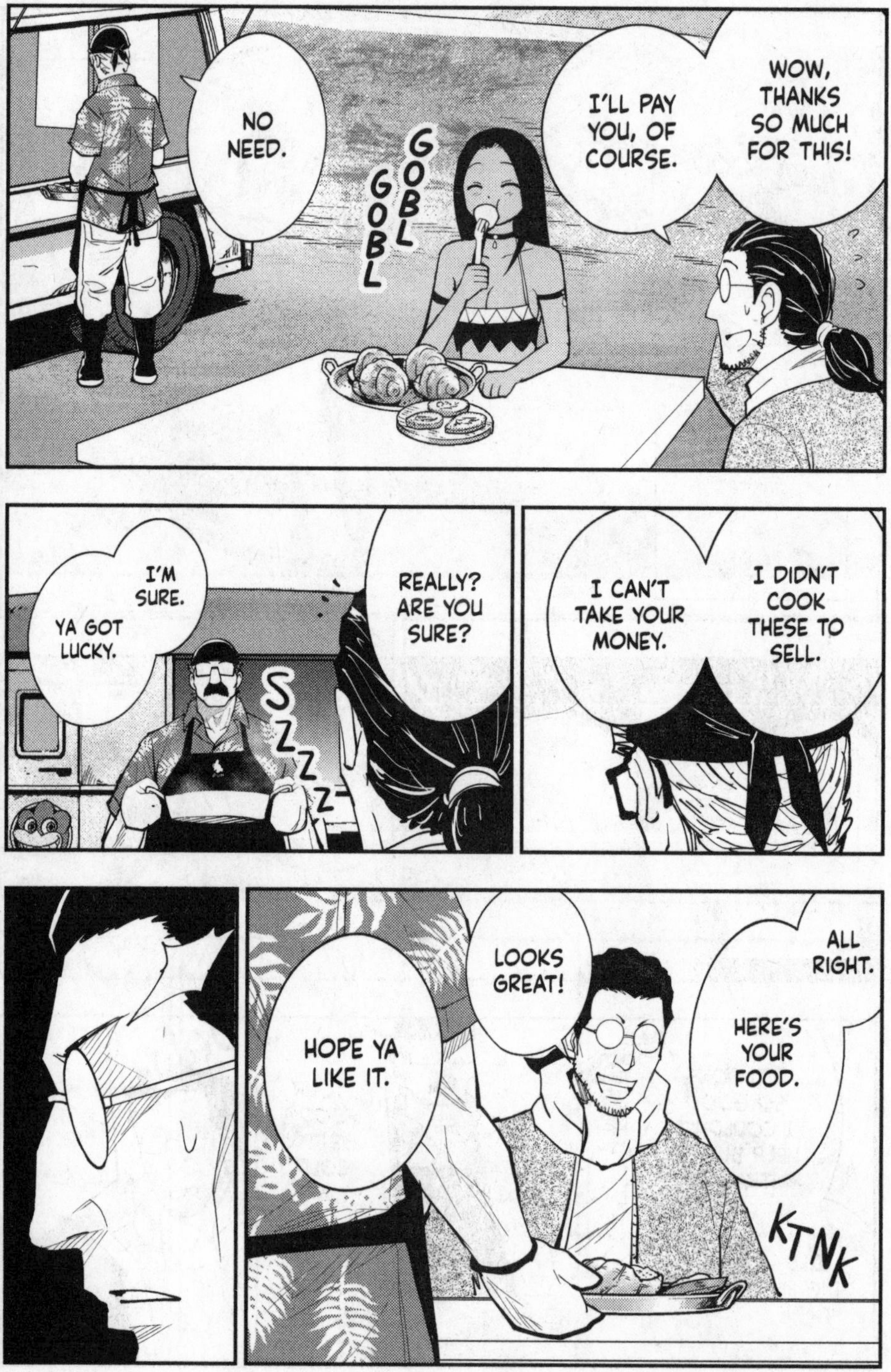
WOW, THANKS SO MUCH FOR THIS!
I'LL PAY YOU, OF COURSE.
GOBL GOBL
NO NEED.
I DIDN'T COOK THESE TO SELL.
I CAN'T TAKE YOUR MONEY.
REALLY? ARE YOU SURE?
SZZZ
I'M SURE.
YA GOT LUCKY.
ALL RIGHT.
HERE'S YOUR FOOD.
KTNK
LOOKS GREAT!
HOPE YA LIKE IT.

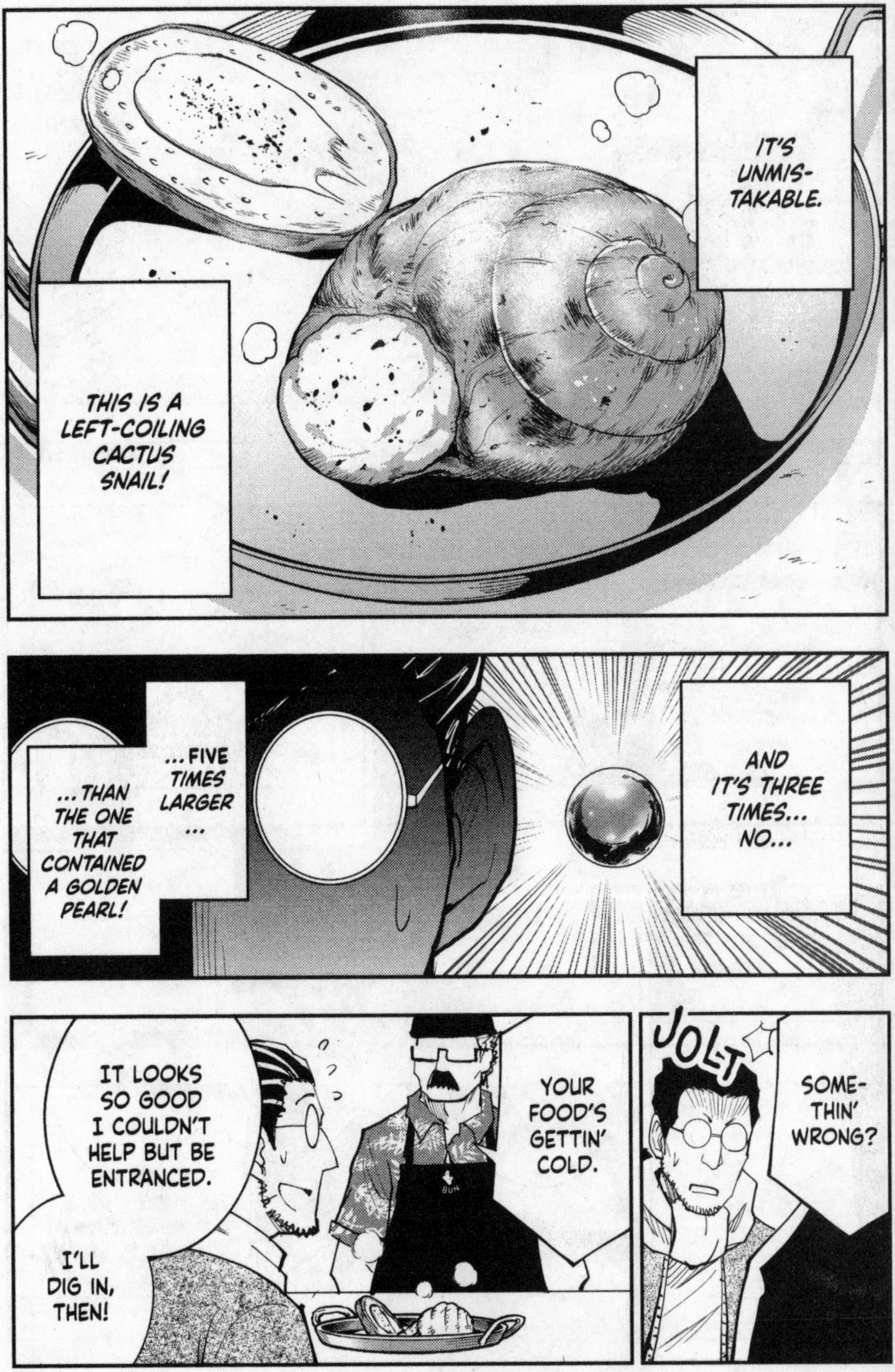
IT'S UNMIS-TAKABLE.
THIS IS A LEFT-COILING CACTUS SNAIL!
AND IT'S THREE TIMES... NO...
...FIVE TIMES LARGER ...
...THAN THE ONE THAT CONTAINED A GOLDEN PEARL!
JOLT
SOME-THIN' WRONG?
YOUR FOOD'S GETTIN' COLD.
IT LOOKS SO GOOD I COULDN'T HELP BUT BE ENTRANCED.
I'LL DIG IN, THEN!

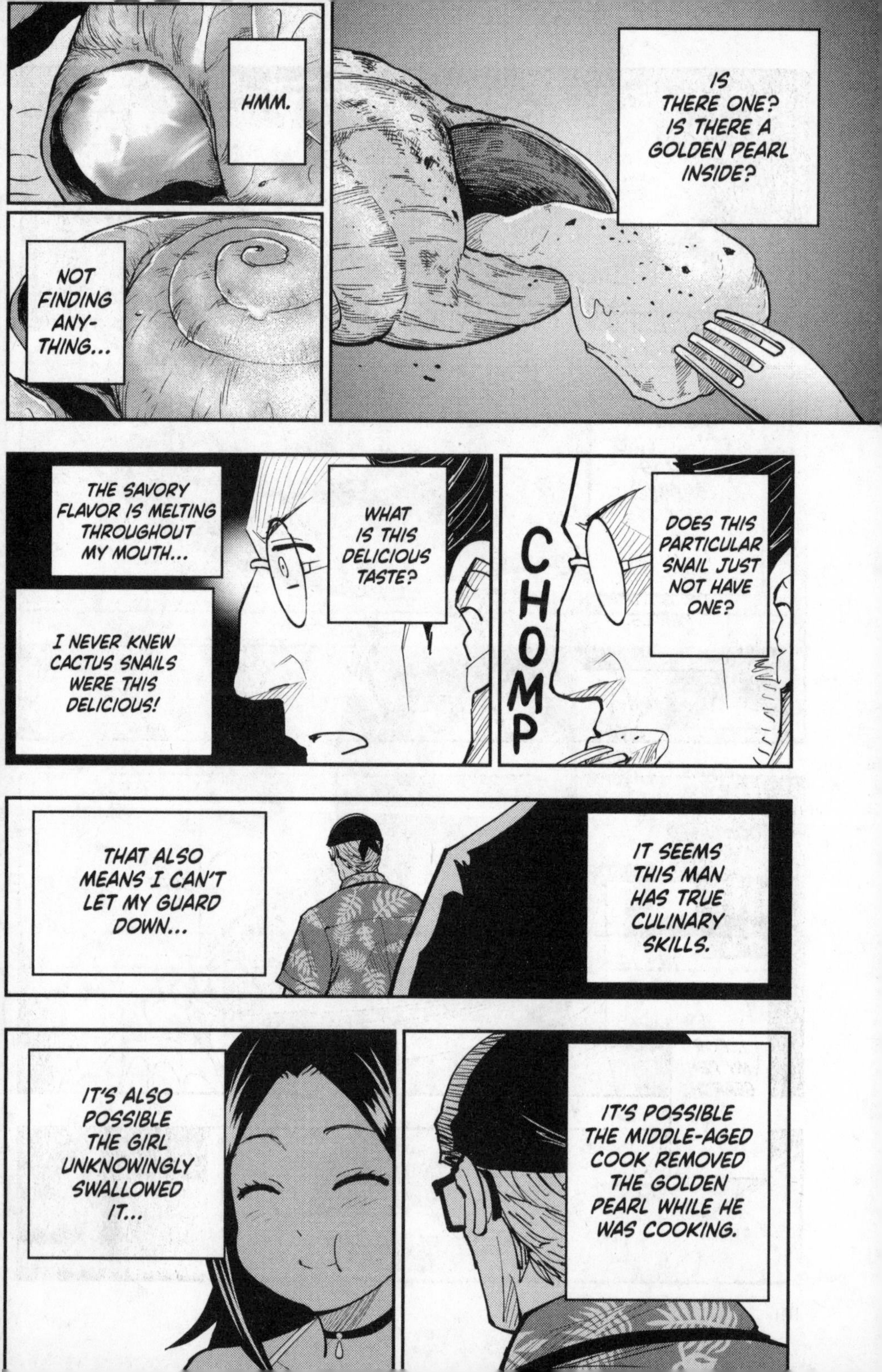
IS THERE ONE? IS THERE A GOLDEN PEARL INSIDE?
HMM.
NOT FINDING ANY-THING...
DOES THIS PARTICULAR SNAIL JUST NOT HAVE ONE?
CHOMP
WHAT IS THIS DELICIOUS TASTE?
THE SAVORY FLAVOR IS MELTING THROUGHOUT MY MOUTH...
I NEVER KNEW CACTUS SNAILS WERE THIS DELICIOUS!
IT SEEMS THIS MAN HAS TRUE CULINARY SKILLS.
THAT ALSO MEANS I CAN'T LET MY GUARD DOWN...
IT'S POSSIBLE THE MIDDLE-AGED COOK REMOVED THE GOLDEN PEARL WHILE HE WAS COOKING.
IT'S ALSO POSSIBLE THE GIRL UNKNOWINGLY SWALLOWED IT...

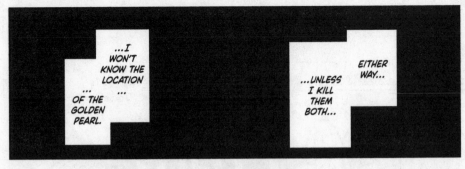

...I WON'T KNOW THE LOCATION ... ... OF THE GOLDEN PEARL.

...UNLESS I KILL THEM BOTH...

EITHER WAY...

...I MIGHT EVEN BE ABLE TO START MASS-PRODUCING THE GOLDEN PEARLS.

...AND SUCCESS-FULLY FARM LEFT-COILING SNAILS...

IF I CONTINUE MY RESEARCH ON THE CACTUS SNAILS IN THIS OASIS...

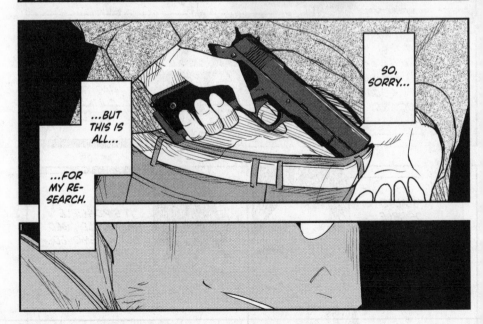

SO, SORRY...

...BUT THIS IS ALL...

...FOR MY RE-SEARCH.

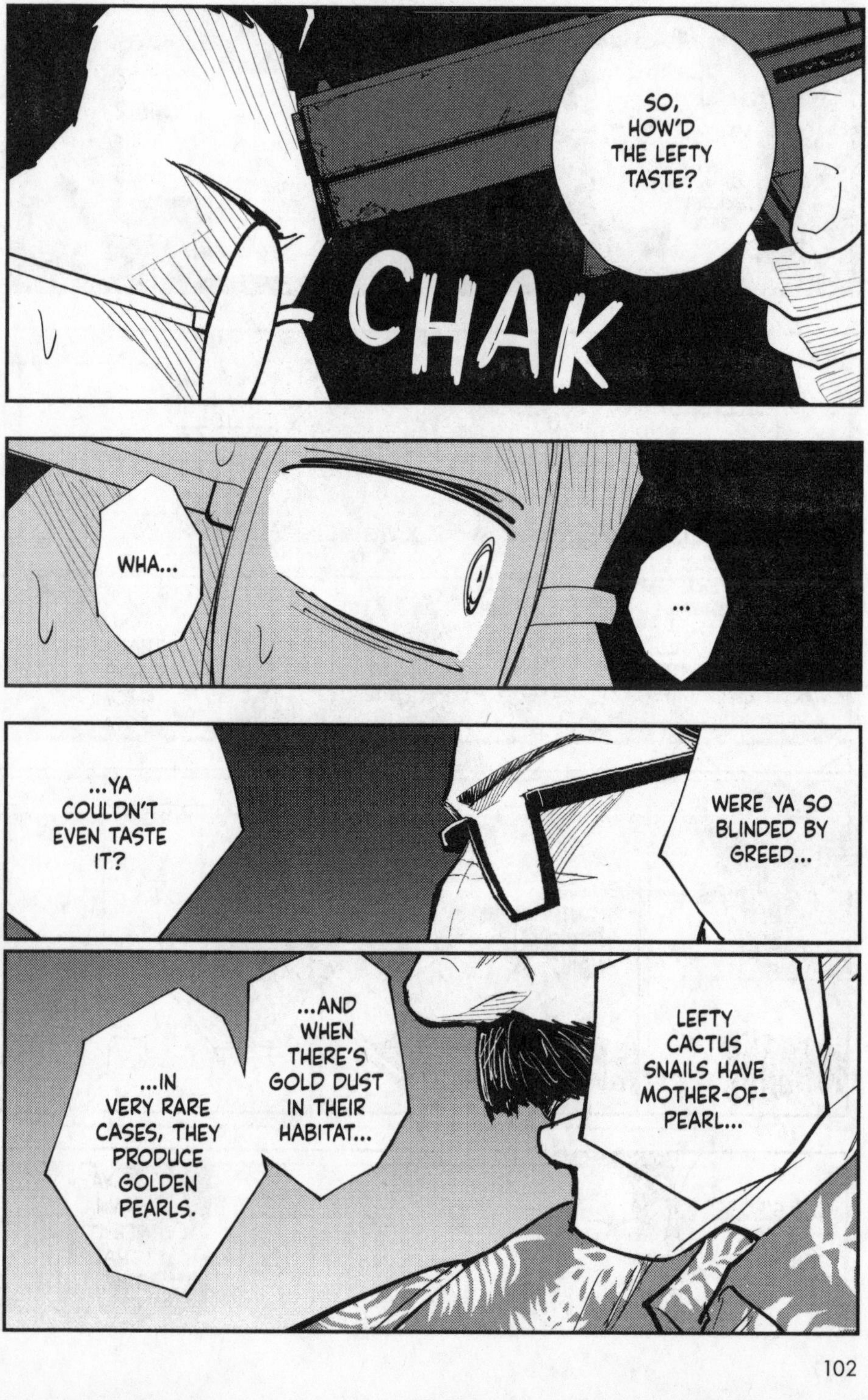
SO, HOW'D THE LEFTY TASTE?
CHAK
...
WHA...
WERE YA SO BLINDED BY GREED...
...YA COULDN'T EVEN TASTE IT?
LEFTY CACTUS SNAILS HAVE MOTHER-OF-PEARL...
...AND WHEN THERE'S GOLD DUST IN THEIR HABITAT...
...IN VERY RARE CASES, THEY PRODUCE GOLDEN PEARLS.

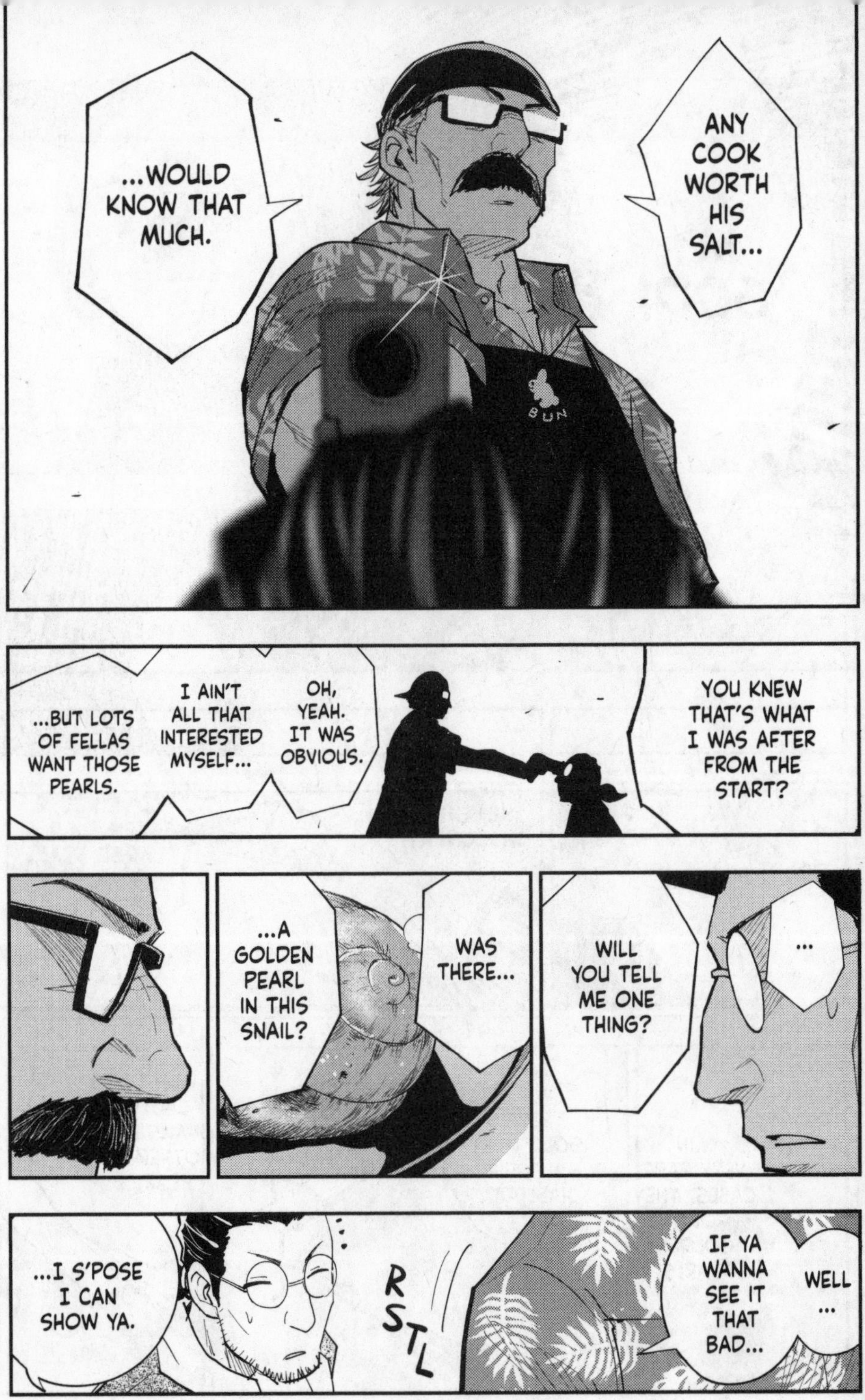
ANY COOK WORTH HIS SALT...
...WOULD KNOW THAT MUCH.
YOU KNEW THAT'S WHAT I WAS AFTER FROM THE START?
OH, YEAH. IT WAS OBVIOUS.
I AIN'T ALL THAT INTERESTED MYSELF...
...BUT LOTS OF FELLAS WANT THOSE PEARLS.
...
WILL YOU TELL ME ONE THING?
WAS THERE...
...A GOLDEN PEARL IN THIS SNAIL?
WELL...
IF YA WANNA SEE IT THAT BAD...
RSTL
...I S'POSE I CAN SHOW YA.

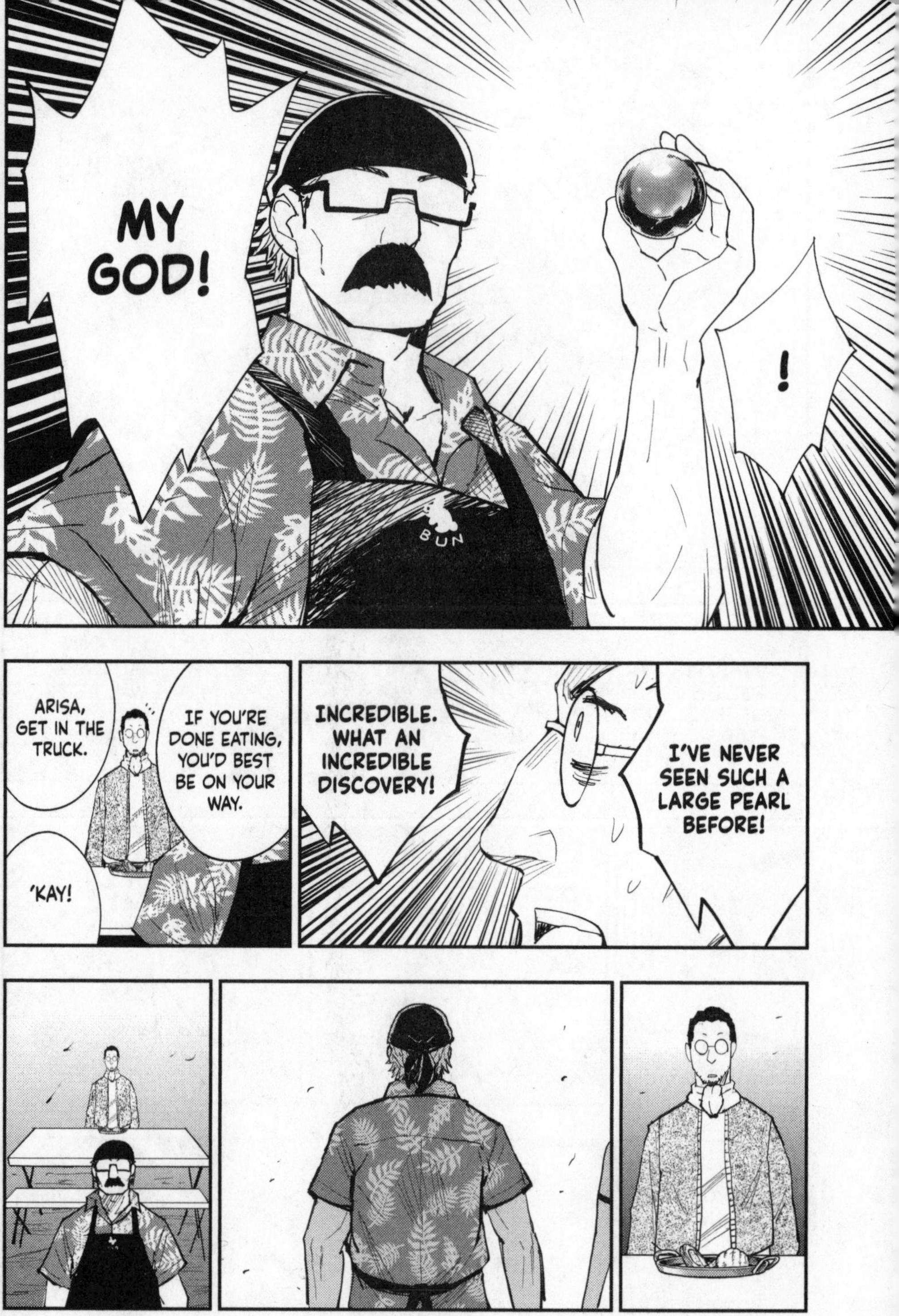
!
MY GOD!
I'VE NEVER SEEN SUCH A LARGE PEARL BEFORE!
INCREDIBLE. WHAT AN INCREDIBLE DISCOVERY!
IF YOU'RE DONE EATING, YOU'D BEST BE ON YOUR WAY.
ARISA, GET IN THE TRUCK.
'KAY!

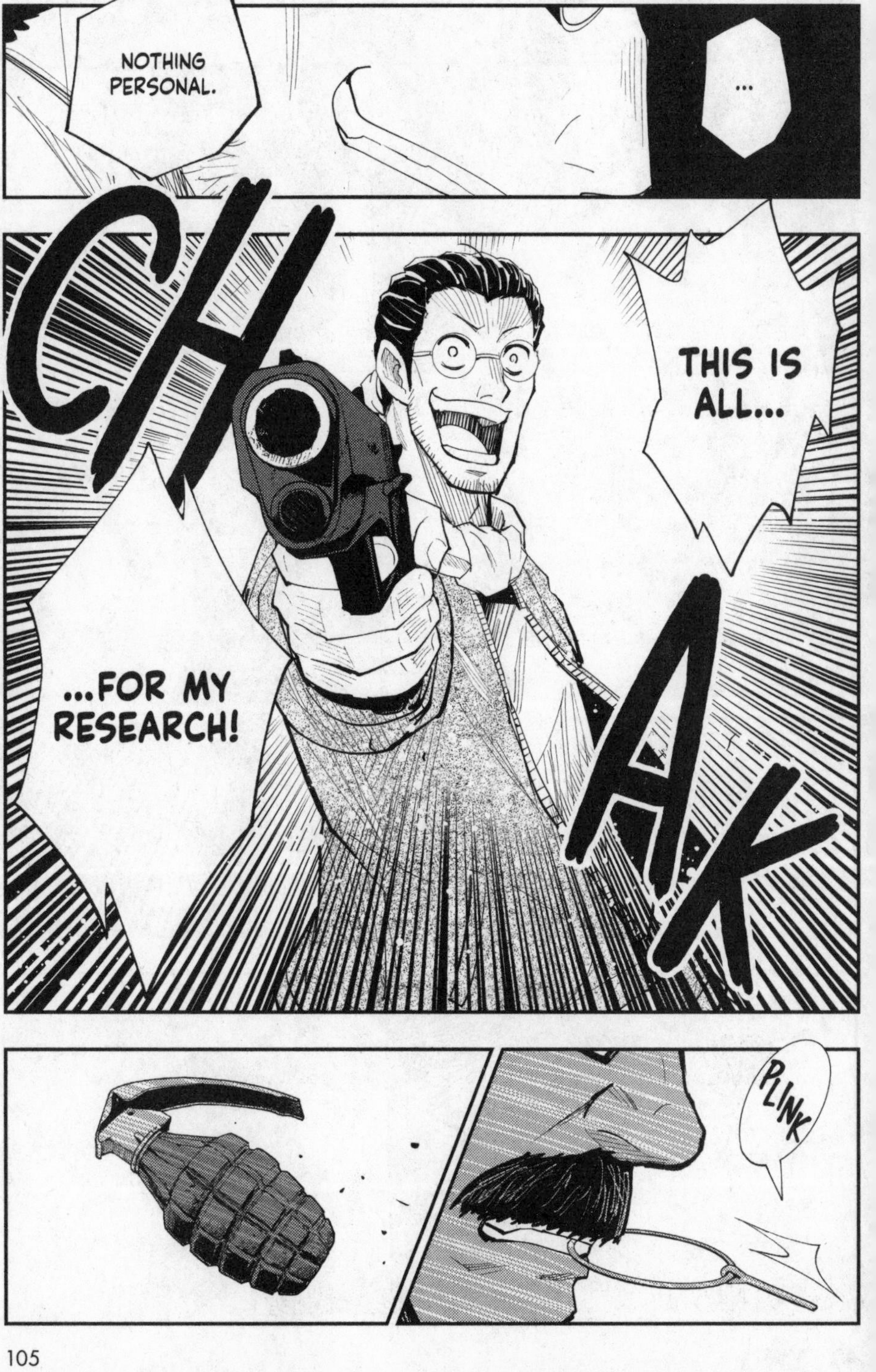
...
NOTHING PERSONAL.
THIS IS ALL...
CH
AK
...FOR MY RESEARCH!
PLINK

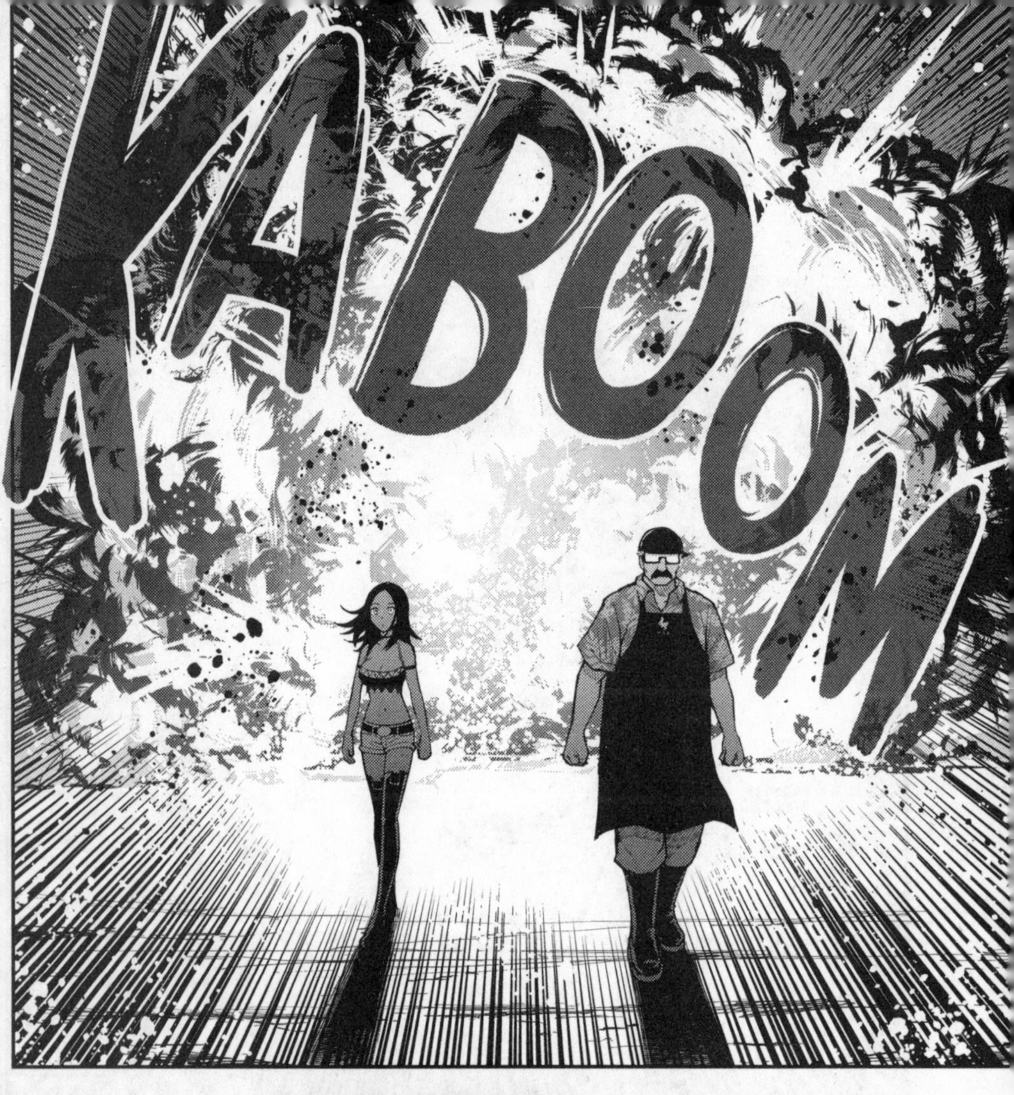
KABOOM

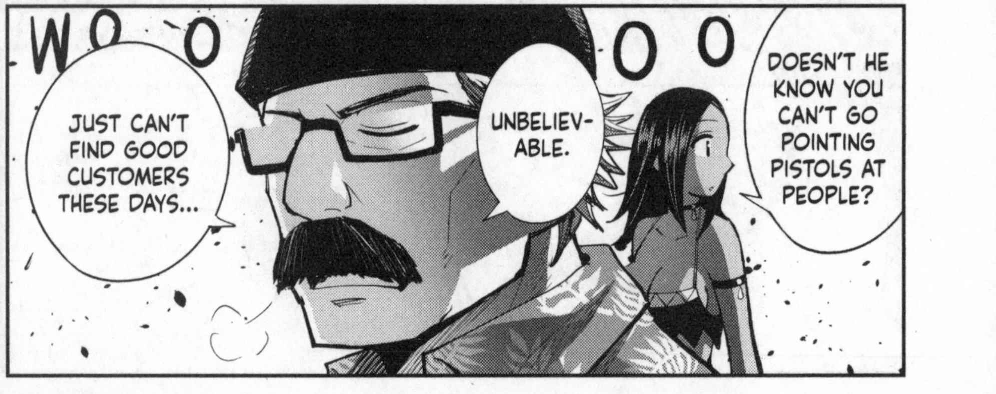
DOESN'T HE KNOW YOU CAN'T GO POINTING PISTOLS AT PEOPLE?
UNBELIEV-ABLE.
JUST CAN'T FIND GOOD CUSTOMERS THESE DAYS...
WO O O O

#8 PORK STEAK

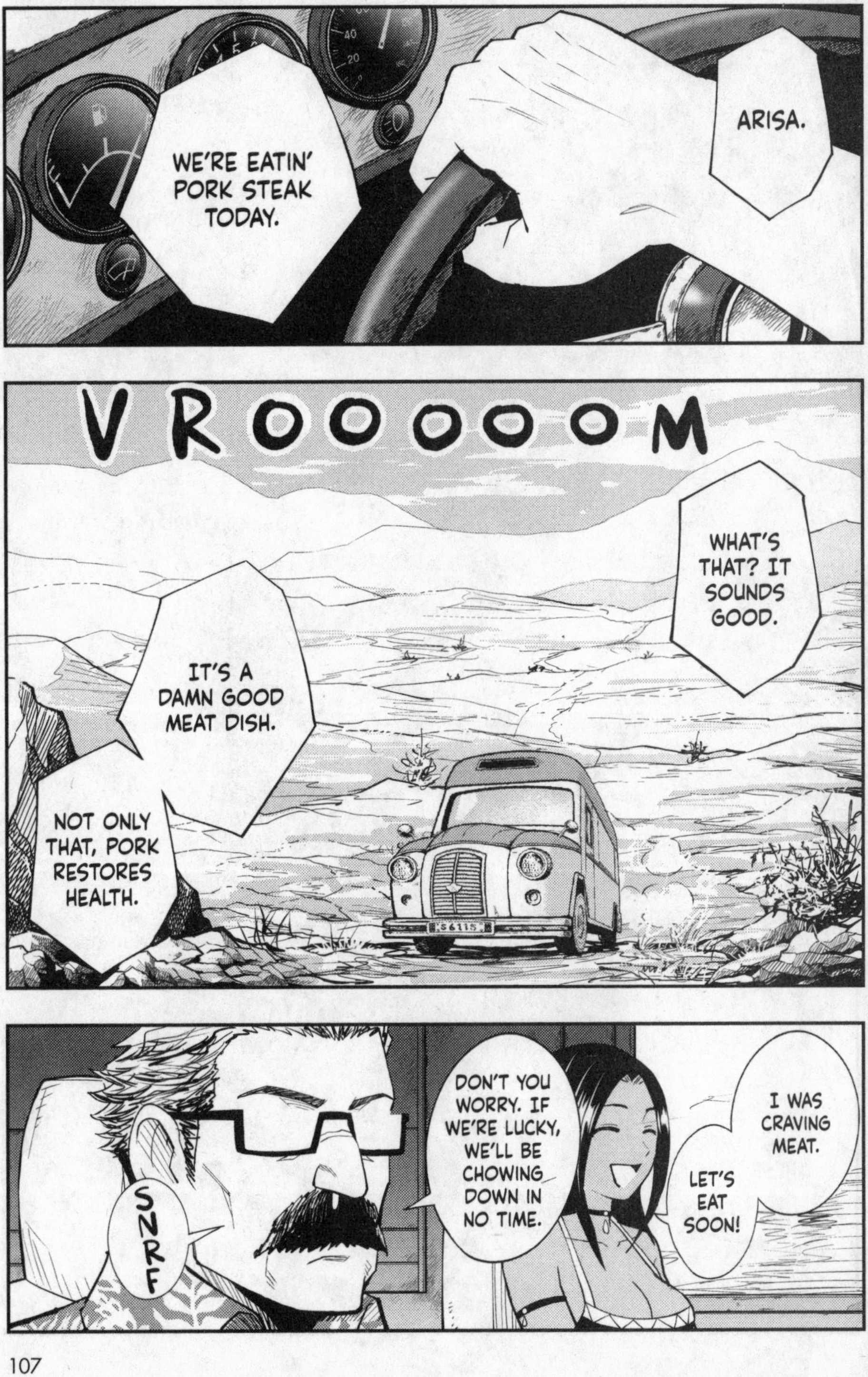
ARISA.
WE'RE EATIN' PORK STEAK TODAY.
VROOOOOM
WHAT'S THAT? IT SOUNDS GOOD.
IT'S A DAMN GOOD MEAT DISH.
NOT ONLY THAT, PORK RESTORES HEALTH.
I WAS CRAVING MEAT.
LET'S EAT SOON!
DON'T YOU WORRY. IF WE'RE LUCKY, WE'LL BE CHOWING DOWN IN NO TIME.
SNRF

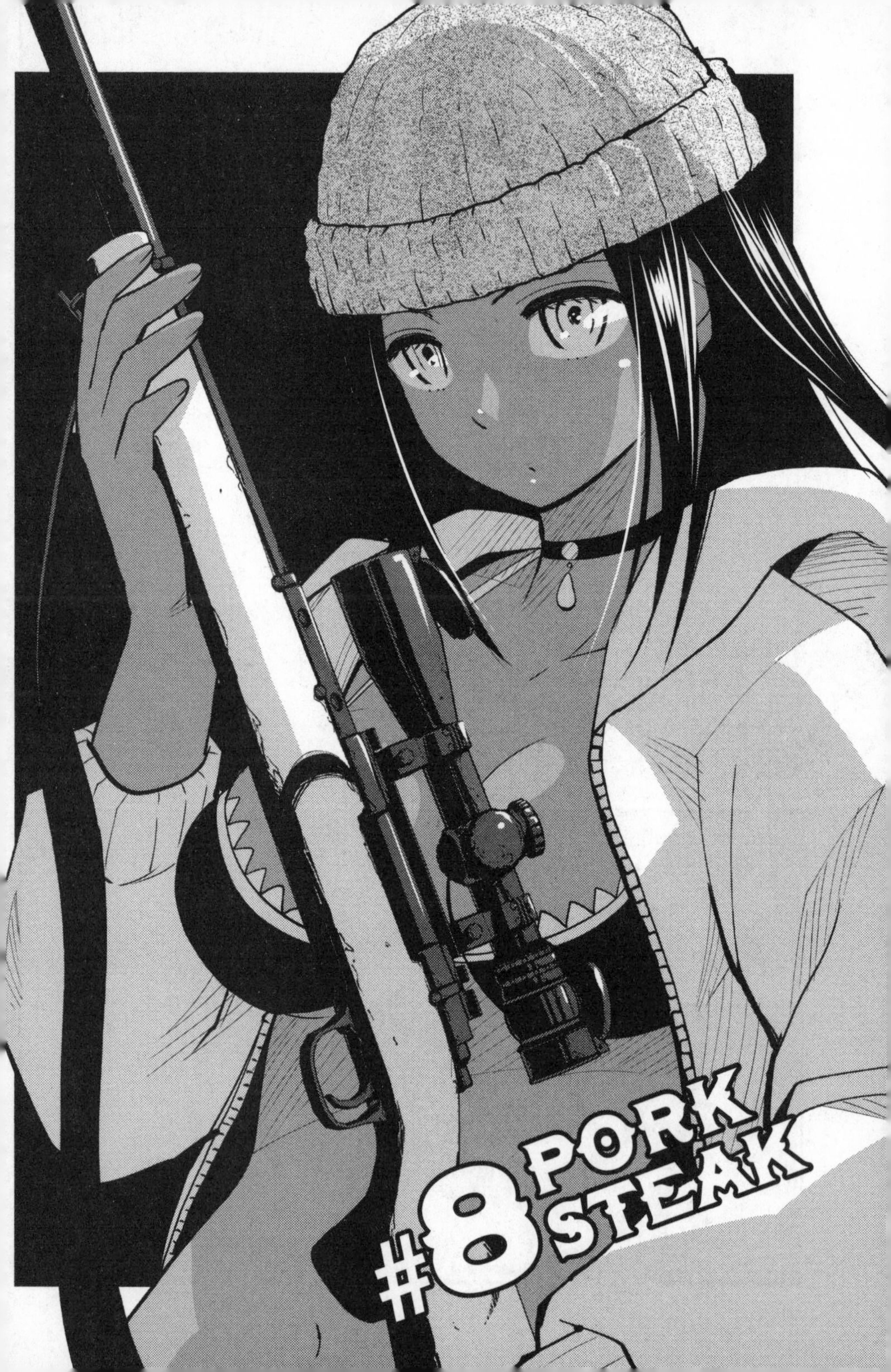
#8
PORK STEAK

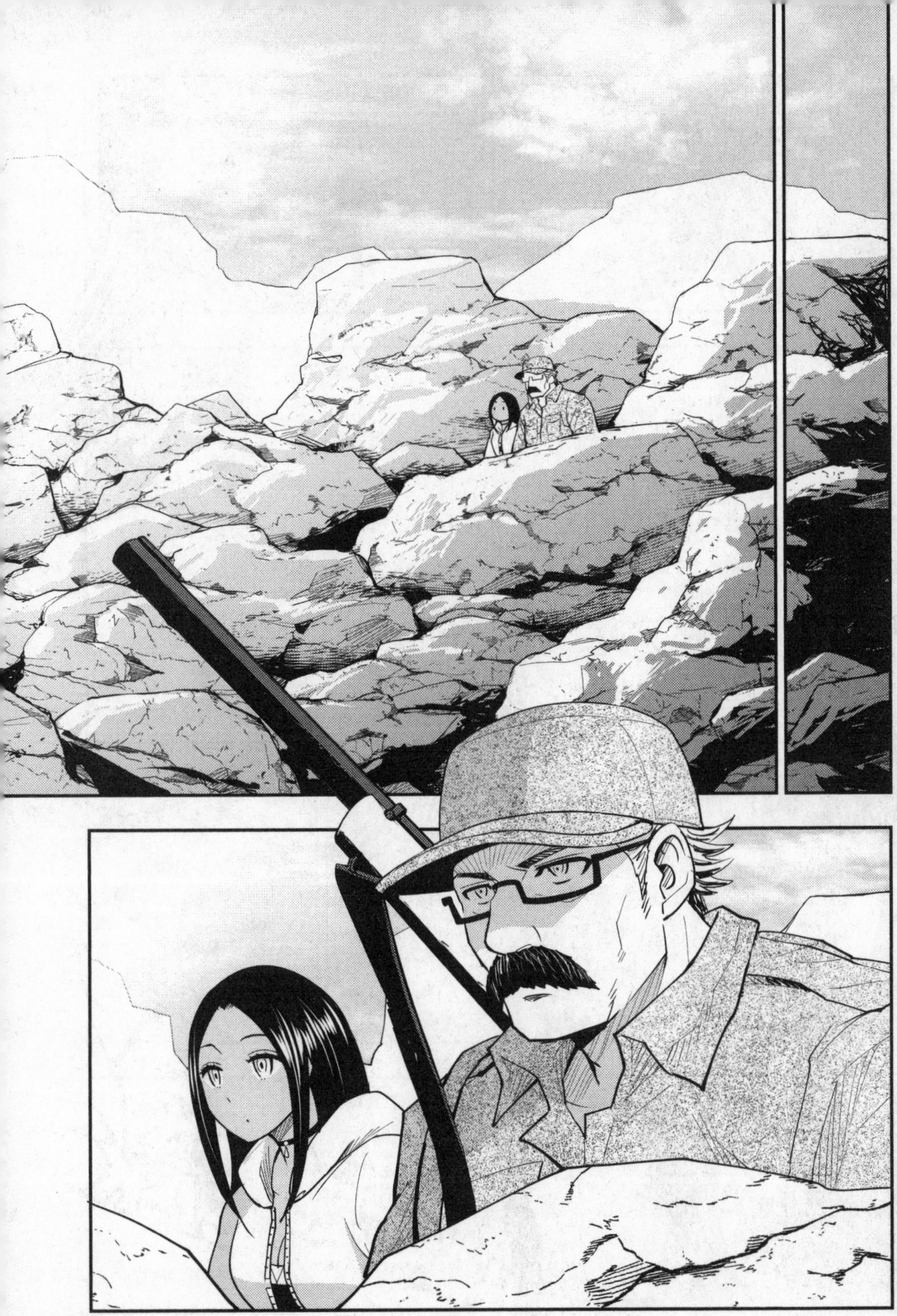

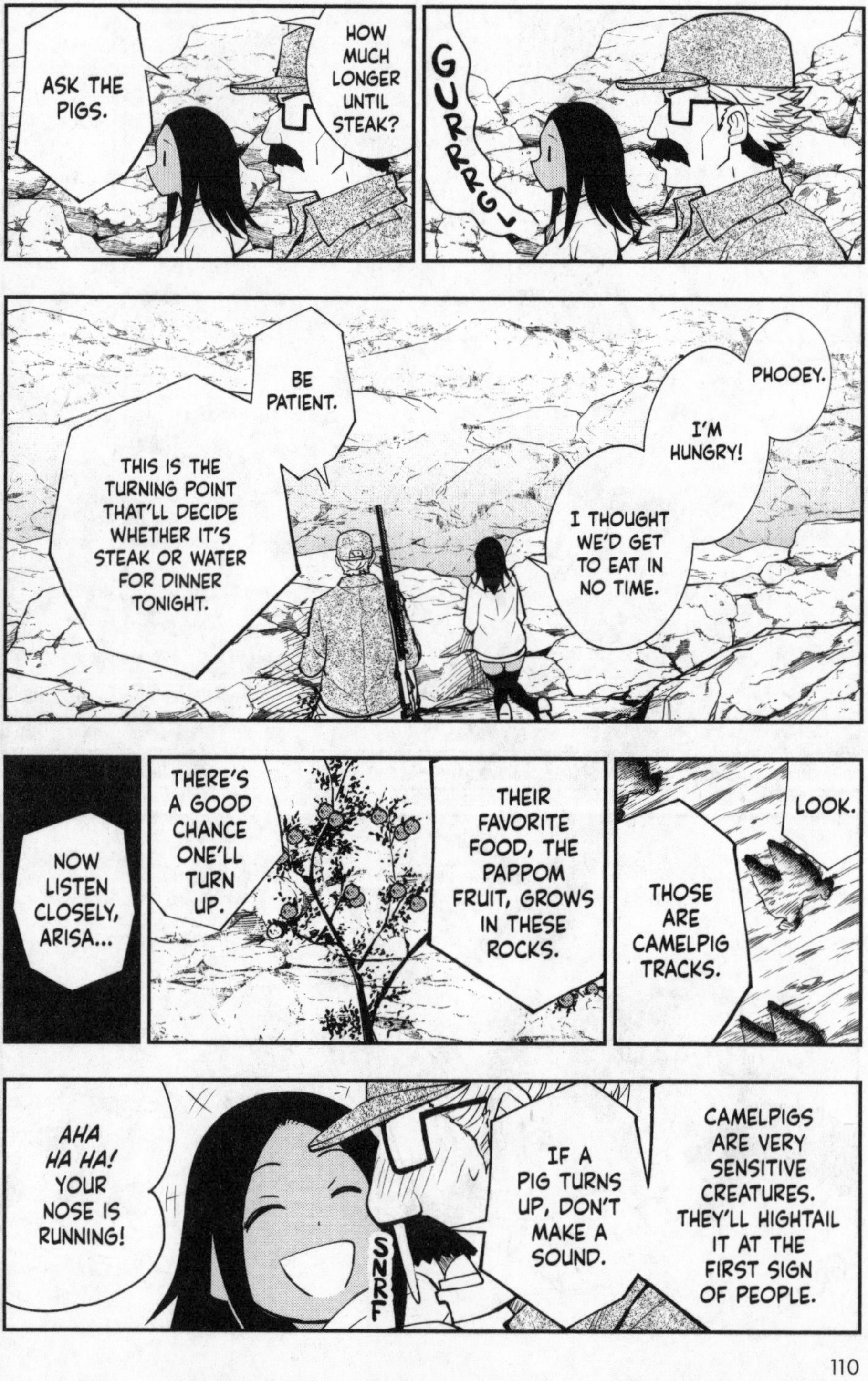

GURRRG
HOW MUCH LONGER UNTIL STEAK?
ASK THE PIGS.
PHOOEY.
I'M HUNGRY!
I THOUGHT WE'D GET TO EAT IN NO TIME.
BE PATIENT.
THIS IS THE TURNING POINT THAT'LL DECIDE WHETHER IT'S STEAK OR WATER FOR DINNER TONIGHT.
LOOK.
THOSE ARE CAMELPIG TRACKS.
THEIR FAVORITE FOOD, THE PAPPOM FRUIT, GROWS IN THESE ROCKS.
THERE'S A GOOD CHANCE ONE'LL TURN UP.
NOW LISTEN CLOSELY, ARISA...
CAMELPIGS ARE VERY SENSITIVE CREATURES. THEY'LL HIGHTAIL IT AT THE FIRST SIGN OF PEOPLE.
IF A PIG TURNS UP, DON'T MAKE A SOUND.
SNRF
AHA HA HA! YOUR NOSE IS RUNNING!

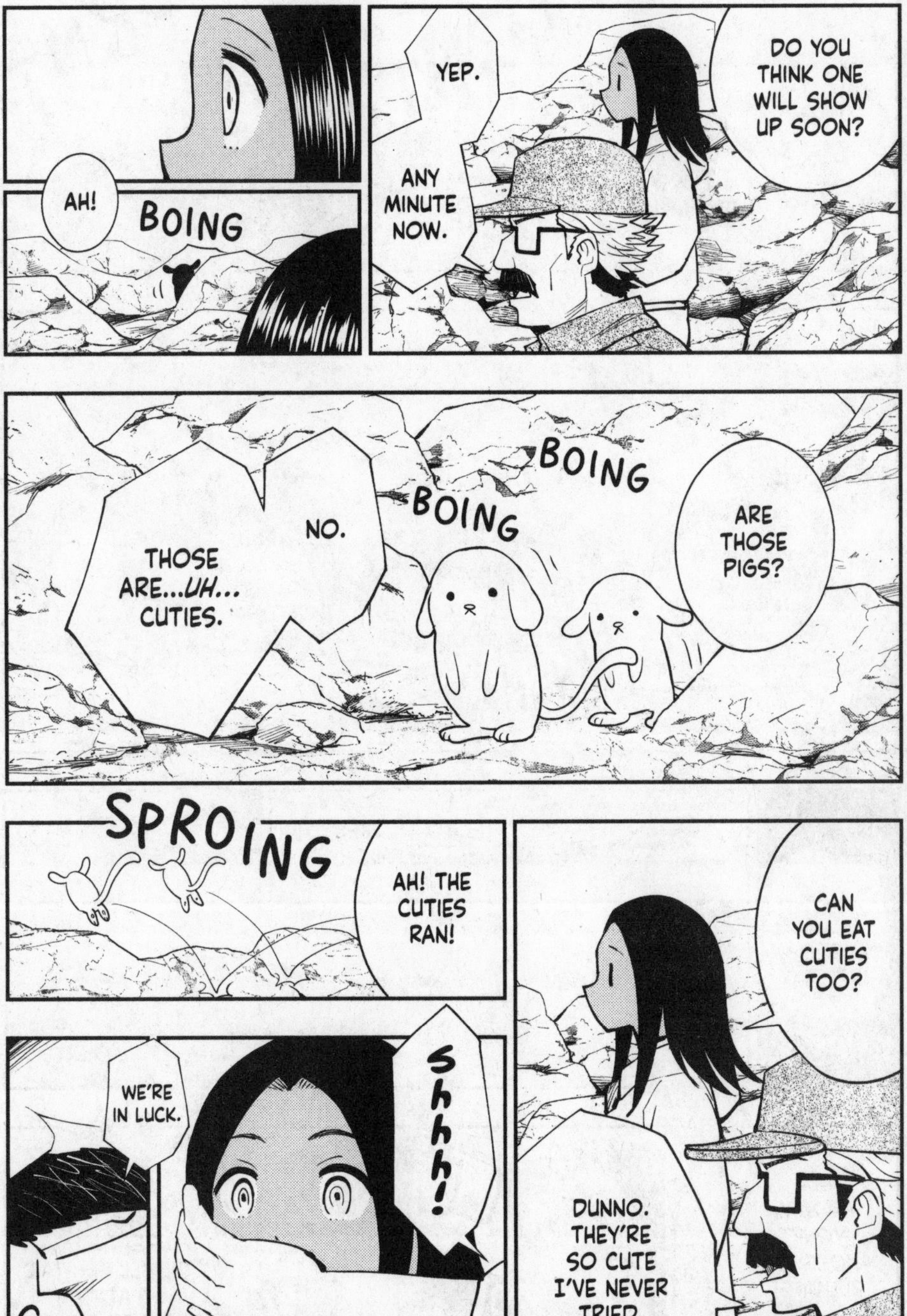
DO YOU THINK ONE WILL SHOW UP SOON?
YEP.
ANY MINUTE NOW.
AH!
BOING
ARE THOSE PIGS?
BOING
BOING
NO.
THOSE ARE...UH... CUTIES.
CAN YOU EAT CUTIES TOO?
DUNNO. THEY'RE SO CUTE I'VE NEVER TRIED.
AH! THE CUTIES RAN!
SPROING
Shhh!
MMF
WE'RE IN LUCK.
GRIN

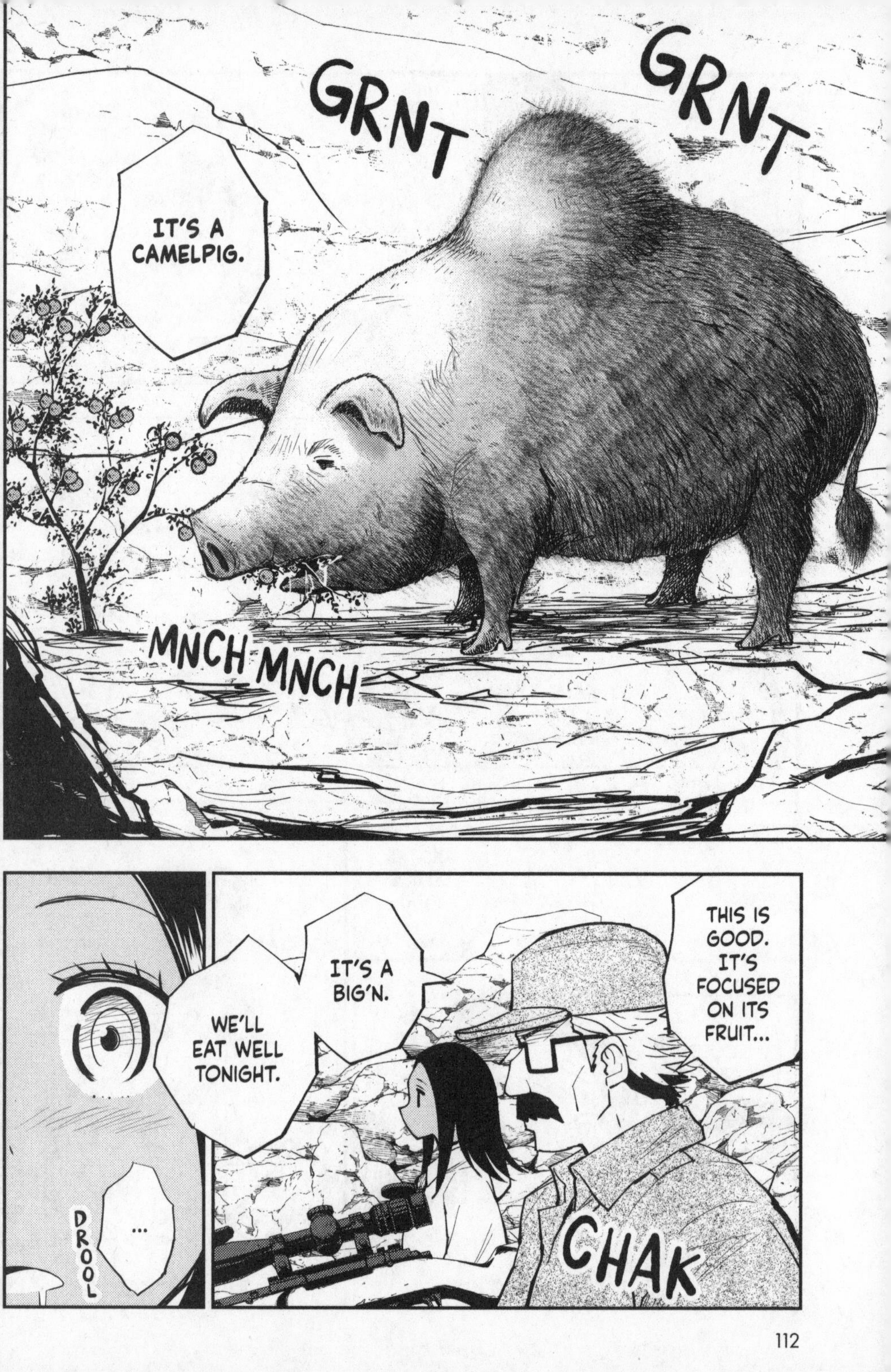
GRNT
GRNT
IT'S A CAMELPIG.
MNCH MNCH
THIS IS GOOD. IT'S FOCUSED ON ITS FRUIT...
IT'S A BIG'N.
WE'LL EAT WELL TONIGHT.
CHAK
...
DROOL

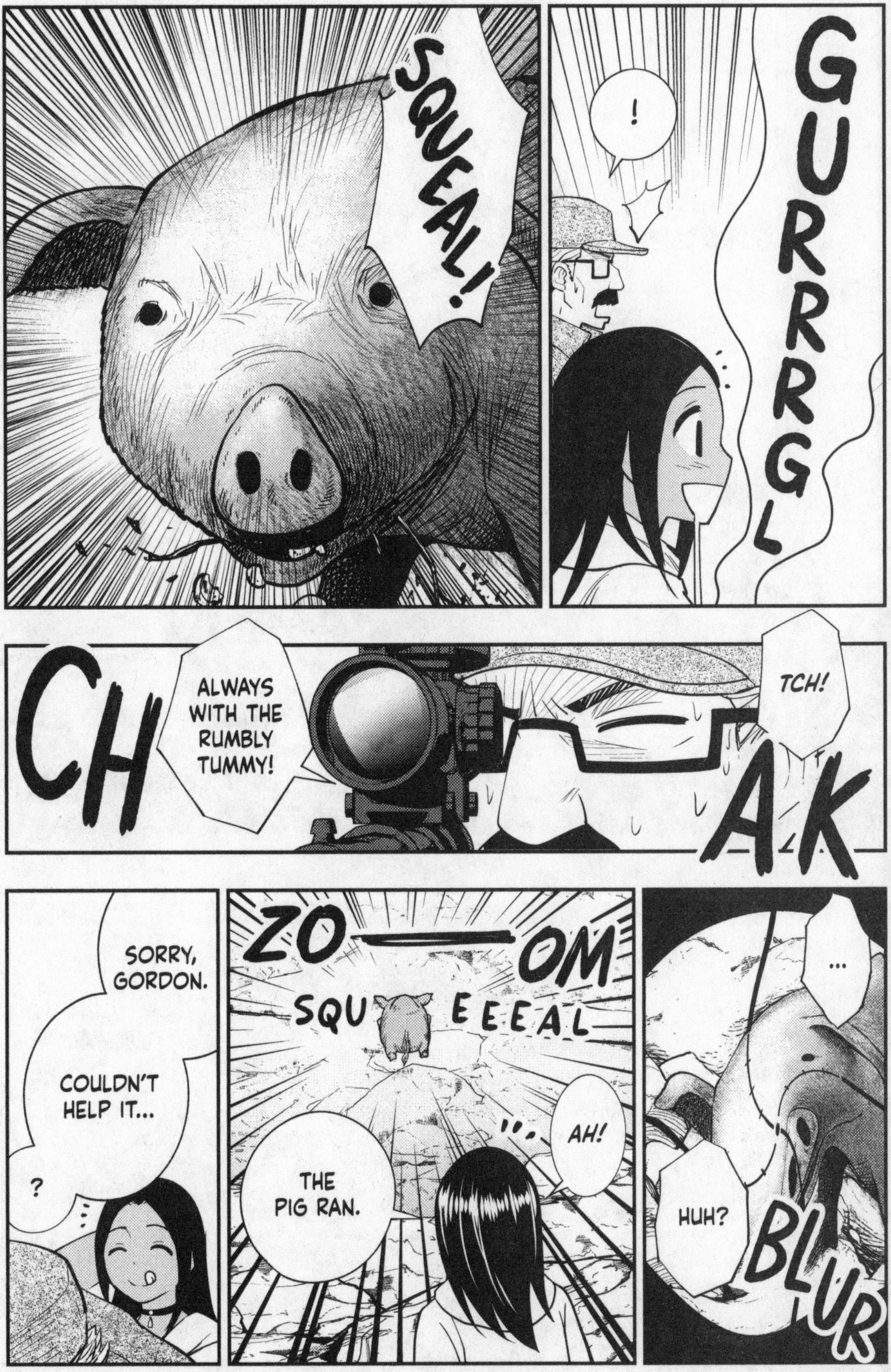

GURRRGL
!
SQUEAL!
TCH!
ALWAYS WITH THE RUMBLY TUMMY!
CHAK
...
HUH?
BLUR
ZO—OM
SQUEEEAL
AH!
THE PIG RAN.
SORRY, GORDON.
COULDN'T HELP IT...
?

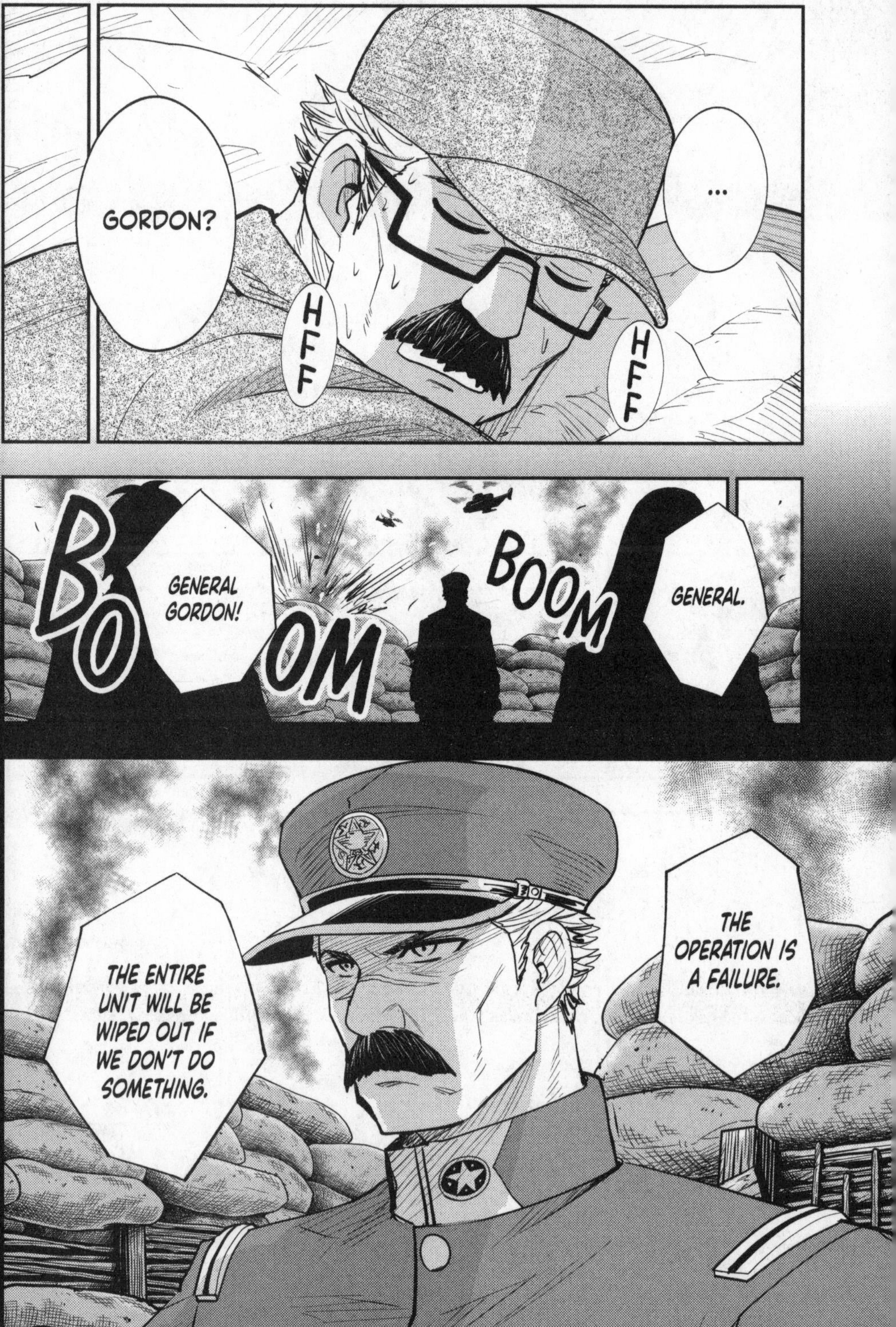
...
HFF
GORDON?
HFF
GENERAL.
BOOM
GENERAL GORDON!
BOOM
THE OPERATION IS A FAILURE.
THE ENTIRE UNIT WILL BE WIPED OUT IF WE DON'T DO SOMETHING.

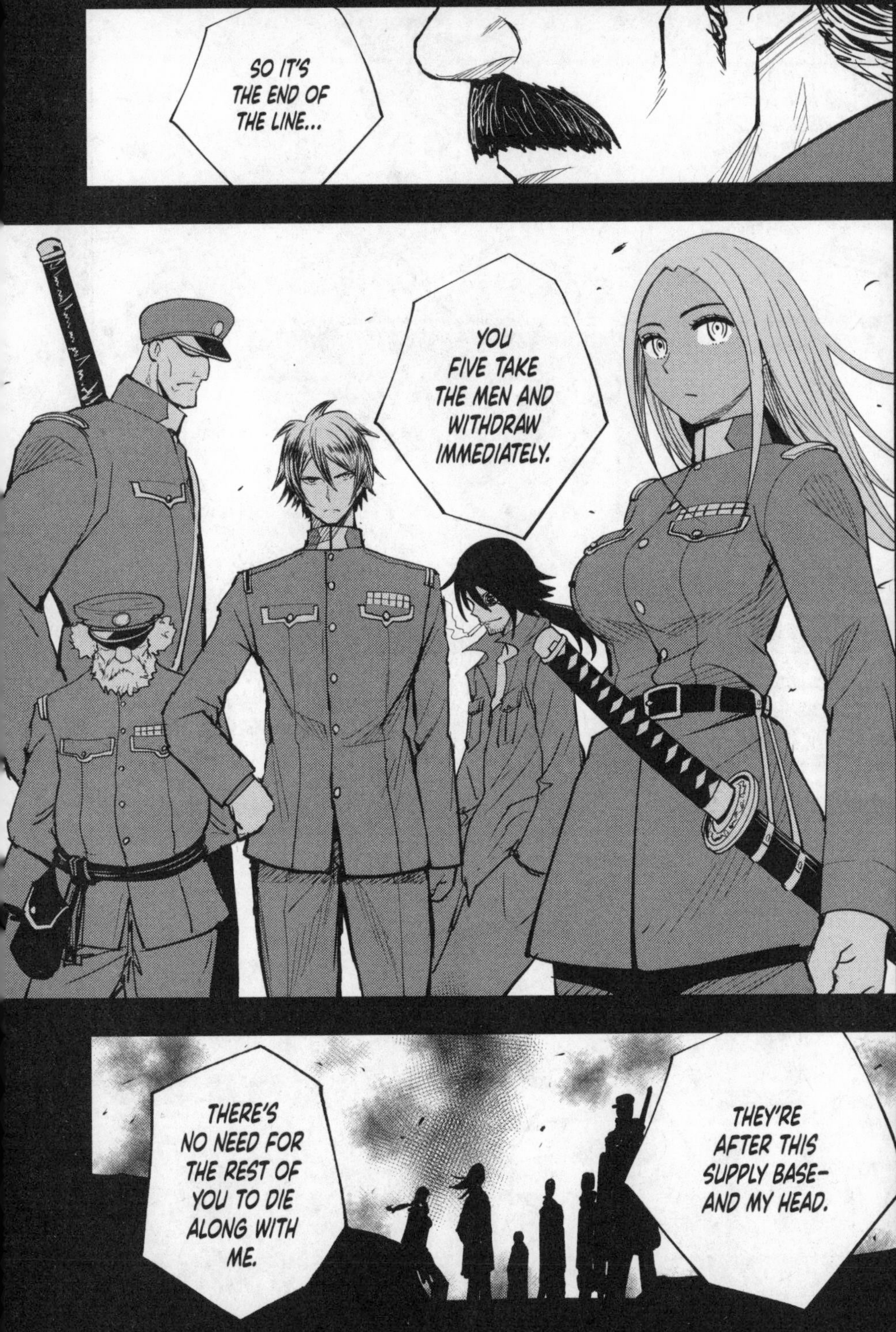
SO IT'S THE END OF THE LINE...
YOU FIVE TAKE THE MEN AND WITHDRAW IMMEDIATELY.
THEY'RE AFTER THIS SUPPLY BASE-AND MY HEAD.
THERE'S NO NEED FOR THE REST OF YOU TO DIE ALONG WITH ME.

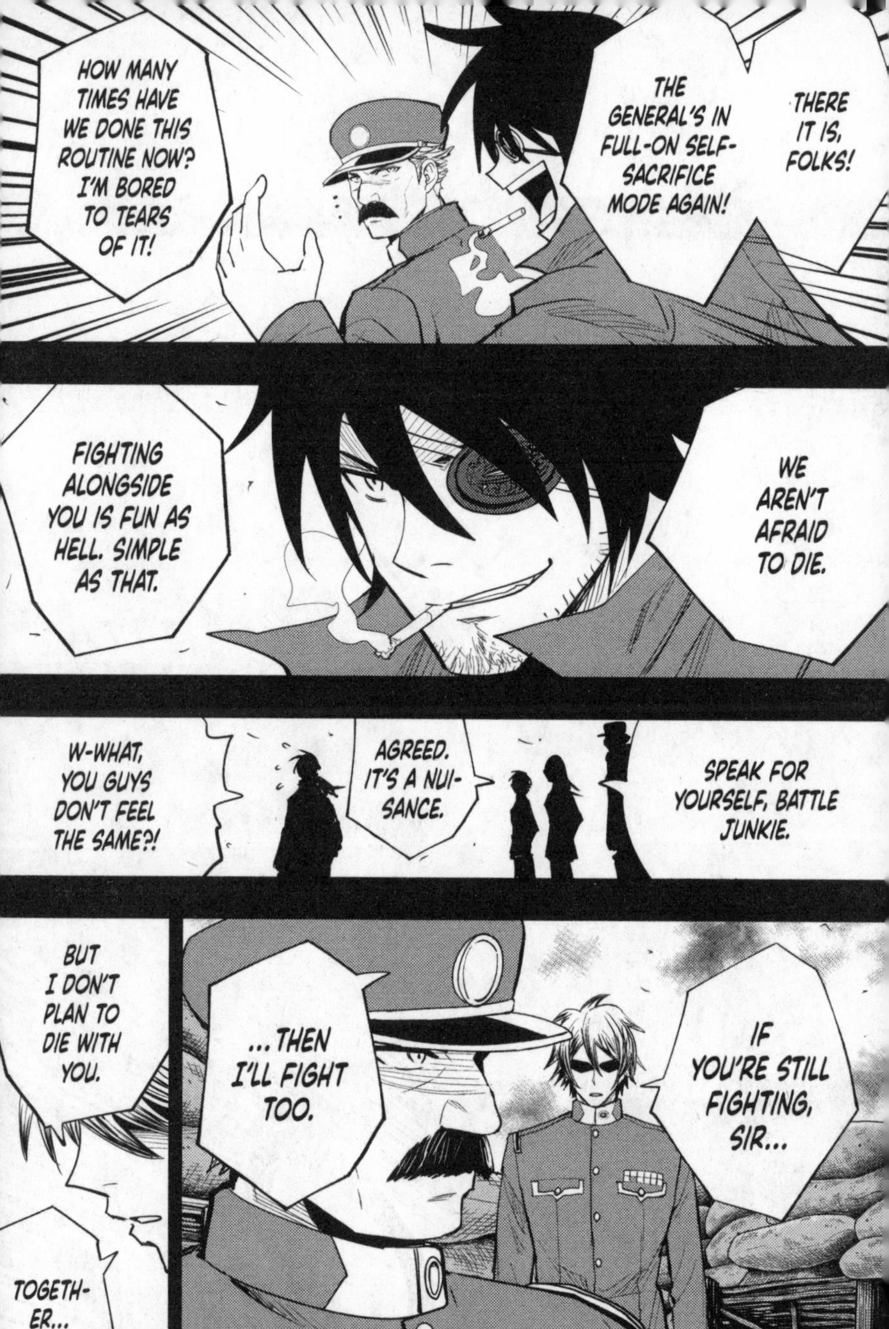
THERE IT IS, FOLKS!
THE GENERAL'S IN FULL-ON SELF-SACRIFICE MODE AGAIN!
HOW MANY TIMES HAVE WE DONE THIS ROUTINE NOW? I'M BORED TO TEARS OF IT!
WE AREN'T AFRAID TO DIE.
FIGHTING ALONGSIDE YOU IS FUN AS HELL. SIMPLE AS THAT.
SPEAK FOR YOURSELF, BATTLE JUNKIE.
AGREED. IT'S A NUI-SANCE.
W-WHAT, YOU GUYS DON'T FEEL THE SAME?!
IF YOU'RE STILL FIGHTING, SIR...
...THEN I'LL FIGHT TOO.
BUT I DON'T PLAN TO DIE WITH YOU.
TOGETH-ER...

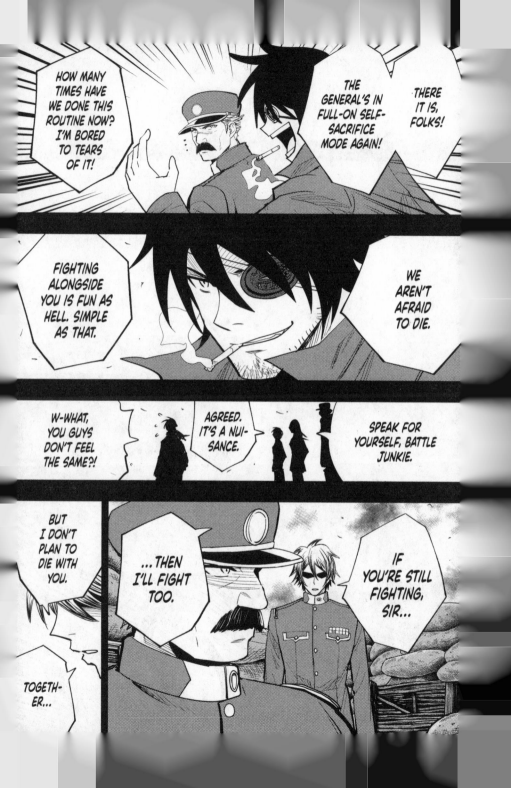

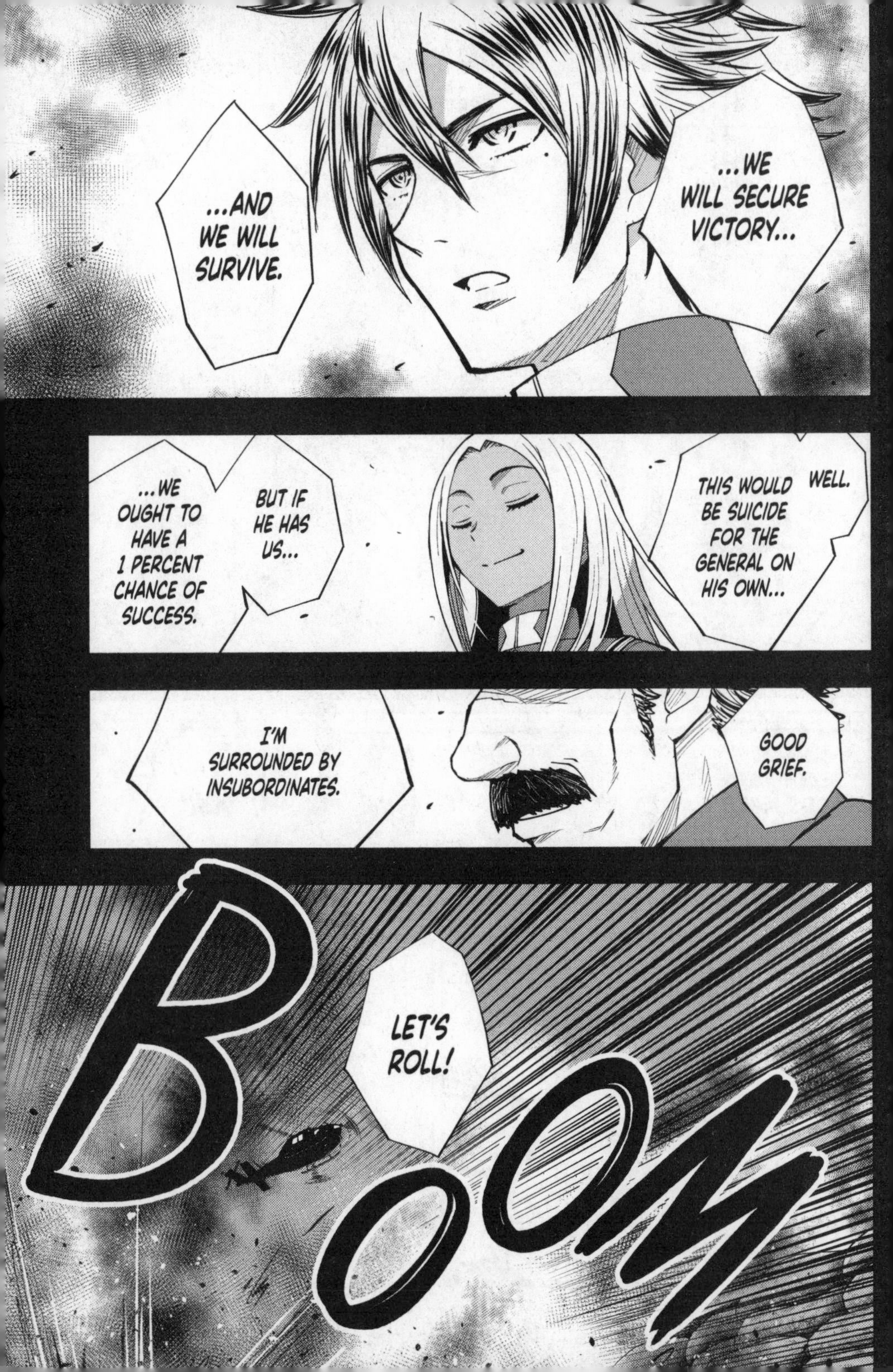
...WE WILL SECURE VICTORY...
...AND WE WILL SURVIVE.
WELL.
THIS WOULD BE SUICIDE FOR THE GENERAL ON HIS OWN...
BUT IF HE HAS US...
...WE OUGHT TO HAVE A 1 PERCENT CHANCE OF SUCCESS.
GOOD GRIEF.
I'M SURROUNDED BY INSUBORDINATES.
LET'S ROLL!
BOOM

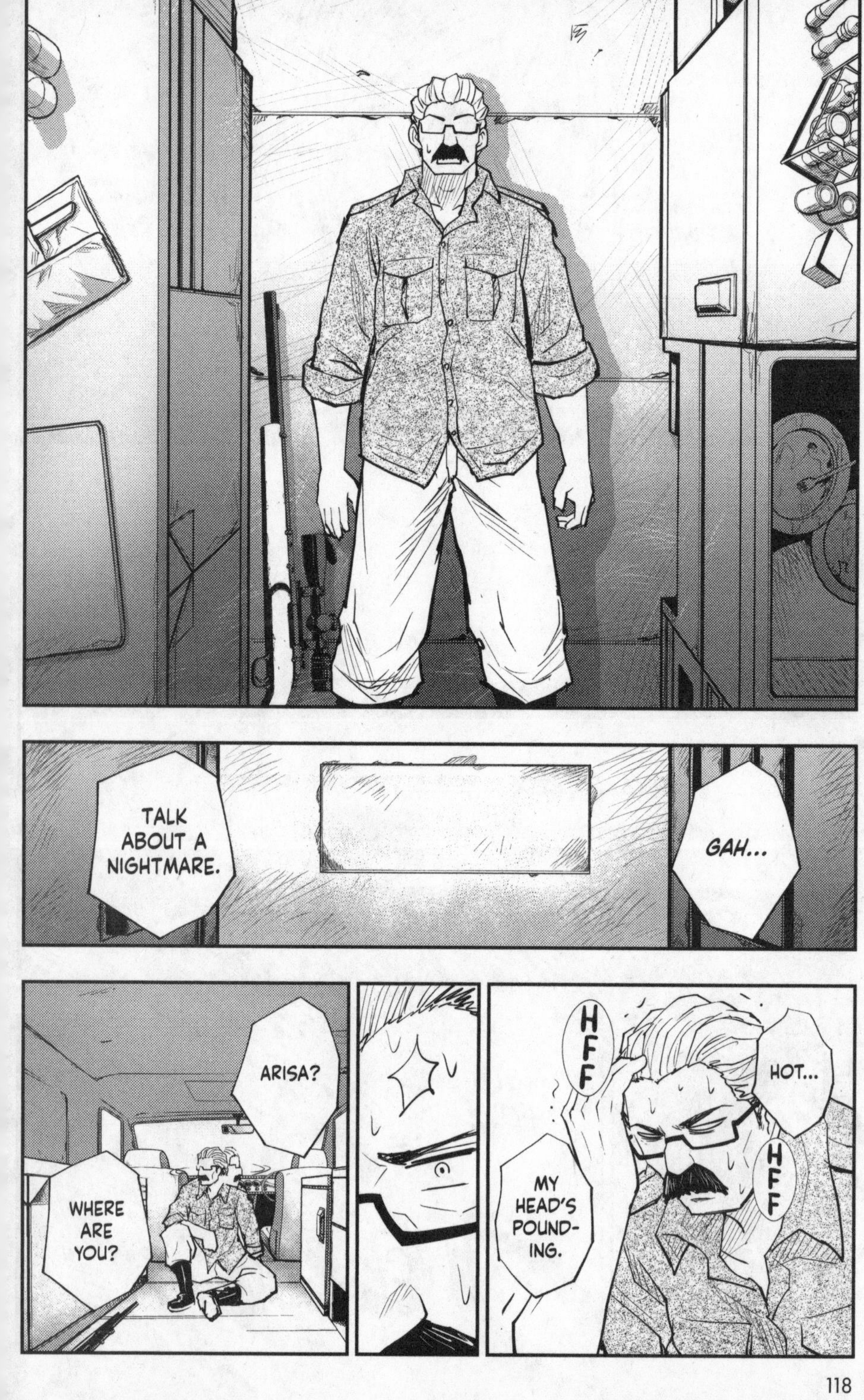
GAH...
TALK ABOUT A NIGHTMARE.
HOT...
HFF
HFF
MY HEAD'S POUND- ING.
ARISA?
WHERE ARE YOU?

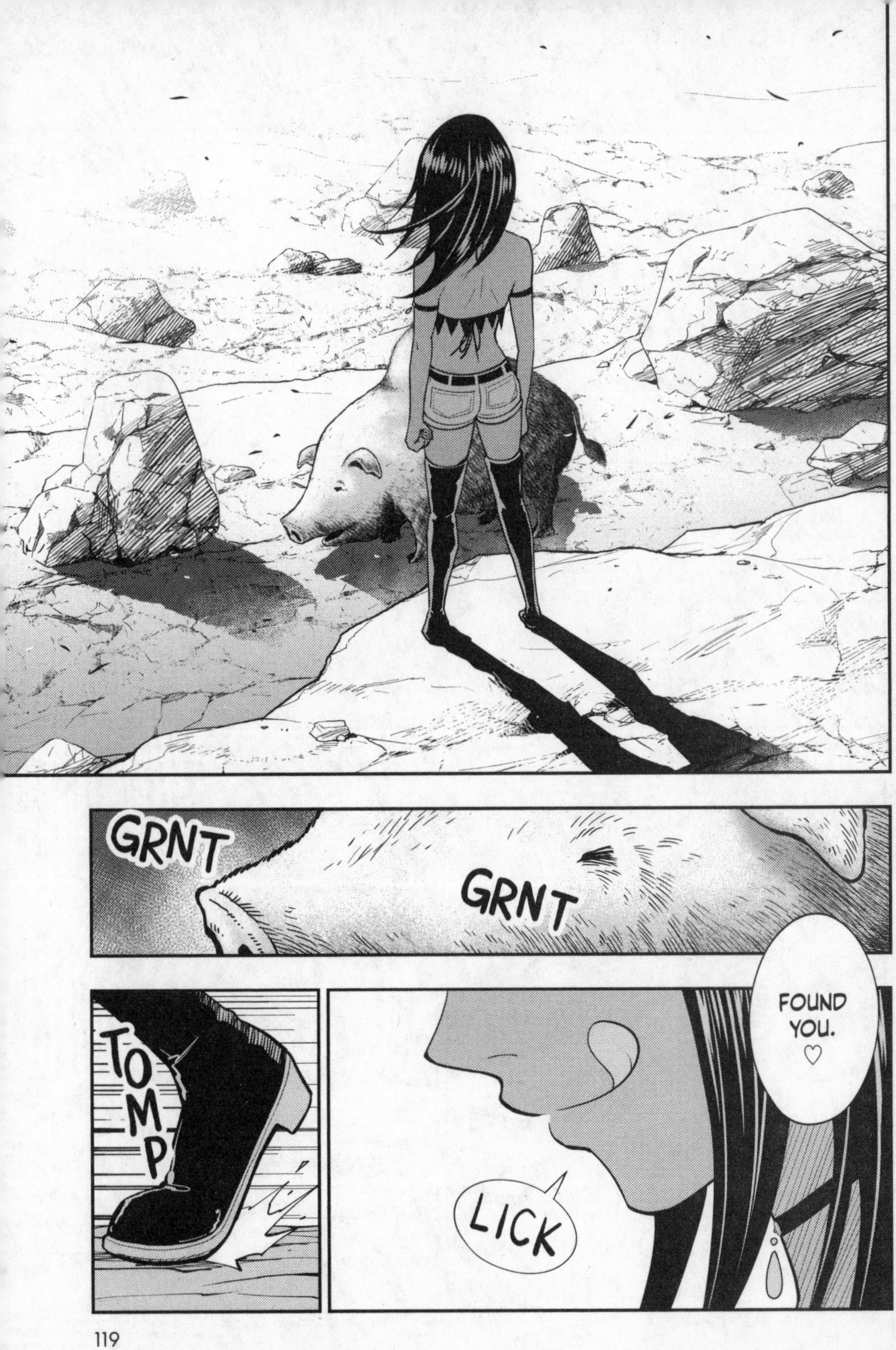
GRNT
GRNT
FOUND YOU. ♡
LICK
TOMP

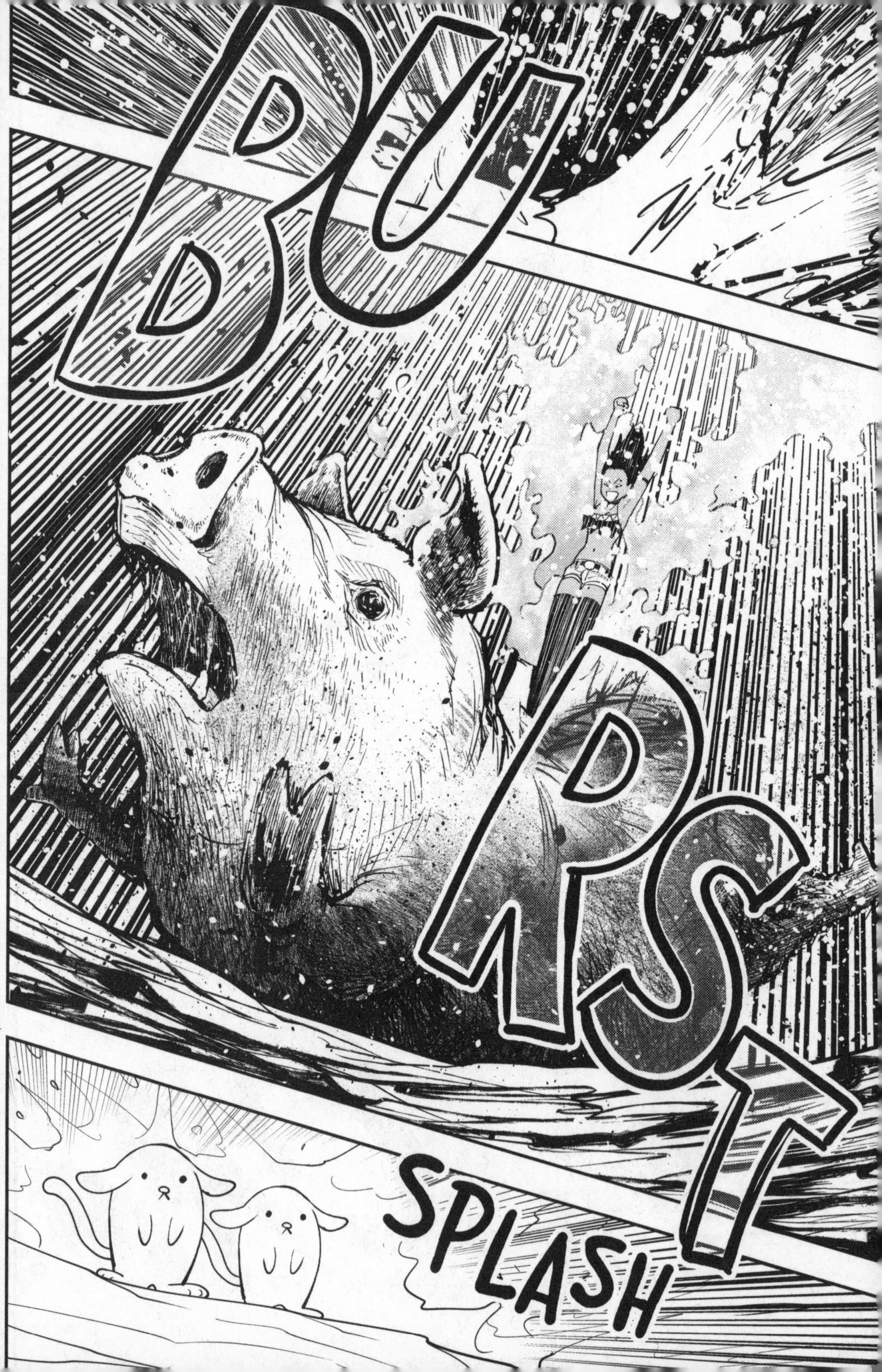
BURST
SPLASH

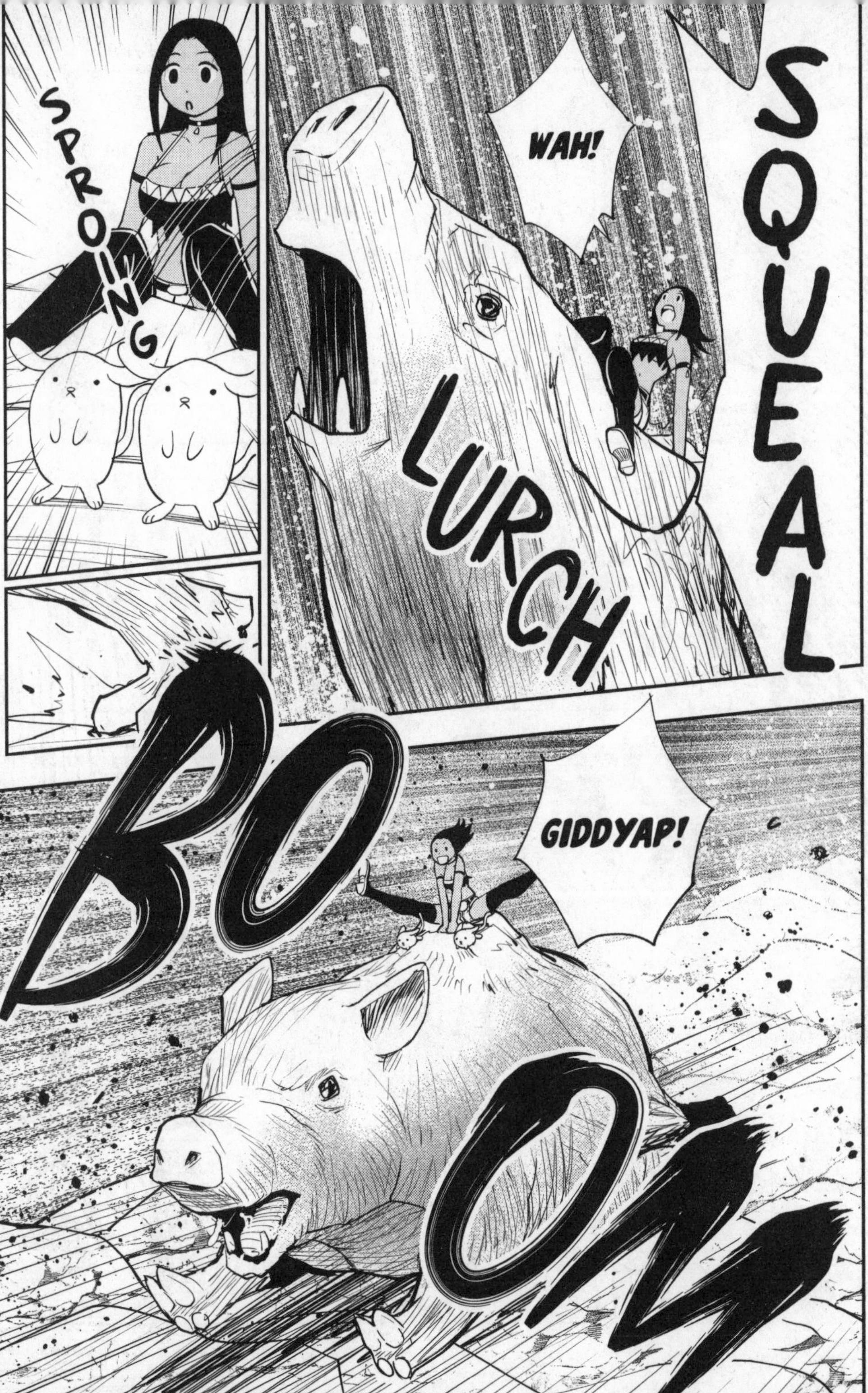
SQUEAL
WAH!
LURCH
SPROING
GIDDYAP!
BOOM

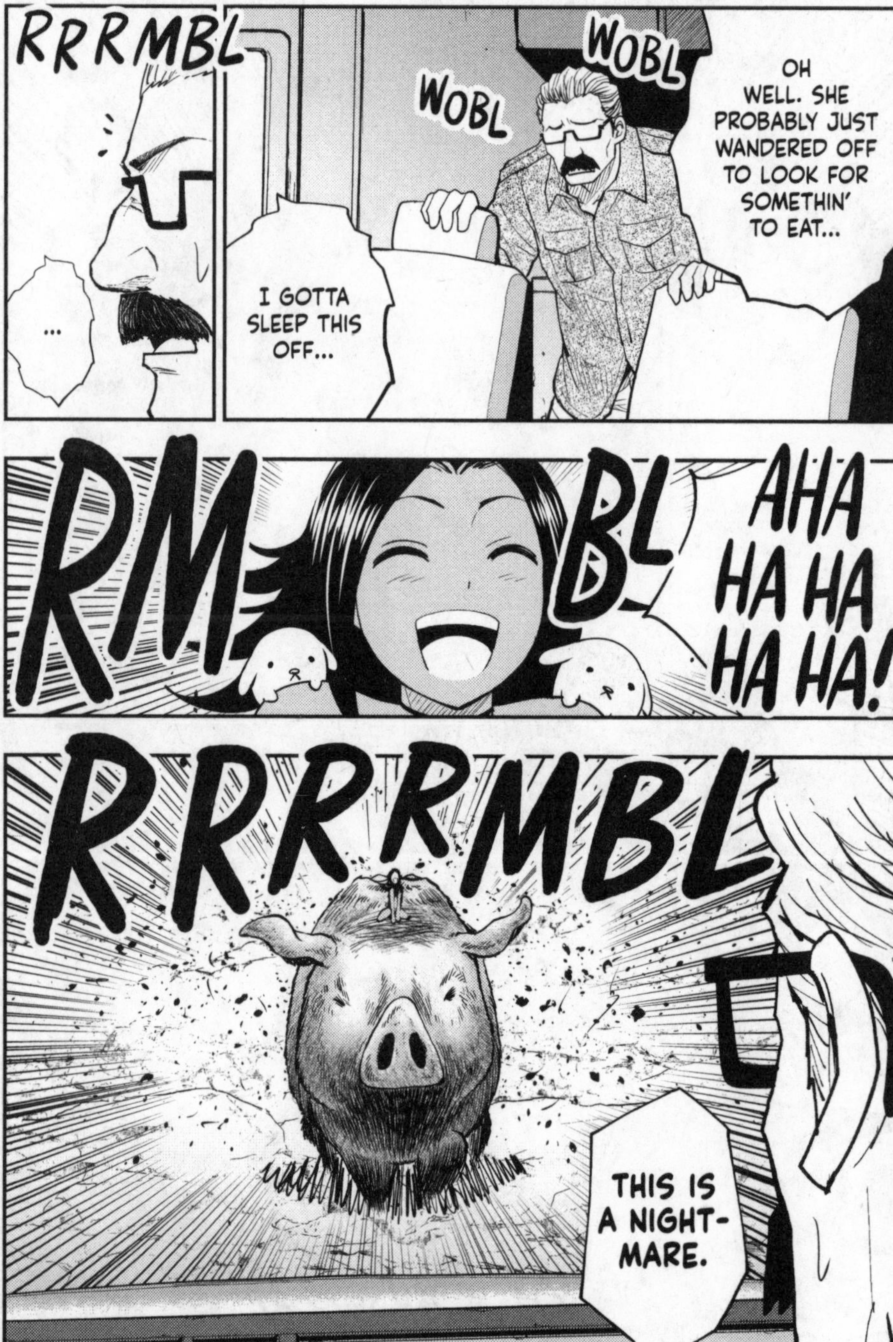
WOBL
WOBL
OH WELL. SHE PROBABLY JUST WANDERED OFF TO LOOK FOR SOMETHIN' TO EAT...
I GOTTA SLEEP THIS OFF...
RRRMBL
...
AHA HA HA HA HA!
RMBL
RRRRMBL
THIS IS A NIGHT-MARE.

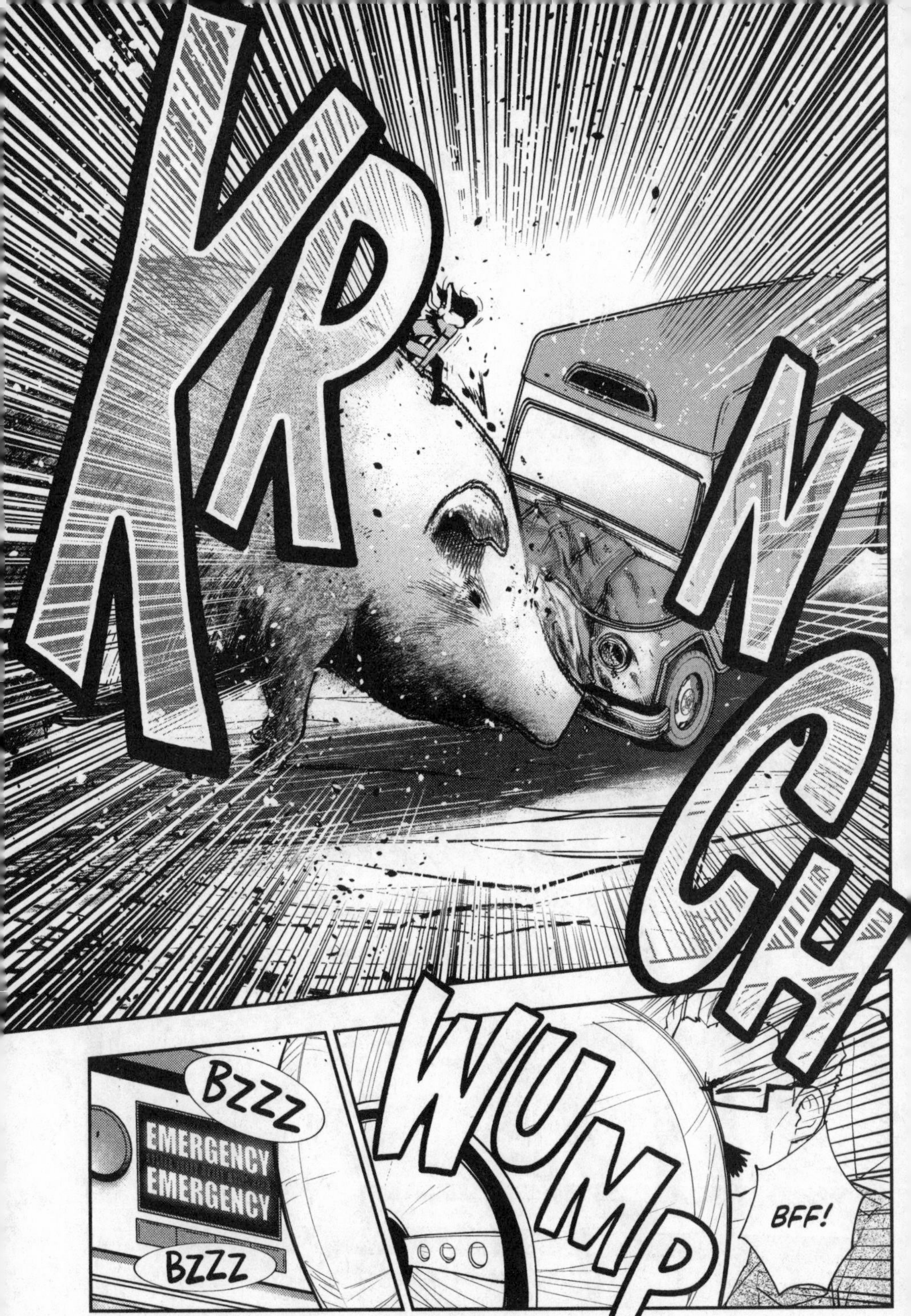
KRNCH
BFF!
WUMP
Bzzz
EMERGENCY
EMERGENCY
BZZZ

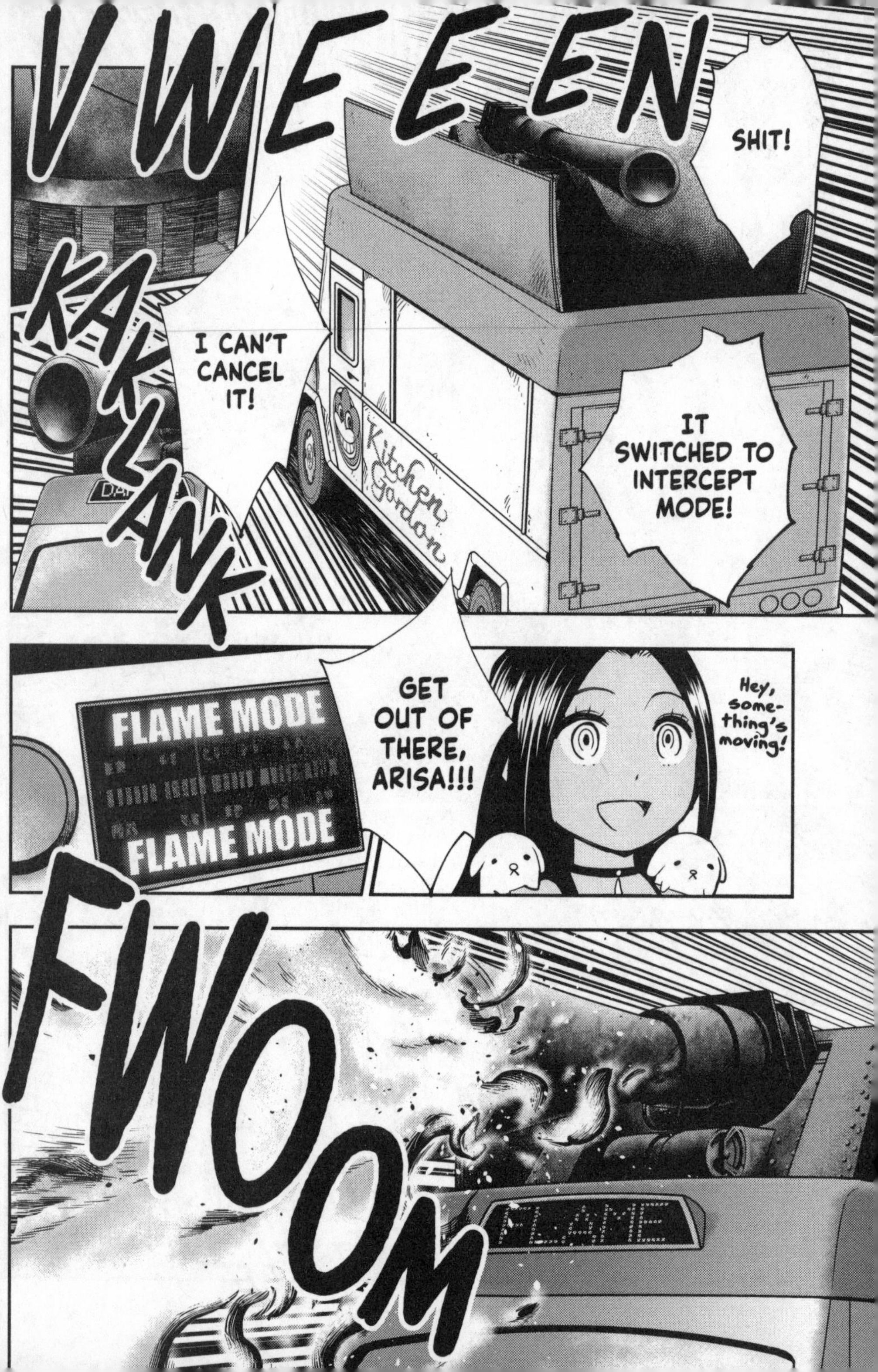
VWEEEN
SHIT!
IT SWITCHED TO INTERCEPT MODE!
I CAN'T CANCEL IT!
Kitchen Gordon
KAKLANK
Hey, something's moving!
GET OUT OF THERE, ARISA!!!
FLAME MODE
FLAME MODE
FWOOM
FLAME

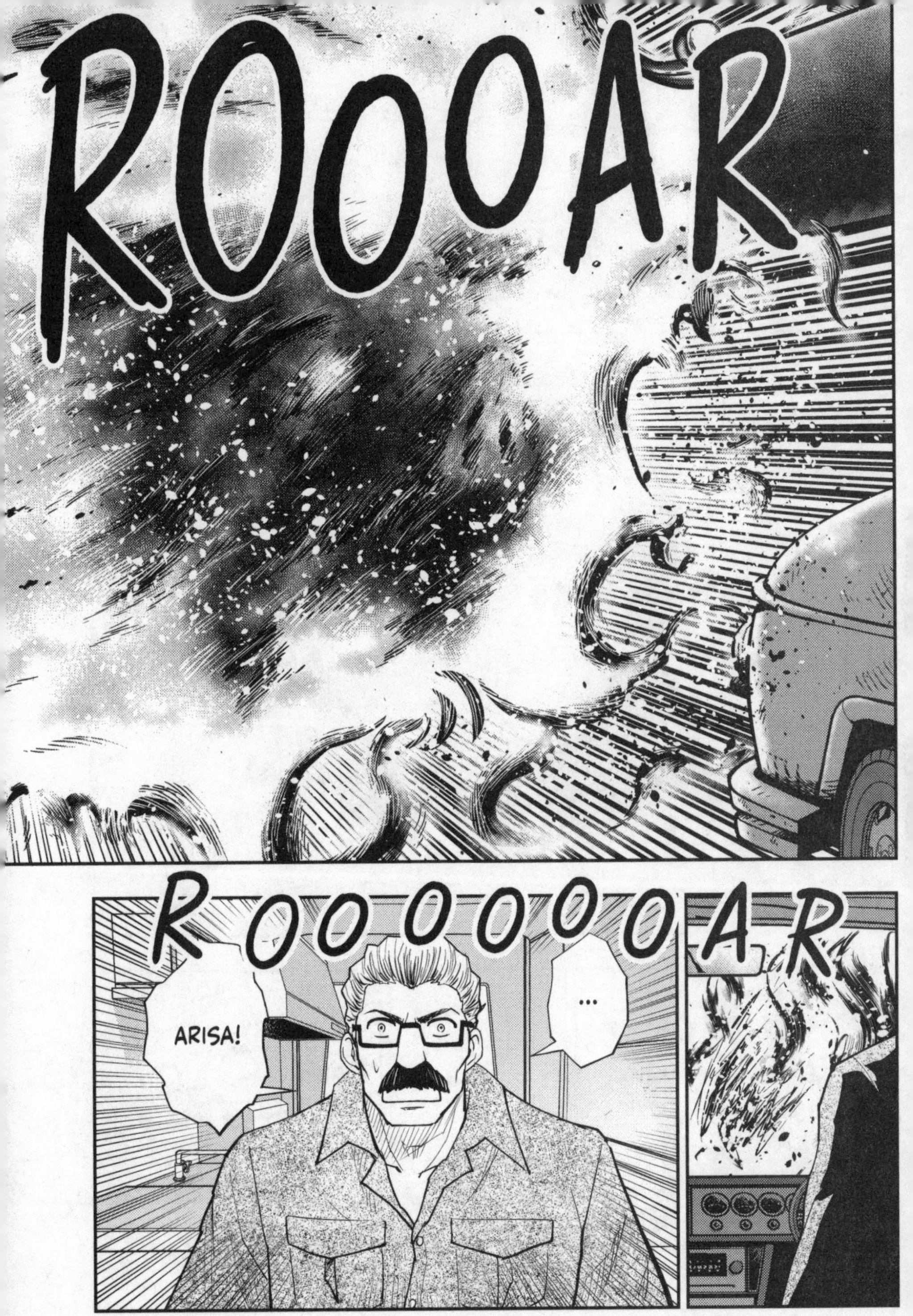
ROOOAR
ROOOOOOAR
...
ARISA!

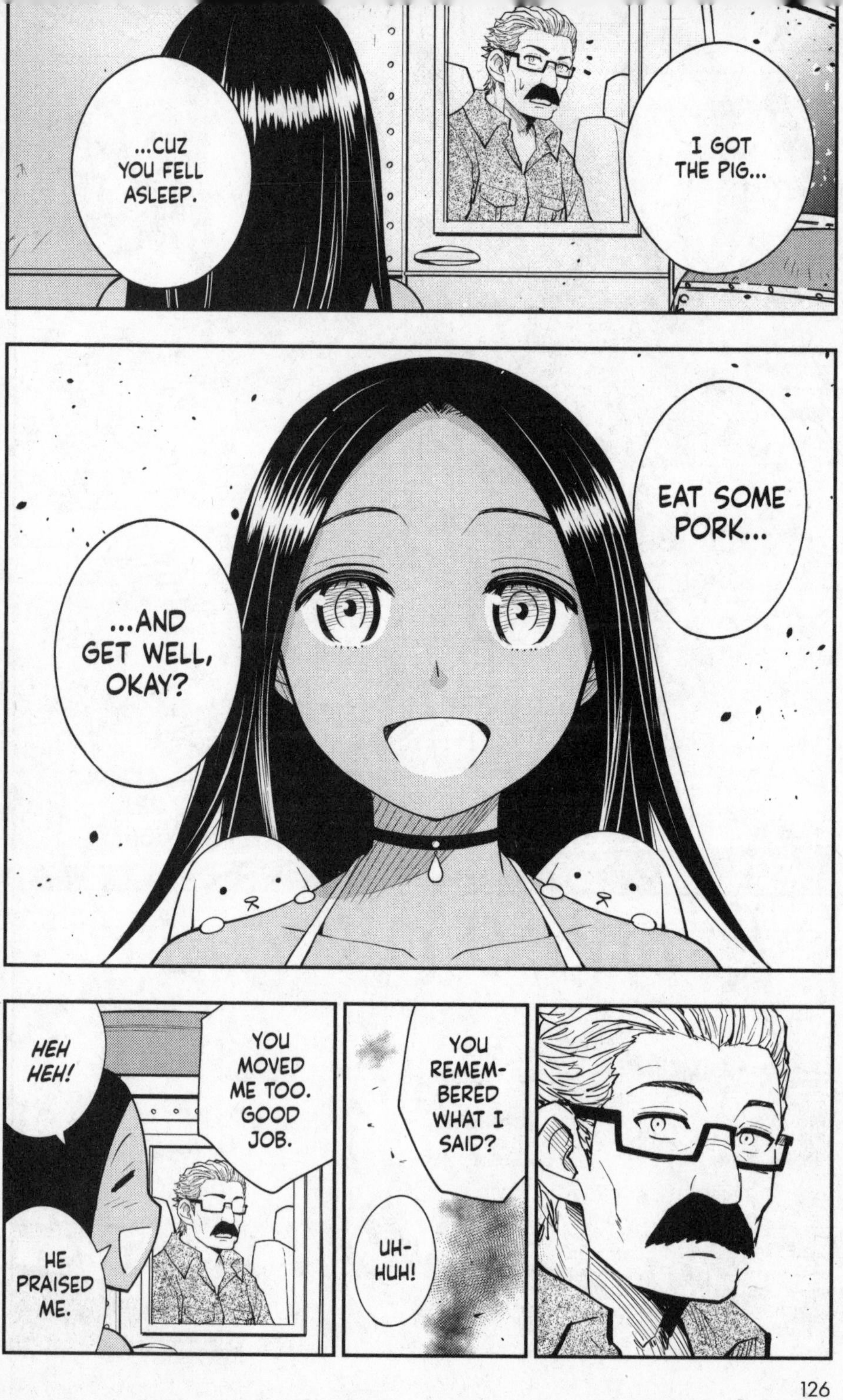
I GOT THE PIG...
...CUZ YOU FELL ASLEEP.
EAT SOME PORK...
...AND GET WELL, OKAY?
YOU REMEM-BERED WHAT I SAID?
UH-HUH!
YOU MOVED ME TOO. GOOD JOB.
HEH HEH!
HE PRAISED ME.

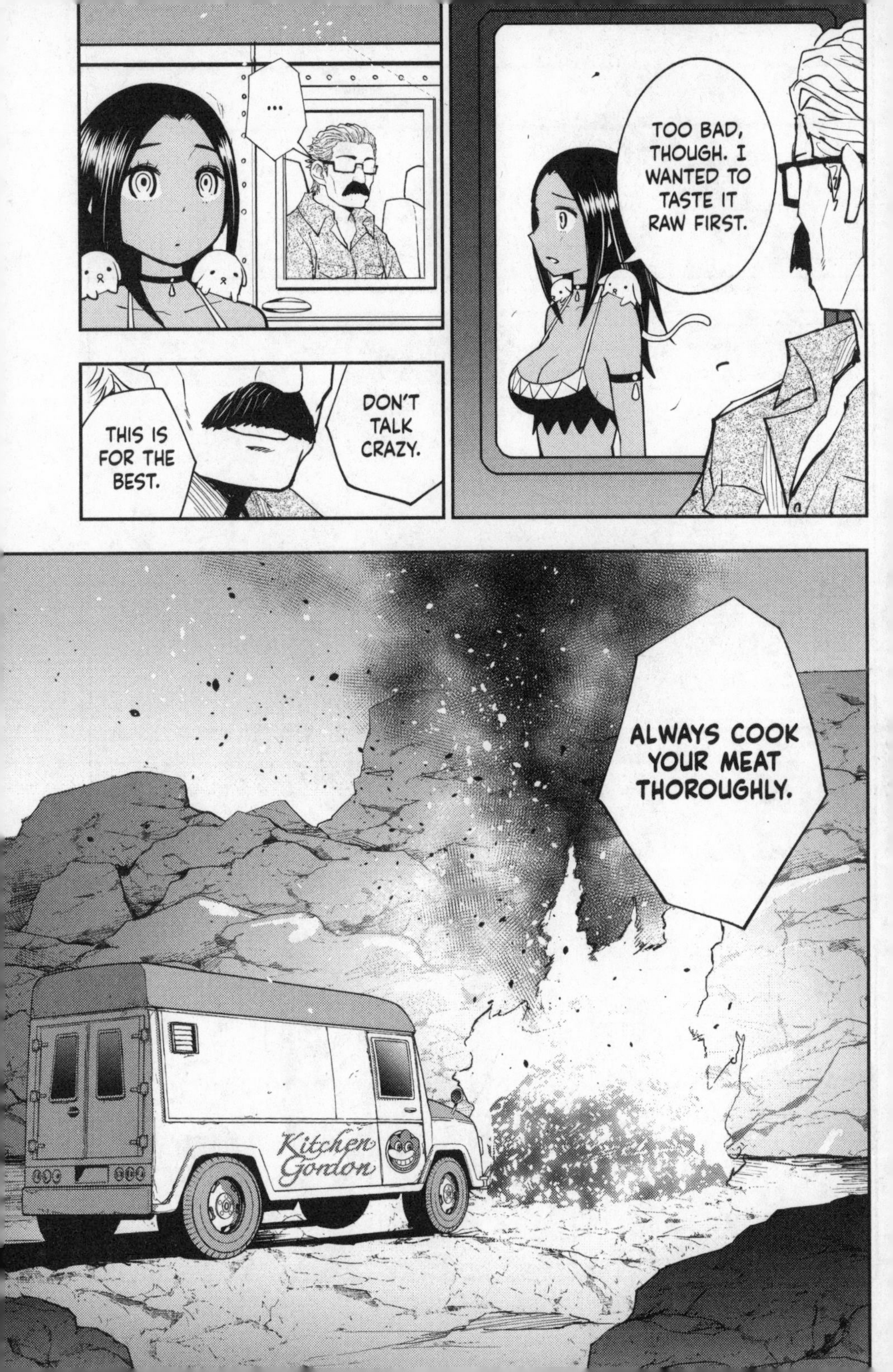
TOO BAD, THOUGH. I WANTED TO TASTE IT RAW FIRST.
...
DON'T TALK CRAZY.
THIS IS FOR THE BEST.
ALWAYS COOK YOUR MEAT THOROUGHLY.
Kitchen Gondon

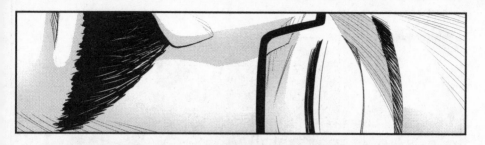

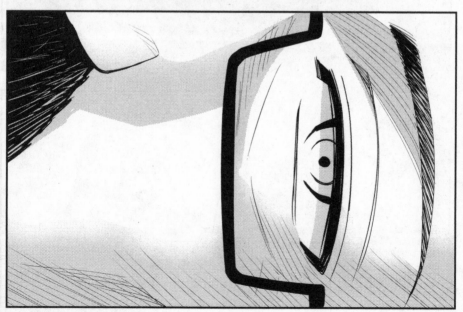

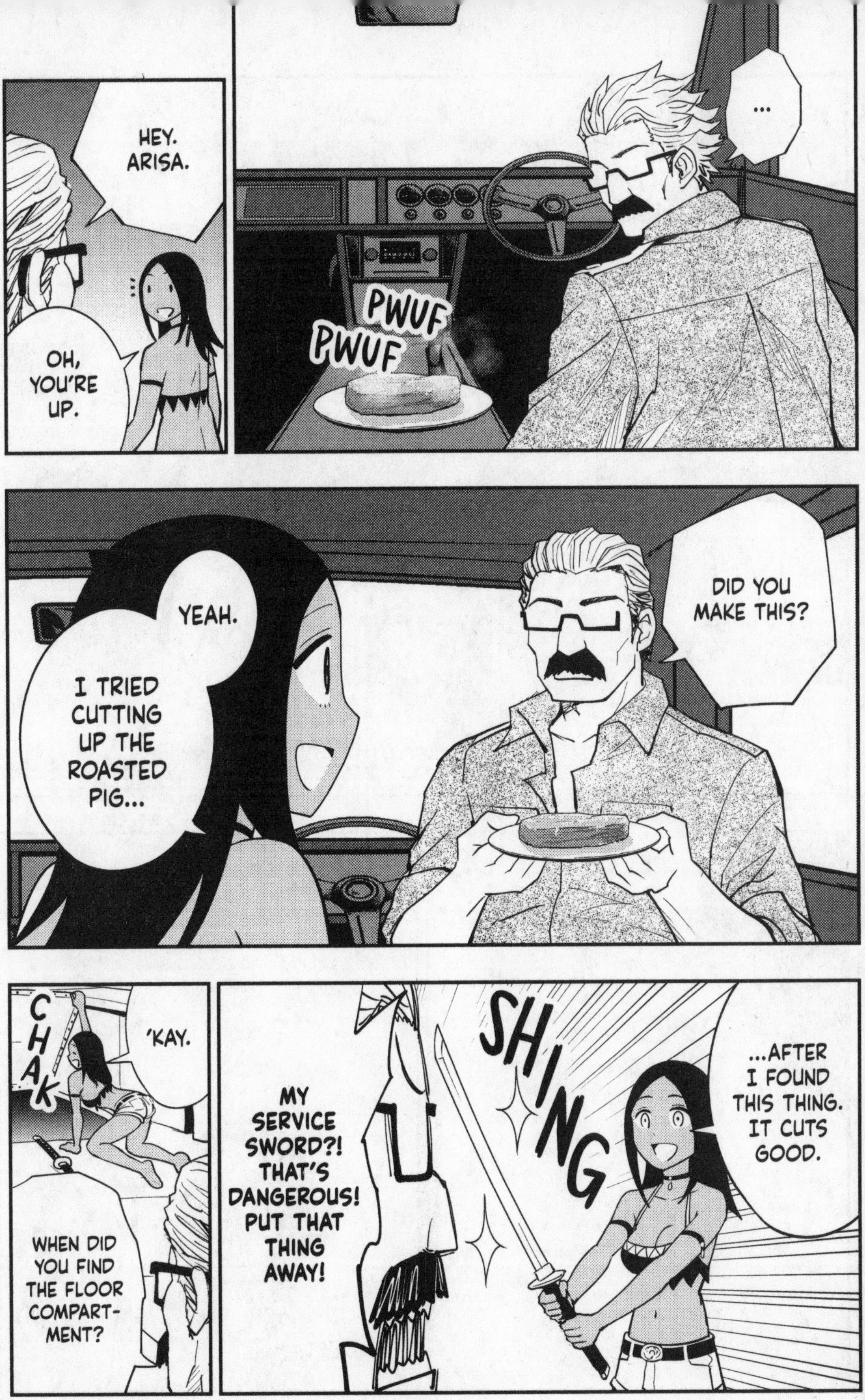
...
PWUF
PWUF
HEY. ARISA.
OH, YOU'RE UP.
DID YOU MAKE THIS?
YEAH.
I TRIED CUTTING UP THE ROASTED PIG...
...AFTER I FOUND THIS THING. IT CUTS GOOD.
SHING
MY SERVICE SWORD?! THAT'S DANGEROUS! PUT THAT THING AWAY!
CHAK
'KAY.
WHEN DID YOU FIND THE FLOOR COMPART-MENT?

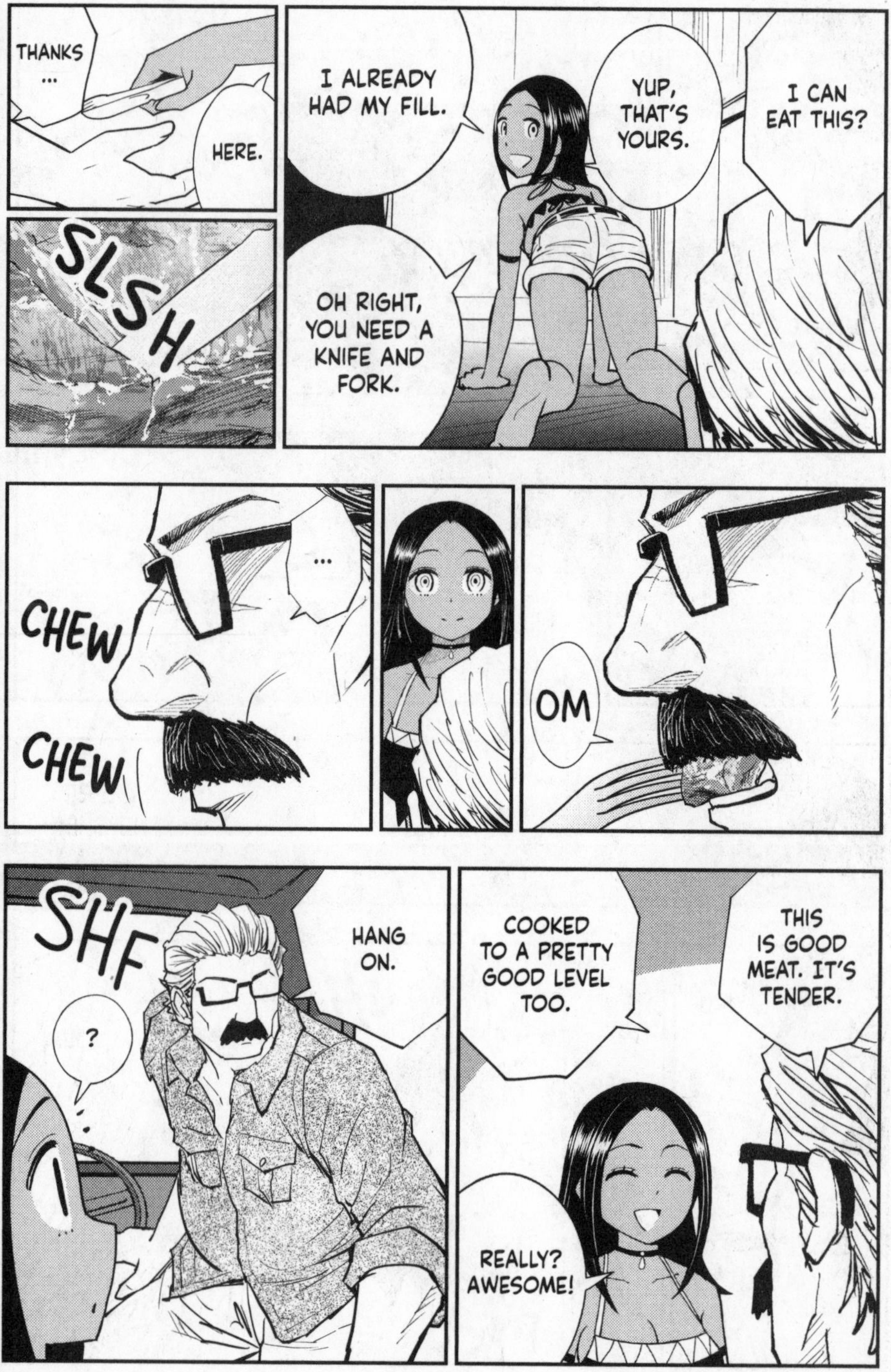
I CAN EAT THIS?
YUP, THAT'S YOURS.
I ALREADY HAD MY FILL.
OH RIGHT, YOU NEED A KNIFE AND FORK.
HERE.
THANKS ...
SLSH
OM
...
CHEW
CHEW
THIS IS GOOD MEAT. IT'S TENDER.
COOKED TO A PRETTY GOOD LEVEL TOO.
REALLY? AWESOME!
HANG ON.
SHF
?

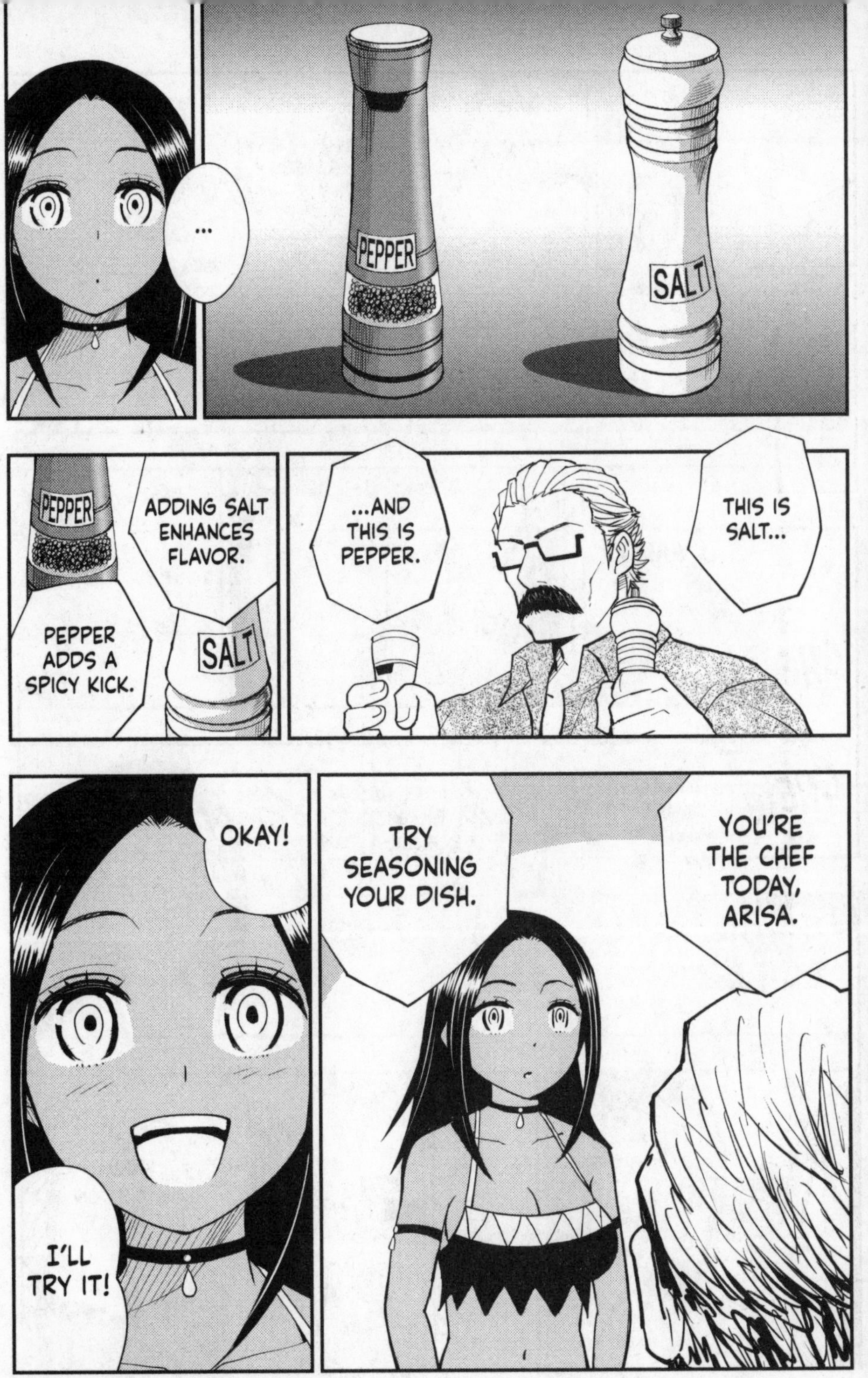
PEPPER
SALT
...
THIS IS SALT...
...AND THIS IS PEPPER.
PEPPER
ADDING SALT ENHANCES FLAVOR.
SALT
PEPPER ADDS A SPICY KICK.
YOU'RE THE CHEF TODAY, ARISA.
TRY SEASONING YOUR DISH.
OKAY!
I'LL TRY IT!

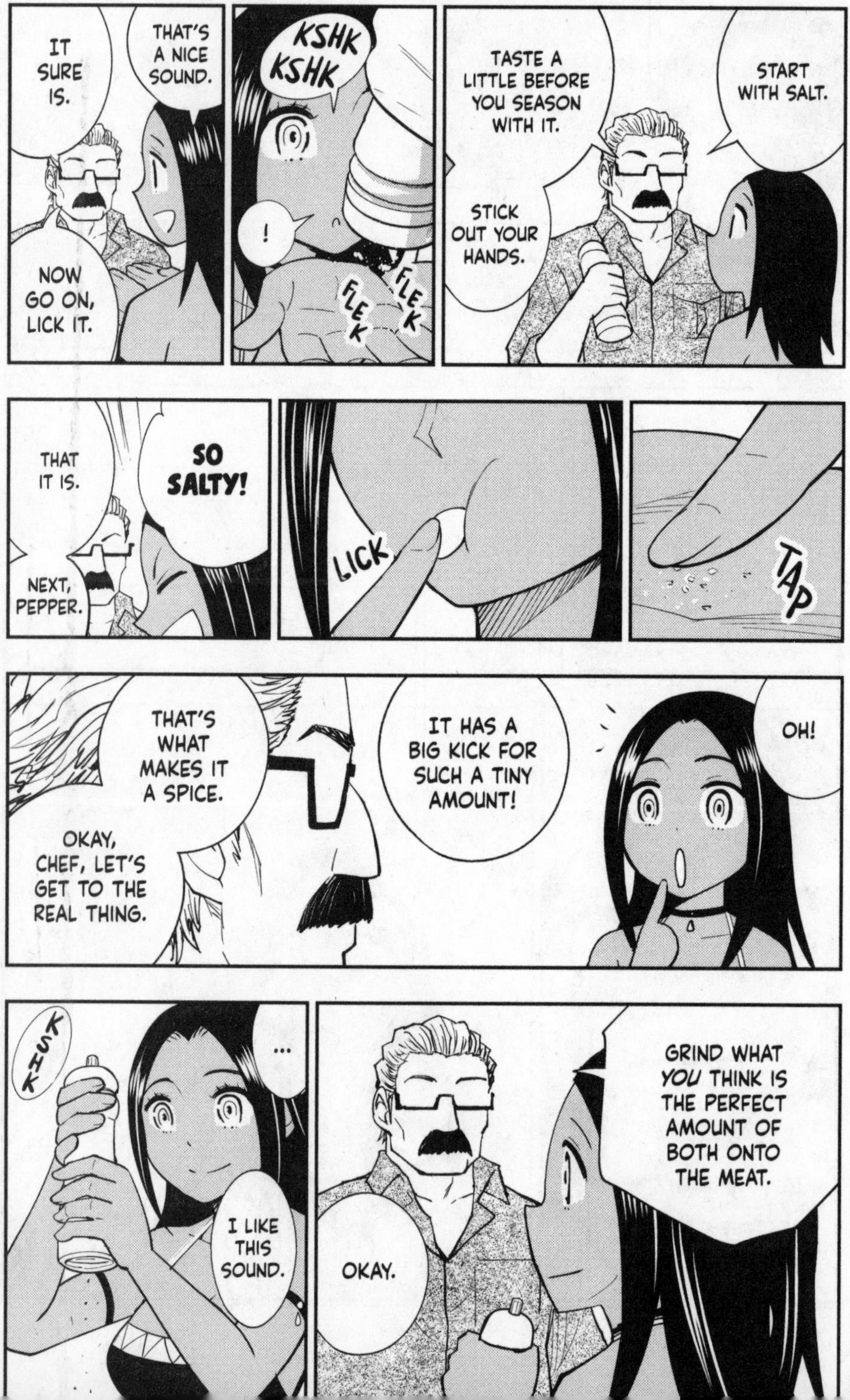
START WITH SALT.
TASTE A LITTLE BEFORE YOU SEASON WITH IT.
STICK OUT YOUR HANDS.
KSHK KSHK
!
FLEK
FLEK
THAT'S A NICE SOUND.
IT SURE IS.
NOW GO ON, LICK IT.
TAP
LICK
SO SALTY!
THAT IT IS.
NEXT, PEPPER.
OH!
IT HAS A BIG KICK FOR SUCH A TINY AMOUNT!
THAT'S WHAT MAKES IT A SPICE.
OKAY, CHEF, LET'S GET TO THE REAL THING.
GRIND WHAT *YOU* THINK IS THE PERFECT AMOUNT OF BOTH ONTO THE MEAT.
OKAY.
KSHK
...
I LIKE THIS SOUND.

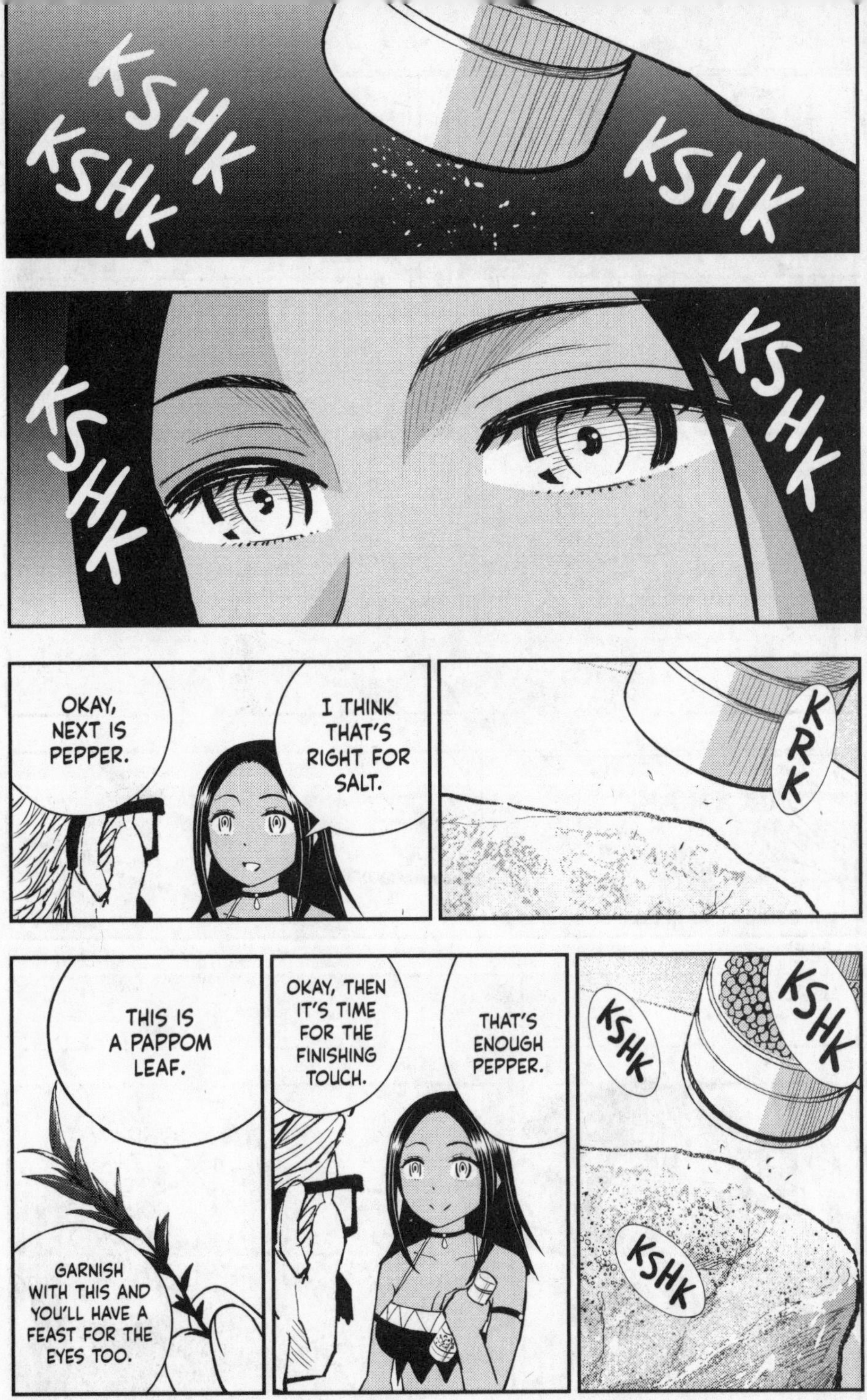
KSHK
KSHK
KSHK
KSHK
KSHK
KRK
I THINK THAT'S RIGHT FOR SALT.
OKAY, NEXT IS PEPPER.
KSHK
KSHK
KSHK
THAT'S ENOUGH PEPPER.
OKAY, THEN IT'S TIME FOR THE FINISHING TOUCH.
THIS IS A PAPPOM LEAF.
GARNISH WITH THIS AND YOU'LL HAVE A FEAST FOR THE EYES TOO.

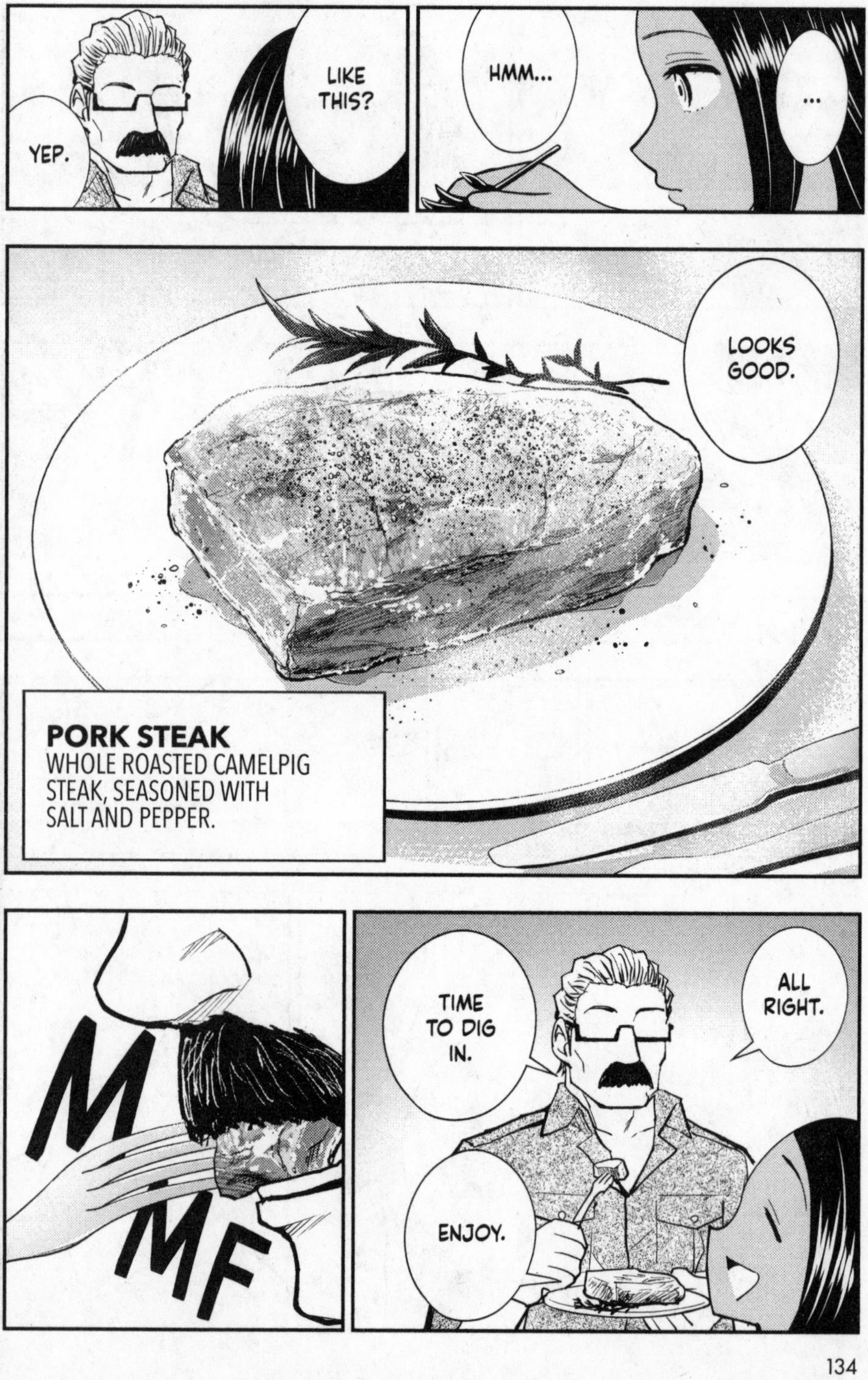
...
HMM...
LIKE THIS?
YEP.
LOOKS GOOD.
PORK STEAK
WHOLE ROASTED CAMELPIG STEAK, SEASONED WITH SALT AND PEPPER.
ALL RIGHT.
TIME TO DIG IN.
ENJOY.
MMMF

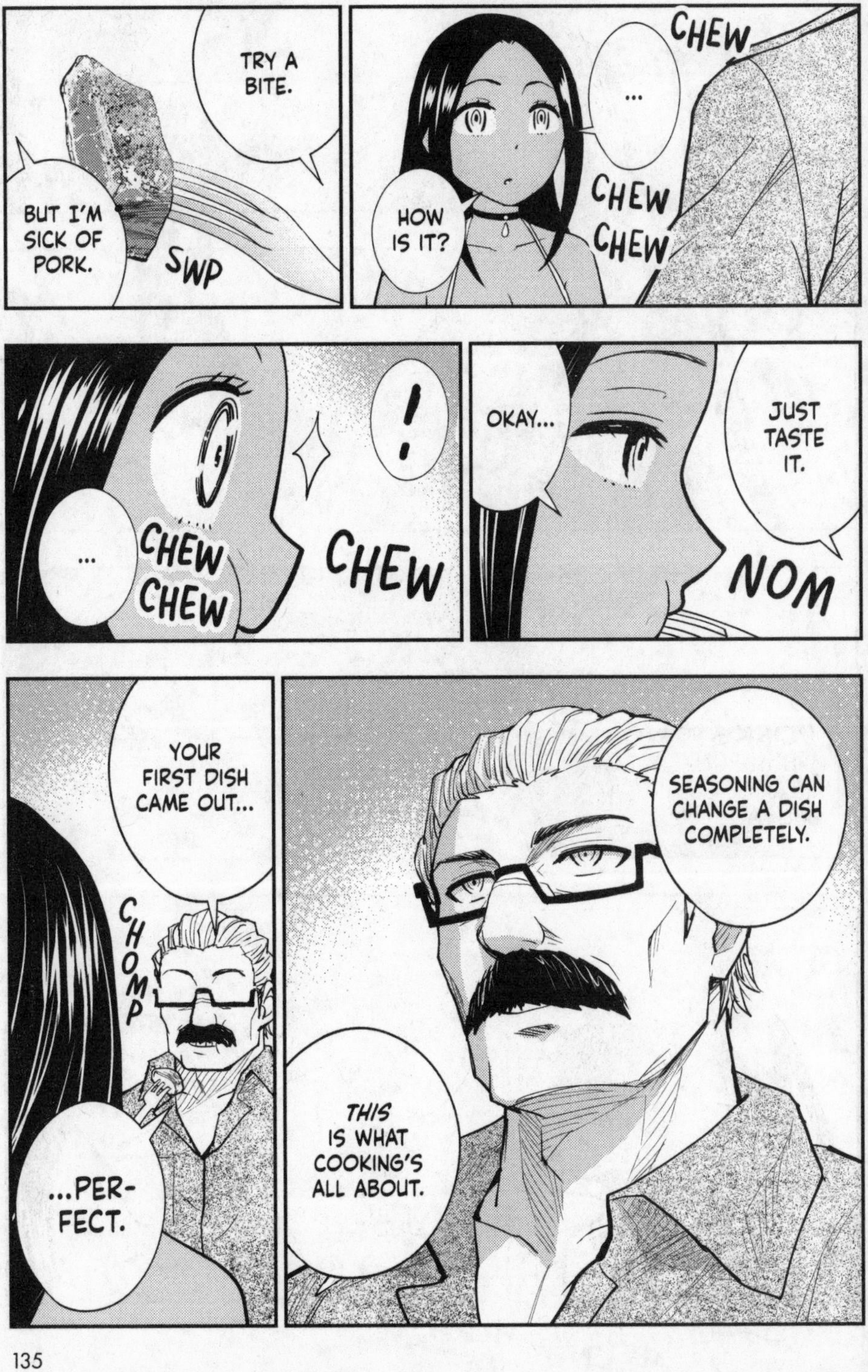
CHEW
...
CHEW CHEW
HOW IS IT?
TRY A BITE.
BUT I'M SICK OF PORK.
SWP
JUST TASTE IT.
OKAY...
NOM
!
CHEW
...
CHEW CHEW
SEASONING CAN CHANGE A DISH COMPLETELY.
THIS IS WHAT COOKING'S ALL ABOUT.
YOUR FIRST DISH CAME OUT...
CHOMP
...PER-FECT.

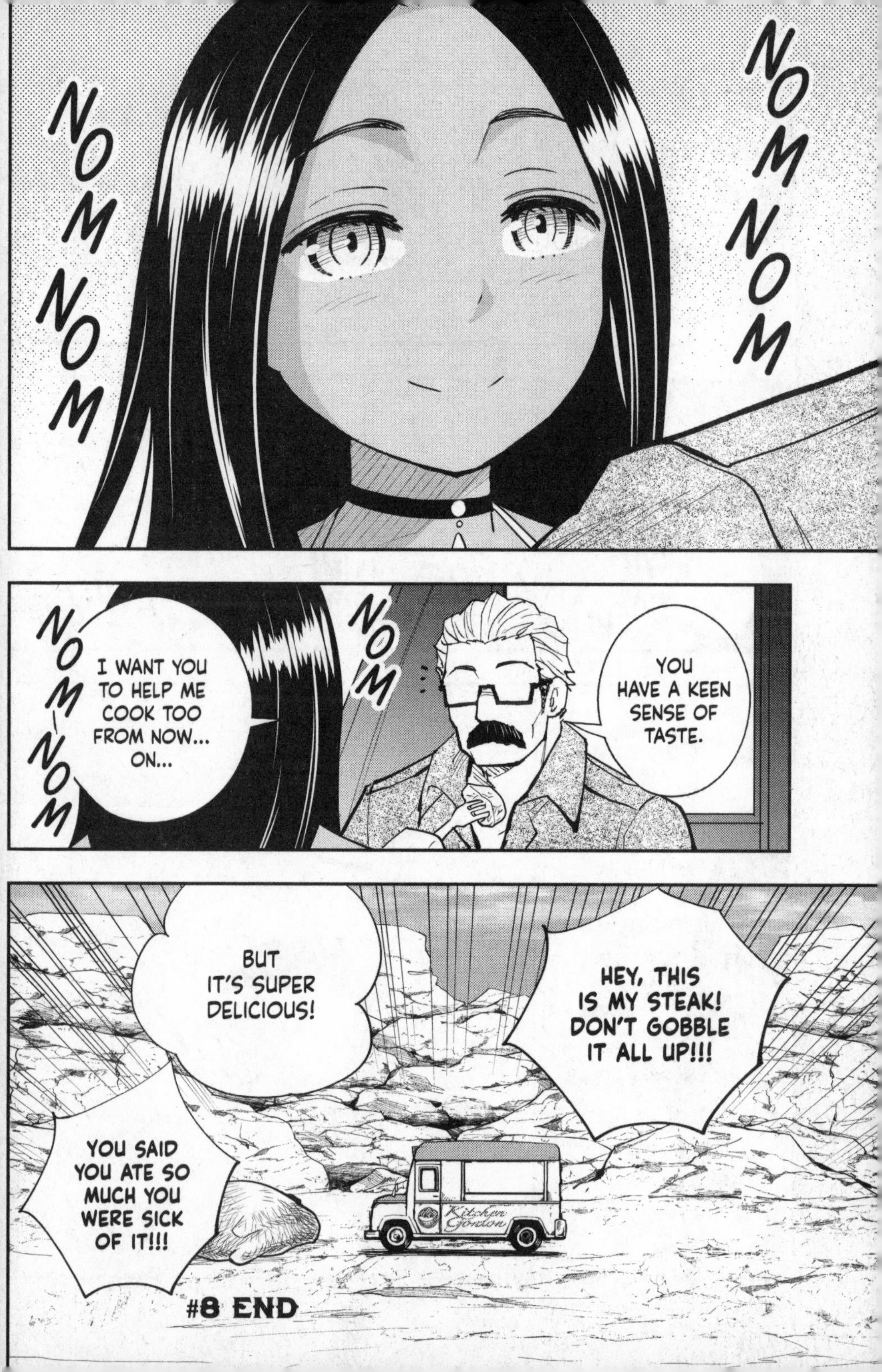

NOM NOM NOM
NOM NOM NOM
YOU HAVE A KEEN SENSE OF TASTE.
NOM NOM
I WANT YOU TO HELP ME COOK TOO FROM NOW... ON...
NOM-NOM-NOM
HEY, THIS IS MY STEAK! DON'T GOBBLE IT ALL UP!!!
BUT IT'S SUPER DELICIOUS!
YOU SAID YOU ATE SO MUCH YOU WERE SICK OF IT!!!
Kitchen Gordon
#8 END

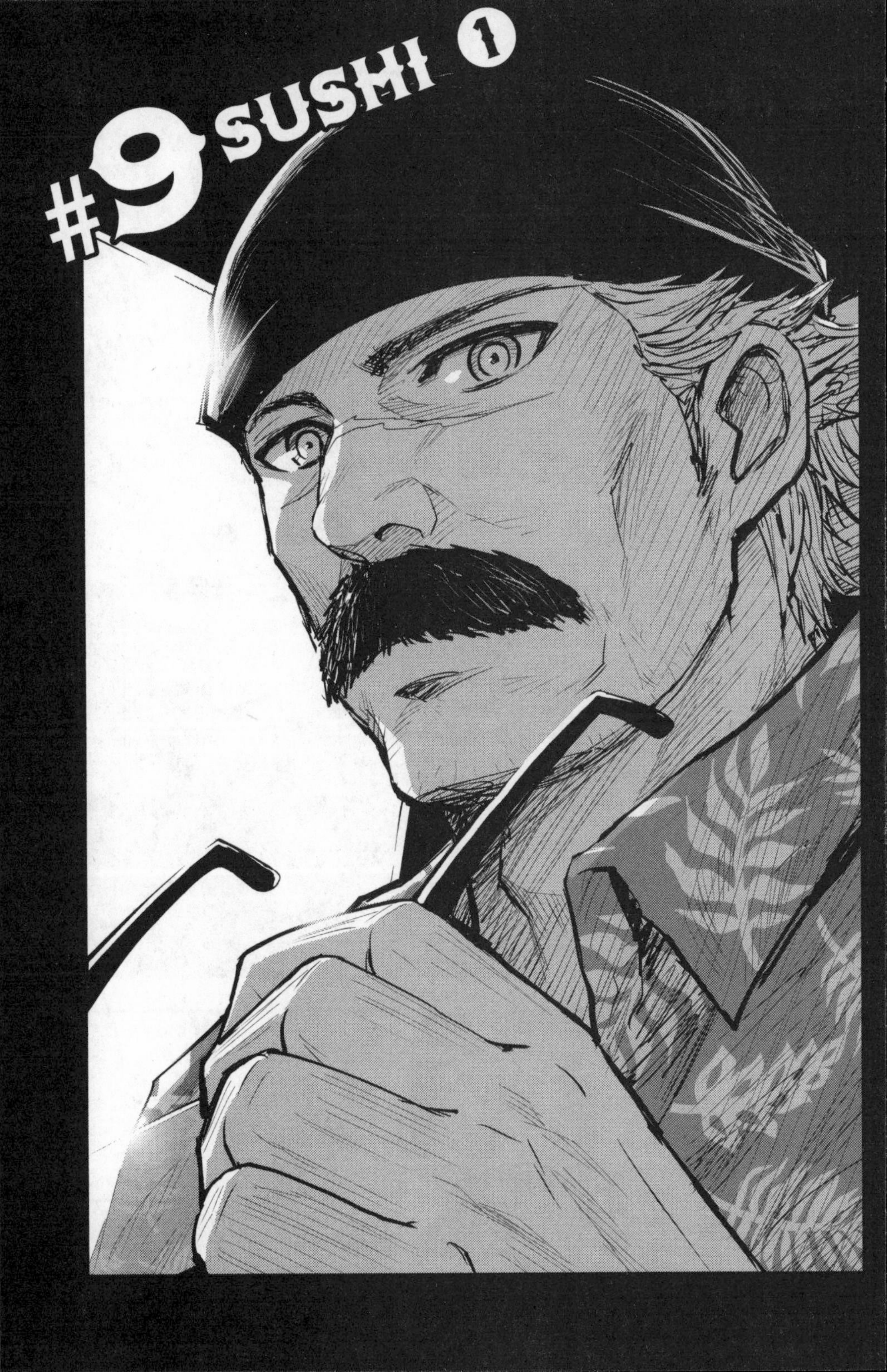
#9 SUSHI 1

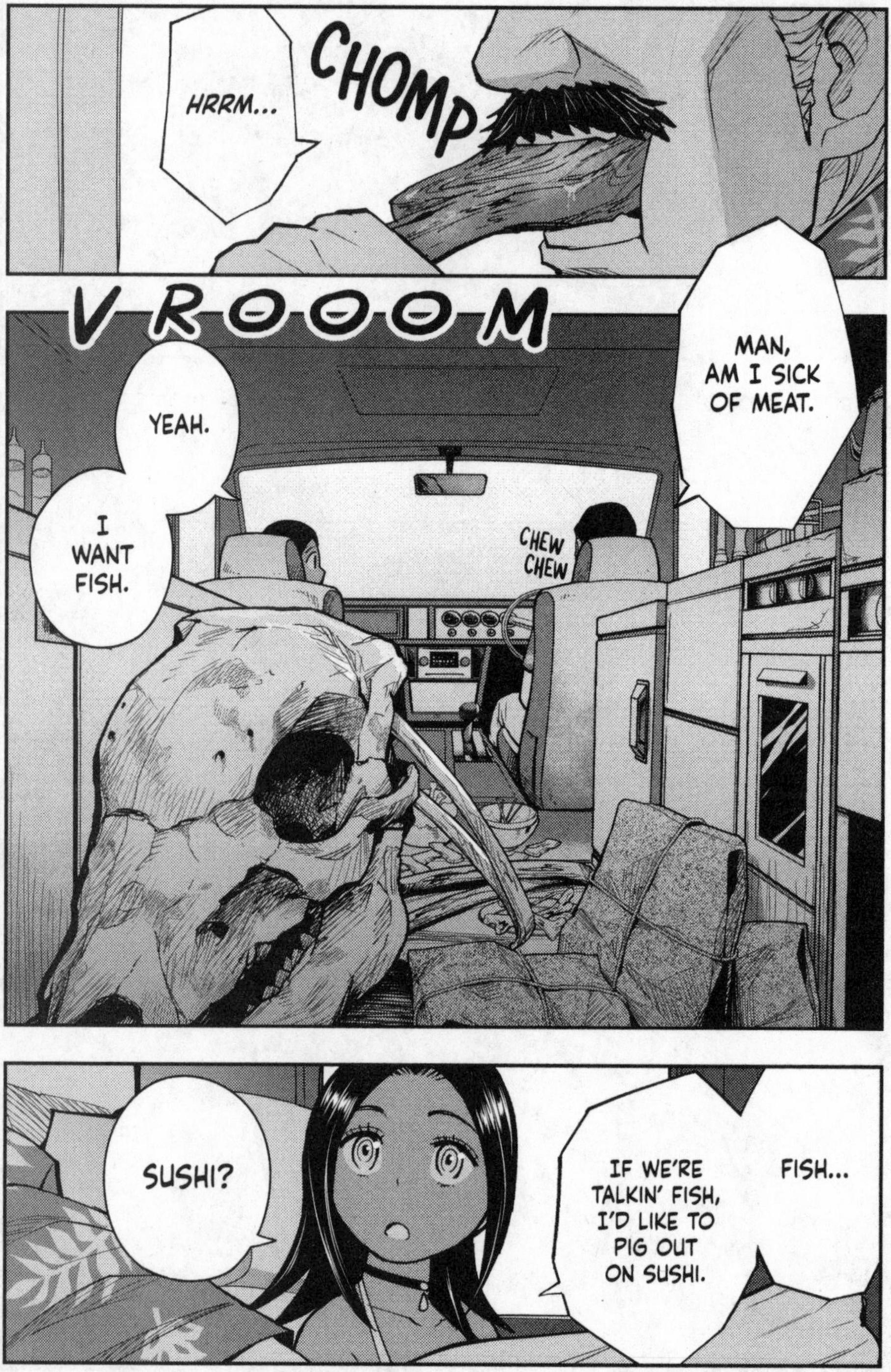
CHOMP
HRRM...
VROOOM
MAN, AM I SICK OF MEAT.
CHEW CHEW
YEAH.
I WANT FISH.
FISH...
IF WE'RE TALKIN' FISH, I'D LIKE TO PIG OUT ON SUSHI.
SUSHI?

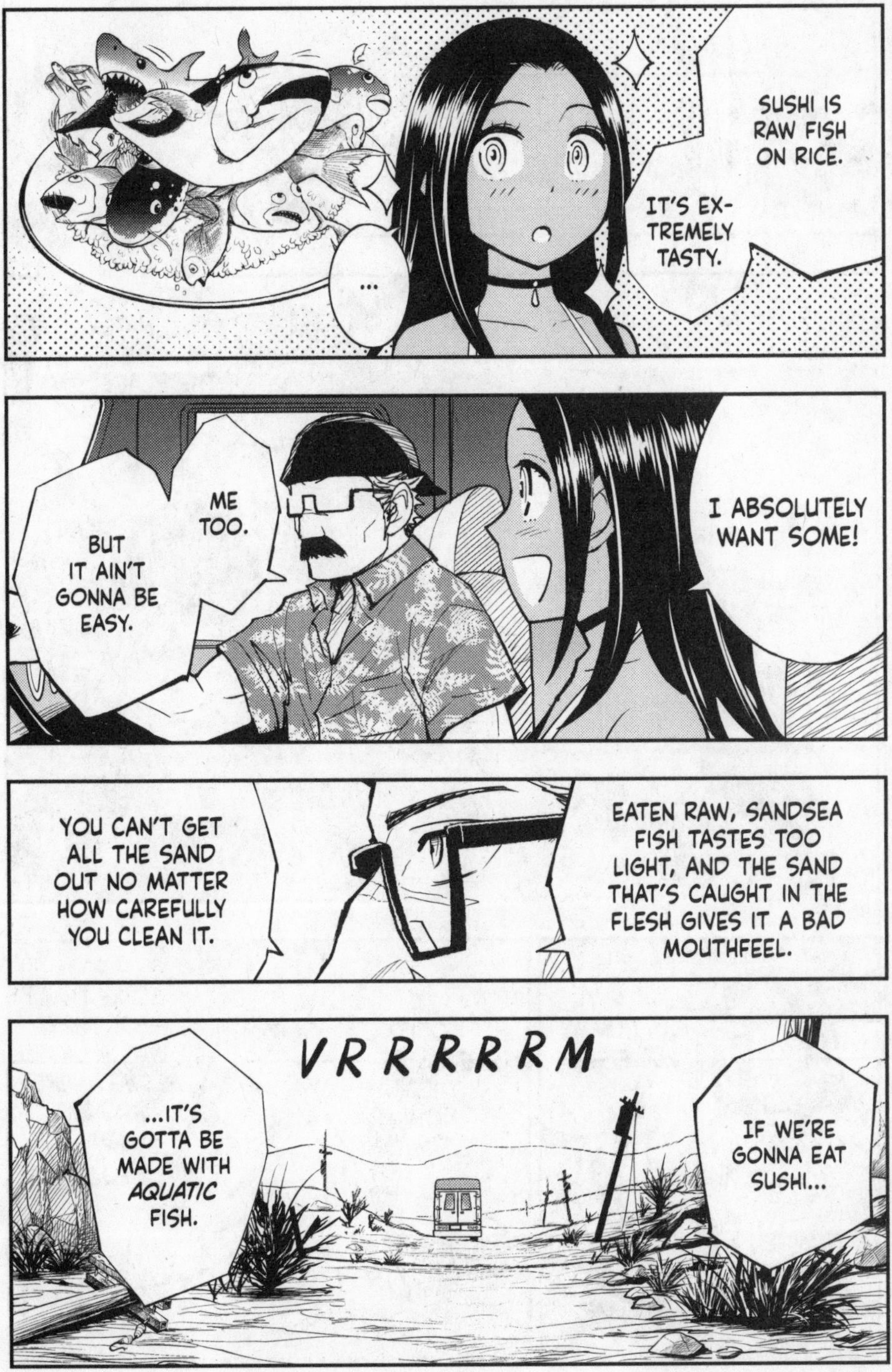
SUSHI IS RAW FISH ON RICE.
IT'S EX-TREMELY TASTY.
...
I ABSOLUTELY WANT SOME!
ME TOO.
BUT IT AIN'T GONNA BE EASY.
EATEN RAW, SANDSEA FISH TASTES TOO LIGHT, AND THE SAND THAT'S CAUGHT IN THE FLESH GIVES IT A BAD MOUTHFEEL.
YOU CAN'T GET ALL THE SAND OUT NO MATTER HOW CAREFULLY YOU CLEAN IT.
IF WE'RE GONNA EAT SUSHI...
VRRRRRM
...IT'S GOTTA BE MADE WITH *AQUATIC* FISH.

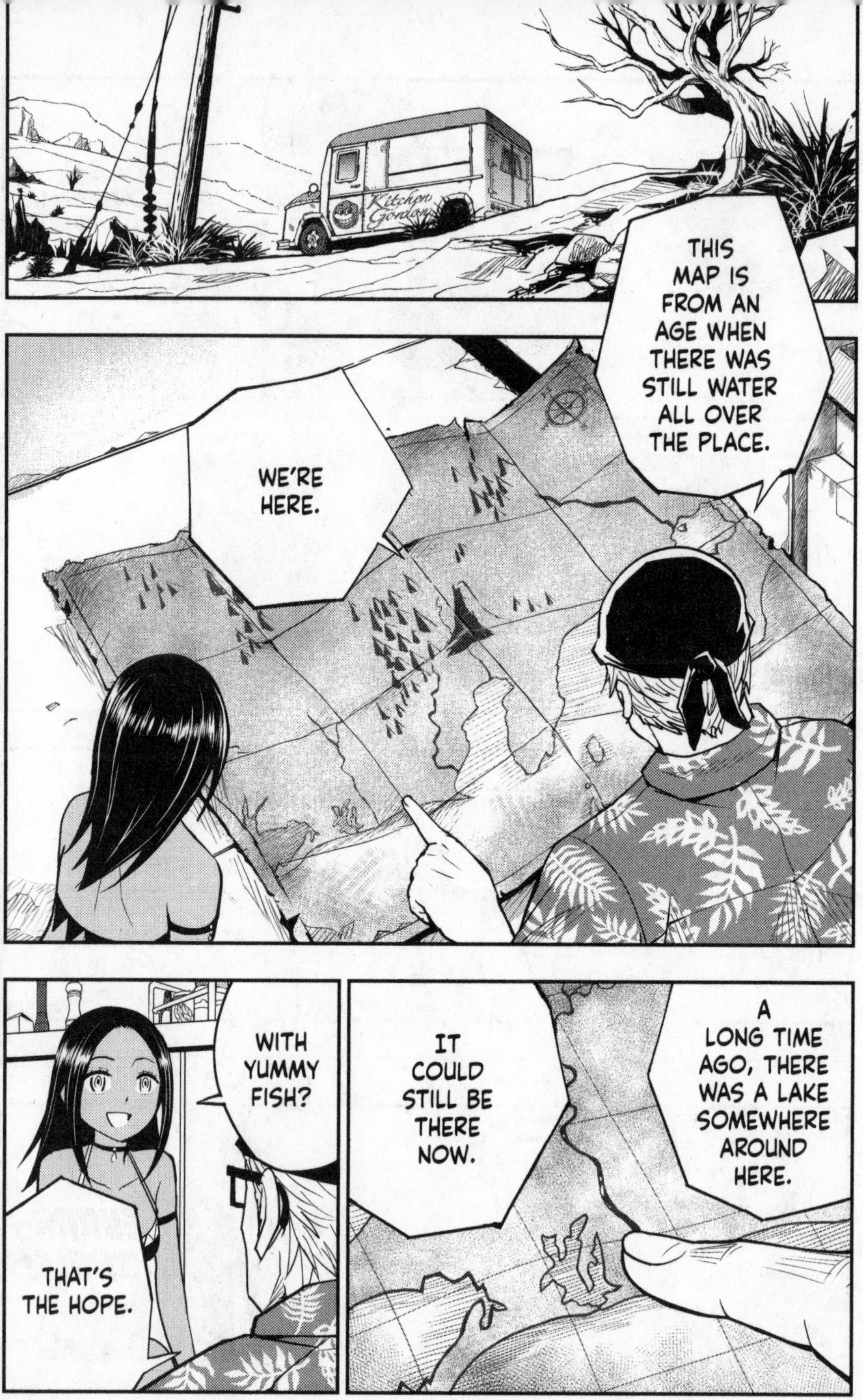
THIS MAP IS FROM AN AGE WHEN THERE WAS STILL WATER ALL OVER THE PLACE.
WE'RE HERE.
A LONG TIME AGO, THERE WAS A LAKE SOMEWHERE AROUND HERE.
IT COULD STILL BE THERE NOW.
WITH YUMMY FISH?
THAT'S THE HOPE.

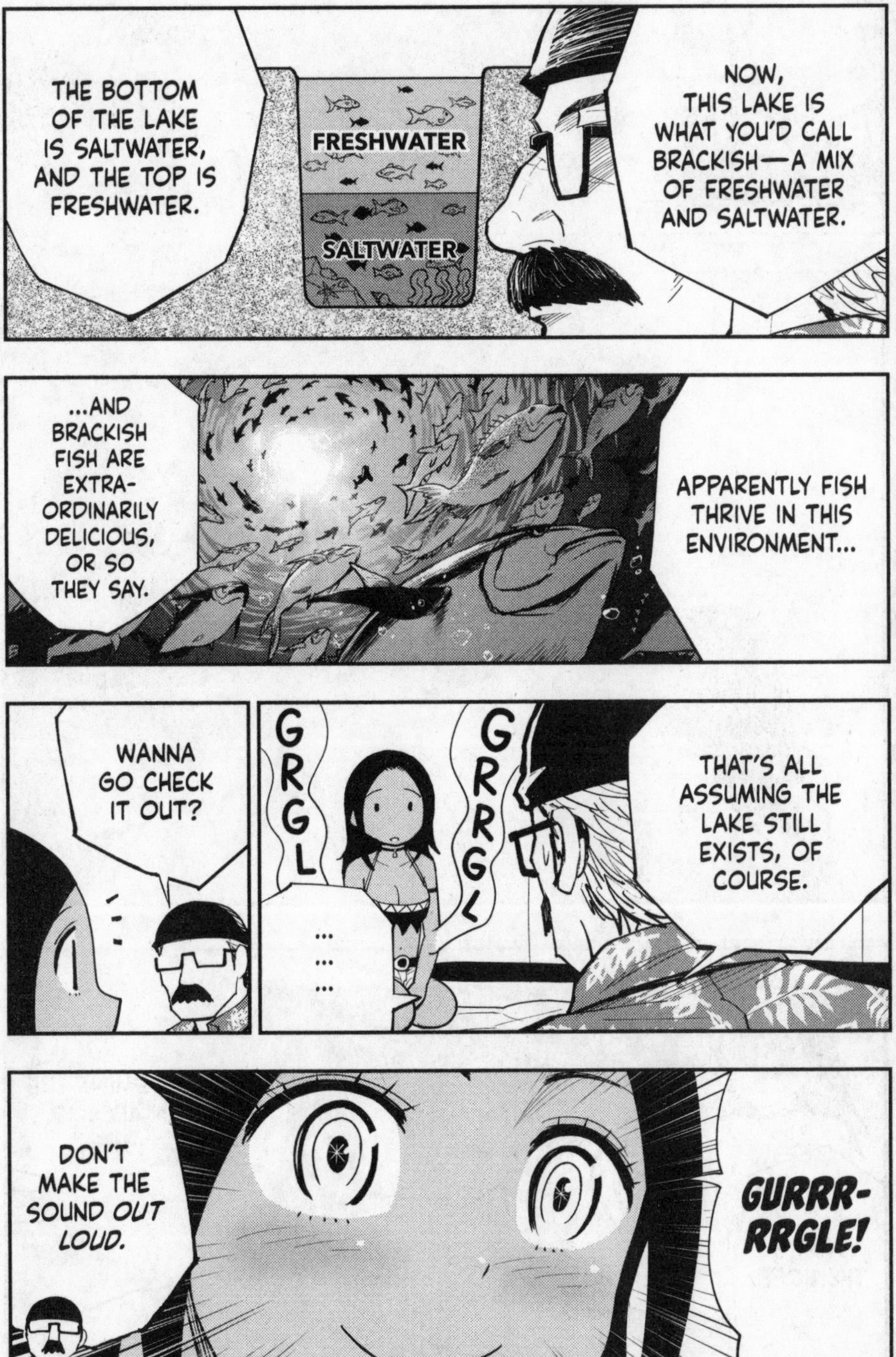
NOW, THIS LAKE IS WHAT YOU'D CALL BRACKISH—A MIX OF FRESHWATER AND SALTWATER.
THE BOTTOM OF THE LAKE IS SALTWATER, AND THE TOP IS FRESHWATER.
FRESHWATER
SALTWATER
APPARENTLY FISH THRIVE IN THIS ENVIRONMENT...
...AND BRACKISH FISH ARE EXTRA-ORDINARILY DELICIOUS, OR SO THEY SAY.
THAT'S ALL ASSUMING THE LAKE STILL EXISTS, OF COURSE.
GRRRGL
GRGL
...
...
...
WANNA GO CHECK IT OUT?
GURRR-RRGLE!
DON'T MAKE THE SOUND *OUT LOUD.*

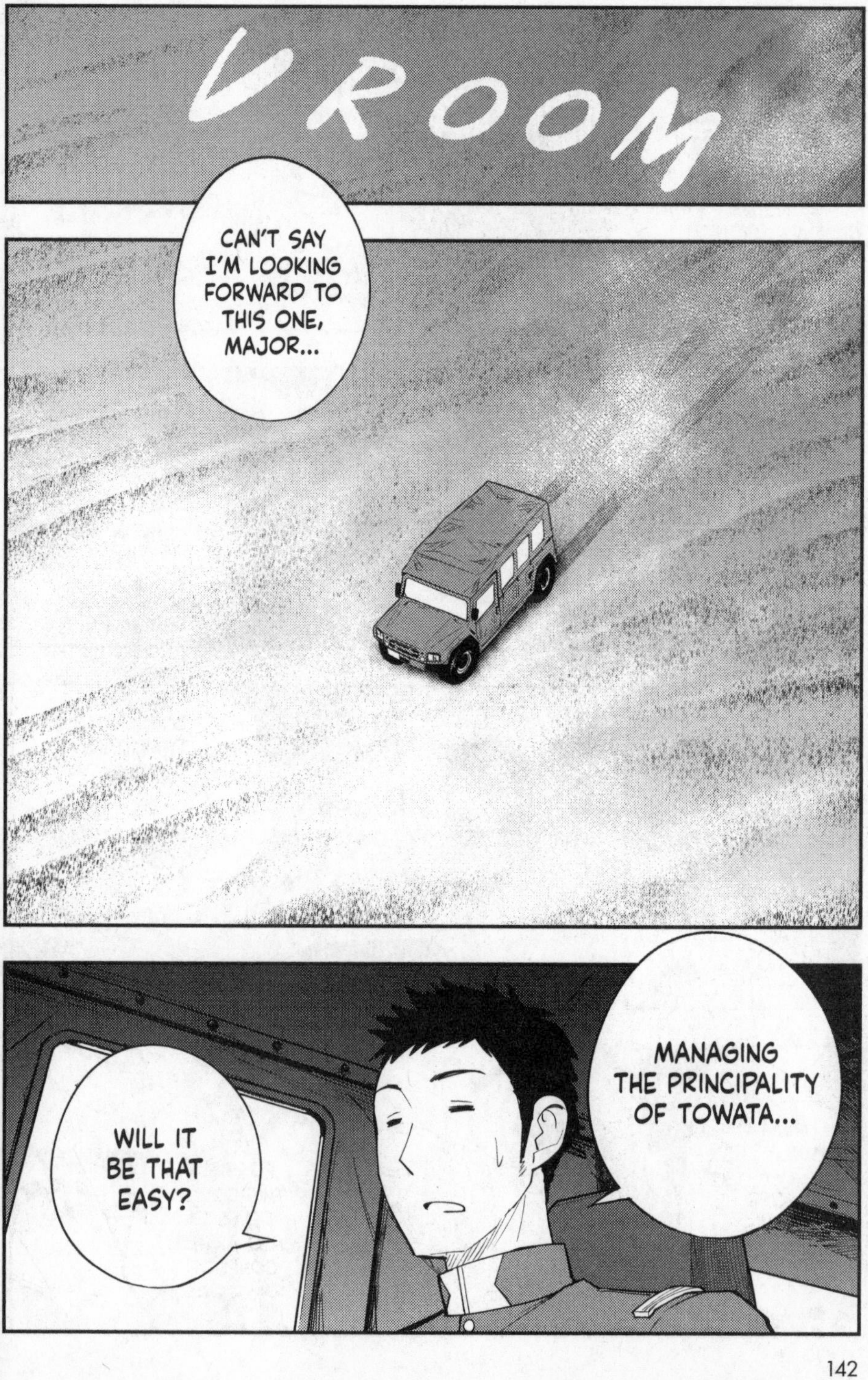
VROOM
CAN'T SAY I'M LOOKING FORWARD TO THIS ONE, MAJOR...
MANAGING THE PRINCIPALITY OF TOWATA...
WILL IT BE THAT EASY?

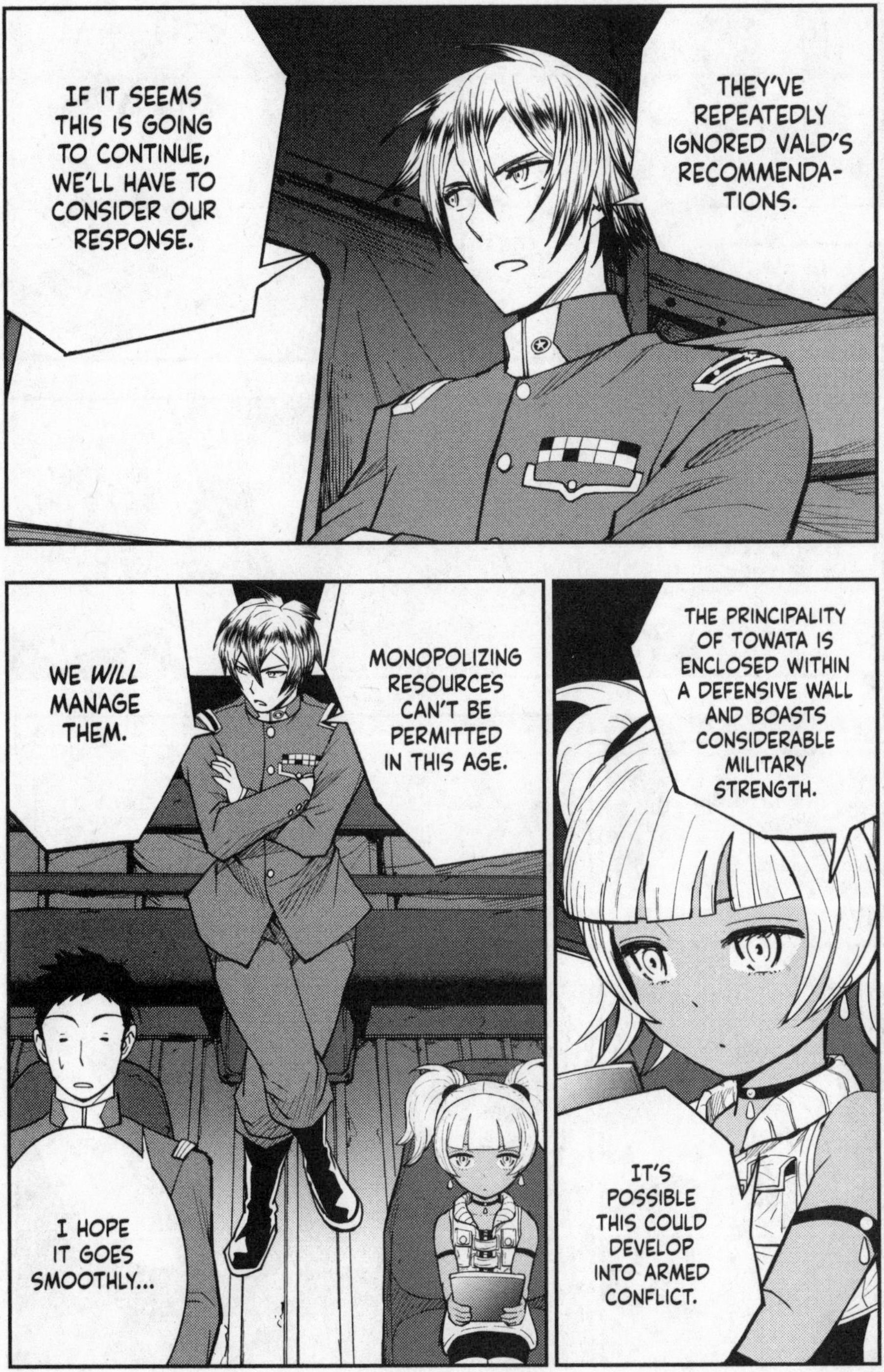
THEY'VE REPEATEDLY IGNORED VALD'S RECOMMENDA-TIONS.
IF IT SEEMS THIS IS GOING TO CONTINUE, WE'LL HAVE TO CONSIDER OUR RESPONSE.
THE PRINCIPALITY OF TOWATA IS ENCLOSED WITHIN A DEFENSIVE WALL AND BOASTS CONSIDERABLE MILITARY STRENGTH.
IT'S POSSIBLE THIS COULD DEVELOP INTO ARMED CONFLICT.
MONOPOLIZING RESOURCES CAN'T BE PERMITTED IN THIS AGE.
WE *WILL* MANAGE THEM.
I HOPE IT GOES SMOOTHLY...

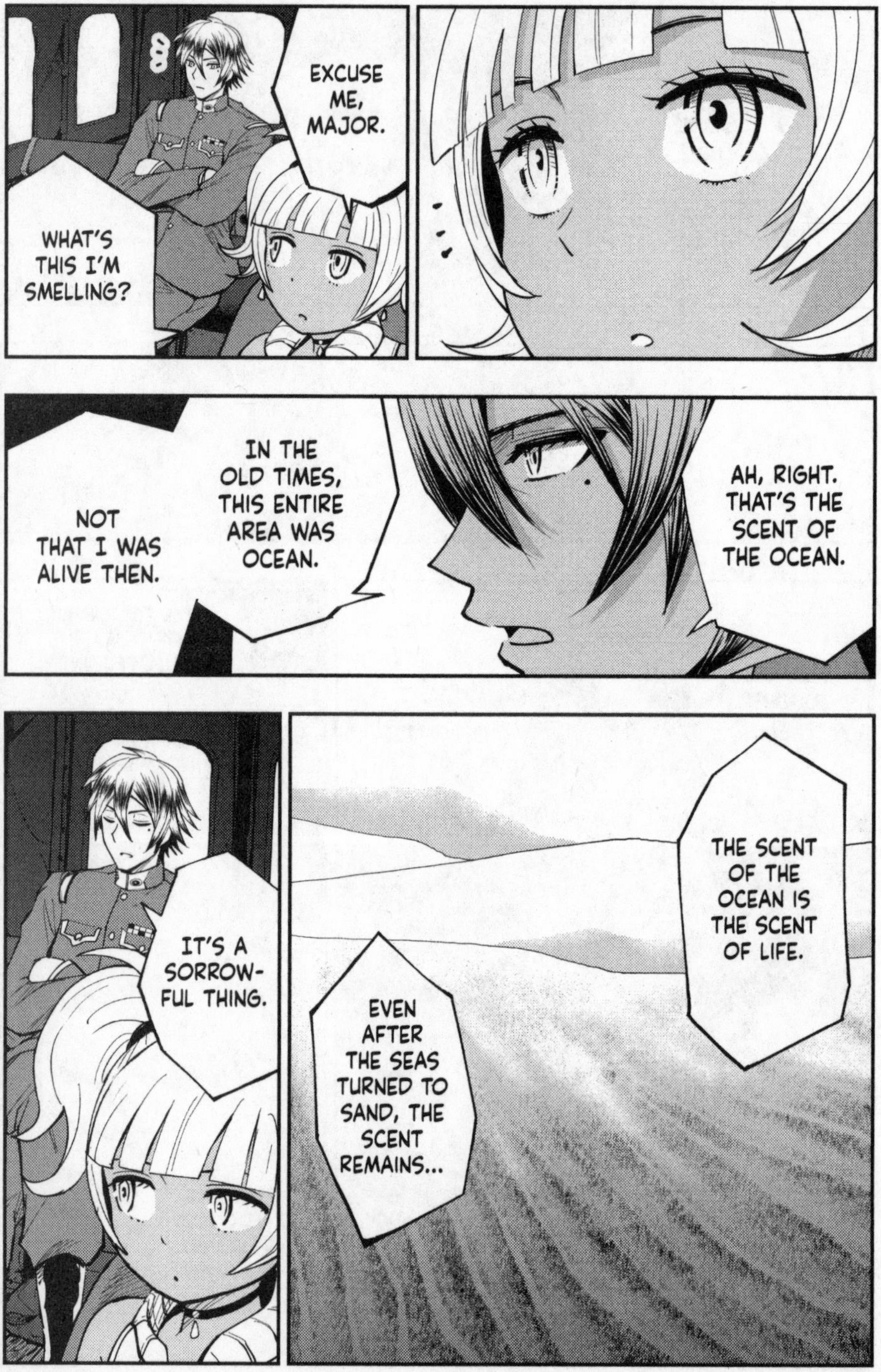
EXCUSE ME, MAJOR.
WHAT'S THIS I'M SMELLING?
AH, RIGHT. THAT'S THE SCENT OF THE OCEAN.
IN THE OLD TIMES, THIS ENTIRE AREA WAS OCEAN.
NOT THAT I WAS ALIVE THEN.
THE SCENT OF THE OCEAN IS THE SCENT OF LIFE.
EVEN AFTER THE SEAS TURNED TO SAND, THE SCENT REMAINS...
IT'S A SORROWFUL THING.

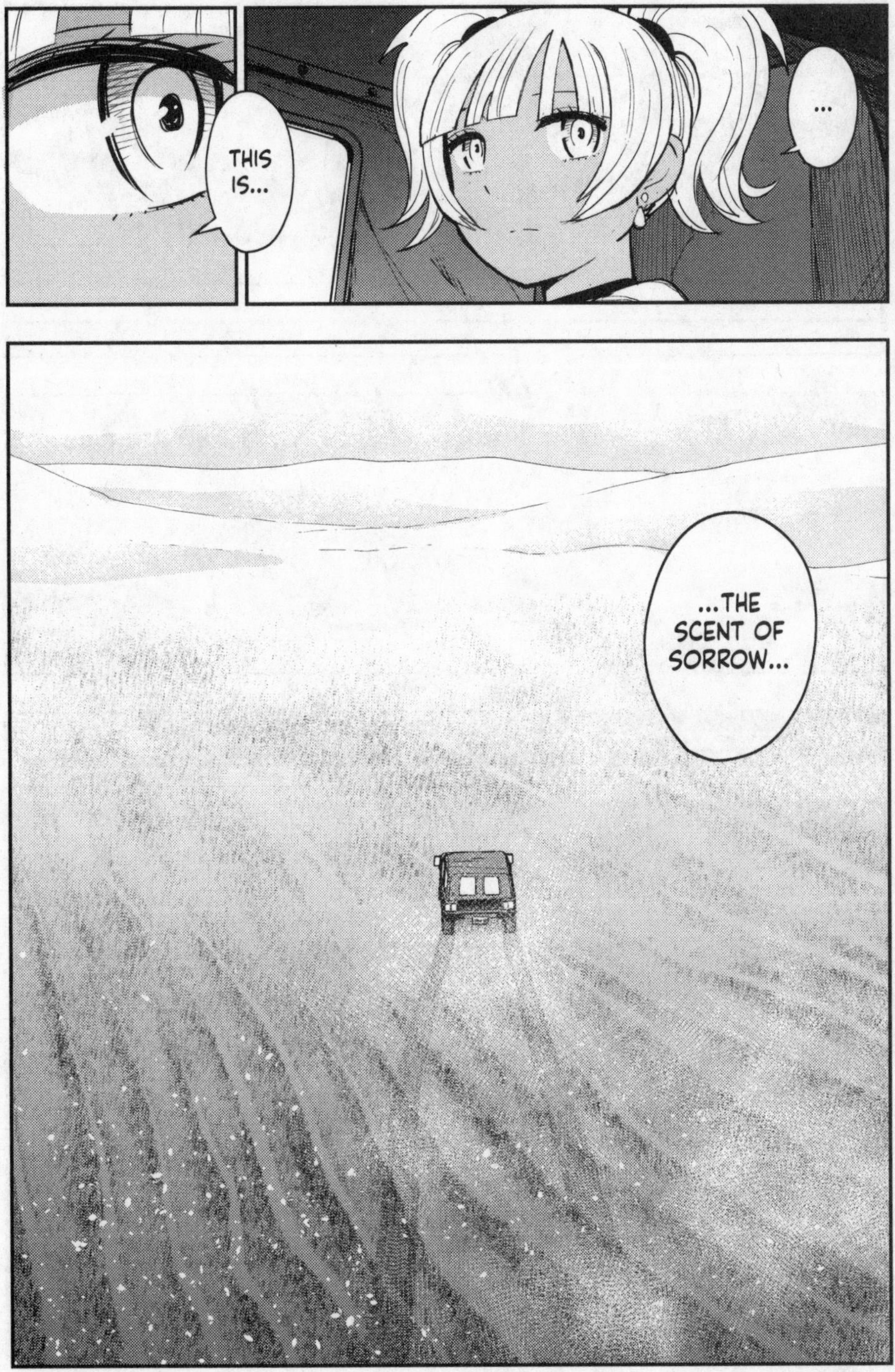
...
THIS IS...
...THE SCENT OF SORROW...

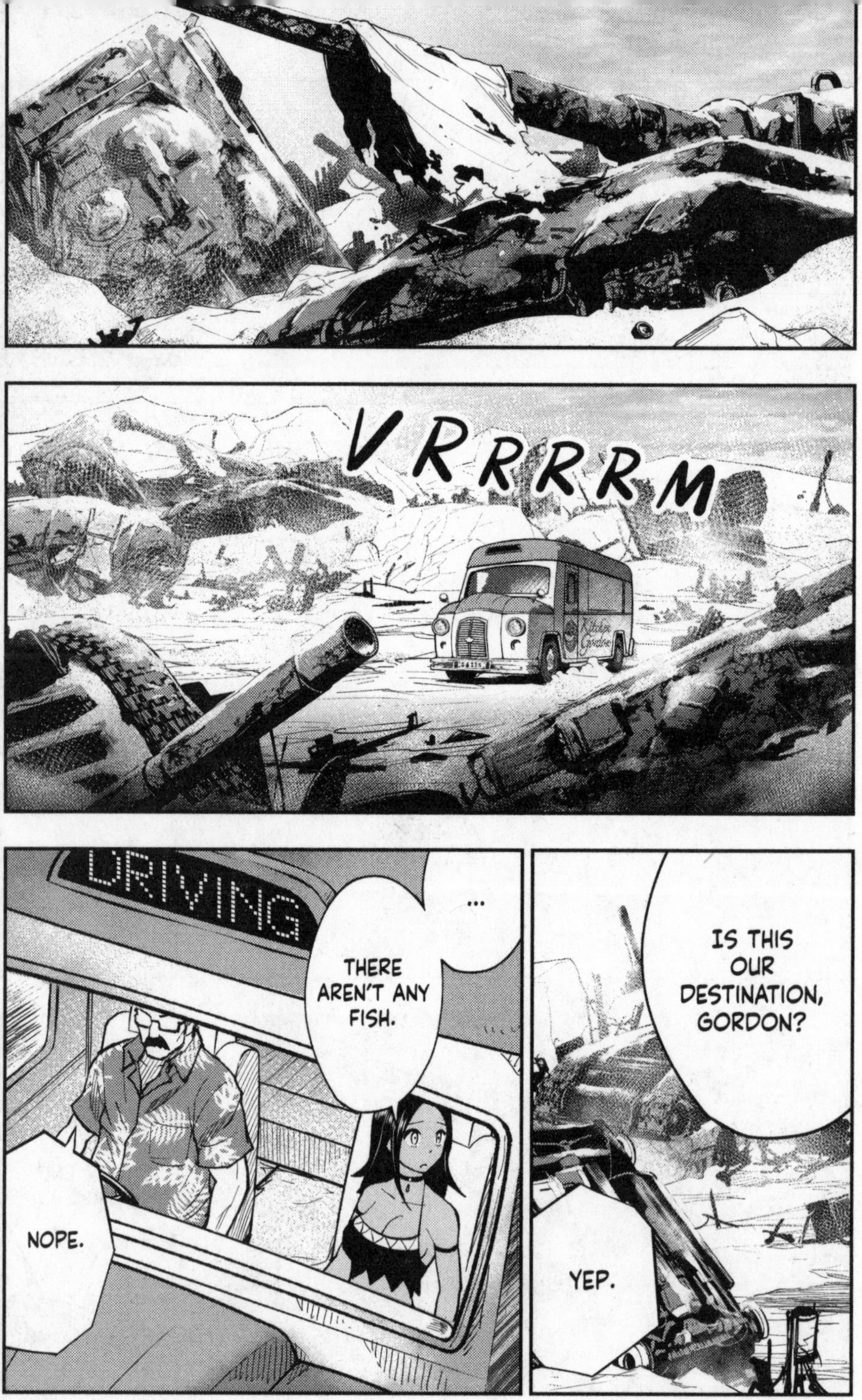
VRRRRM
IS THIS OUR DESTINATION, GORDON?
YEP.
... THERE AREN'T ANY FISH.
DRIVING
NOPE.

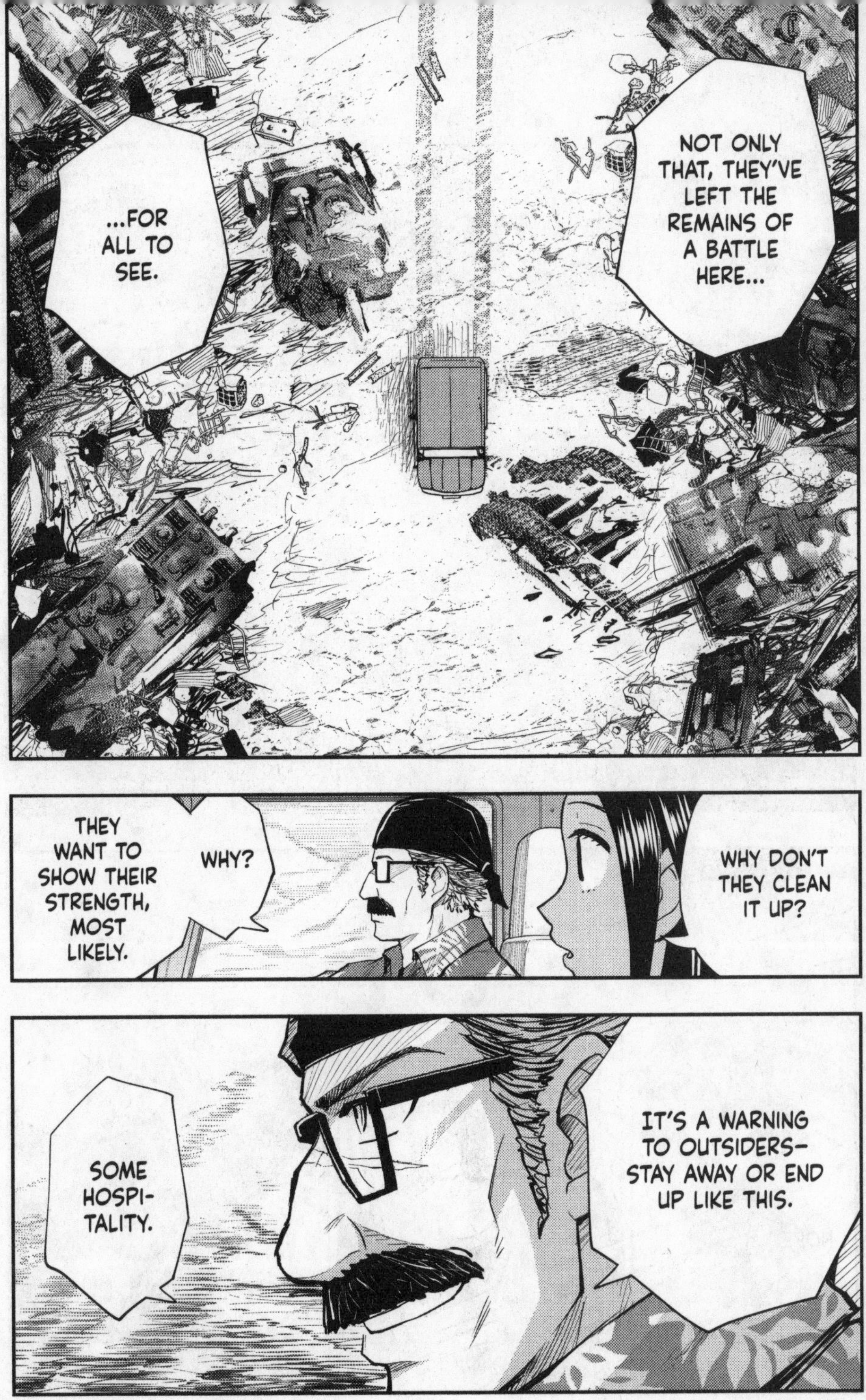
NOT ONLY THAT, THEY'VE LEFT THE REMAINS OF A BATTLE HERE...
...FOR ALL TO SEE.
WHY DON'T THEY CLEAN IT UP?
WHY?
THEY WANT TO SHOW THEIR STRENGTH, MOST LIKELY.
IT'S A WARNING TO OUTSIDERS— STAY AWAY OR END UP LIKE THIS.
SOME HOSPI- TALITY.

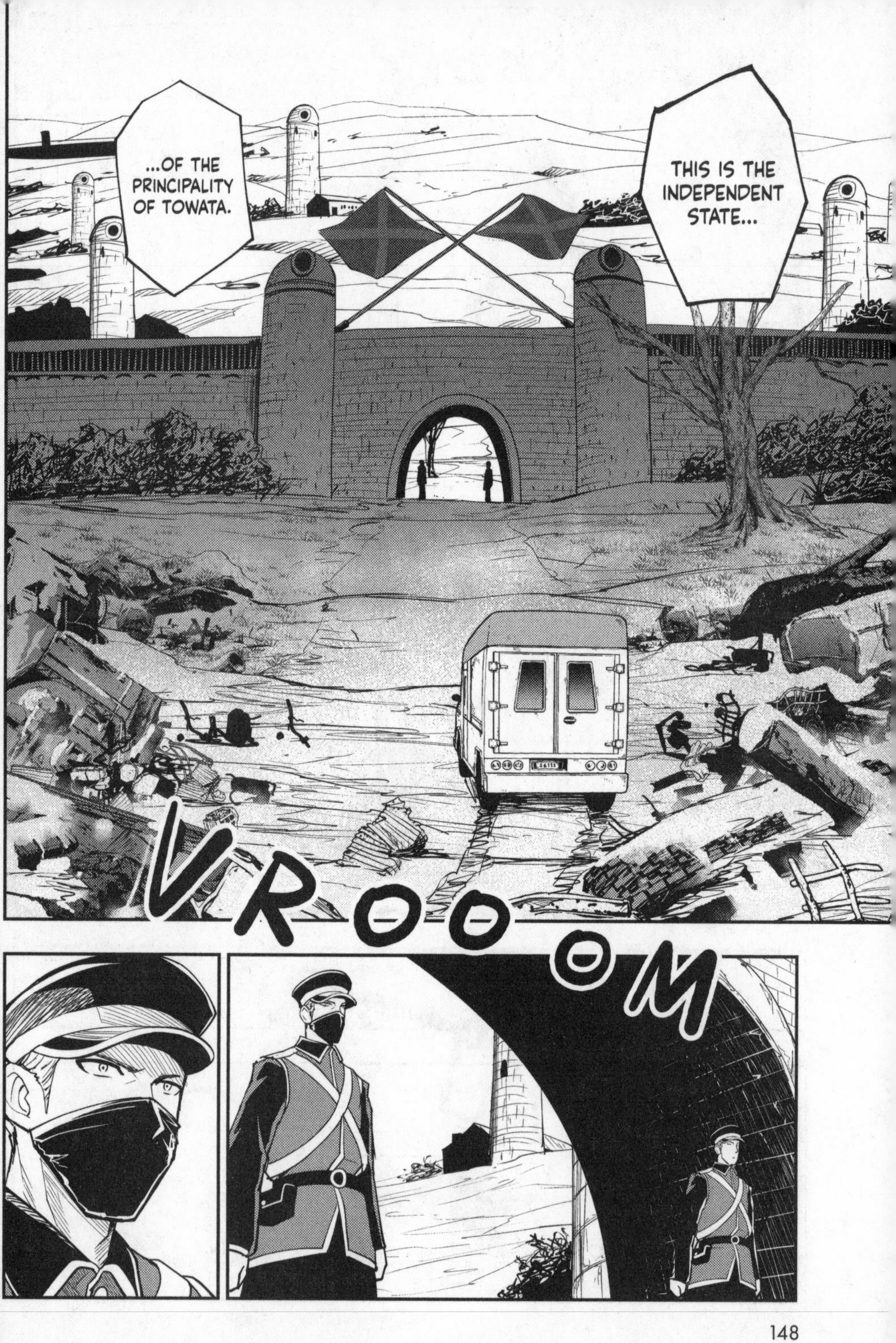
THIS IS THE INDEPENDENT STATE...
...OF THE PRINCIPALITY OF TOWATA.
VROOOOM

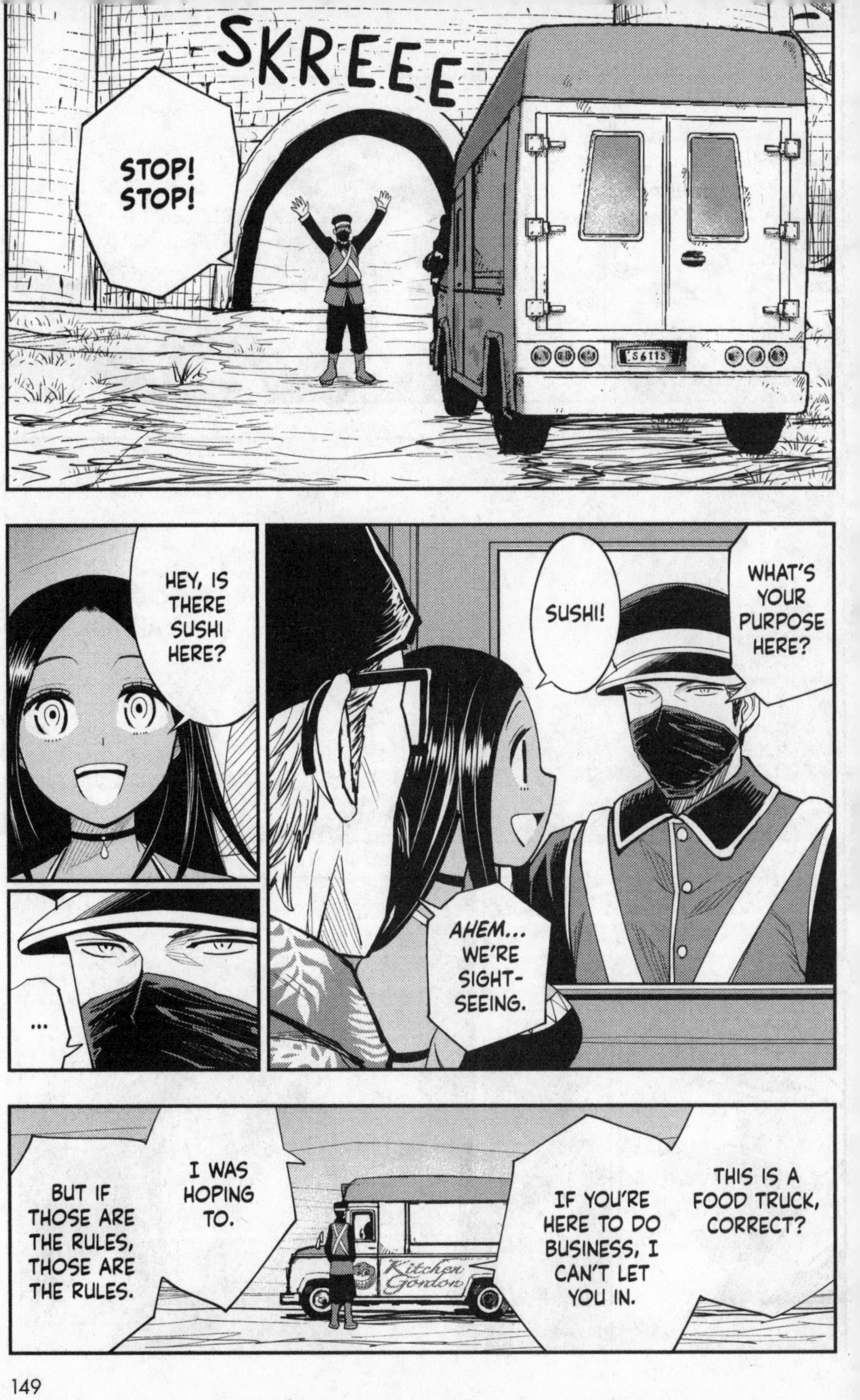
SKREEE
STOP! STOP!
WHAT'S YOUR PURPOSE HERE?
SUSHI!
AHEM... WE'RE SIGHT-SEEING.
HEY, IS THERE SUSHI HERE?
...
THIS IS A FOOD TRUCK, CORRECT?
IF YOU'RE HERE TO DO BUSINESS, I CAN'T LET YOU IN.
Kitchen Gondon
I WAS HOPING TO.
BUT IF THOSE ARE THE RULES, THOSE ARE THE RULES.

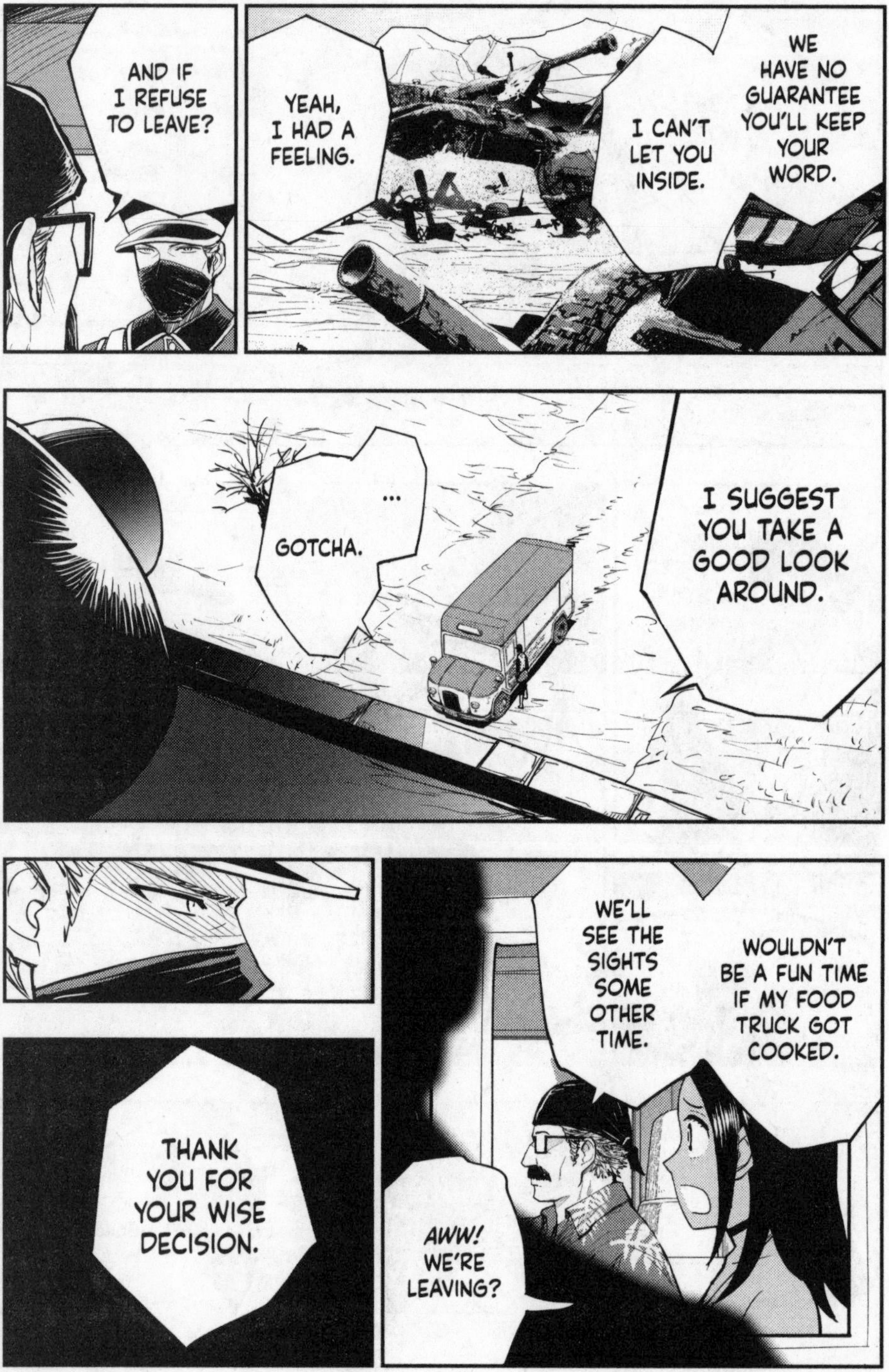
WE HAVE NO GUARANTEE YOU'LL KEEP YOUR WORD.
I CAN'T LET YOU INSIDE.
YEAH, I HAD A FEELING.
AND IF I REFUSE TO LEAVE?
I SUGGEST YOU TAKE A GOOD LOOK AROUND.
...
GOTCHA.
WOULDN'T BE A FUN TIME IF MY FOOD TRUCK GOT COOKED.
WE'LL SEE THE SIGHTS SOME OTHER TIME.
AWW! WE'RE LEAVING?
THANK YOU FOR YOUR WISE DECISION.

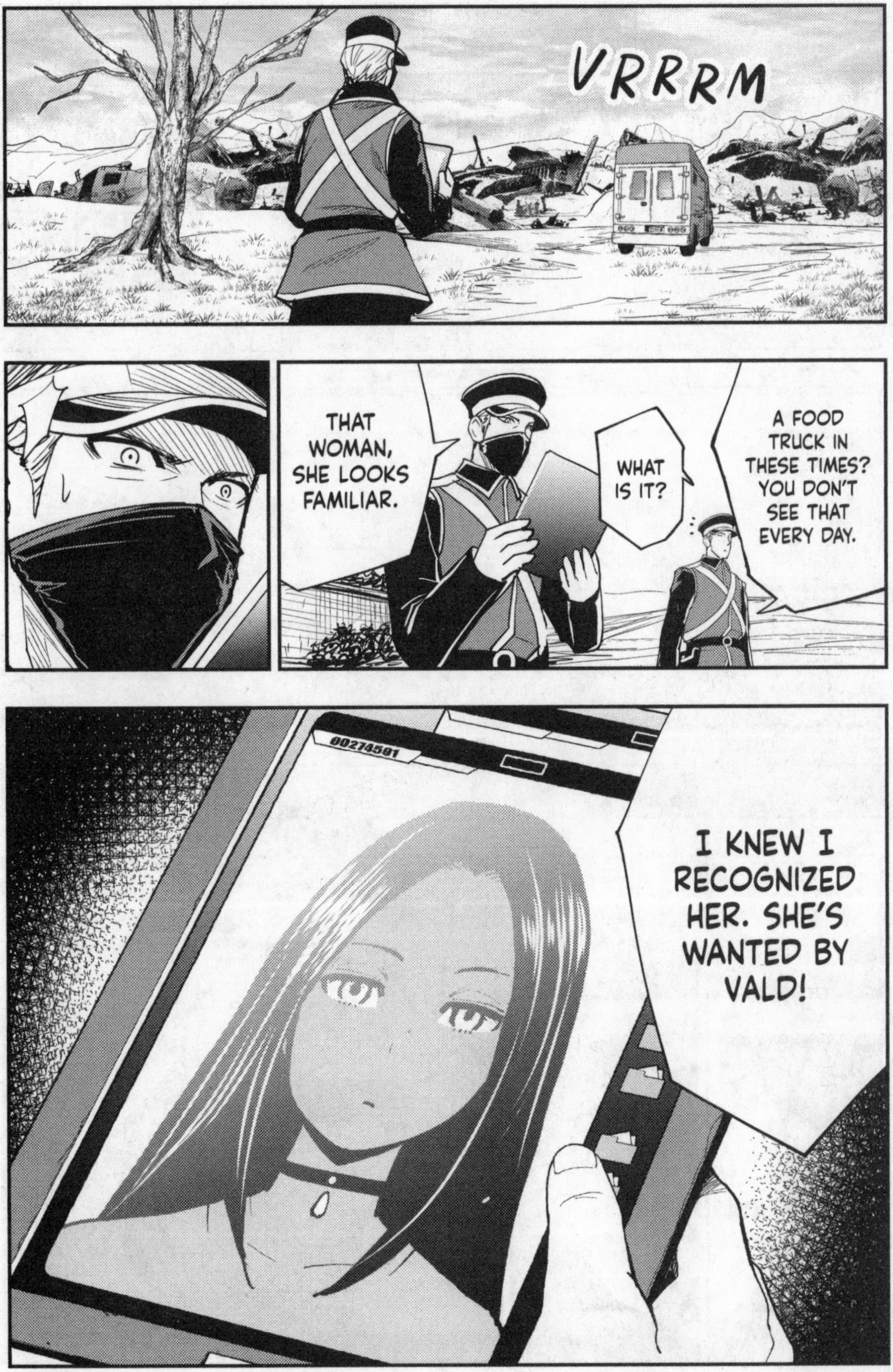
VRRRM
A FOOD TRUCK IN THESE TIMES? YOU DON'T SEE THAT EVERY DAY.
WHAT IS IT?
THAT WOMAN, SHE LOOKS FAMILIAR.
I KNEW I RECOGNIZED HER. SHE'S WANTED BY VALD!

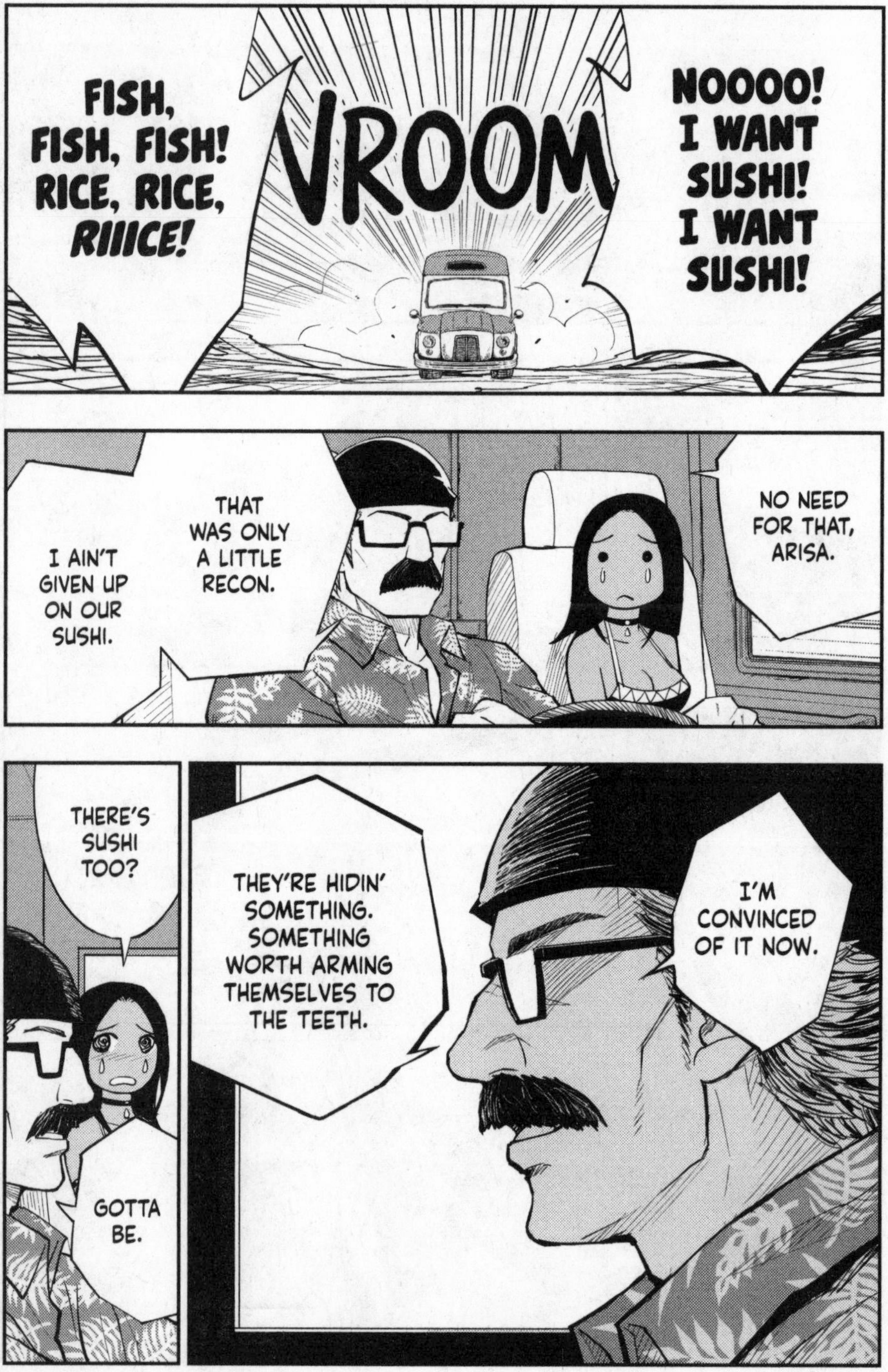
NOOOO! I WANT SUSHI! I WANT SUSHI!
VROOM
FISH, FISH, FISH! RICE, RICE, *RIIICE!*
NO NEED FOR THAT, ARISA.
THAT WAS ONLY A LITTLE RECON.
I AIN'T GIVEN UP ON OUR SUSHI.
I'M CONVINCED OF IT NOW.
THEY'RE HIDIN' SOMETHING. SOMETHING WORTH ARMING THEMSELVES TO THE TEETH.
THERE'S SUSHI TOO?
GOTTA BE.

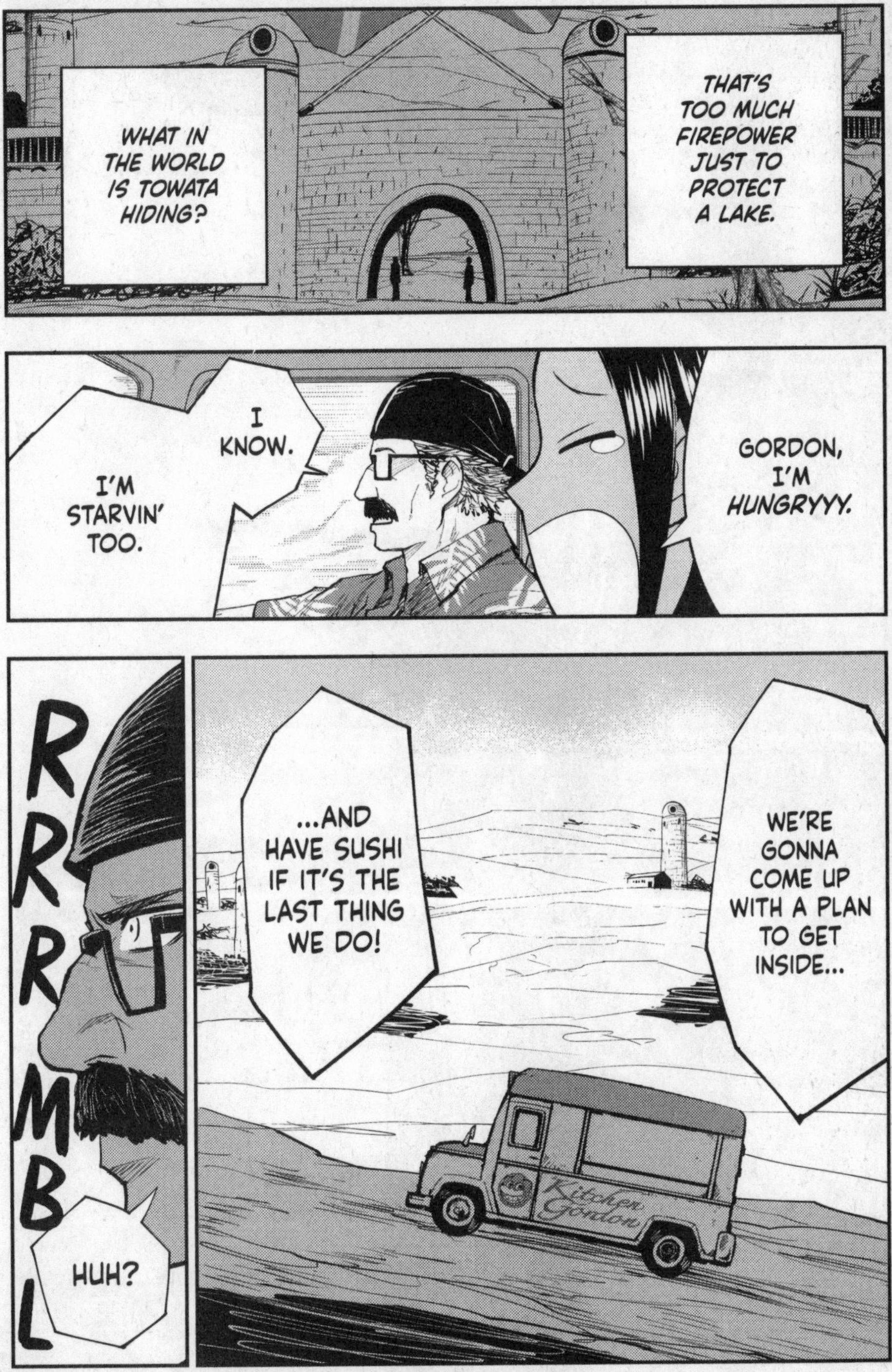
THAT'S TOO MUCH FIREPOWER JUST TO PROTECT A LAKE.
WHAT IN THE WORLD IS TOWATA HIDING?
GORDON, I'M HUNGRYYY.
I KNOW.
I'M STARVIN' TOO.
WE'RE GONNA COME UP WITH A PLAN TO GET INSIDE...
...AND HAVE SUSHI IF IT'S THE LAST THING WE DO!
Kitchen Gordon
RRRRMBL
HUH?

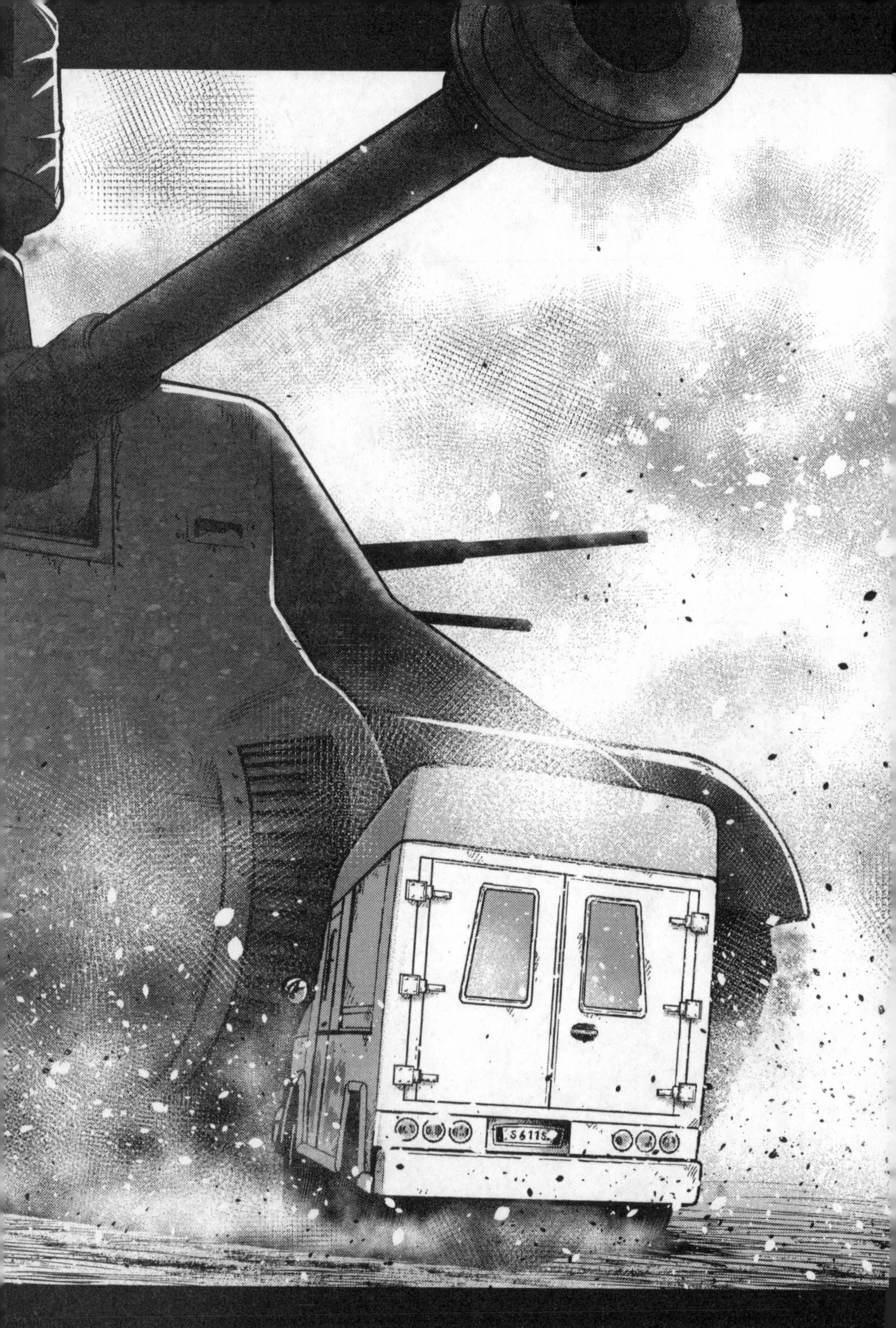

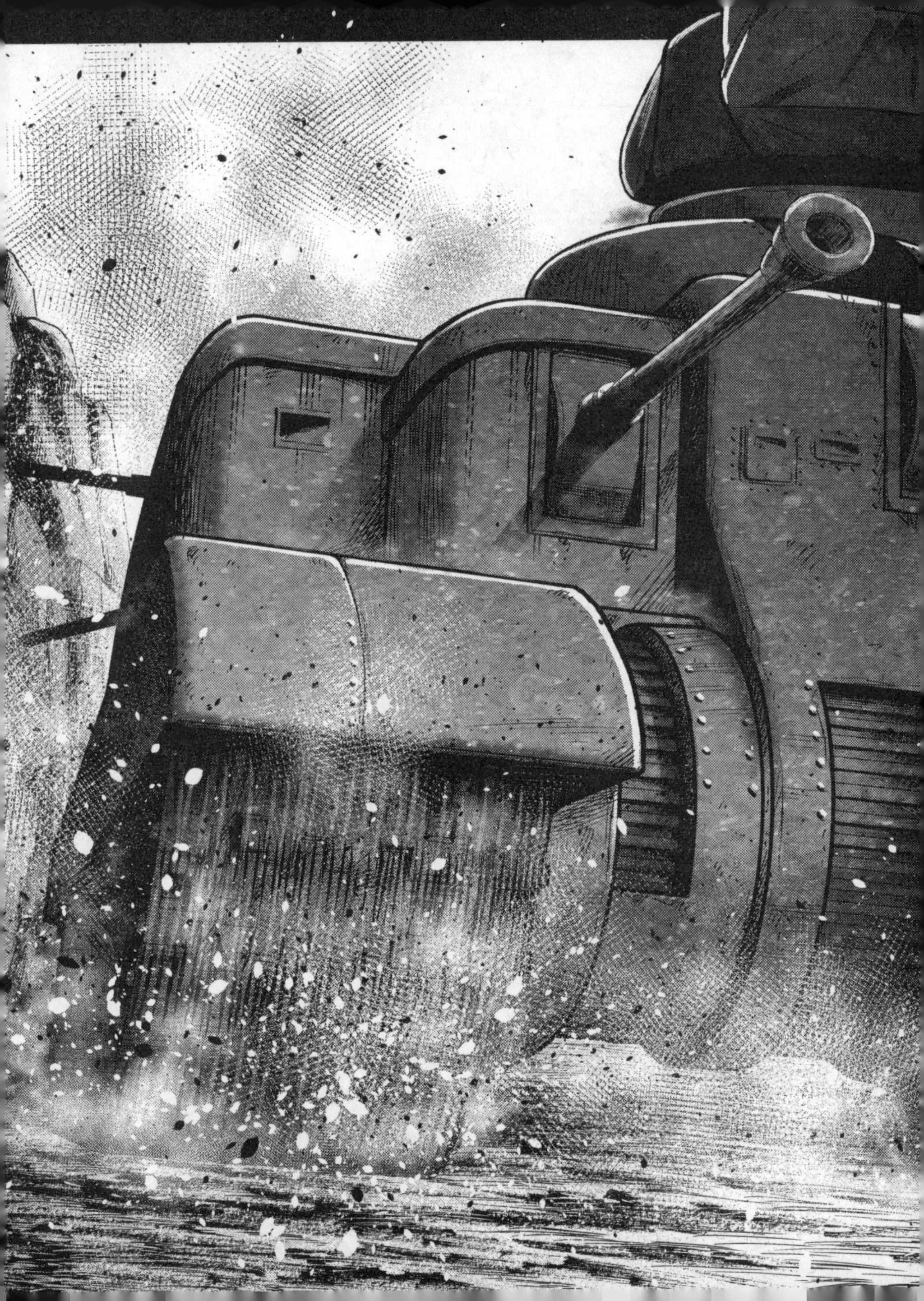

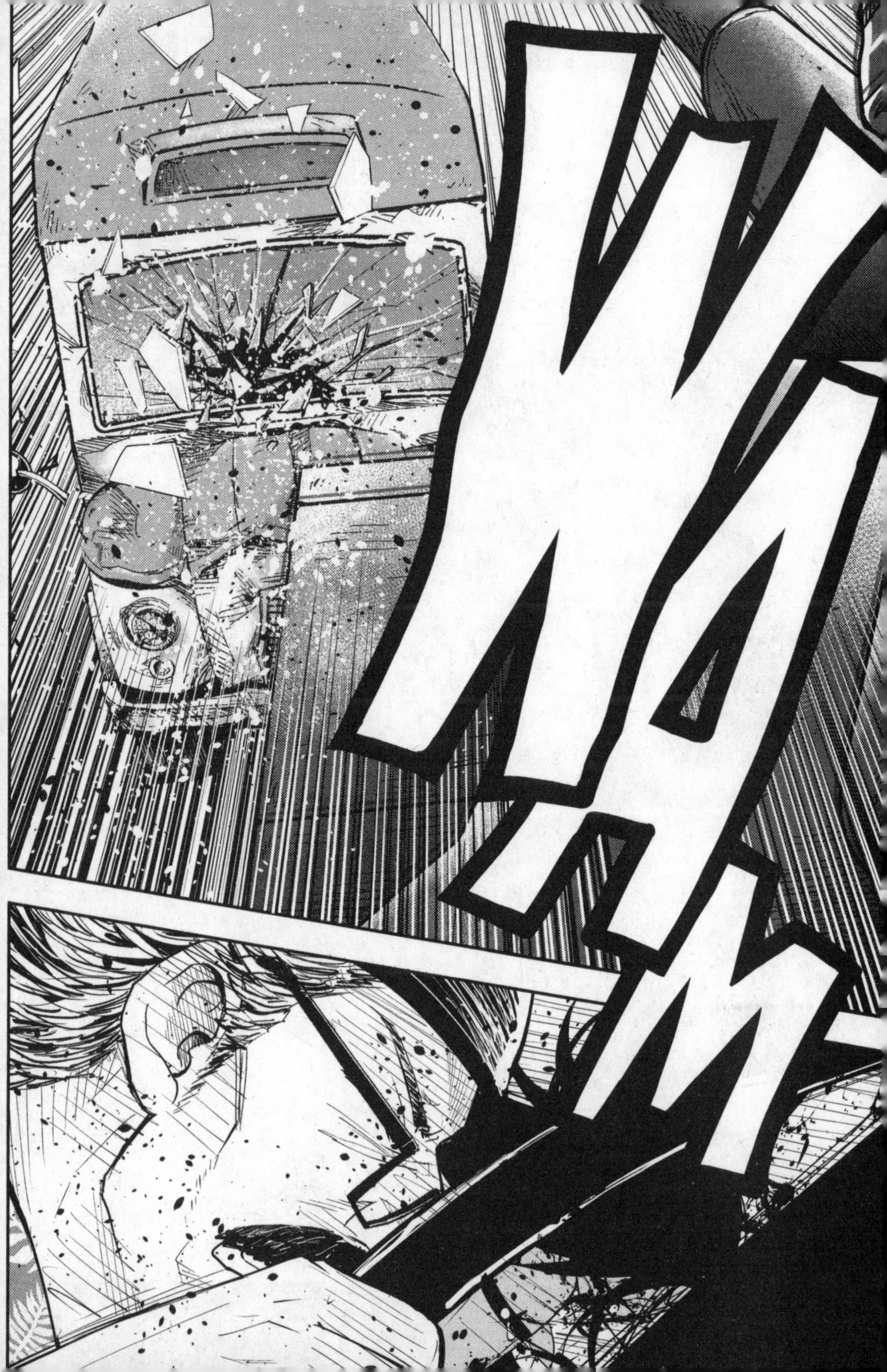
WHAM

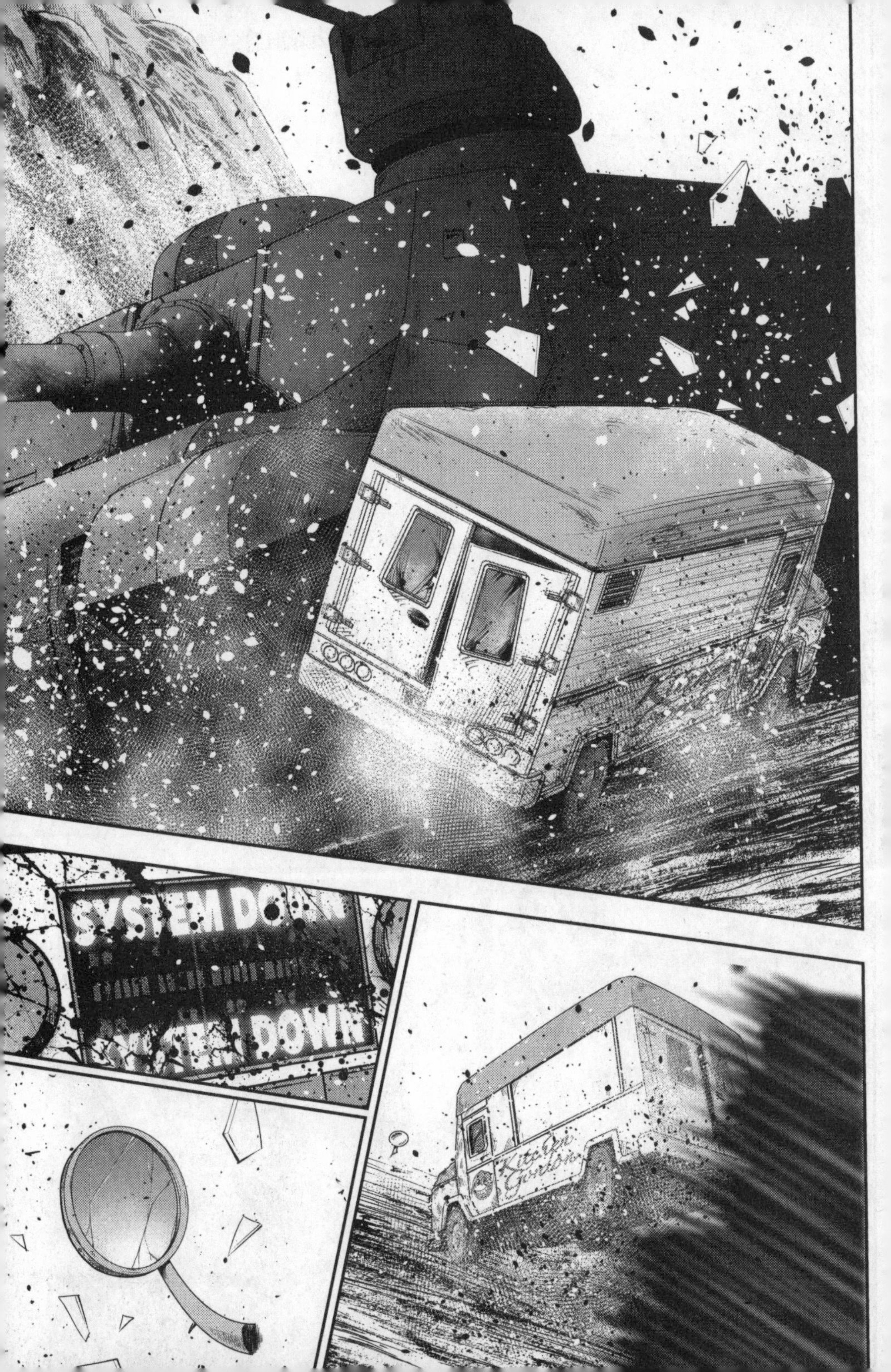
Kitchen Gordon
SYSTEM DOWN

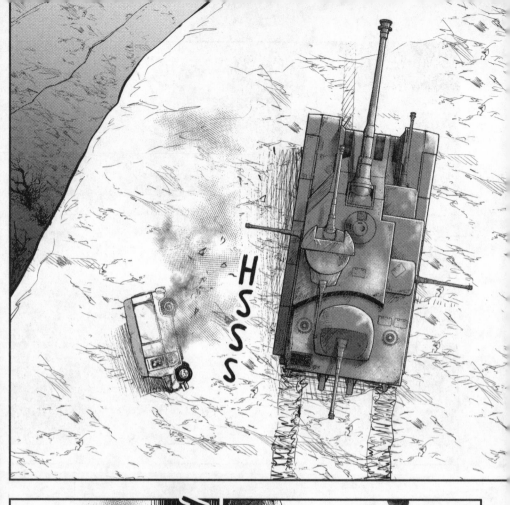

HSSS

TMP

KLNK

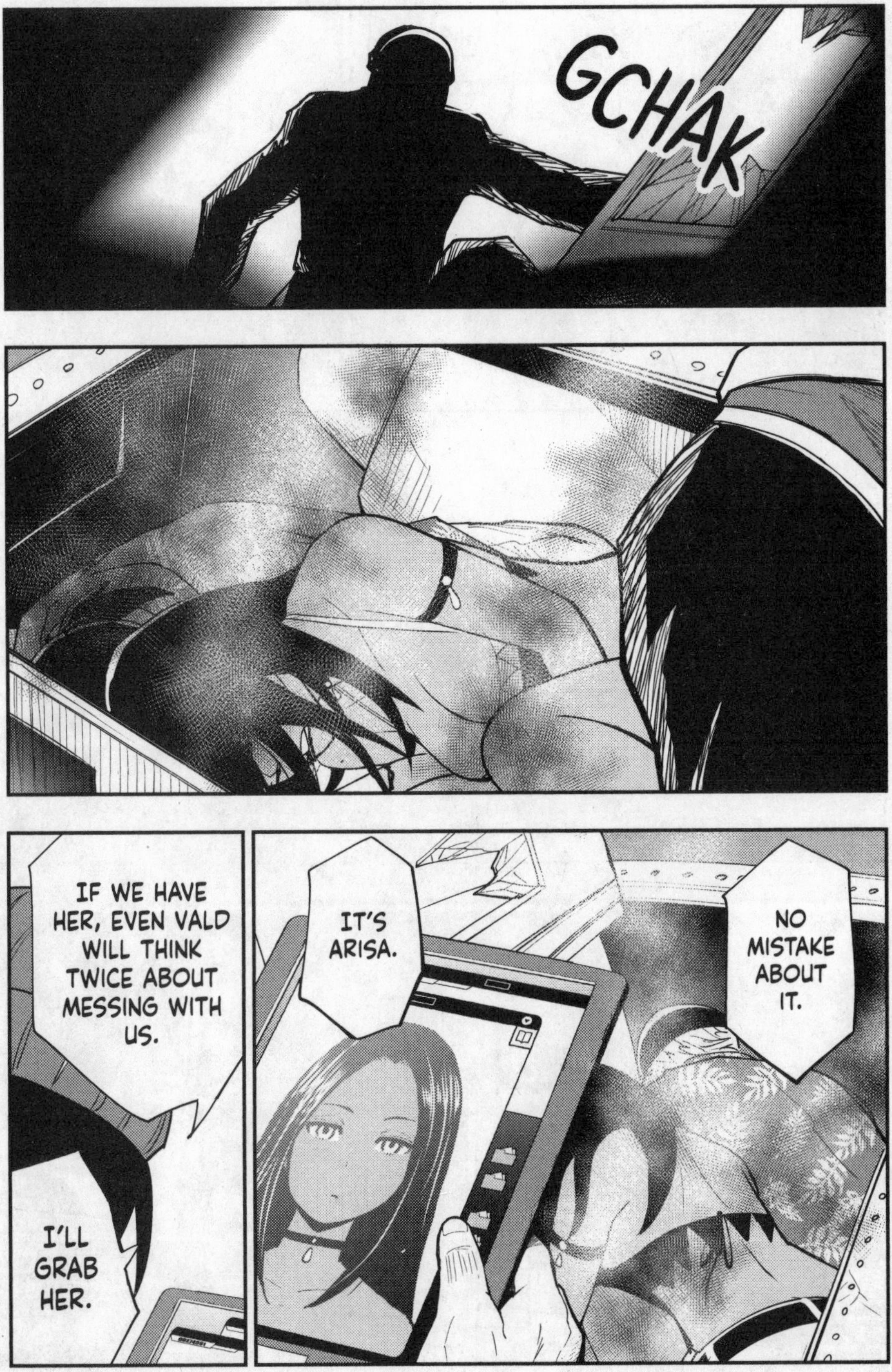
GCHAK
NO MISTAKE ABOUT IT.
IT'S ARISA.
IF WE HAVE HER, EVEN VALD WILL THINK TWICE ABOUT MESSING WITH US.
I'LL GRAB HER.

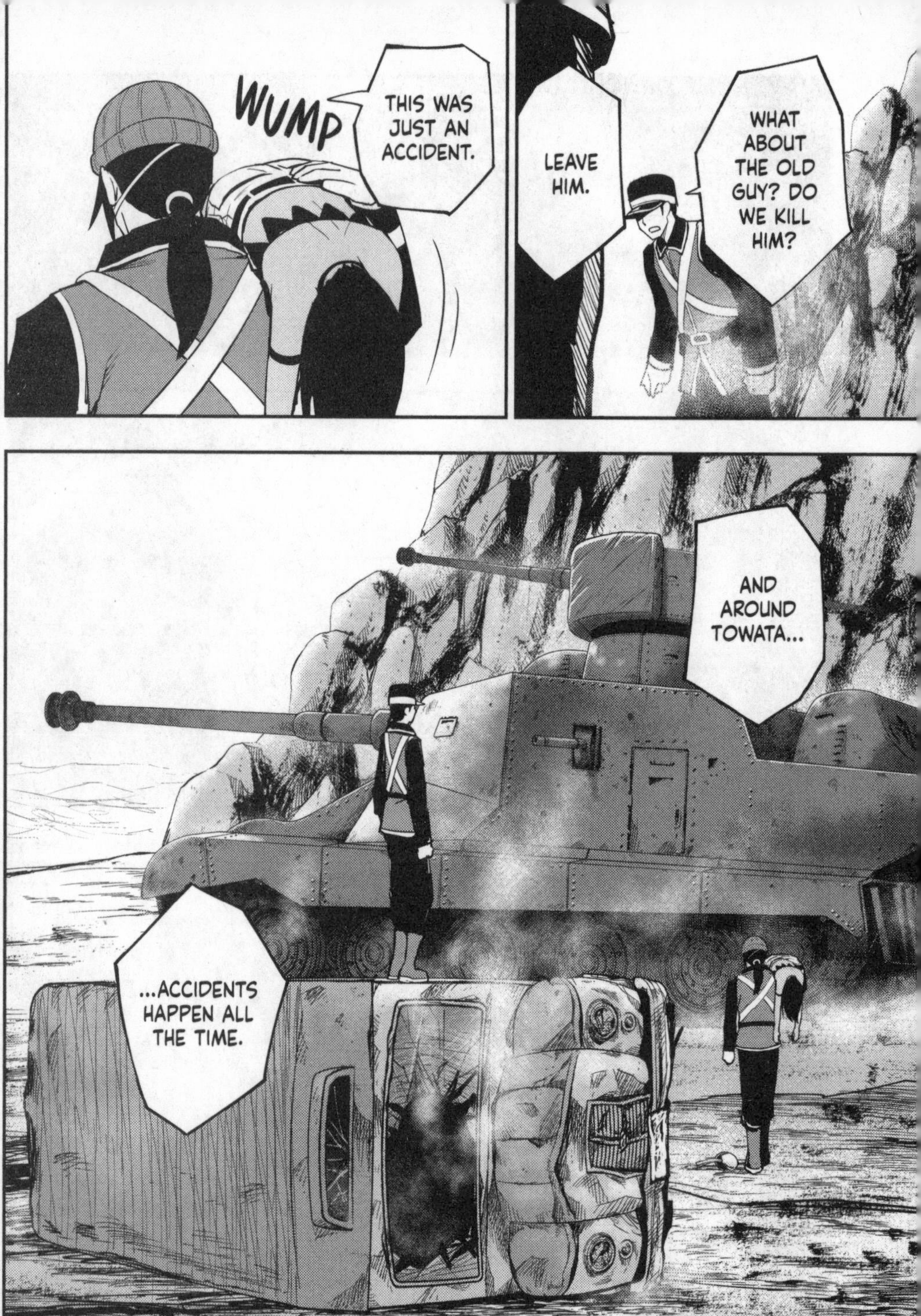
WHAT ABOUT THE OLD GUY? DO WE KILL HIM?
LEAVE HIM.
WUMP
THIS WAS JUST AN ACCIDENT.
AND AROUND TOWATA...
...ACCIDENTS HAPPEN ALL THE TIME.
#9 END

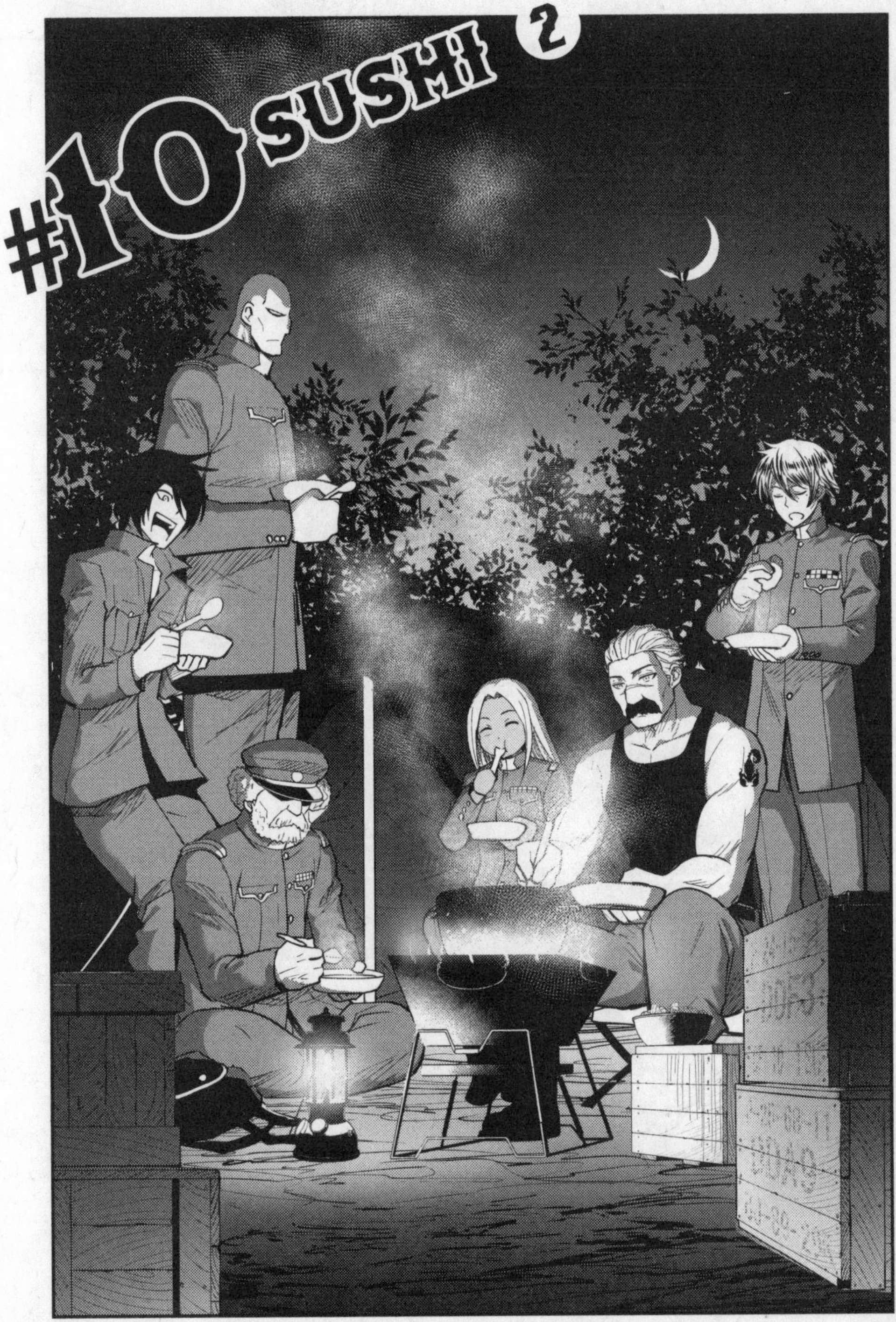
#10 SUSHI 2

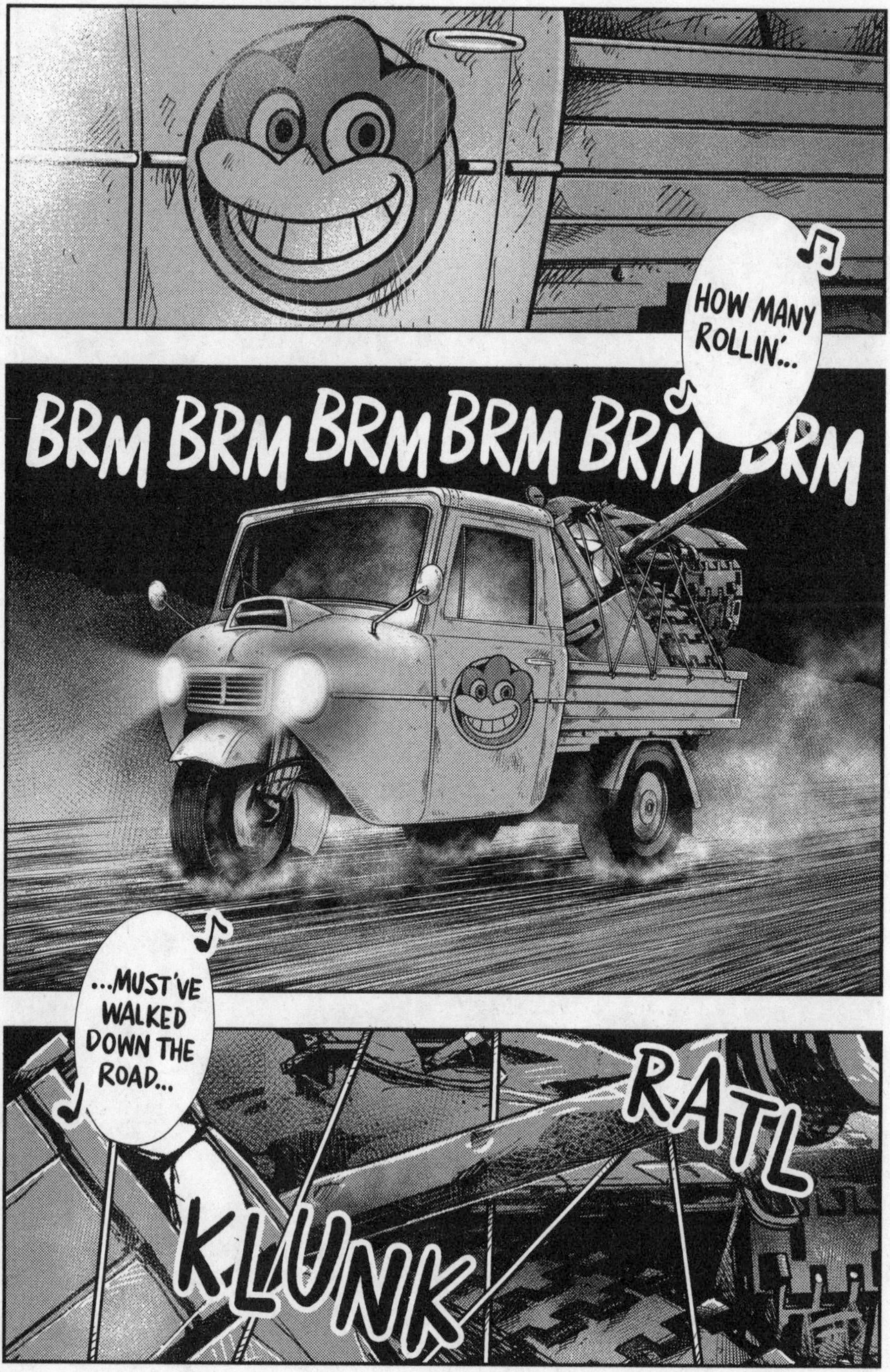
HOW MANY ROLLIN'...
BRM BRM BRM BRM BRM BRM
...MUST'VE WALKED DOWN THE ROAD...
RATL
KLUNK

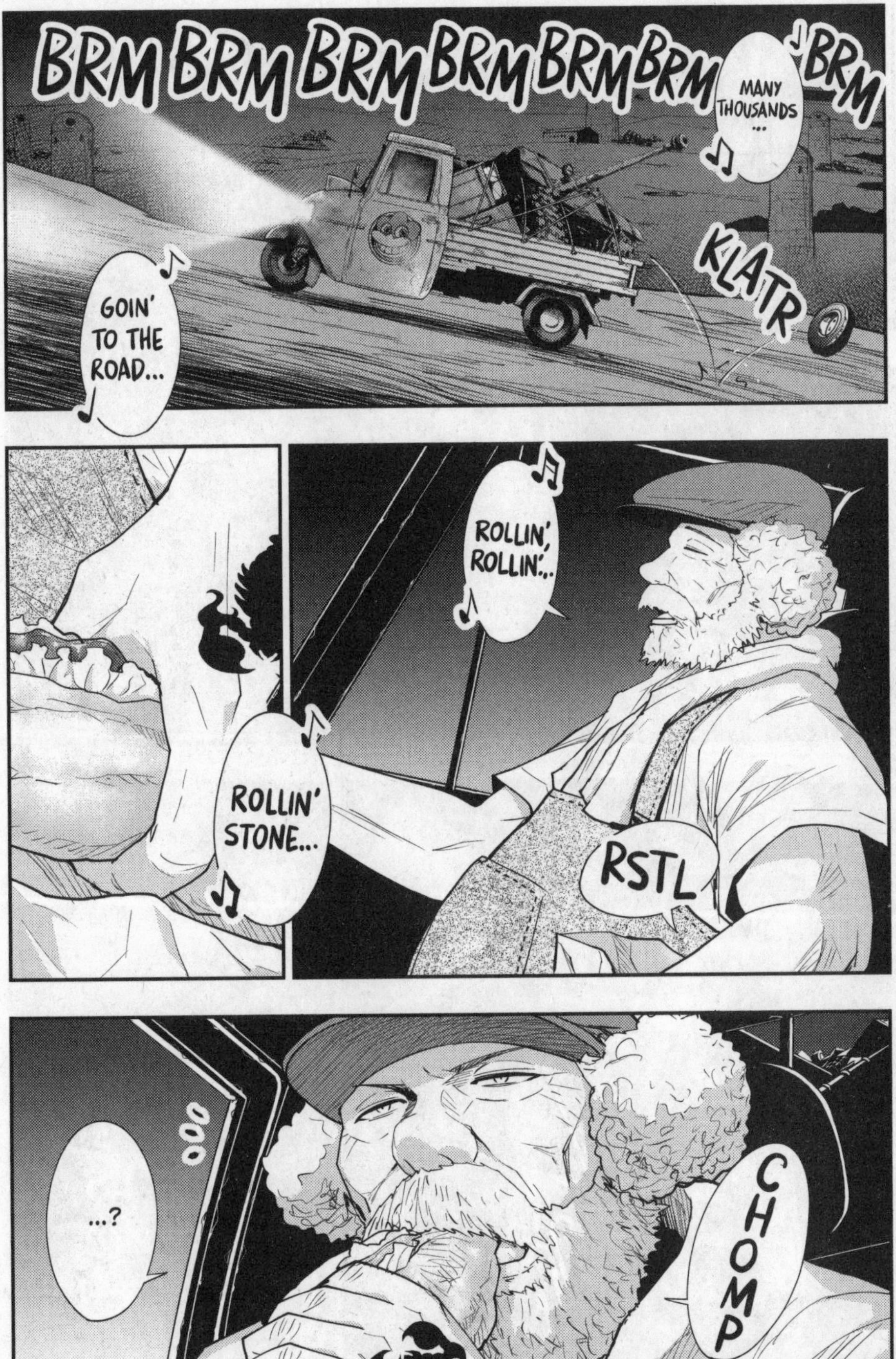
BRM BRM BRM BRM BRM BRM BRM
MANY THOUSANDS...
KLATR
GOIN' TO THE ROAD...
ROLLIN', ROLLIN'...
RSTL
ROLLIN' STONE...
CHOMP
...?
ooo

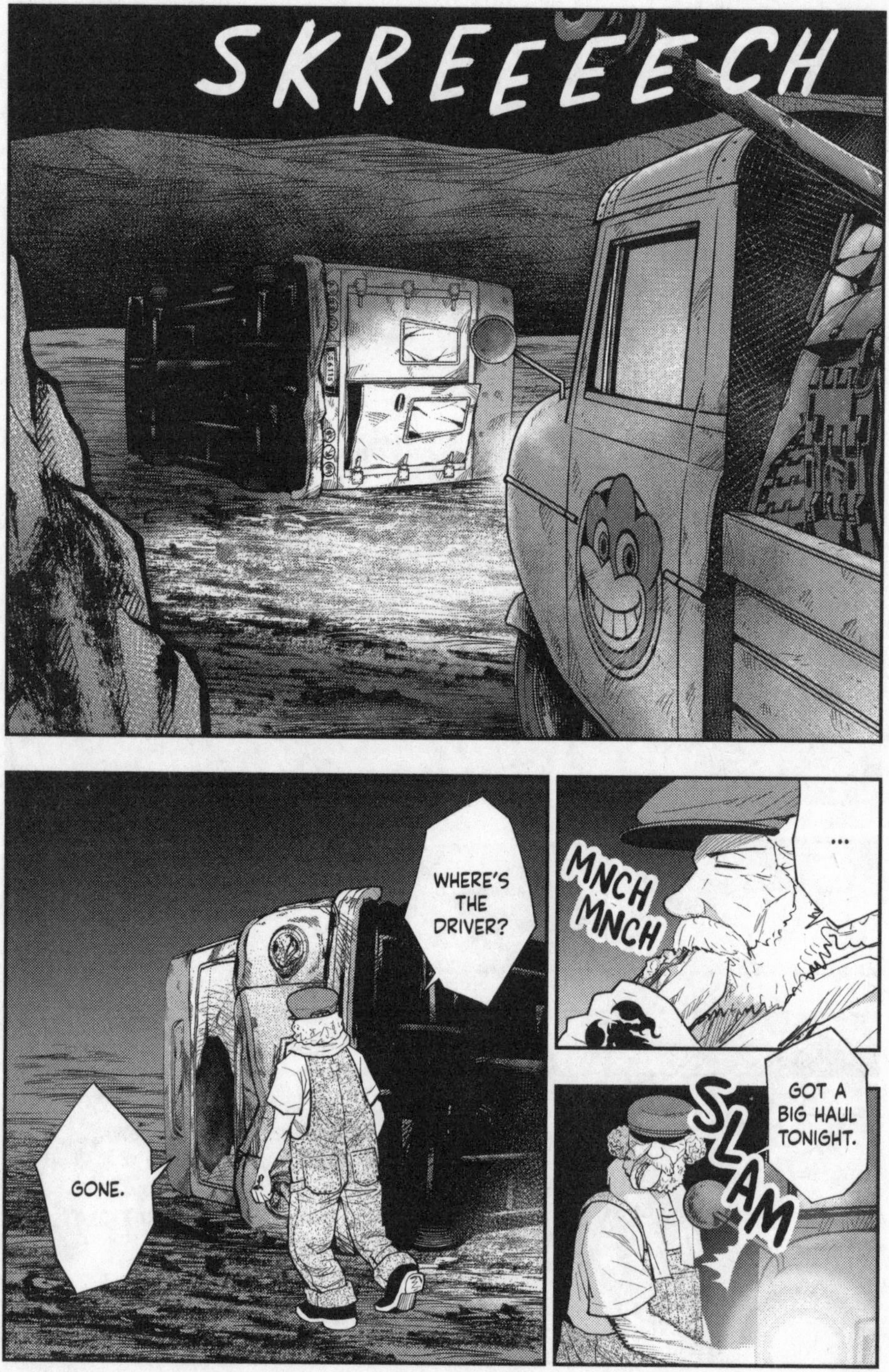
SKREEEECH
...
MNCH MNCH
GOT A BIG HAUL TONIGHT.
SLAM
WHERE'S THE DRIVER?
GONE.

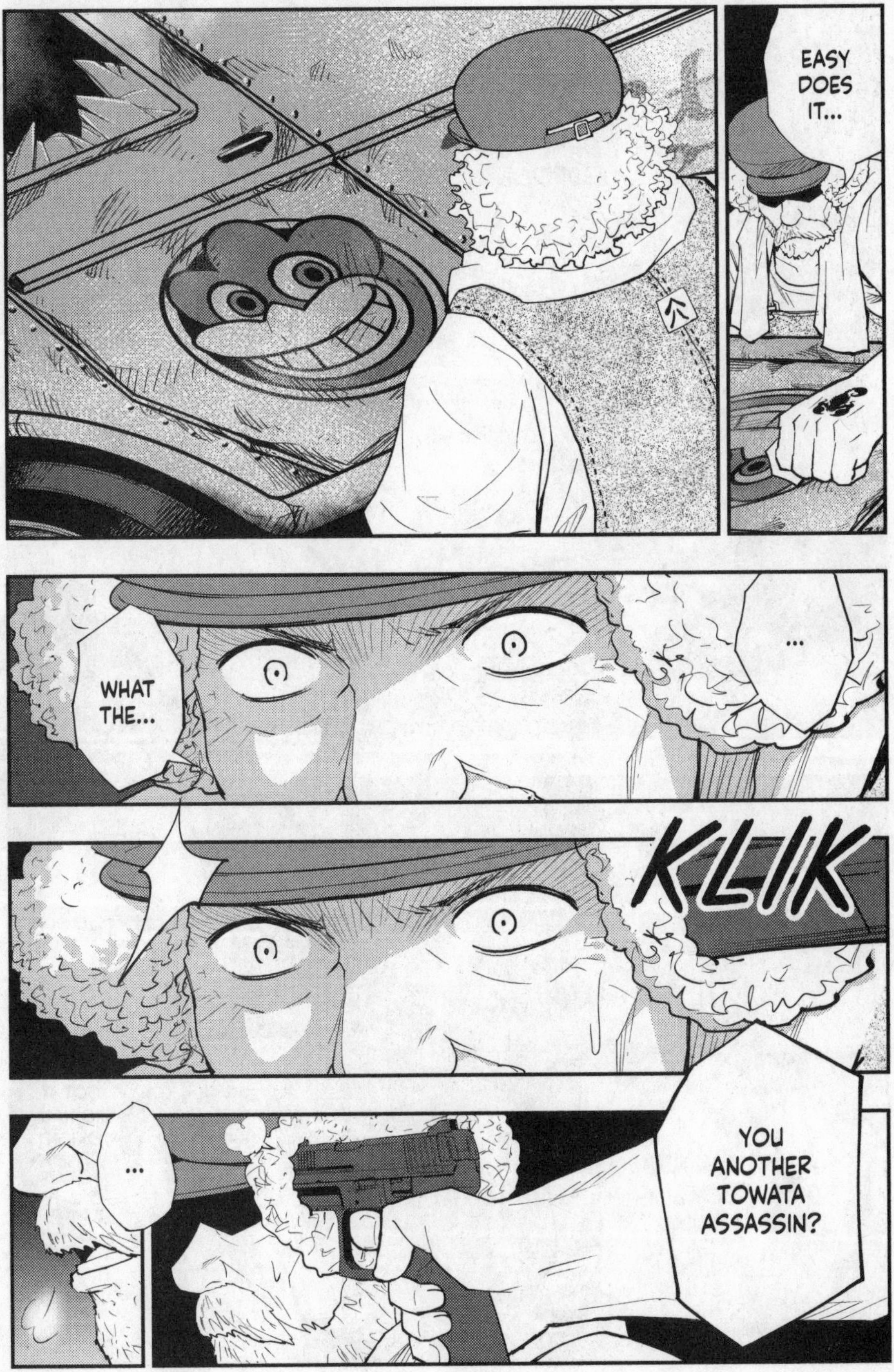
EASY DOES IT...
...
WHAT THE...
KLIK
YOU ANOTHER TOWATA ASSASSIN?
...

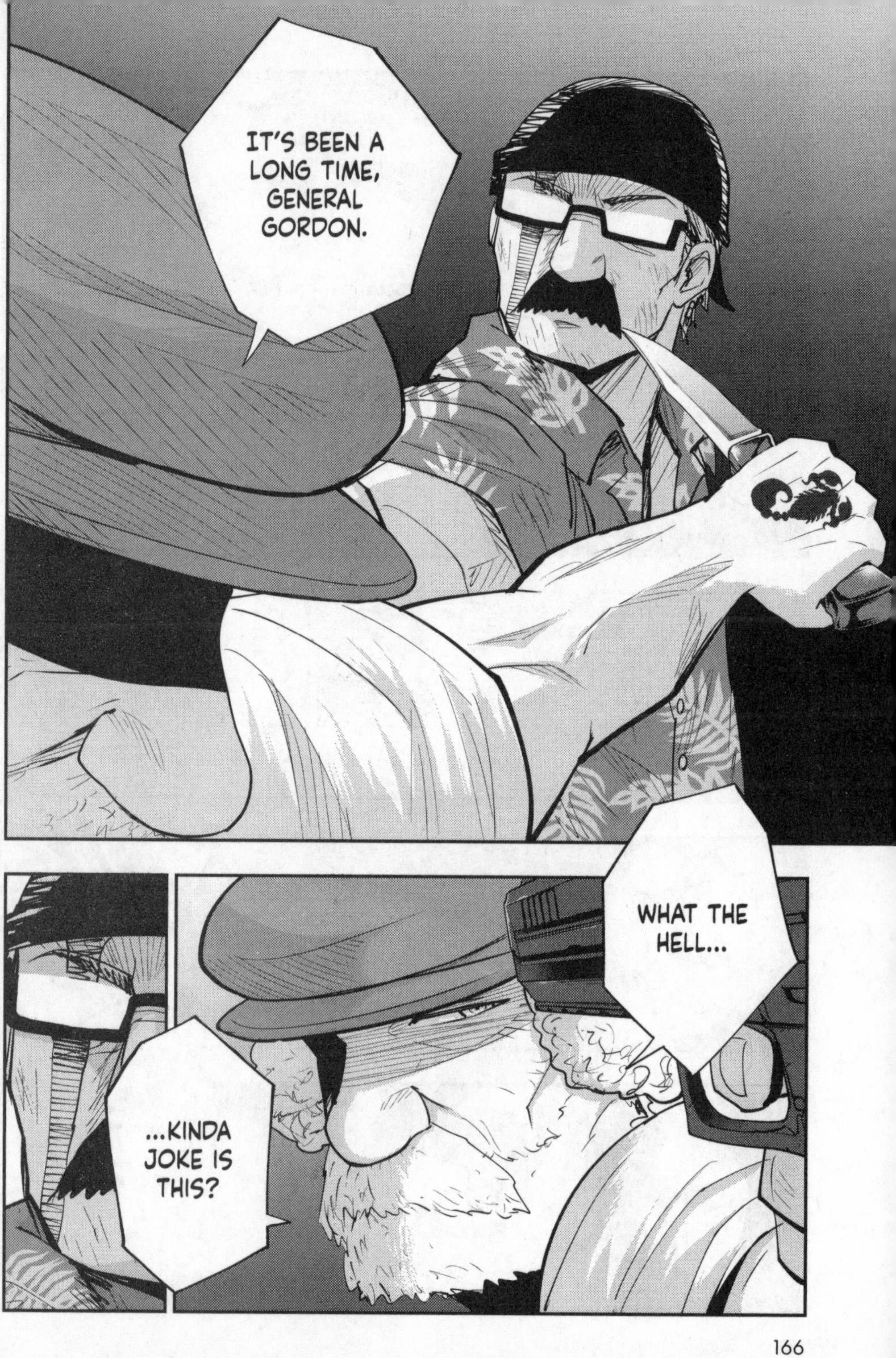
IT'S BEEN A LONG TIME, GENERAL GORDON.
WHAT THE HELL...
...KINDA JOKE IS THIS?

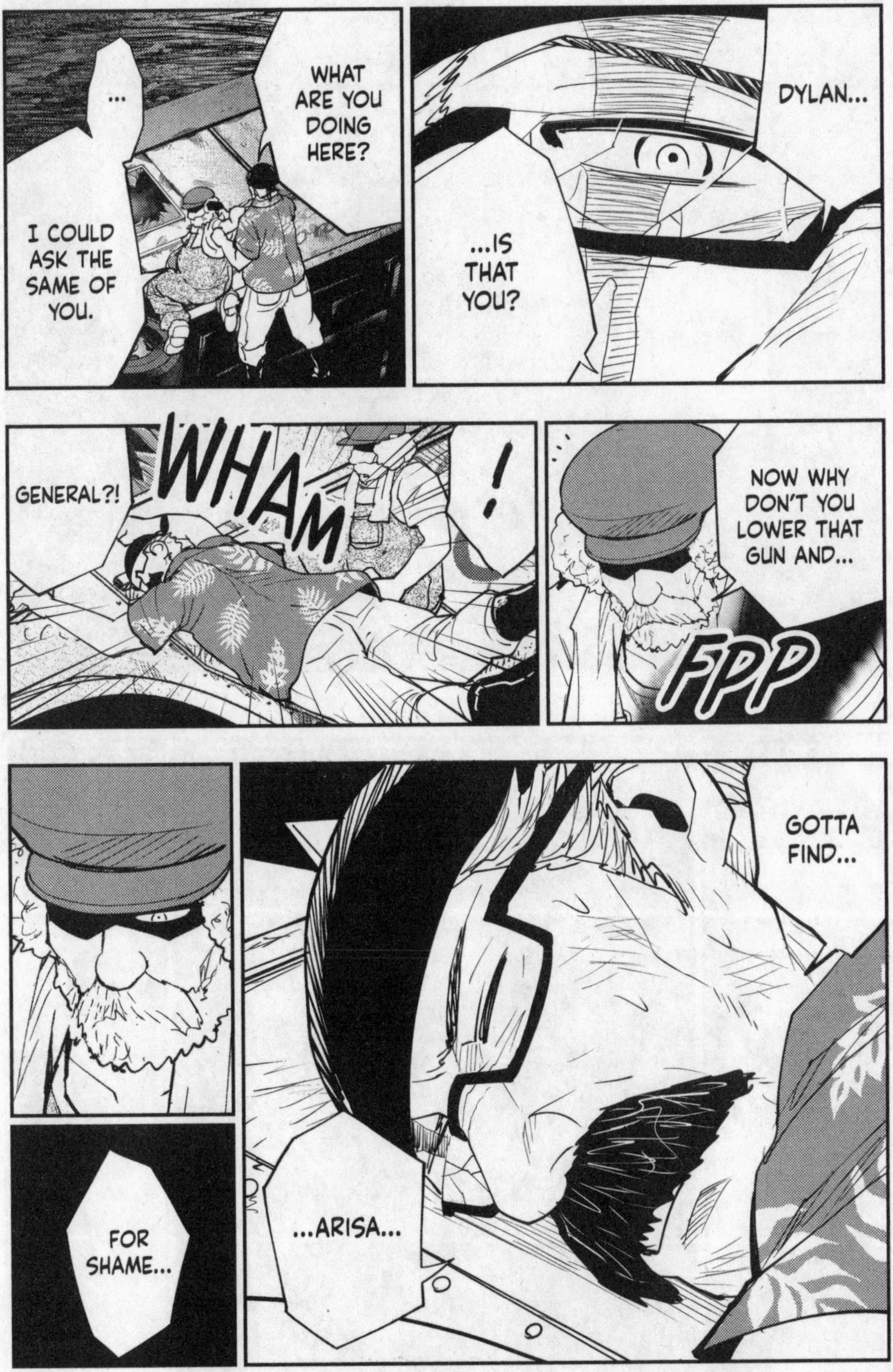
DYLAN...
...IS THAT YOU?
WHAT ARE YOU DOING HERE?
...
I COULD ASK THE SAME OF YOU.
NOW WHY DON'T YOU LOWER THAT GUN AND...
FPP
!
WHAM
GENERAL?!
GOTTA FIND...
...ARISA...
FOR SHAME...

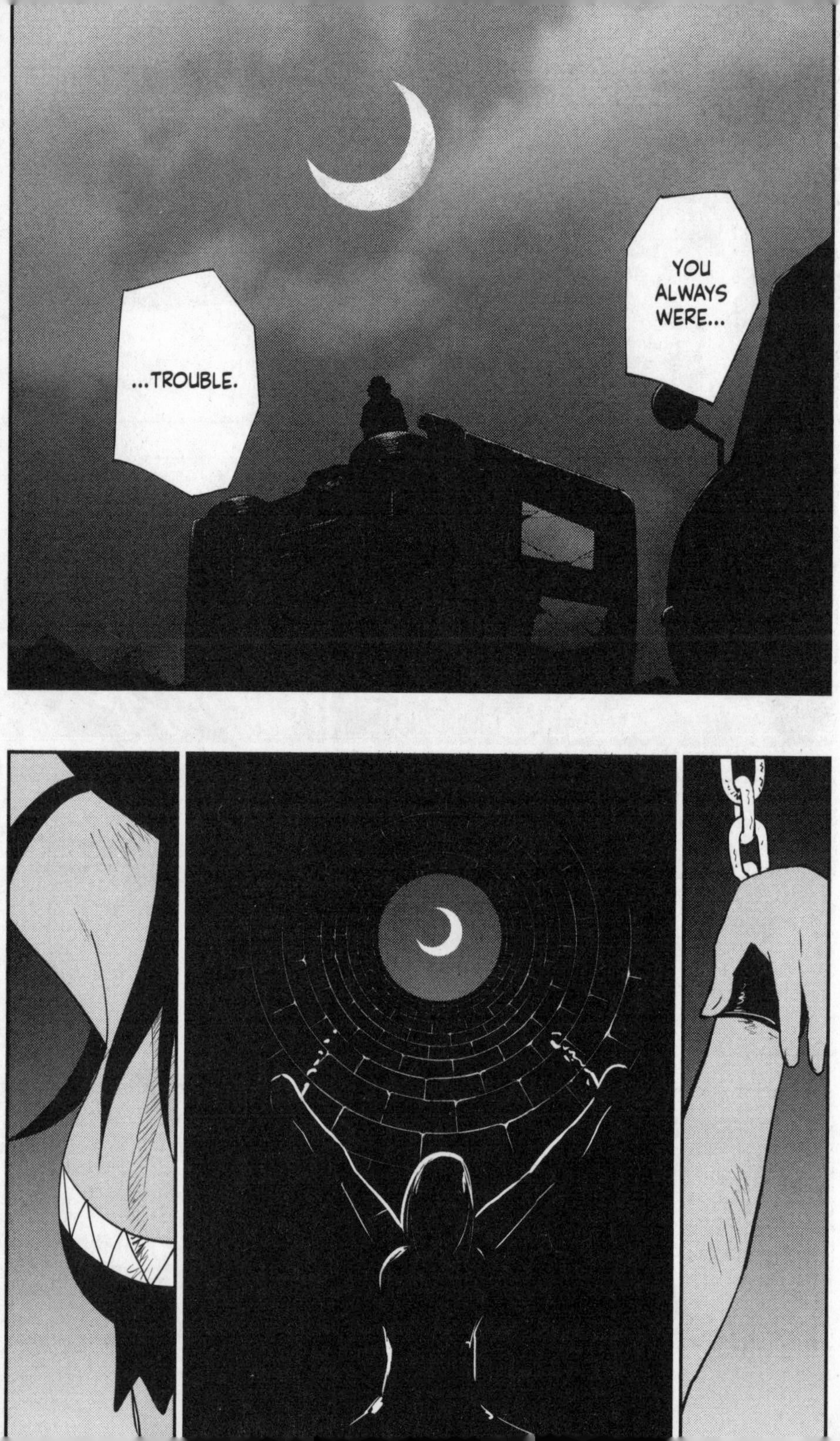
YOU ALWAYS WERE...
...TROUBLE.

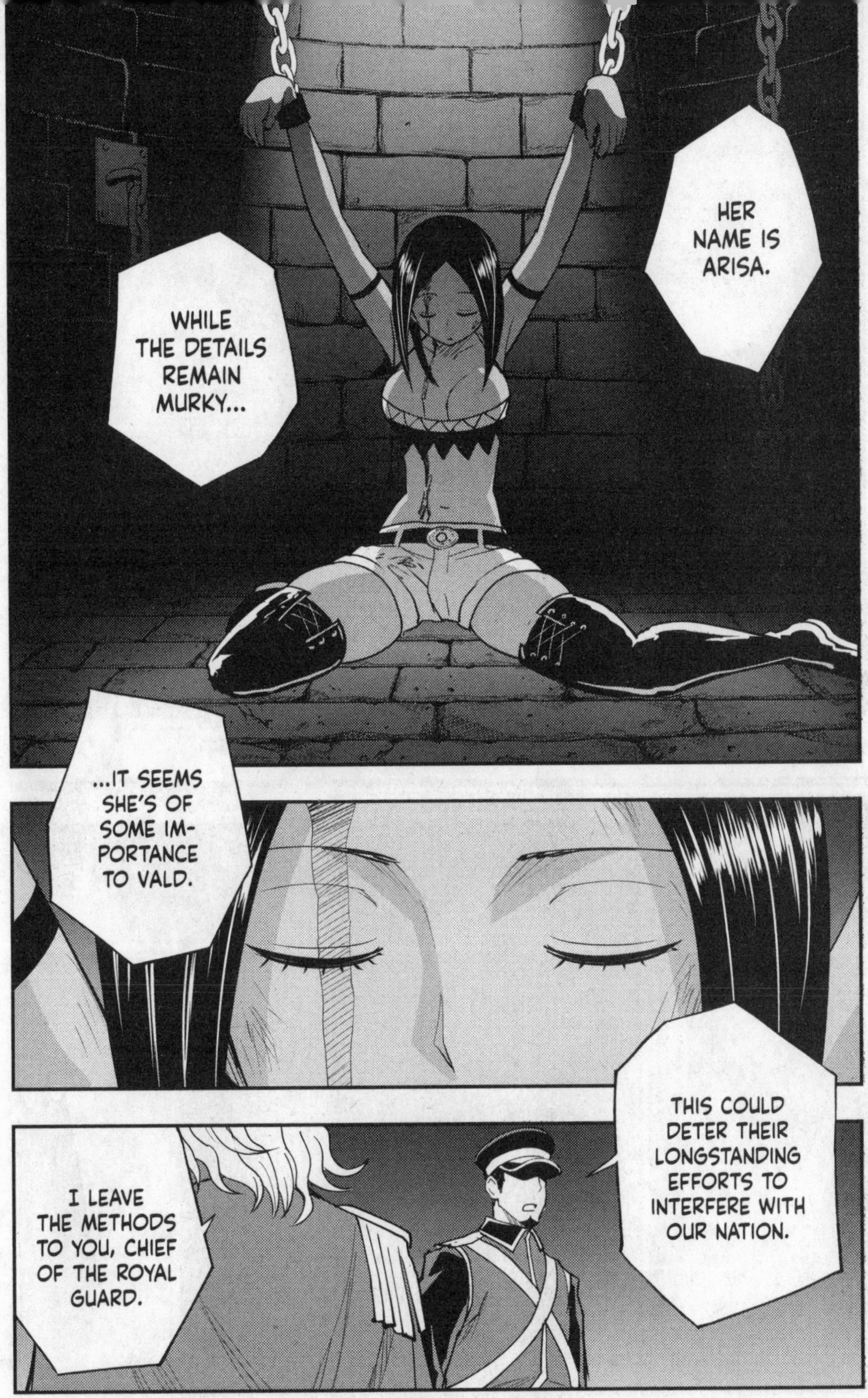
HER NAME IS ARISA.
WHILE THE DETAILS REMAIN MURKY...
...IT SEEMS SHE'S OF SOME IM-PORTANCE TO VALD.
THIS COULD DETER THEIR LONGSTANDING EFFORTS TO INTERFERE WITH OUR NATION.
I LEAVE THE METHODS TO YOU, CHIEF OF THE ROYAL GUARD.

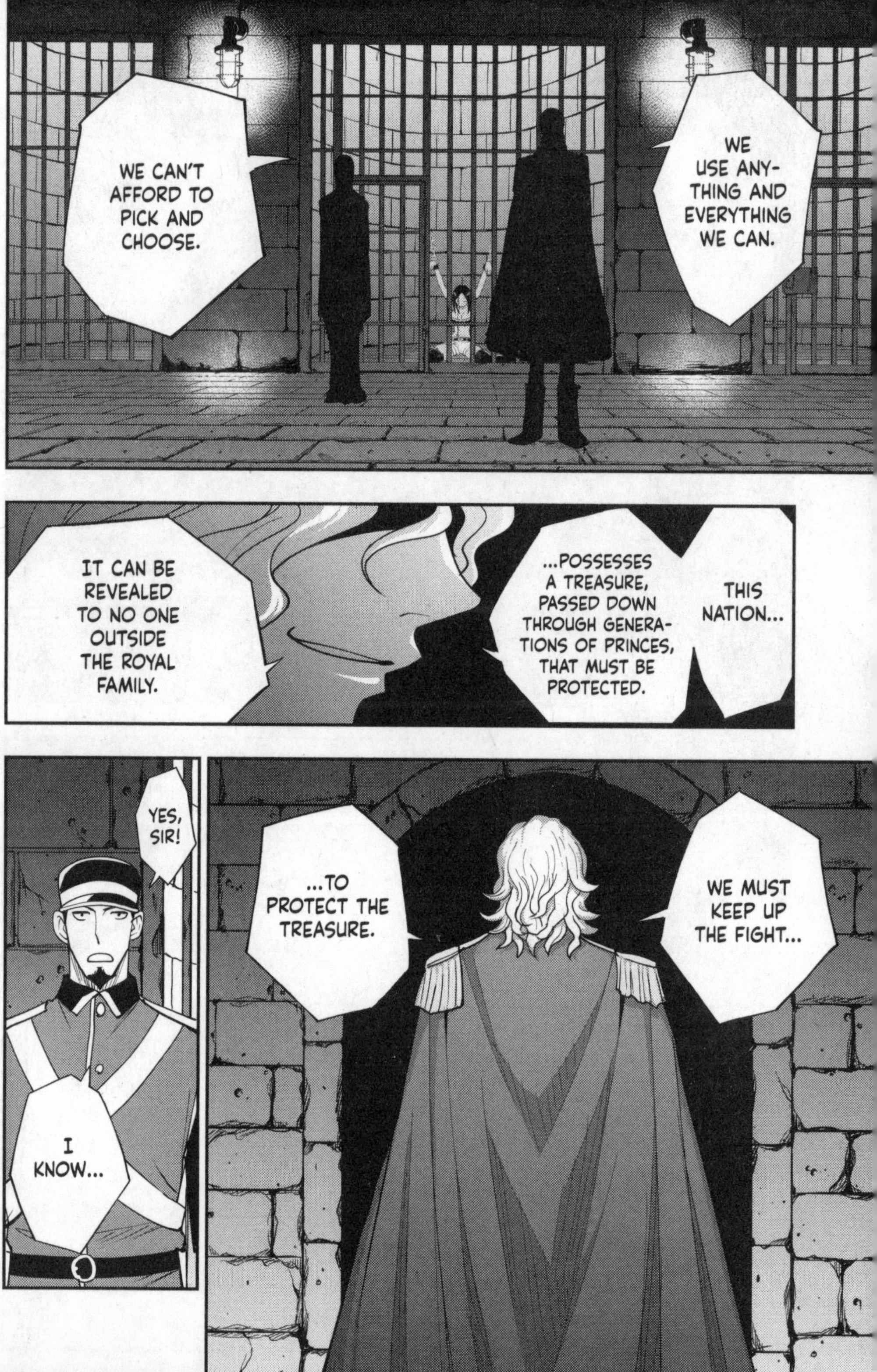
WE USE ANYTHING AND EVERYTHING WE CAN.
WE CAN'T AFFORD TO PICK AND CHOOSE.
THIS NATION...
...POSSESSES A TREASURE, PASSED DOWN THROUGH GENERATIONS OF PRINCES, THAT MUST BE PROTECTED.
IT CAN BE REVEALED TO NO ONE OUTSIDE THE ROYAL FAMILY.
WE MUST KEEP UP THE FIGHT...
...TO PROTECT THE TREASURE.
YES, SIR!
I KNOW...

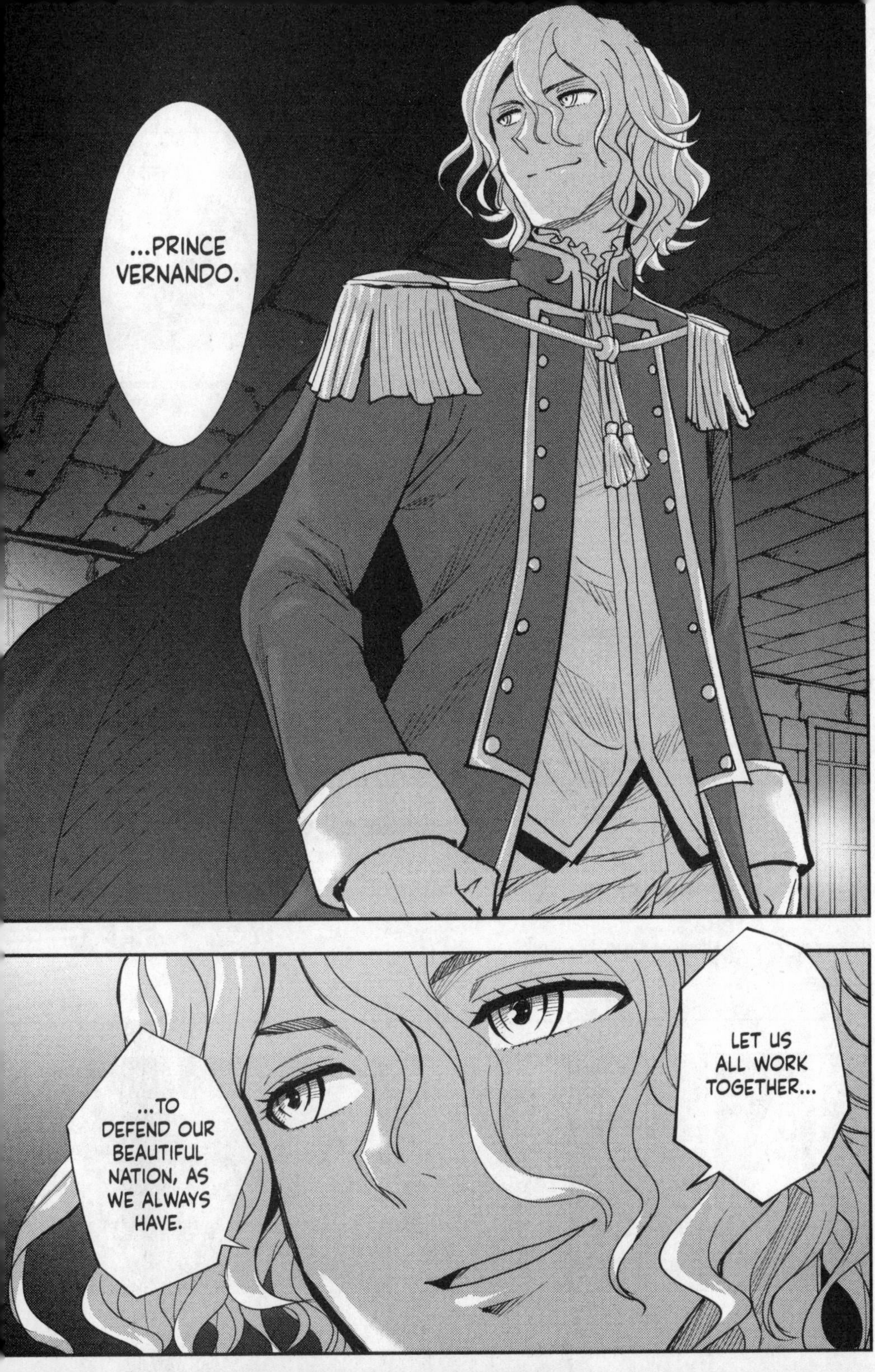
...PRINCE VERNANDO.
LET US ALL WORK TOGETHER...
...TO DEFEND OUR BEAUTIFUL NATION, AS WE ALWAYS HAVE.

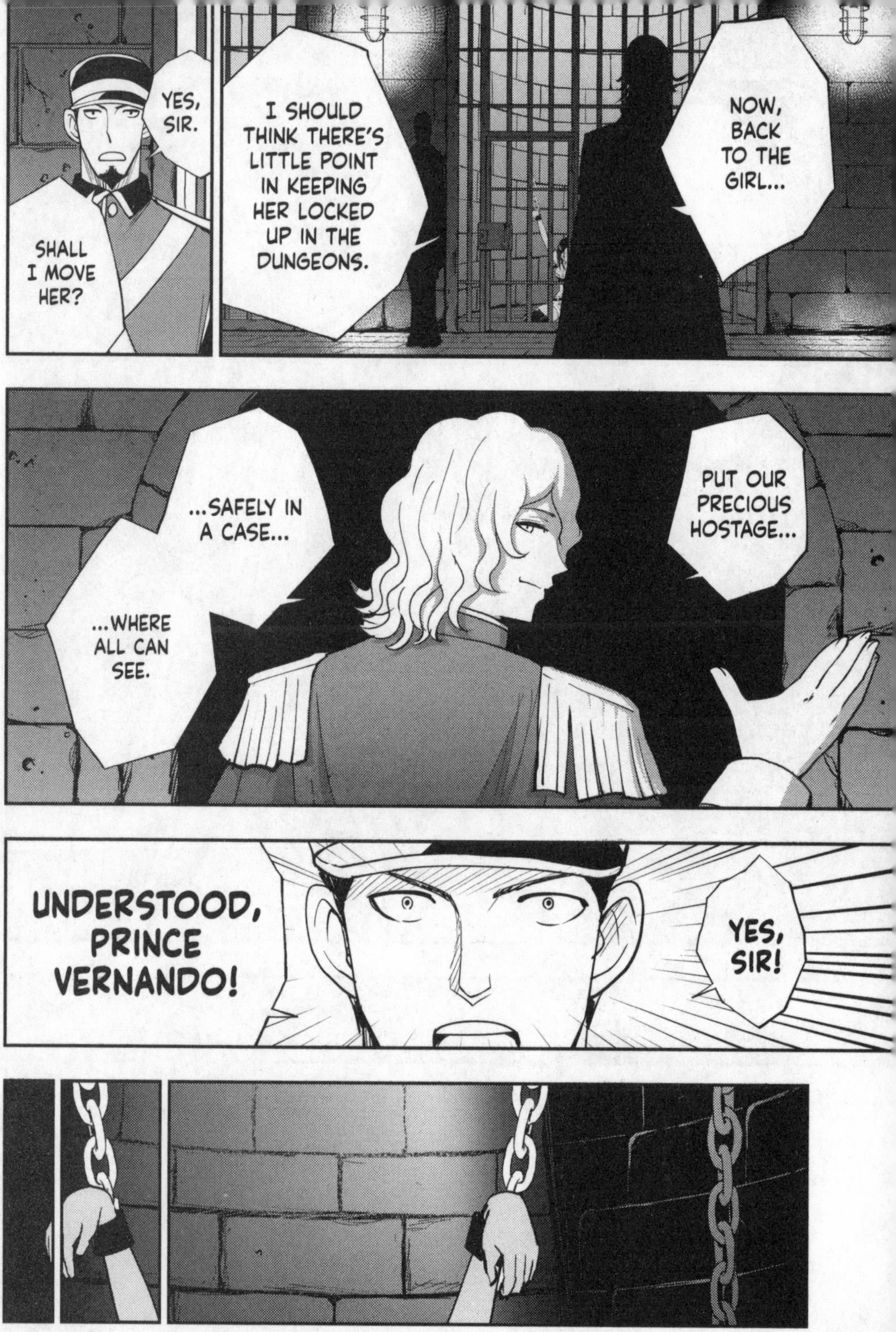
NOW, BACK TO THE GIRL...
I SHOULD THINK THERE'S LITTLE POINT IN KEEPING HER LOCKED UP IN THE DUNGEONS.
YES, SIR.
SHALL I MOVE HER?
PUT OUR PRECIOUS HOSTAGE...
...SAFELY IN A CASE...
...WHERE ALL CAN SEE.
YES, SIR!
UNDERSTOOD, PRINCE VERNANDO!

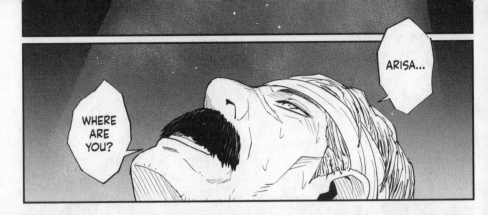

ARISA...

WHERE ARE YOU?

YOU'RE AWAKE?

IT'S HOT...

WHERE AM I?

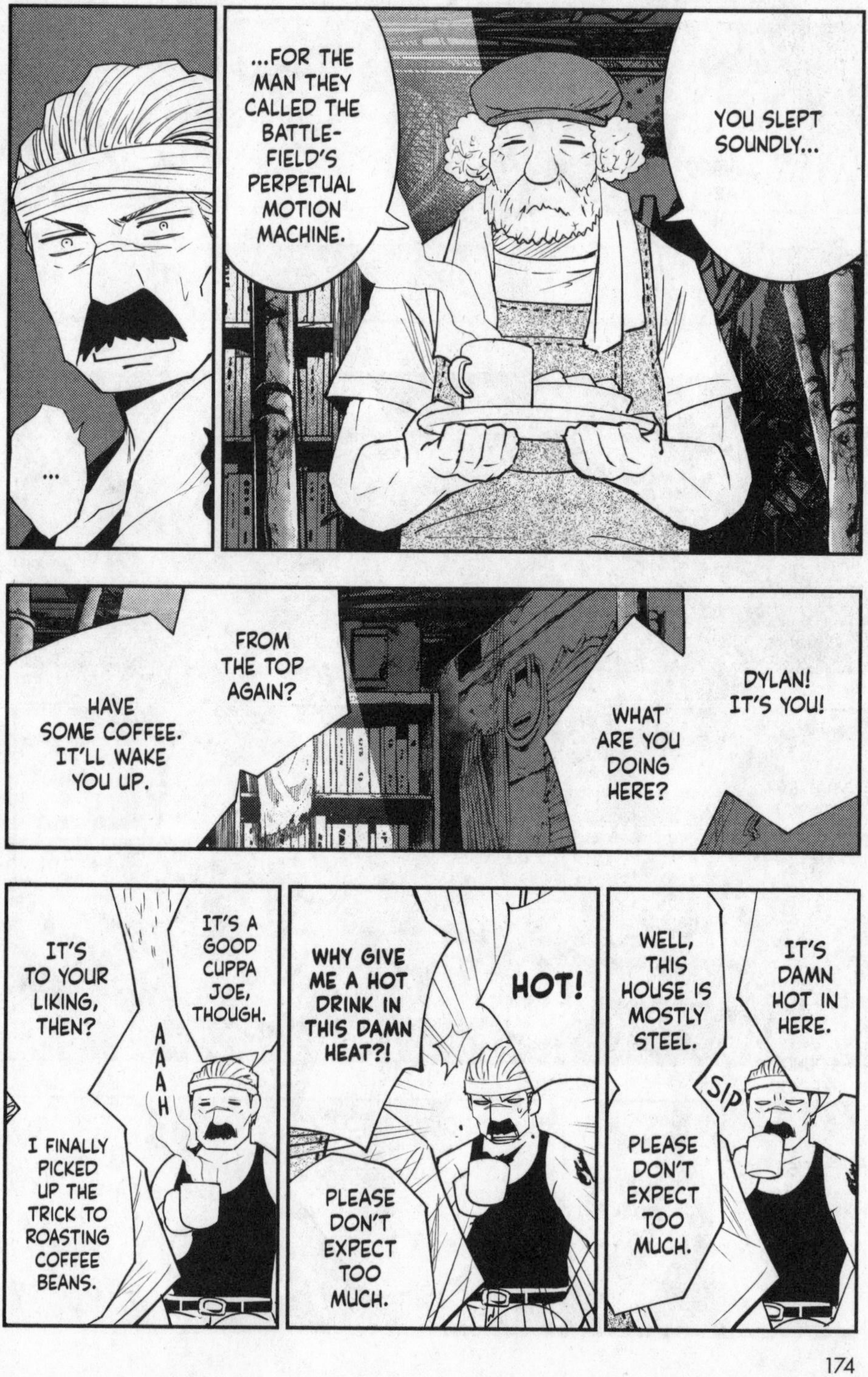
YOU SLEPT SOUNDLY...
...FOR THE MAN THEY CALLED THE BATTLE-FIELD'S PERPETUAL MOTION MACHINE.
...
DYLAN! IT'S YOU!
WHAT ARE YOU DOING HERE?
FROM THE TOP AGAIN?
HAVE SOME COFFEE. IT'LL WAKE YOU UP.
IT'S DAMN HOT IN HERE.
WELL, THIS HOUSE IS MOSTLY STEEL.
SIP
PLEASE DON'T EXPECT TOO MUCH.
HOT!
WHY GIVE ME A HOT DRINK IN THIS DAMN HEAT?!
PLEASE DON'T EXPECT TOO MUCH.
IT'S A GOOD CUPPA JOE, THOUGH.
IT'S TO YOUR LIKING, THEN?
AAAH
I FINALLY PICKED UP THE TRICK TO ROASTING COFFEE BEANS.

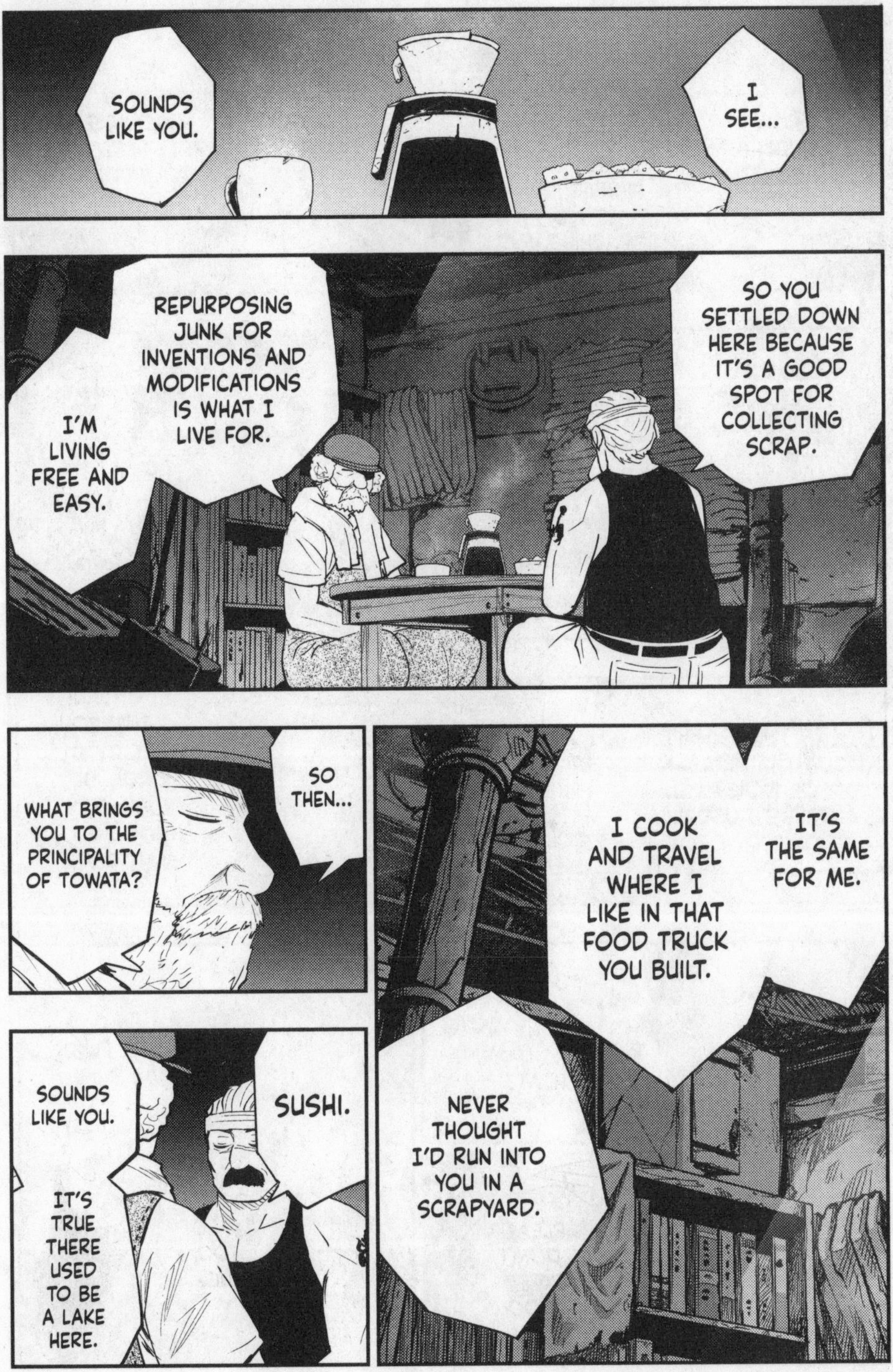
I SEE...
SOUNDS LIKE YOU.
SO YOU SETTLED DOWN HERE BECAUSE IT'S A GOOD SPOT FOR COLLECTING SCRAP.
REPURPOSING JUNK FOR INVENTIONS AND MODIFICATIONS IS WHAT I LIVE FOR.
I'M LIVING FREE AND EASY.
IT'S THE SAME FOR ME.
I COOK AND TRAVEL WHERE I LIKE IN THAT FOOD TRUCK YOU BUILT.
NEVER THOUGHT I'D RUN INTO YOU IN A SCRAPYARD.
SO THEN...
WHAT BRINGS YOU TO THE PRINCIPALITY OF TOWATA?
SUSHI.
SOUNDS LIKE YOU.
IT'S TRUE THERE USED TO BE A LAKE HERE.

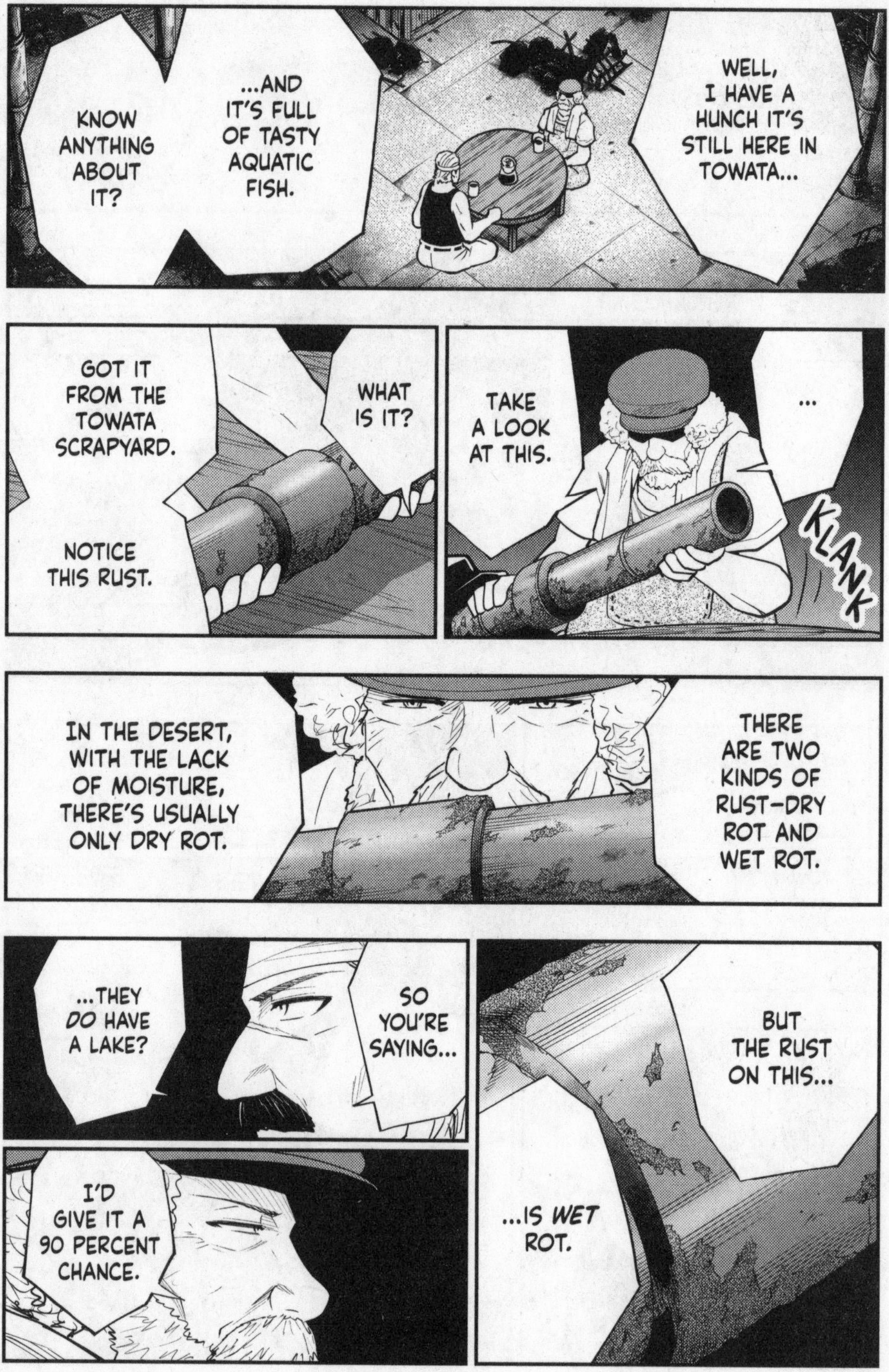
WELL, I HAVE A HUNCH IT'S STILL HERE IN TOWATA...
...AND IT'S FULL OF TASTY AQUATIC FISH.
KNOW ANYTHING ABOUT IT?
...
TAKE A LOOK AT THIS.
KLANK
WHAT IS IT?
GOT IT FROM THE TOWATA SCRAPYARD.
NOTICE THIS RUST.
THERE ARE TWO KINDS OF RUST–DRY ROT AND WET ROT.
IN THE DESERT, WITH THE LACK OF MOISTURE, THERE'S USUALLY ONLY DRY ROT.
BUT THE RUST ON THIS...
...IS *WET* ROT.
SO YOU'RE SAYING...
...THEY *DO* HAVE A LAKE?
I'D GIVE IT A 90 PERCENT CHANCE.

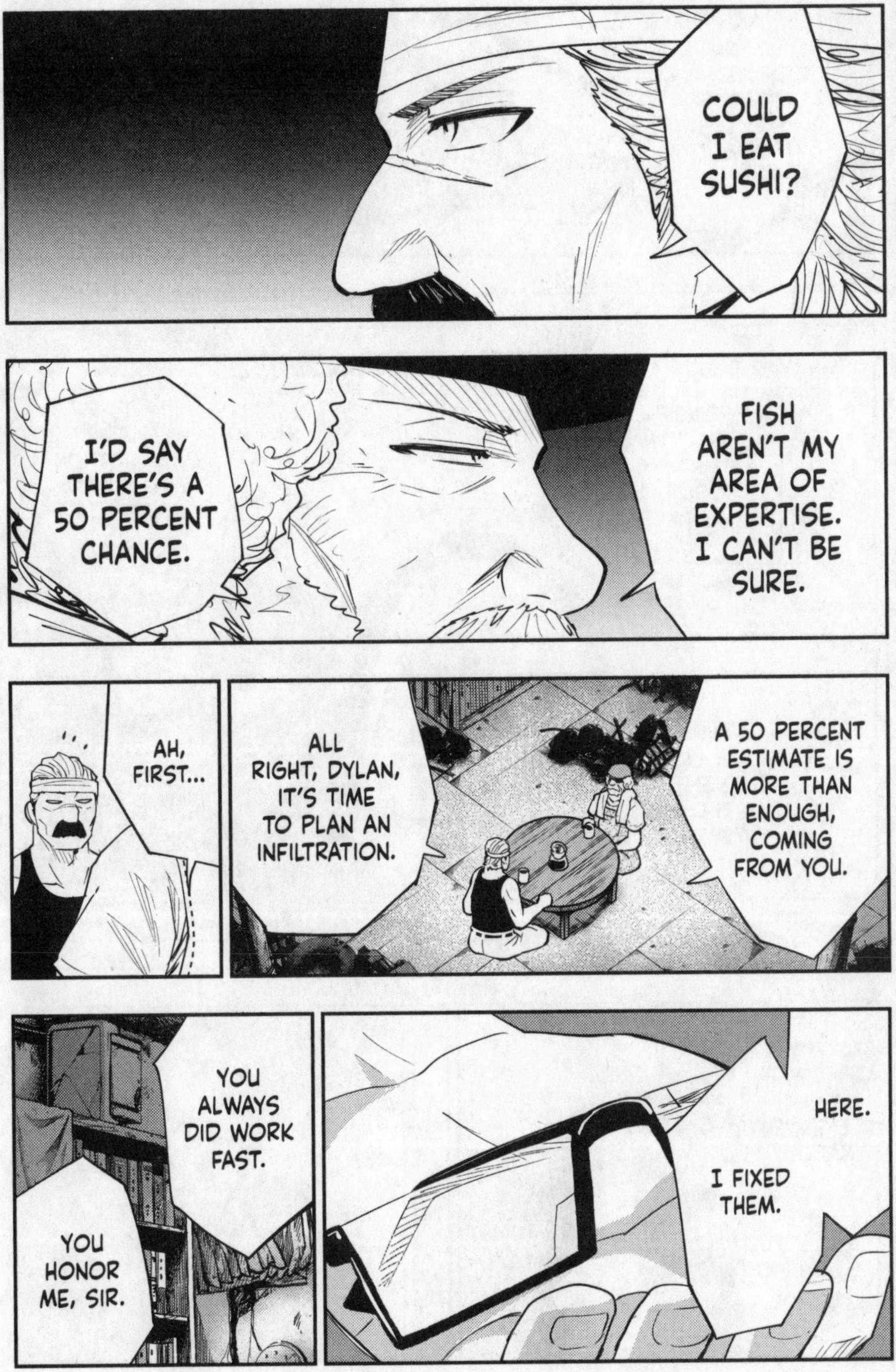
COULD I EAT SUSHI?
FISH AREN'T MY AREA OF EXPERTISE. I CAN'T BE SURE.
I'D SAY THERE'S A 50 PERCENT CHANCE.
A 50 PERCENT ESTIMATE IS MORE THAN ENOUGH, COMING FROM YOU.
ALL RIGHT, DYLAN, IT'S TIME TO PLAN AN INFILTRATION.
AH, FIRST...
HERE.
I FIXED THEM.
YOU ALWAYS DID WORK FAST.
YOU HONOR ME, SIR.

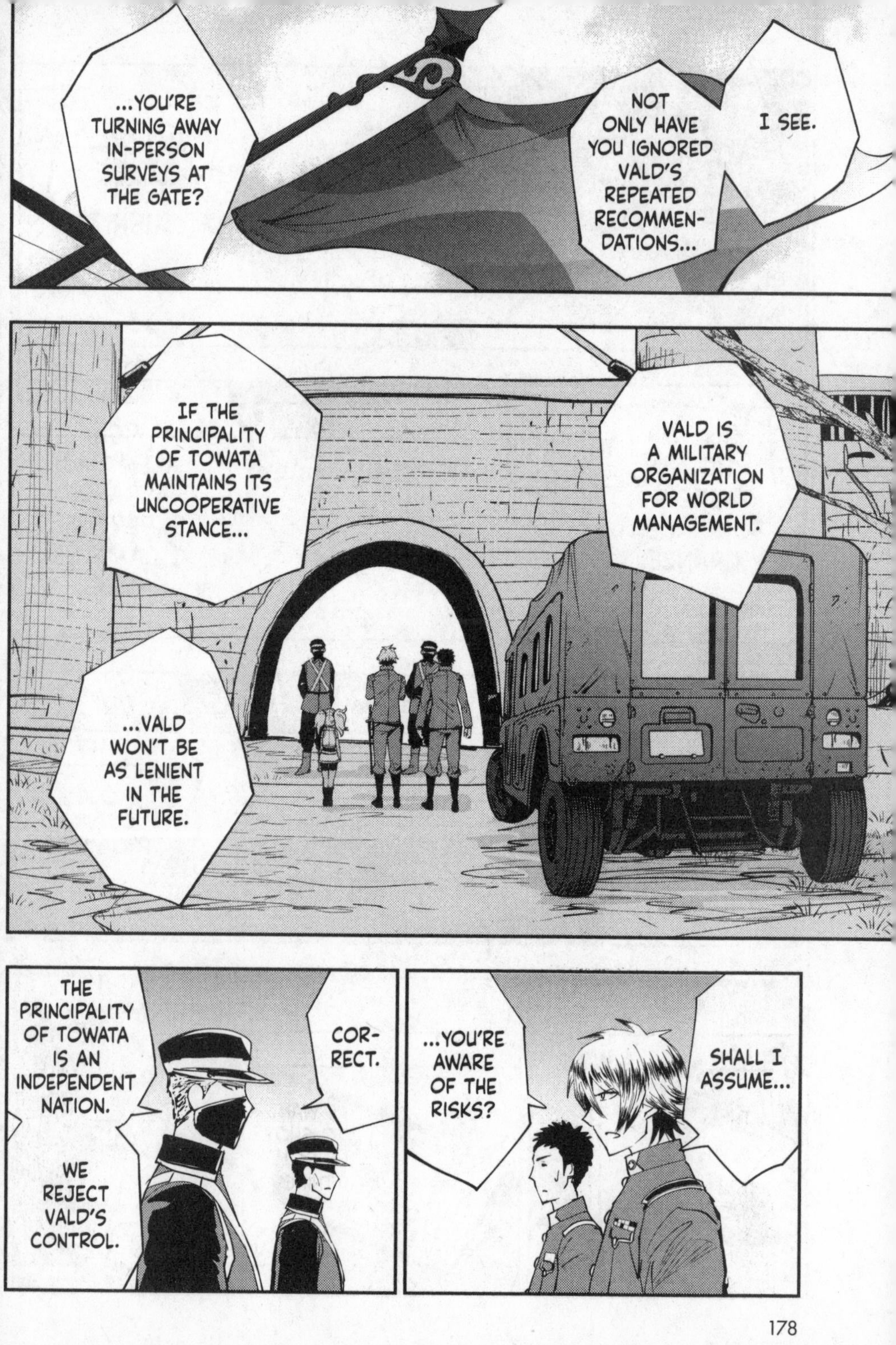
I SEE.
NOT ONLY HAVE YOU IGNORED VALD'S REPEATED RECOMMEN-DATIONS...
...YOU'RE TURNING AWAY IN-PERSON SURVEYS AT THE GATE?
VALD IS A MILITARY ORGANIZATION FOR WORLD MANAGEMENT.
IF THE PRINCIPALITY OF TOWATA MAINTAINS ITS UNCOOPERATIVE STANCE...
...VALD WON'T BE AS LENIENT IN THE FUTURE.
SHALL I ASSUME...
...YOU'RE AWARE OF THE RISKS?
COR-RECT.
THE PRINCIPALITY OF TOWATA IS AN INDEPENDENT NATION.
WE REJECT VALD'S CONTROL.

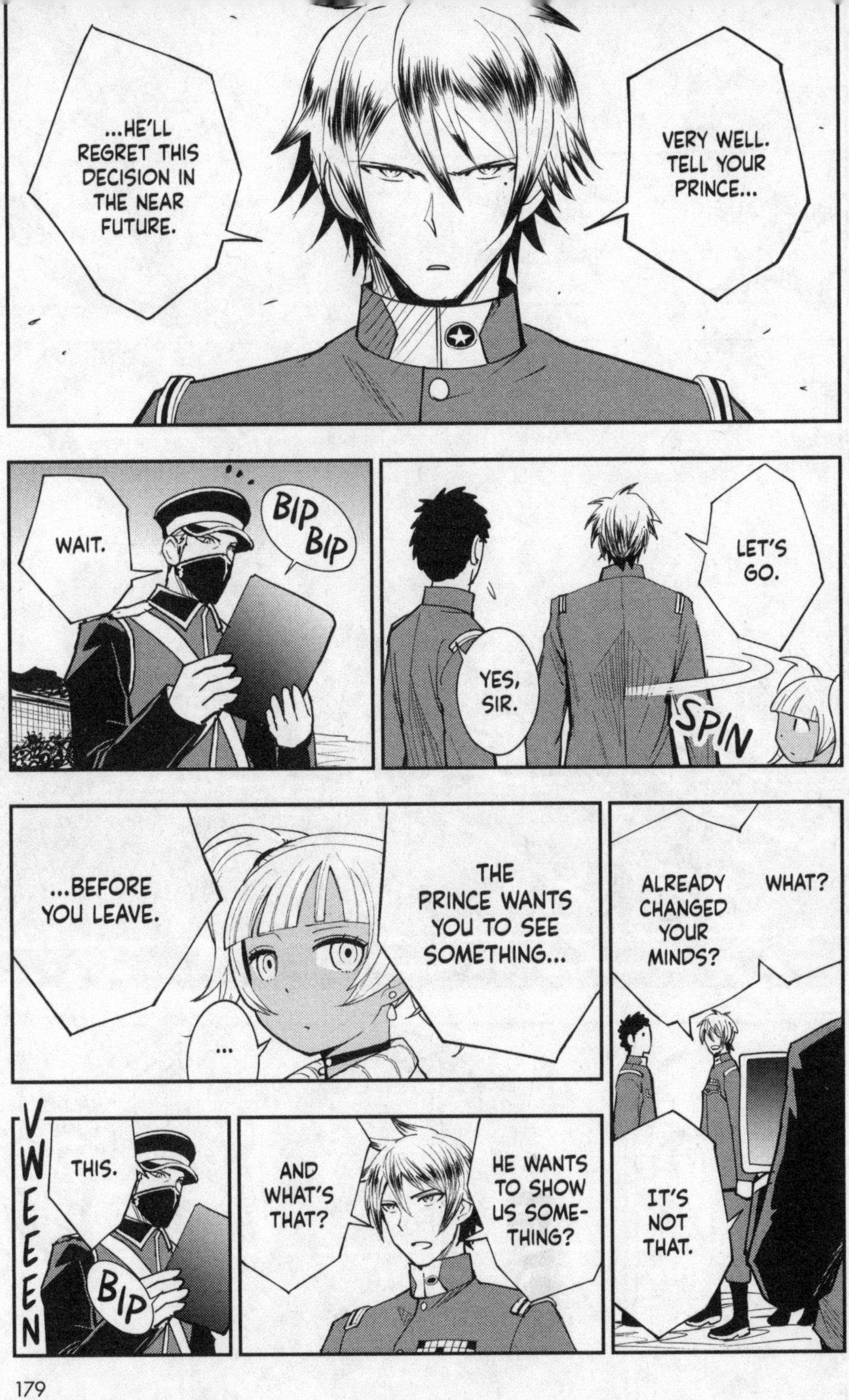
VERY WELL. TELL YOUR PRINCE...
...HE'LL REGRET THIS DECISION IN THE NEAR FUTURE.
LET'S GO.
YES, SIR.
SPIN
BIP BIP
WAIT.
WHAT?
ALREADY CHANGED YOUR MINDS?
IT'S NOT THAT.
THE PRINCE WANTS YOU TO SEE SOMETHING...
...BEFORE YOU LEAVE.
...
HE WANTS TO SHOW US SOME-THING?
AND WHAT'S THAT?
THIS.
BIP
VWEEEN

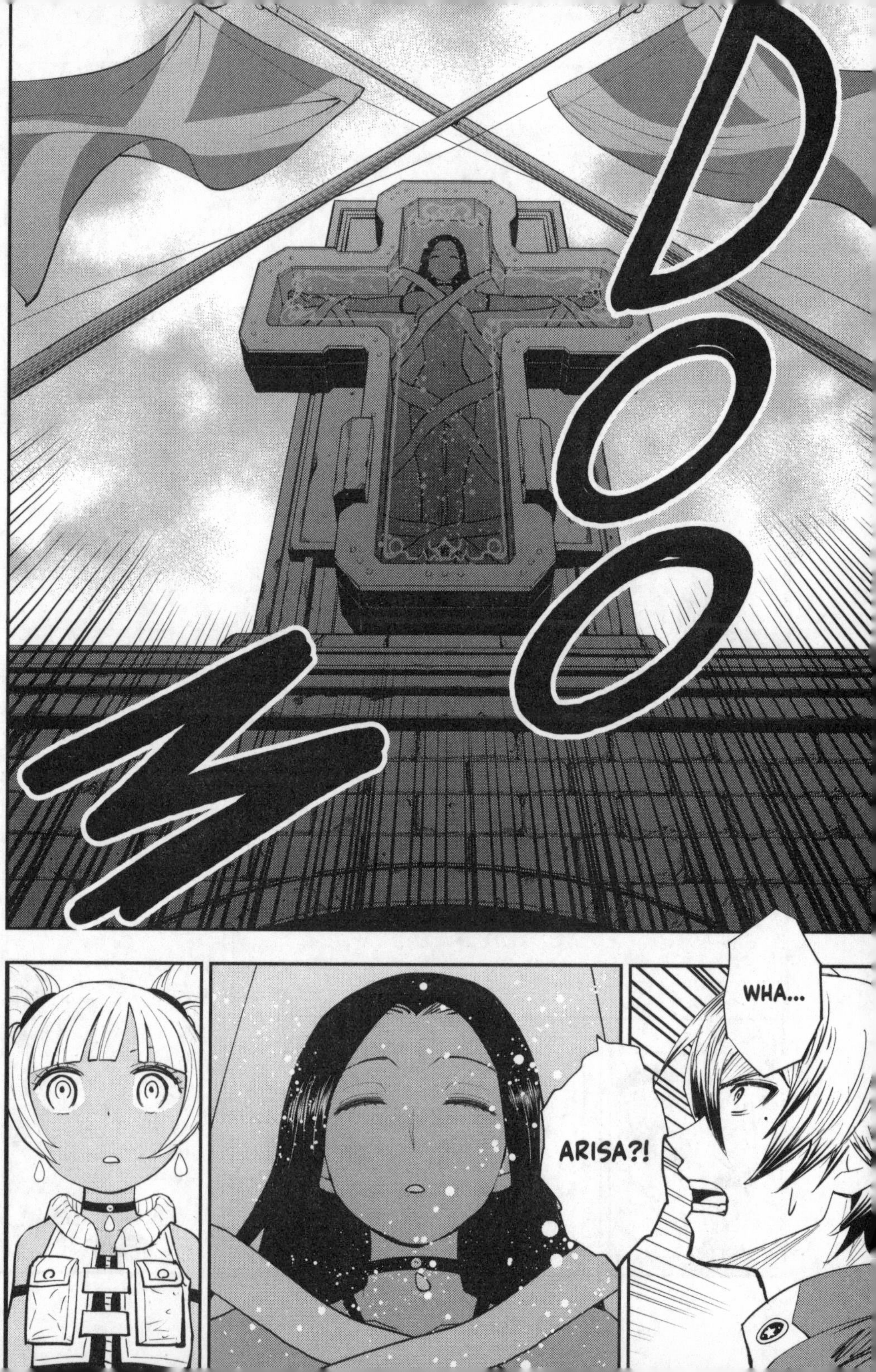
DOOM
WHA...
ARISA?!

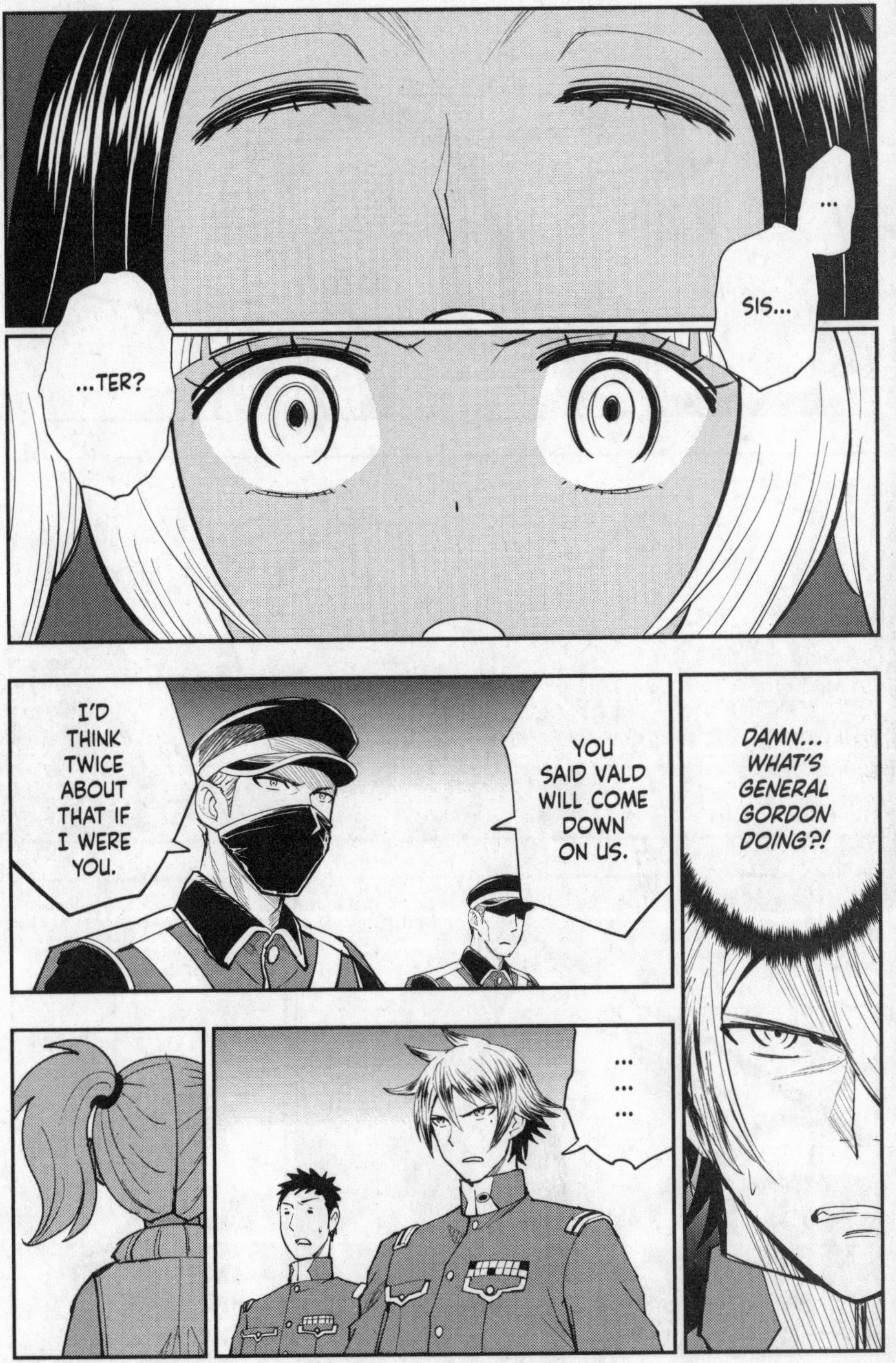

...
SIS...
...TER?
DAMN... WHAT'S GENERAL GORDON DOING?!
YOU SAID VALD WILL COME DOWN ON US.
I'D THINK TWICE ABOUT THAT IF I WERE YOU.
... ...

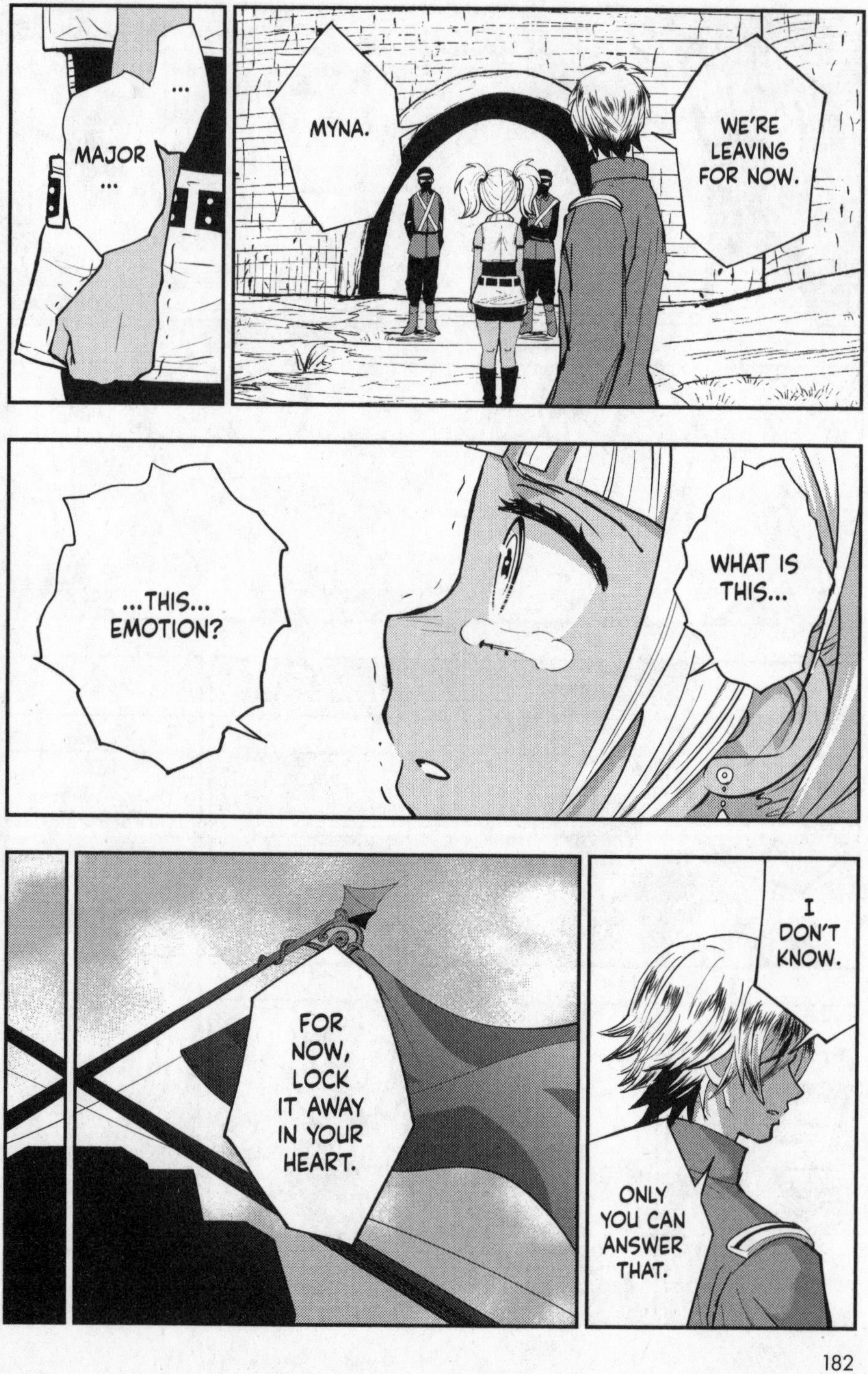
WE'RE LEAVING FOR NOW.
MYNA.
...
MAJOR ...
WHAT IS THIS...
...THIS... EMOTION?
I DON'T KNOW.
ONLY YOU CAN ANSWER THAT.
FOR NOW, LOCK IT AWAY IN YOUR HEART.

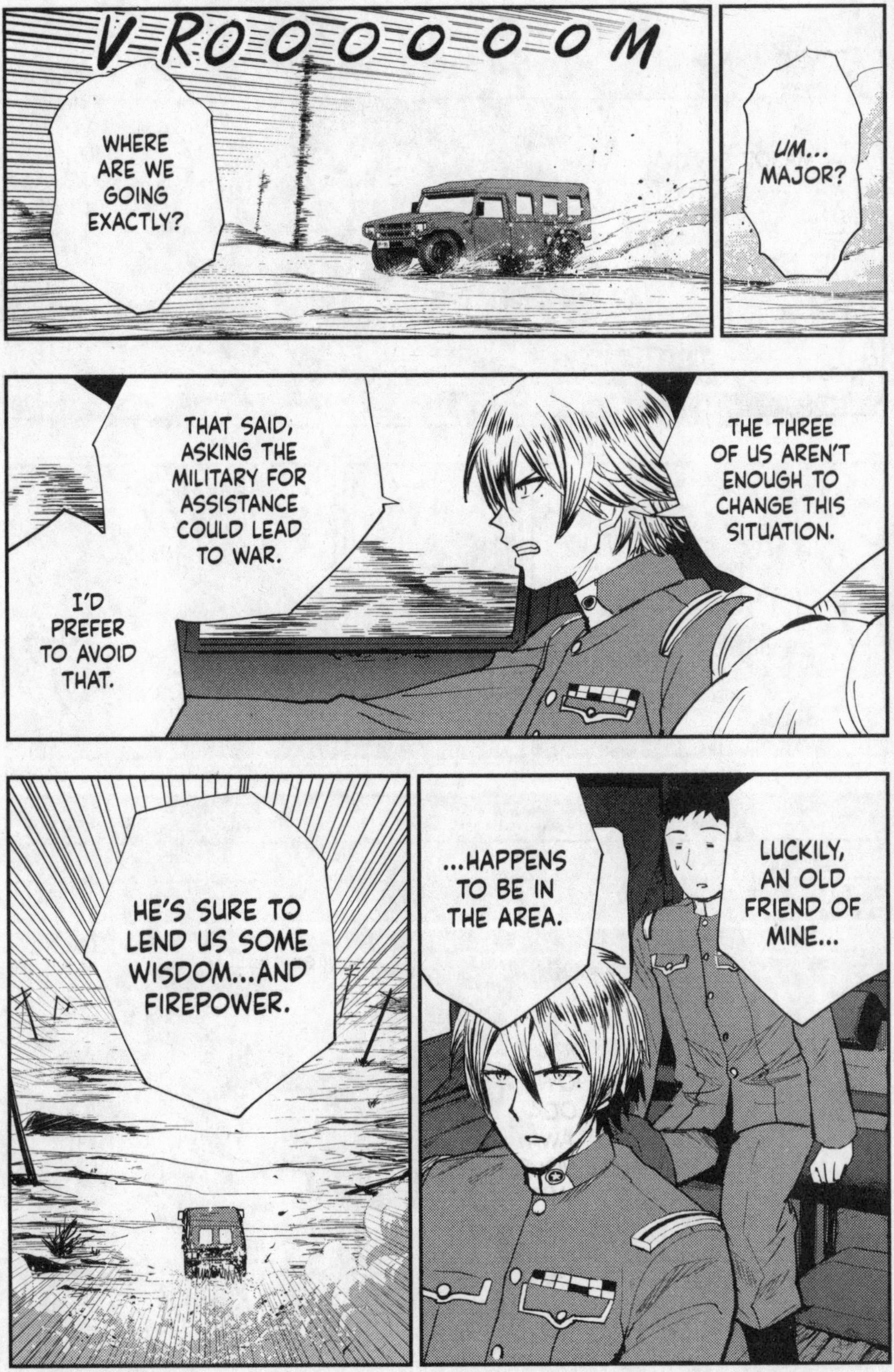
UM... MAJOR?
VROOOOOOM
WHERE ARE WE GOING EXACTLY?
THE THREE OF US AREN'T ENOUGH TO CHANGE THIS SITUATION.
THAT SAID, ASKING THE MILITARY FOR ASSISTANCE COULD LEAD TO WAR.
I'D PREFER TO AVOID THAT.
LUCKILY, AN OLD FRIEND OF MINE...
...HAPPENS TO BE IN THE AREA.
HE'S SURE TO LEND US SOME WISDOM...AND FIREPOWER.

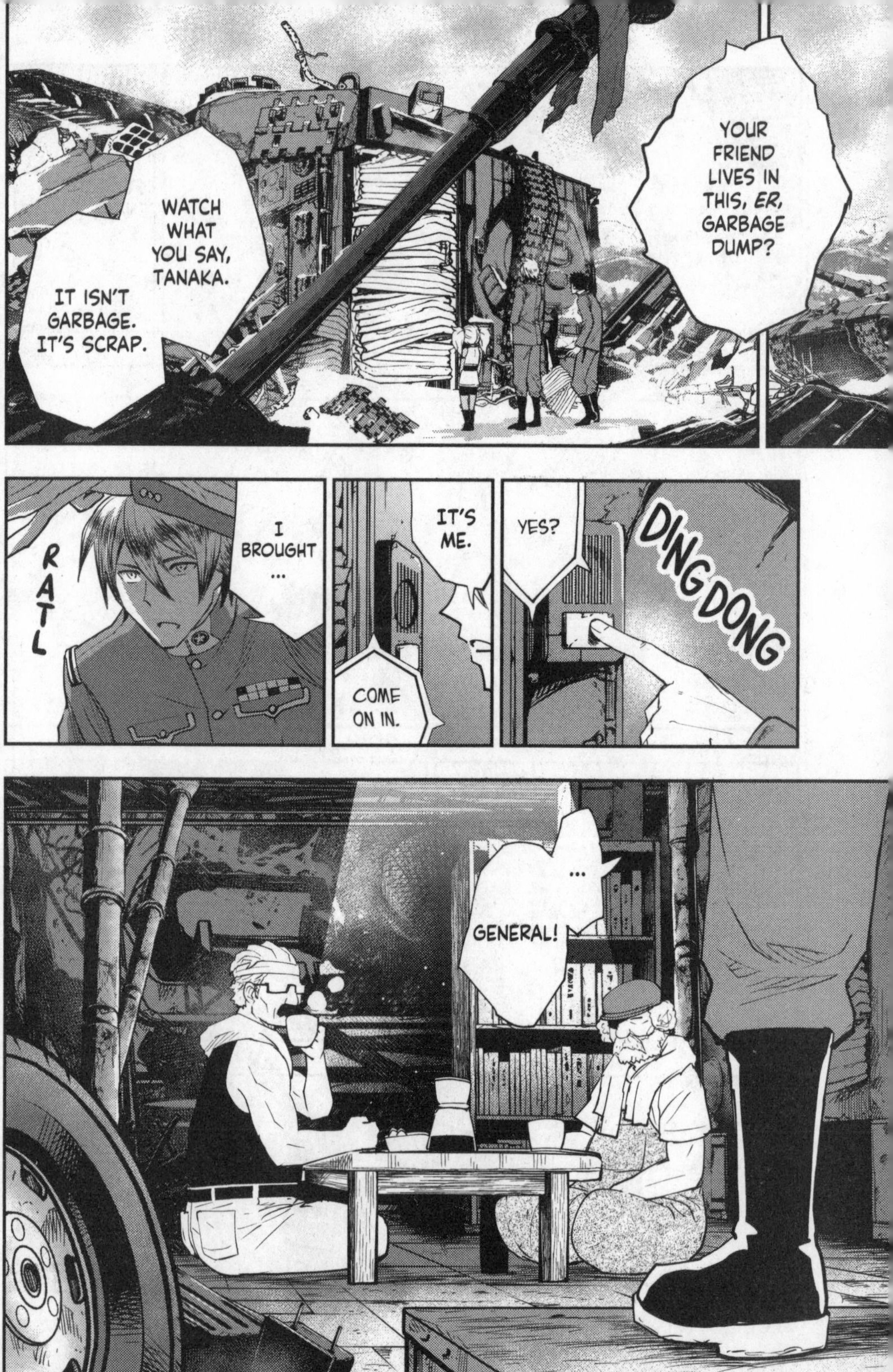
YOUR FRIEND LIVES IN THIS, *ER*, GARBAGE DUMP?
WATCH WHAT YOU SAY, TANAKA.
IT ISN'T GARBAGE. IT'S SCRAP.
DING DONG
YES?
IT'S ME.
COME ON IN.
RATL
I BROUGHT ...
... GENERAL!

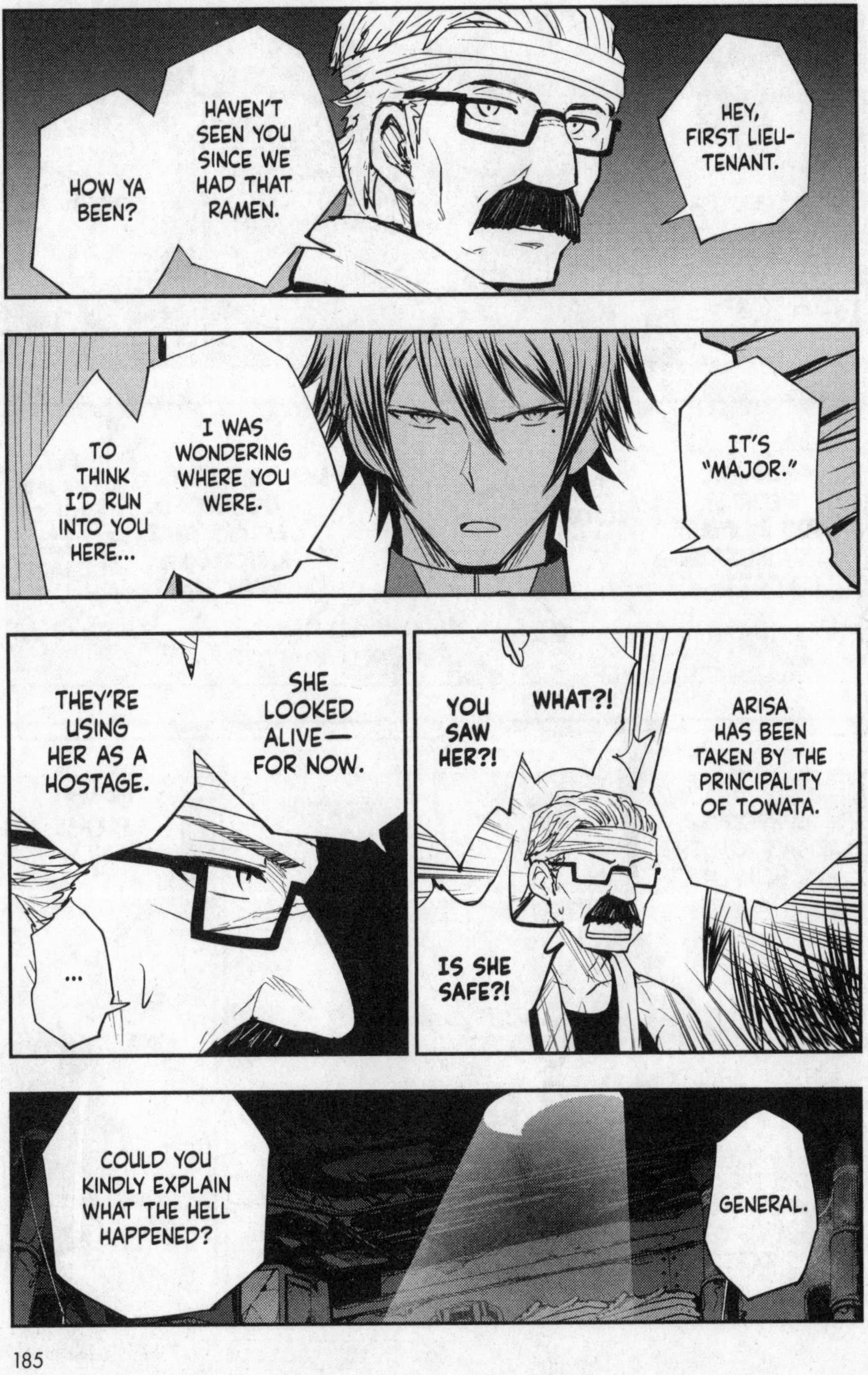
HEY, FIRST LIEU-TENANT.
HAVEN'T SEEN YOU SINCE WE HAD THAT RAMEN.
HOW YA BEEN?
IT'S "MAJOR."
I WAS WONDERING WHERE YOU WERE.
TO THINK I'D RUN INTO YOU HERE...
ARISA HAS BEEN TAKEN BY THE PRINCIPALITY OF TOWATA.
WHAT?!
YOU SAW HER?!
IS SHE SAFE?!
SHE LOOKED ALIVE— FOR NOW.
THEY'RE USING HER AS A HOSTAGE.
...
GENERAL.
COULD YOU KINDLY EXPLAIN WHAT THE HELL HAPPENED?

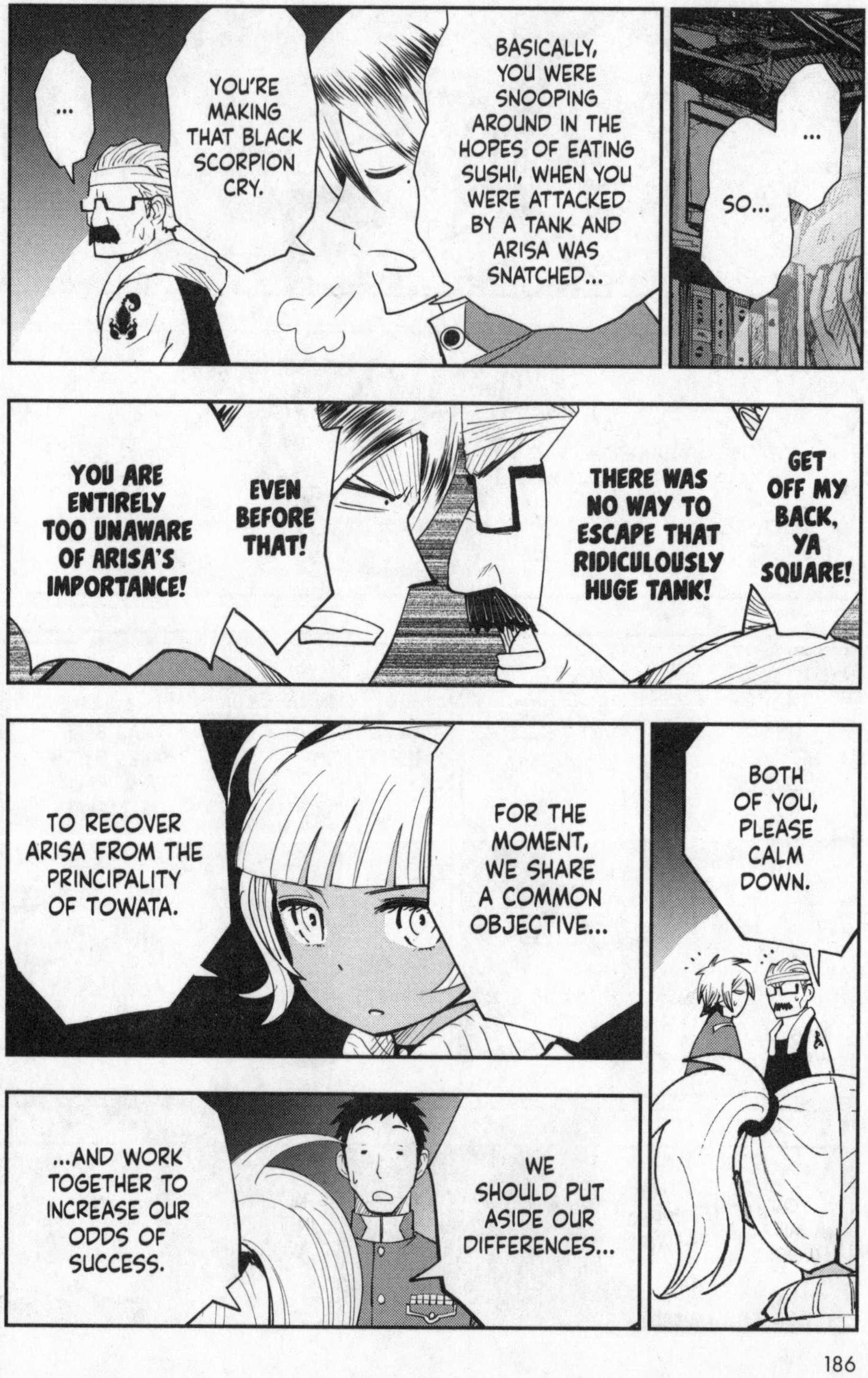
...
SO...
BASICALLY, YOU WERE SNOOPING AROUND IN THE HOPES OF EATING SUSHI, WHEN YOU WERE ATTACKED BY A TANK AND ARISA WAS SNATCHED...
YOU'RE MAKING THAT BLACK SCORPION CRY.
...
GET OFF MY BACK, YA SQUARE!
THERE WAS NO WAY TO ESCAPE THAT RIDICULOUSLY HUGE TANK!
EVEN BEFORE THAT!
YOU ARE ENTIRELY TOO UNAWARE OF ARISA'S IMPORTANCE!
BOTH OF YOU, PLEASE CALM DOWN.
FOR THE MOMENT, WE SHARE A COMMON OBJECTIVE...
TO RECOVER ARISA FROM THE PRINCIPALITY OF TOWATA.
WE SHOULD PUT ASIDE OUR DIFFERENCES...
...AND WORK TOGETHER TO INCREASE OUR ODDS OF SUCCESS.

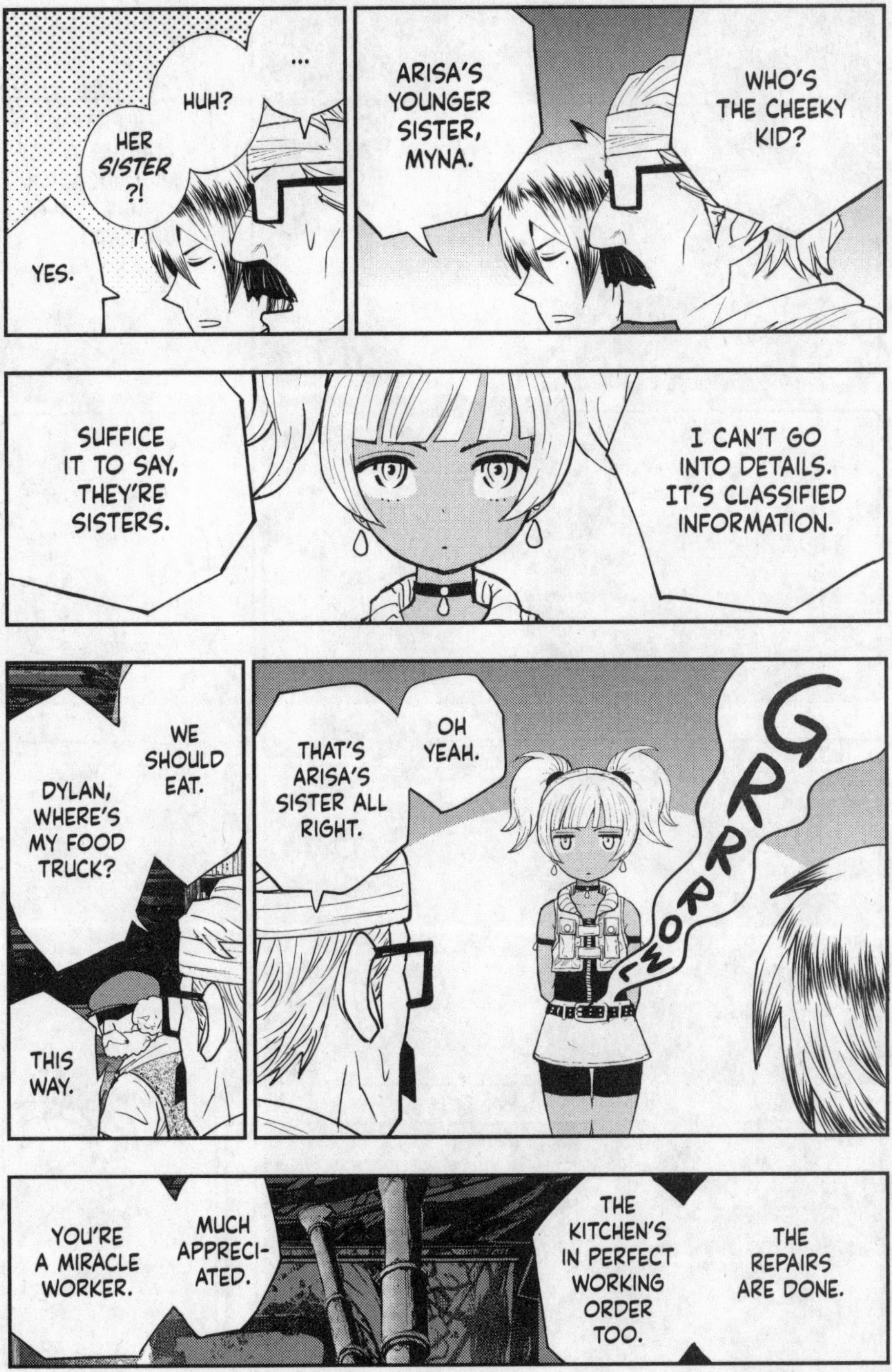
WHO'S THE CHEEKY KID?
ARISA'S YOUNGER SISTER, MYNA.
...
HUH?
HER *SISTER* ?!
YES.
I CAN'T GO INTO DETAILS. IT'S CLASSIFIED INFORMATION.
SUFFICE IT TO SAY, THEY'RE SISTERS.
GRRROWL
OH YEAH.
THAT'S ARISA'S SISTER ALL RIGHT.
WE SHOULD EAT.
DYLAN, WHERE'S MY FOOD TRUCK?
THIS WAY.
THE REPAIRS ARE DONE.
THE KITCHEN'S IN PERFECT WORKING ORDER TOO.
MUCH APPRECIATED.
YOU'RE A MIRACLE WORKER.

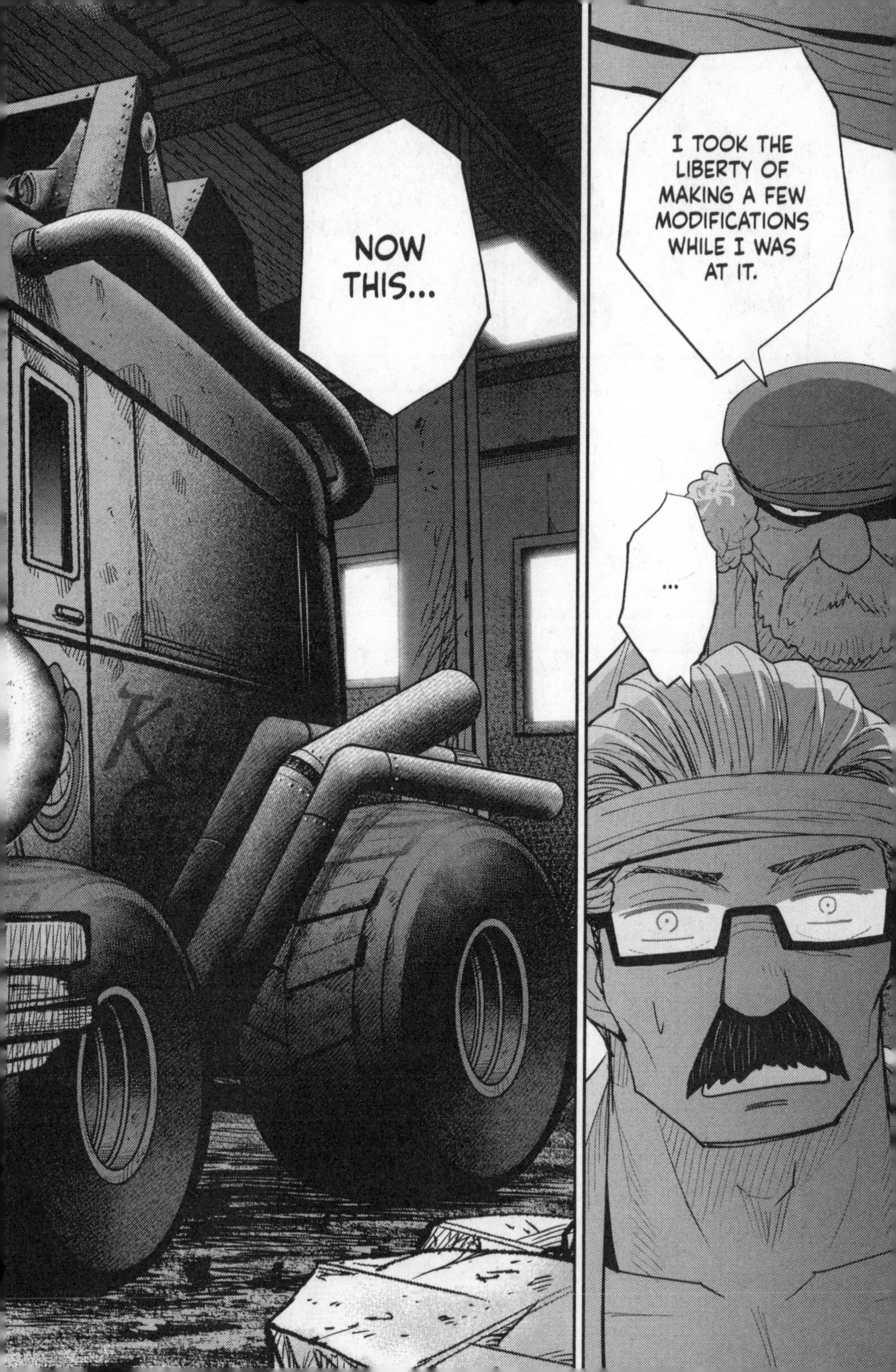
I TOOK THE LIBERTY OF MAKING A FEW MODIFICATIONS WHILE I WAS AT IT.
...
NOW THIS...

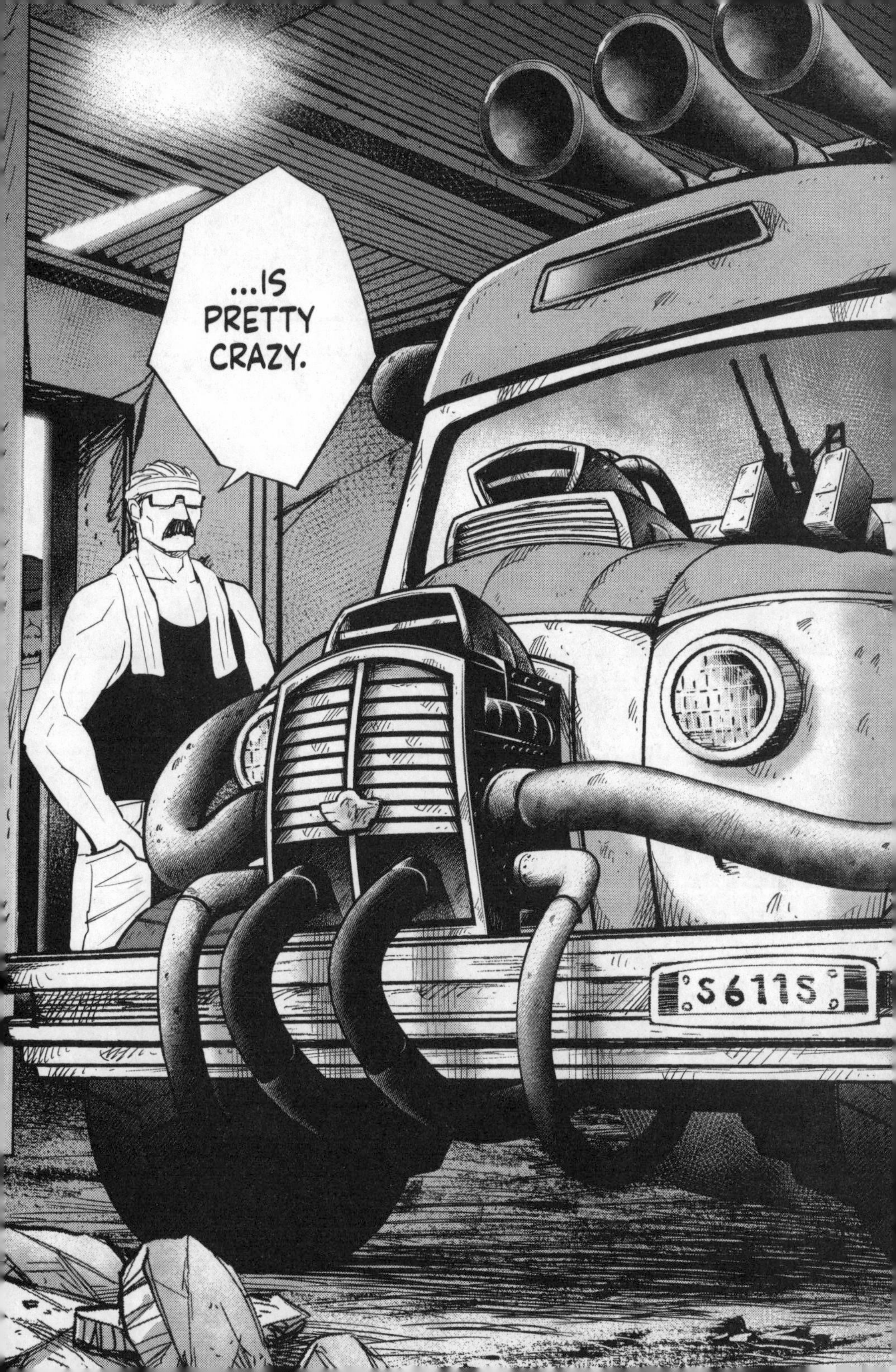
...IS PRETTY CRAZY.
S611S

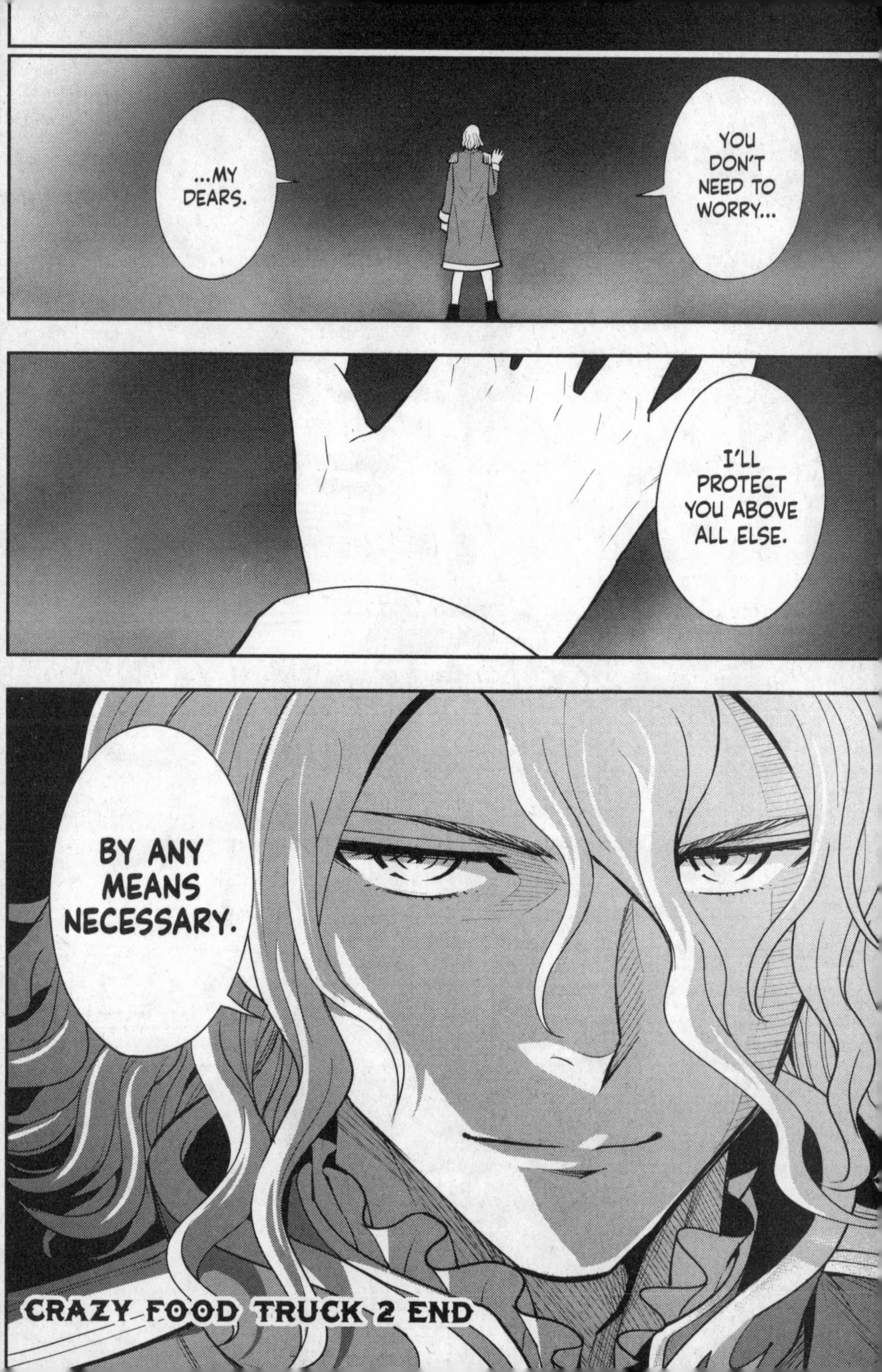
YOU DON'T NEED TO WORRY...
...MY DEARS.
I'LL PROTECT YOU ABOVE ALL ELSE.
BY ANY MEANS NECESSARY.
CRAZY FOOD TRUCK 2 END

CRAZY FOOD TRUCK TO BE CONTINUED NEXT STOP VOL. 3.

CRAZY STAFF

MANGA
ROKUROU OGAKI

ART
TATSUYA HAINOKI
KAKU NINOMIYA
SEI FUKUI
KOUSUKE MINE
TSUMURI RIKUGAI

EDITING
YOSHINOSUKE SUMINO

COVER DESIGN
RYOUSUKE TAKEUCHI [CRAZY FORCE]

ROKUROU OGAKI

I'm hooked on saunas. They used to be too hot for me, but ever since I learned the "sauna → cold plunge → take a break" combo, I can't live without them. And the postsauna meal and alcohol are delicious. Apparently, the reason it feels so good is that the combination of extreme heat and cold triggers an adrenaline rush, and during the subsequent rest period, your brain releases endorphins in spades. This is actually similar to manga work. When a deadline's looming, you can't sleep or rest, and you want to draw the best work you can, so you feel this constant mortal danger as you gradually fill in the hopelessly blank pages. And when you somehow manage to finish the chapter, what a feeling of release... And the postdeadline food and alcohol are so, so delicious. And then, tipsy, you drift into a deep sleep... It's the best. It's a sauna, in a way. There may be no greater high in life than rest and a reward after a difficult struggle. I'd be happy if this manga serves as a poststruggle reward for you!

Before his 2013 debut in *Shonen Sunday S* with *Unlimited Psychic Squad*, Rokurou Ogaki worked as an assistant for manga artists Junpei Goto and Kenjiro Hata. In addition to *Crazy Food Truck*, he's also the manga artist of the *Akudama Drive* anime's manga adaptation. Fun fact: Rokurou Ogaki's pen name is a reference to "rock and roll"! Rock on!

CRAZY FOOD TRUCK

VOLUME 2
VIZ SIGNATURE EDITION

-

STORY AND ART BY
ROKUROU OGAKI

TRANSLATION: **AMANDA HALEY**
ENGLISH ADAPTATION: **JENNIFER LEBLANC**
TOUCH-UP ART & LETTERING: **PHIL CHRISTIE**
DESIGN: **JIMMY PRESLER**
EDITOR: **JENNIFER LEBLANC**

CRAZY FOOD TRUCK volume 2
© Rokurou Ogaki 2020
All rights reserved.
English translation rights arranged with SHINCHOSHA Publishing Co., Ltd.
through Tuttle-Mori Agency, Inc, Tokyo

Printed in Canada

Published by VIZ Media, LLC
P.O. Box 77010
San Francisco, CA 94107

10 9 8 7 6 5 4 3 2 1
First printing, September 2022

VIZ MEDIA   VIZ SIGNATURE
viz.com   vizsignature.com

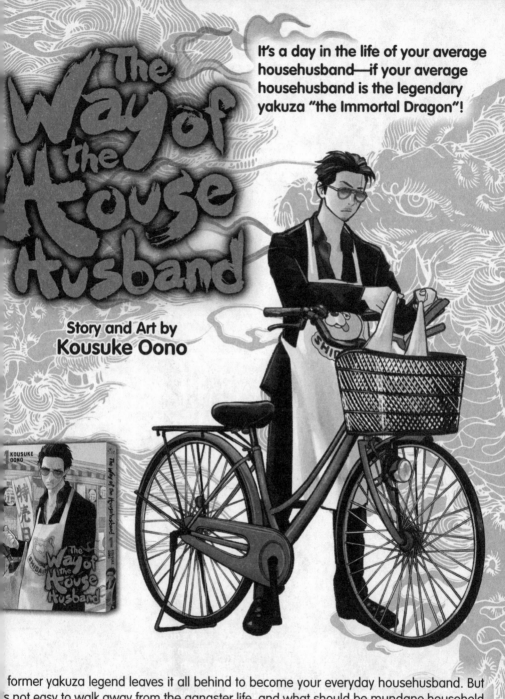

It's a day in the life of your average househusband—if your average househusband is the legendary yakuza "the Immortal Dragon"!

The Way of the House Husband

Story and Art by
Kousuke Oono

...former yakuza legend leaves it all behind to become your everyday househusband. But
...s not easy to walk away from the gangster life, and what should be mundane household
...asks are anything but!

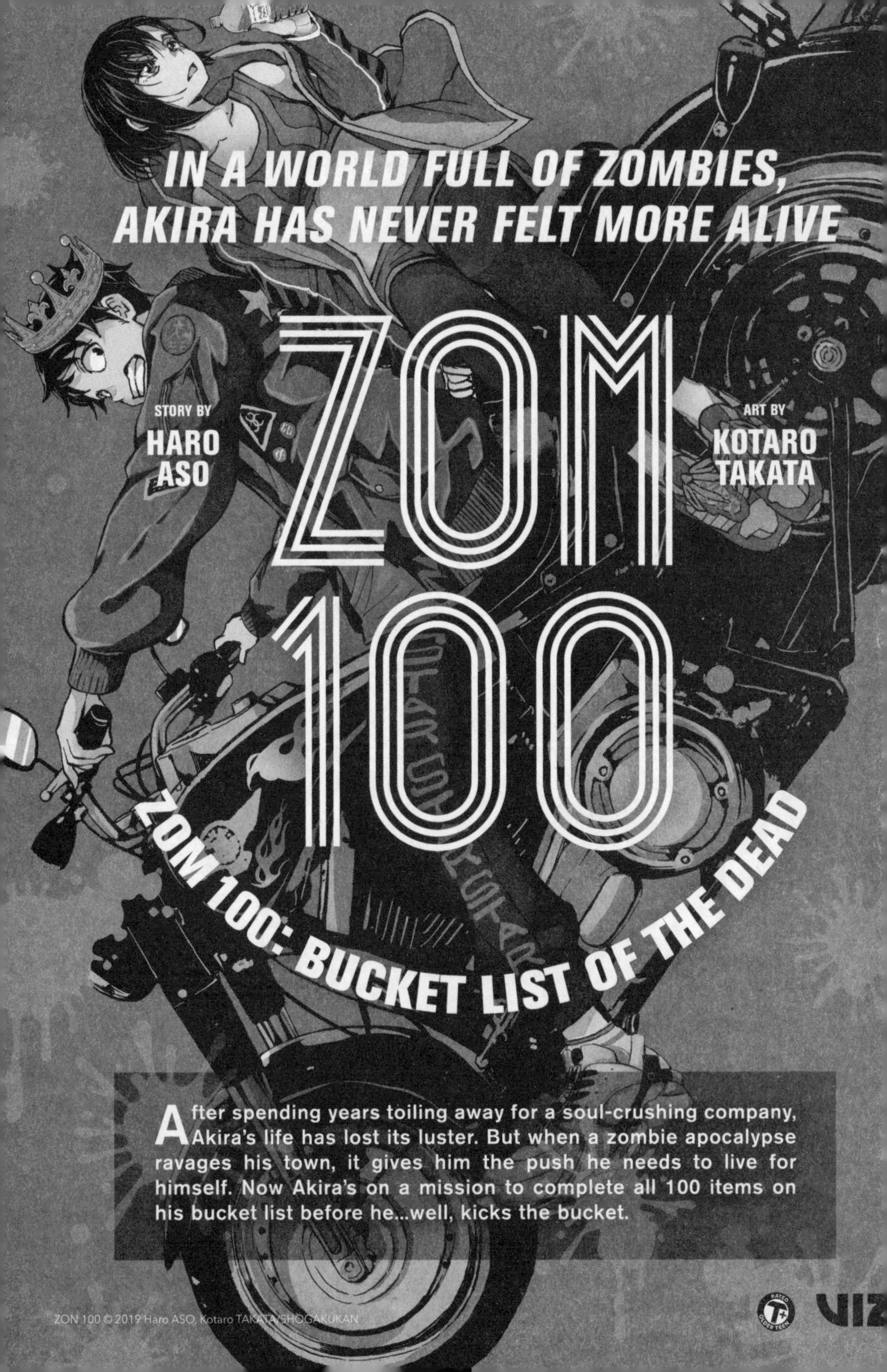

IN A WORLD FULL OF ZOMBIES,
AKIRA HAS NEVER FELT MORE ALIVE
STORY BY
HARO ASO
ZOM 100
ART BY
KOTARO TAKATA
ZOM 100: BUCKET LIST OF THE DEAD
After spending years toiling away for a soul-crushing company, Akira's life has lost its luster. But when a zombie apocalypse ravages his town, it gives him the push he needs to live for himself. Now Akira's on a mission to complete all 100 items on his bucket list before he...well, kicks the bucket.
ZON 100 © 2019 Haro ASO, Kotaro TAKATA/SHOGAKUKAN
RATED T+ OLDER TEEN
VIZ

No. 5

A powerfully imagined vision of the future from TAIYO MATSUMOTO, creator of the Eisner Award–winning *CATS OF THE LOUVRE* and *TEKKONKINKREET*.

In a world where most of the earth has become a harsh desert, the Rainbow Council of the Peace Corps has a growing crisis on its hands. No. 5, one member of a team of superpowered global security guardians and a top marksman, has gone rogue. Now the other guardians have to hunt down No. 5 and his mysterious companion, Matryoshka. But why did No. 5 turn against the council, and what will it mean for the future of the world?

RATED TEEN   VIZ

TOKYO GHOUL

C O M P L E T E   B O X   S E T

STORY AND ART BY **SUI ISHIDA**

KEN KANEKI is an ordinary college student until a violent encounter turns him into the first half-human, half-Ghoul hybrid. Trapped between two worlds, he must survive Ghoul turf wars, learn more about Ghoul society and master his new powers.

Box set collects all fourteen volumes of the original *Tokyo Ghoul* series. Includes an exclusive double-sided poster.

COLLECT THE COMPLETE SERIES